# Dust Off the Gold Medal

The oldest and most prestigious children's literature award, the Newbery Medal has since 1922 been granted annually by the American Library Association to the children's book it deems "most distinguished." Medal books enjoy an outsized influence on American children's literature, figuring perennially on publishers' lists, on library and bookstore shelves, and in school curricula. As such, they offer a compelling window into the history of US children's literature and publishing, as well as into changing societal attitudes about which books are "best" for America's schoolchildren. Yet literary scholars have disproportionately ignored the Medal winners in their research. This volume provides a critically- and historically-grounded scholarly analysis of representative but understudied Newbery Medal books from the 1920s through the 2010s, interrogating the disjunction between the books' omnipresence and influence, on the one hand, and the critical silence surrounding them, on the other. *Dust Off the Gold Medal* makes a case for closing these scholarly gaps by revealing neglected texts' insights into the politics of children's literature prizing and by demonstrating how neglected titles illuminate critical debates currently central to the field of children's literature. In particular, the essays shed light on the hidden elements of diversity apparent in the neglected Newbery canon while illustrating how the books respond—sometimes in quite subtle ways—to contemporaneous concerns around race, class, gender, disability, nationalism, and globalism.

**Sara L. Schwebel** is the Director of the Center for Children's Books and a Professor of Information Sciences at the University of Illinois Urbana-Champaign. She is the author of *Child-Sized History: Fictions of the Past in U.S. Classrooms* (2011) and the editor of *Island of the Blue Dolphins: The Complete Reader's Edition* (2016) and the Lone Woman and Last Indians Digital Archive.

**Jocelyn Van Tuyl** is a Professor of French at New College of Florida. She is the author of *André Gide and the Second World War: A Novelist's Occupation* (2006), which was supported by a grant from the National Endowment for the Humanities, and the author-translator of *André Gide et la Seconde Guerre mondiale: l'Occupation d'un homme de lettres* (2017).

**Children's Literature and Culture**
Jack Zipes, *Founding Series Editor*
Philip Nel, *Series Editor, 2011–2018*
Kenneth Kidd and Elizabeth Marshall, *Current Series Editors*

Founded by Jack Zipes in 1994, Children's Literature and Culture is the longest-running series devoted to the study of children's literature and culture from a national and international perspective. Dedicated to promoting original research in children's literature and children's culture, in 2011 the series expanded its focus to include childhood studies, and it seeks to explore the legal, historical, and philosophical conditions of different childhoods. An advocate for scholarship from around the globe, the series recognizes innovation and encourages interdisciplinarity. Children's Literature and Culture offers cutting-edge, upper-level scholarly studies and edited collections considering topics such as gender, race, picture books, childhood, nation, religion, technology, and many others. Titles are characterized by dynamic interventions into established subjects and innovative studies on emerging topics.

Titles include:
**Rulers of Literary Playgrounds**
Politics of Intergenerational Play in Children's Literature
*Edited by Justyna Deszcz-Tryhubczak and Irena Barbara Kalla*

**Antarctica in British Children's Literature**
*Sinéad Moriarty*

**Dust Off the Gold Medal**
Rediscovering Children's Literature at the Newbery Centennial
*Edited by Sara L. Schwebel and Jocelyn Van Tuyl*

**Sexuality in Literature for Children and Young Adults**
*Edited by Paul Venzo and Kristine Moruzi*

For more information about this series, please visit: https://www.routledge.com/Childrens-Literature-and-Culture/book-series/SE0686

# Dust Off the Gold Medal

## Rediscovering Children's Literature at the Newbery Centennial

Edited by Sara L. Schwebel
and Jocelyn Van Tuyl

Routledge
Taylor & Francis Group
NEW YORK AND LONDON

First published 2022
by Routledge

605 Third Avenue, New York, NY 10158
and by Routledge

2 Park Square, Milton Park, Abingdon, Oxon, OX14 4RN

*Routledge is an imprint of the Taylor & Francis Group, an informa business*



*Library of Congress Cataloging-in-Publication Data*
A catalog record for this title has been requested

ISBN: 978-0-367-33721-6 (hbk)
ISBN: 978-1-032-04809-3 (pbk)
ISBN: 978-0-367-33722-3 (ebk)

DOI: 10.4324/9780367337223

To Miriam and Benjy Schwebel, who were born while we worked on this project

S. L. S.

And to Mileva Van Tuyl, who grew up

J. V. T.

# Contents

# Figures

# Acknowledgments

It is a great pleasure to thank the many people and institutions who helped in the creation of this volume.

Our thanks to Katharine Capshaw, Karen Chandler, Kenneth Kidd, and Ebony Elizabeth Thomas for initial review of the project; Anastasia Ulanowicz for early encouragement; and Michelle Ann Abate and Salamishah Tillet for help identifying contributors.

Paige Kuester provided outstanding research assistance in the American Library Association (ALA) archives. Numerous librarians contributed invaluable support, especially: Cara Setsu Bertram, Archival Operations and Reference Specialist, ALA Archives; Salvatore V. De Sando, Archives Assistant, ALA Archives; and Mara Thacker, South Asian Studies & Global Popular Culture Librarian, University of Illinois Urbana-Champaign. Thank you to Scott Swanson and Helen Salkeld for their assistance with image preparation. Thanks, too, to the librarians and interlibrary loan staff at the New College of Florida, University of South Carolina, and University of Illinois Urbana-Champaign libraries.

The University of Illinois Urbana-Champaign School of Information Sciences provided generous support for this project. Additional financial support came from New College of Florida.

Our thanks to Michelle Salyga, Bryony Reece, and the entire team at Taylor & Francis, as well as to Kenneth Kidd and Elizabeth Marshall, editors of Routledge's Children's Literature and Culture series.

As always, we thank our families, friends, and colleagues for their patience and support.

Above all, we are grateful to our contributors, who demonstrated exceptional grace and persistence as we requested revision after revision in our effort to shape chapters into a unified volume. (What's worse than a perfectionist editor? Two of them, with different disciplinary backgrounds!) During the writing of this volume, our contributors battled COVID-19 and other illnesses; they made job changes and faced personal challenges; they had babies—several of them; they dealt with the hardships of a pandemic and with the trauma of the racism, injustice, and inequity that it brought to the fore. We can't thank them warmly enough for the superlative work they did while facing these many challenges.

Then, after all the struggles of the first pandemic year, we unexpectedly lost our colleague and contributor Beverly Lyon Clark. Bev was an intellectual giant and a true friend. We feel her absence acutely, and hope to honor her memory with this volume.

# Contributors

**Giselle Liza Anatol** is a Professor of English at the University of Kansas. Her monograph *The Things That Fly in the Night* explores representations of female vampires in folklore and literature from the circum-Caribbean and African diaspora. She has also published three edited collections—*Bringing Light to* Twilight: *Perspectives on the Pop Culture Phenomenon*, *Reading Harry Potter: Critical Essays*, and *Reading Harry Potter Again*—along with articles on writing for youth by Jacqueline Woodson, Langston Hughes, and Marilyn Nelson.

**Mary K. Bercaw Edwards** is an Associate Professor of English and the Director of Maritime Studies at the University of Connecticut. She is the author of *Melville's Sources*, *Cannibal Old Me: Spoken Sources in Melville's Early* Works, and *Sailor Talk: Labor, Utterance, and Meaning in the Works of Melville, Conrad, and London*. A Coast Guard-licensed captain, she has 58,000 miles at sea, all under sail. Her love of the South Pacific grew from the two years her family spent there during their circumnavigation aboard their thirty-eight-foot sail boat.

**Poushali Bhadury** is an Assistant Professor of Children's Literature at Middle Tennessee State University. Specializing in international and comparative children's and young adult literature, she has contributed to scholarly journals such as *Children's Literature Association Quarterly*, *Journal of Lesbian Studies*, *The Lion and the Unicorn*, and *South Asian Review*. She is currently completing a monograph on Bengali children's publishing.

**Beverly Lyon Clark** was a Professor of English and Women's and Gender Studies at Wheaton College in Massachusetts, where she taught for forty-four years. The author of *Kiddie Lit: The Cultural Construction of Children's Literature in America*, *Regendering the School Story: Sassy Sissies and Tattling Tomboys*, and *The Afterlife of "Little Women*," she also edited or coedited works by or about Louisa May

Alcott, Mark Twain, Flannery O'Connor, Carson McCullers, and Evelyn Sharp. A tremendously influential literary figure in the field of children's literature, Clark mentored generations of teachers and scholars.

**Sara K. Day** is an Assistant Professor of English at Truman State University, where she teaches courses in children's and young adult literature, popular literature, and film. She is the author of *Reading Like a Girl: Narrative Intimacy in Contemporary American Young Adult Literature* and is currently the editor of the *Children's Literature Association Quarterly*. Her research interests include young adult literature, gender studies, narrative theory, and fandom studies.

**Rebekah May Degener** is an Assistant Professor of Elementary and Literacy Education at Minnesota State University, Mankato. Her research interests include representations of female athletes in children's literature, racial equity in literacy education, and fostering teacher candidates' beliefs about racial justice and critical literacy. Her work has appeared in *Children's Literature in Education*, *Children's Literature in English Language Education*, and the *Journal of Adolescent & Adult Literacy*.

**Gregory Eiselein** is a Professor of English and a University Distinguished Teaching Scholar at Kansas State University, where he also serves as the director of the first-year experience program, K-State First. He is the author of *Literature and Humanitarian Reform in the Civil War Era* and numerous articles on American literature and culture. He is also the editor or coeditor of several books including, with Anne K. Phillips, the Norton Critical Edition of *Little Women*.

**Paige Gray** is a Professor of Liberal Arts and Writing at the Savannah College of Art and Design. She is the author of *Cub Reporters: American Children's Literature and Journalism in the Golden Age*. Her work has appeared in academic journals such as *Children's Literature* and the *Children's Literature Association Quarterly* as well as popular-press outlets including *Time.com* and *The Conversation*.

**Kathleen T. Horning** is the Director of the Cooperative Children's Book Center, a library of the School of Education at the University of Wisconsin-Madison. She is the author of *From Cover to Cover: Evaluating and Reviewing Children's Books* and several articles on the history of the Newbery and Caldecott Medals. She teaches a popular online class about the history of the Newbery Medal for the Association of Library Services for Children division of the American Library Association.

**Adrienne Kertzer** is the author of *My Mother's Voice: Children, Literature, and the Holocaust*, which received the ChLA Honor Book Award and the Canadian Jewish Book Award for Scholarship on a Jewish Subject. Her influential essays on Holocaust representation, maternal narratives, and traumatic memory have appeared in a wide range of scholarly journals. Now Professor Emerita of the University of Calgary, she has recently published an essay on traumatic memory, agency, and the American identity of Holocaust time travelers in *Literary Cultures and Twentieth-Century Childhoods*.

**Kenneth B. Kidd** is a Professor of English at the University of Florida. He has coedited four essay collections, most recently *Queer as Camp*, and is the author of three books: *Making American Boys*, *Freud in Oz*, and *Theory for Beginners, or Children's Literature Otherwise*. He has also published highly influential scholarship on the Newbery Award and prizing in children's literature. With Elizabeth Marshall, he coedits the Routledge series Children's Literature and Culture.

**Anna Lockhart** is a writer, editor, and independent scholar. She holds a master's degree in English with a focus on Children's Literature and postcolonial literature from Rutgers University-Camden. Her academic publications include scholarship on the role of play, gender and animality in Laura Ingalls Wilder's *Little House* series. She has also worked extensively in features and magazine writing.

**Megan L. Musgrave** is an Associate Professor of English at Indiana University-Purdue University at Indianapolis, where she teaches courses in children's literature, young adult literature, Native American literature, women's studies, and pedagogy. Her research focuses on the intersections between young adult literature and culture, digital media, and activism. She is the author of *Digital Citizenship in Twenty-First Century Young Adult Literature: Imaginary Activism*.

**Anne K. Phillips** is the Donnelly Professor of English and Associate Head of the Department of English at Kansas State University. With Gregory Eiselein, she has coedited *The Alcott Encyclopedia*, the Norton Critical Edition of *Little Women*, and a special issue of *Women's Studies* on the newness of *Little Women*. With Miranda Green-Barteet, she coedited *Reconsidering Laura Ingalls Wilder: Little House and Beyond*. Past president of the Children's Literature Association and the Louisa May Alcott Society, she remains active in US children's literature, nineteenth century to the present.

**Rachel L. Rickard Rebellino** is an Instructor at Bowling Green State University, where she teaches undergraduate and graduate classes in children's and young adult literature. Her research focuses on narrative form, digital youth cultures, girlhood studies, and the role of youth literature in facilitating conversations around equity and justice. Her work has been published in *The ALAN Review*, *English Journal*, and *The Lion and the Unicorn*.

**Paul Ringel** is an Associate Professor of History at High Point University. He is the author of *Commercializing Childhood: Children's Magazines, Urban Gentility, and the Ideal of the Child Consumer in the United States, 1823–1918* and numerous articles about children's literature and American children's consumer cultures. His current work includes The William Penn Project, a public history project on a segregated Black high school in High Point, North Carolina.

**Donelle Ruwe** is Professor and Chair of English at Northern Arizona University. She is the author of *British Children's Poetry in the Romantic Era: Verse, Riddle, and Rhyme*, the editor of *Culturing the Child, 1660–1830: Essays in Memory of Mitzi Myers*, and the coeditor, with James Leve, of *Children, Childhood, and Musical Theater*. Her poetry chapbook *Condiments* has won multiple awards. Ruwe is the co-president of the British Women Writers Association.

**Sara L. Schwebel** is the Director of the Center for Children's Books at the University of Illinois Urbana-Champaign, where she is a Professor of Information Sciences. She is the author of *Child-Sized History: Fictions of the Past in U.S. Classrooms* and the editor of *Island of the Blue Dolphins: The Complete Reader's Edition* and The Lone Woman and Last Indians Digital Archive. She is currently coauthoring, with Ivy Stabell and Anastasia Ulanowicz, a history of US children's literature.

**Jocelyn Van Tuyl** is a Professor of French at New College of Florida. A specialist in the works of Nobel Laureate André Gide, she is the author of *André Gide and the Second World War* and author-translator of *André Gide et la Seconde Guerre mondiale*. Her current research examines the ways midcentury American children's literature was shaped by World War II-era emigrants, exiles, and expats shuttling between the US and France.

# Introduction

## The Gold Medal and the Ivory Tower

*Sara L. Schwebel and Jocelyn Van Tuyl*

We find them in nearly every American library and bookstore: row upon row of shiny gold stickers, a triumphant display of The Best Books for Children. Considered the most distinguished American writing for kids, the Newbery Medal winners are aspirational (or assigned) reading for schoolchildren everywhere. These are books that parents, grandparents, and other adults recognize instantly (thanks to that shiny medal) and gift to children again and again. Intense secrecy surrounds the selection process, and the annual Medal announcement generates excitement in many circles. K-12 educators and librarians have long revered the Award, interviewing Newbery-winning authors, collecting their papers in archives, and publishing on their work. But one group—literature professors—has disproportionately ignored the Medal winners in its scholarship. As we set out to remedy that neglect in this volume, we first trace its origins back to the Medal's inception a century ago.

When Frederic G. Melcher proposed a children's book award at a 1921 meeting of the American Library Association (ALA), he was motivated in large part by the sluggish production of American children's literature. As they had for well over a century, American kids grew up with more British books than American ones—or at least, more *respectable* British books. Thinking about the recently created Pulitzer Prize, Melcher hypothesized that the situation could change if American authors became convinced that producing a beautiful book for children would bring prestige. With the hindsight of a century, it seems that Melcher figured correctly: publicity surrounding the Newbery Medal helped stimulate the production of "literary" American children's books, establish a mechanism for forming a national children's canon, and set a precedent that other nations followed (as the UK did by launching its Carnegie Medal in 1936).

That Melcher proposed the John Newbery name for an American book prize is telling, honoring as it does the eighteenth-century British publisher credited with effectively launching the field of children's literature by tying instruction to delight (Marcus 86). As library scholar Anne Lundin so aptly characterized it, "a publisher honor[ed] a

DOI: 10.4324/9780367337223-NaN-1

publisher" (49) with an award intended to benefit the *business* of children's literature. Moreover, the Newbery solidified a relationship between American book publishers and the growing field of children's librarianship—a marriage that continues to influence the landscape of American children's literature today. Melcher, who was affiliated with a number of bookseller associations as well as *Publishers Weekly* at the time he proposed the Newbery, knew that children's librarians would be fierce advocates for the production of quality children's books—with texts and bindings that could grace a bedroom or nursery for decades—and that librarians' approval of these beautiful books would improve publishers' bottom lines.

Assigning children's librarians the task of annually selecting "the most distinguished contribution to American literature for children" (Association 9) was part of a strategy to keep the Award free from the taint of commercialism. No one was better suited to that task than early-twentieth-century librarians, a group historian Dee Garrison characterizes as "Apostles of Culture." While librarians had turned over the role of evaluating adult literature to newly formed university English departments, they simultaneously solidified their role as gatekeepers of children's literature, a subject ignored by the academy. Eschewing dime novels, syndicate fiction, and comics when filling their child-sized shelves, librarians were apt to argue that reading "bad fiction" was worse than not reading at all. The Newbery Medal, as early children's librarians perceived it, was a bulwark against popular literature. Each Newbery promised excellence in an American tradition—a tradition defined, by default, as White, Protestant, and middle class.

While librarians' selection of Newbery winners was designed to position the prize above commercial interests, their involvement in the process actually enmeshed them in the market. That it did so is not unique to the Newbery—as literary scholar James F. English has convincingly argued, this is the history of cultural prizing more generally: aesthetic value is exchanged for economic value and inextricably linked to the political (English 17–21). But the Newbery's history points to the complex relationship forged between booksellers and children's librarians—to the exclusion of literary scholars. Further, it highlights the tension within the triad of profit, popularity, and prestige—a tension that rests constantly within the Medal (Kidd 166–168; Kidd and Thomas 1–18).

There is no question that the Newbery prize generates considerable profit, promoting individual authors' careers and sometimes securing the viability of small publishing houses (Maughan 24). Children's authors and publishers know it to be a holy grail that confers instant celebrity status in the children's book world. Moreover, by contrast with the current "boom and bust" cycle—in which popular series fiction generates large profits when it first comes out but then fails to maintain marketability—Newbery titles are typically steady sellers.[1] In effect, the gold medal acts as an insurance policy against the books' going permanently out of print: only one Newbery title, James Daugherty's *Daniel Boone* (1939; 1940 Newbery Medal), has met that fate. Librarians thus wield tremendous influence in shaping the children's literature canon, anointing books that endure over generations as "classics."

The Newbery's influence is further amplified by policies and procedures surrounding the selection and announcement of the winner—procedures designed to heighten anticipation and maximize publicity. Secrecy has been an enduring feature of the process (Horning). For many years, obfuscation centered on the ALA's *announcement* of the Award winner, but since 1978 it has extended to all details about the process preceding the Medal announcement; no records of votes or committee discussions about contenders have been archived since that year.[2] Another Newbery tradition is the grand reveal. Taking a page from the bookseller's marketing toolkit, the ALA has secured extensive print, radio, and television coverage of the winner, including, between 2000 and 2009, interviews on the *CBS Today* show, which reached an audience of four million. While some worry that the end of those broadcasts decreased publicity that built prestige and drove sales (Cockcroft), the ALA now live-streams its annual Award announcement, generating considerable buzz.

The hoopla surrounding the Newbery announcement speaks to further tensions inherent in the prize. On the one hand, the Newbery Medal is a celebration "of the people." Public librarians representing the children of their hometown communities, large and small, come together to champion a book that the elite literary establishment—the academy—wouldn't deign to review. On the other hand, the mechanisms of the Newbery Medal *themselves* foster elitism: exasperatingly, both archived records and recent committee members' informal comments reveal that judges repeatedly fret that there are not enough "distinguished" titles to choose from—even going as far as to suggest that the Award not be granted that year.[3] This opinion stands in stark contrast to that of legions of informal Newbery voters who gather in local libraries, school classrooms, and virtual spaces (Goodreads, the *School Library Journal* blog "Heavy Medal") to advocate passionately for the book(s) they nominate for Newbery gold.[4]

In some ways, the voices of "the people"—including their frustration with Newbery selections—matter more now than they did in the past. During the first half-century of the Newbery Medal's history, 80 or more percent of children's books sold in the United States were purchased by institutions (libraries and schools) and less than 20 percent by individuals; in the second decade of the twenty-first century, more than 65 percent of children's books sold were purchased by individuals (Lundin 48–49; Schwebel 20; Rivera 15). Thus, the fate of a book depends less on librarians' selections than in the past, and increasingly rests on the choices of individual consumers. At the same time, children's librarians collectively understand their responsibility to connect to the communities they serve in more inclusive terms than their early twentieth-century predecessors. No longer gatekeepers, they see themselves as media-savvy, visually-literate information facilitators, helping to connect library patrons to resources that meet *their* needs. As a result, series fiction and comics, the kind of books against which the Newbery Medal originally stood, now populate children's library shelves—and the latter can win Newbery gold.[5]

But if children's librarianship has grown, changed, and arguably democratized since its inception in the 1920s, one cohort of gatekeepers remains: the Newbery Award Selection Committee. The librarians and media specialists who occupy coveted spots on the Committee are not infrequently members of an elite themselves: professors of Library Science or administrators rather than "boots-on-the-ground librarians" (Maughan 28); those working librarians who are elected to the Committee, moreover, have often achieved national recognition by writing successful blogs. Some cite the Committee's composition as fostering a trend toward Newbery selections that are noteworthy for their quirkiness and difficulty, perhaps chosen to reflect the Committee's cleverness and sophistication. Are children's books considered "the most distinguished," and therefore worthy of a Medal, only when adults appreciate them more than children? Does anxiety about the low status of children's literature generally—an anxiety that today's elite youth librarians may share with their 1920s predecessors—lead to an insistence on Newbery titles with highbrow aspirations?[6] This elitist tendency should make Newbery Medal books a particularly compelling object of study for professors of literature, who surely share that anxiety about status. But the Newbery books have elicited far less academic interest than one would expect given their considerable influence and distinction.

The history of scholarly attention given (or withheld from) Newbery winners is in many ways the history of children's literature studies as a profession. As English departments formed in American universities and literary scholars sought to professionalize, universities became the guardians of American literature, a role previously held by literary magazines and clubs (Clark 58). In the process, children's literature became increasingly separated and set off from "Literature." While this early-twentieth-century development demoted children's books in terms of status, it also created space for new champions of the genre, and women moved onto center stage. Literary scholar Jacalyn Eddy dubs this founding generation the "bookwomen," and it is largely through their efforts that the Newbery Medal became a measure of status and prestige in its own right. The Medal is perhaps the best and most enduring symbol of their growing circle of influence, which came to encompass specialty bookstores, children's departments in publishing houses, and a demographic dominance in the ALA—and especially its children's division—that paralleled a similar dominance in K-12 schools. This development marks a milestone in what would become two diverging histories of professionalization. While English professors turned their attention elsewhere, library and education professionals nurtured children's literature, which Literature departments would "discover" only decades later.

Because of this fork in the road of literary institutionalization, academic critics developed a sense of "critical condescension" toward children's literature in general (Clark 74), and we see this condescension enduring in their neglect of the Newbery today. During the first half-century of its history, the Newbery garnered scant notice among literary scholars since children's literature as a field had not yet emerged. When it did, in the 1970s, practitioners brought their own biases to the table. In the inaugural 1972 issue of *Children's Literature*, for example, editor Francelia Butler wrote: "Children's literature is almost entirely in the hands of those in education or library science, who emphasize the uses of literature in the classroom, methodology, biographies of current writers, graded reading lists, book reports—good things but not the concern of those in the Humanities" (8). The first generation of children's literature scholars largely ignored the work of education professors and librarians, focusing instead on books they considered important historical models and classics: fables and fairy tales, medieval literature, and Golden Age fiction—all categories that are considered "Literature," not just "children's literature."[7] While these scholars wrote about contemporary Newbery winners on occasion, attention to Newbery titles continued to be uneven and infrequent.[8]

Looking back over a half-century of children's literature scholarship, patterns of attention to Newbery books emerge. At one end of the continuum, some twenty percent of the Medal books have generated significant literary scholarship. Half of those appear on the *Publishers Weekly* list of "All-Time Bestselling Children's Books."[9] Titles on this long-view list are instantly recognizable as Newbery "classics," whether because of popularity with readers (Madeleine L'Engle's *A Wrinkle in Time* [1962; 1963 Newbery Medal]), prominence in school curricula (Esther Forbes's *Johnny Tremain* [1943; 1944 Newbery Medal]), or a combination of the two (Scott O'Dell's *Island of the Blue Dolphins* [1960; 1961 Newbery Medal] and Lois Lowry's *The Giver* [1993; 1994 Newbery Medal]). Still circulating, still widely read, these books have beaten the rap of Newberys as "eat-your-spinach books" (Graff)—novels that adults remember having foisted on them by teachers and librarians. Turning next to the somewhat less popular but widely-studied titles, we find that scholarship tends to beget scholarship, marking a work as valued in the academic marketplace and often leading to further critical attention. Then there is the middle ground: those books—roughly half the Newbery winners—that have elicited scant to moderate scholarly coverage. And at the other end of the spectrum, we find total scholarly silence (or only very brief treatment) for approximately one-third of the Medal books. To be sure, some winners from the Medal's earlier decades are unlikely to have attracted criticism, let alone readership, because of their offensive gender biases and racist attitudes. Looking beyond those troublesome titles, however, we find a large number of works that have remained in the shadows. We speculate that many of these books are not only what Kenneth Kidd calls "middlebrow" (169) but also *middle-aged*: too new to have the status of Golden Age classics, too old to be widely read by the generations of scholars working in the field since the 1970s.

These neglected Newberys are ripe for attention on the occasion of the Medal's centennial, a time when children's literature scholarship is burgeoning. In the past half-century, the field of children's literature studies has grown exponentially: scholarly journals, professional associations, and master's and doctoral programs devoted specifically to children's literature are flourishing in the US and abroad. At the same time, the number and diversity of newly released children's and young adult books grow at a rapid pace.[10] Critical approaches have proliferated, as have the media studied. As we began work on this volume, published calls for papers on children's literature revealed a wide diversity of genres (comics, animation, fandoms), topics (diversity, transnationalism, climate change), and critical lenses (deconstructionism, posthumanism, cognitive approaches). In this frothy and exuberant era, one could argue, there is simply too much competition, too much to write about, for Newbery books to attract attention.

Still, the enticing array of options does not fully explain current neglect. One issue is the fact that the Newbery recognizes only print media at a time when newer media call out for scholars' attention. Another more significant issue concerns current trends in literary scholarship and cultural criticism—indeed, the nature of the Newbery tends to preclude the types of scholarly engagement that are currently at the academic forefront. The Award's core tenet, literary distinction, may have become an obstacle.[11] Librarians Robert Bittner and Michelle Superle, during their service on various youth literature prize committees, found themselves frustrated by the "primary criterion for identifying prize winners in many major awards—'excellence'" (74). This nebulous benchmark is more congenial to the aesthetic evaluations and formal analyses of mid-twentieth-century New Criticism than to current criticism's investment in "ideological considerations related to gender, race, class, and other social variables" (74). If scholars have shunned Newbery books, then, it may be in part because the values espoused by the Medal are ill-suited to present-day scholarly interests, particularly those that relate to diversity.

Furthermore, the criterion of "excellence," applied by predominantly White Newbery committee members, has made for a canon that is notably White in terms of characters, authors, and attitudes. Privileging "literary quality" allowed selection committees to reward books that "contained racist, sexist, or otherwise offensive elements" (Schwebel 109); searching for subjective "distinction" led to "a conspicuous absence of non-white protagonists and authors" among twentieth-century Newbery winners (Miller).[12] Before the 1970s, Newbery-winning books set in the United States showed little if any racial or ethnic diversity, even as African American librarians moved onto Newbery selection committees. Until the 1970s, Newbery-winning *authors* were nearly universally White. In fact, the first Medal books featuring African American protagonists were written by White authors—and even as they attempted to create sympathetic, nuanced, deeply human characters, they wrote in frameworks that reinforced stereotypes and White hegemony.[13] It was not until the mid-1970s, in the wake of the social and political unrest released by the Civil Rights Movement, that African American authors Virginia Hamilton and Mildred D. Taylor won Newbery gold for *M. C. Higgins, the Great* (1974; 1975 Newbery Medal) and *Roll of Thunder, Hear My Cry* (1976; 1977 Newbery Medal), respectively. Then decades of Whiteness again, until the 2000s finally brought Newbery recognition to a sizeable number of authors of color. Even so, Newbery choices have been cautious, with racism addressed primarily through "historical novels ... set no later than the Depression" (Kidd 180).[14] Only with the selection of Kwame Alexander's novel *The Crossover* in 2015 has the Newbery sanctioned discussion of present-day racism in the US. As the first Newbery century drew to its close, then, Newbery books as a body became slightly less White, slightly less distanced in their treatment of race and racism.

To the extent that change *has* occurred, much of the credit is due to two groups that campaigned for diversity in children's literature: the Council on Interracial Books for Children (CIBC), beginning in the 1960s, and We Need Diverse Books (WNDB), launched in the 2010s. Both movements used prizing as a strategy to upend the children's publishing industry. In 1966, the CIBC launched an annual writing contest for "previously unpublished African Americans (and in subsequent years, members of other minority groups)" (Schwebel 20). The CIBC contest helped increase the share of minority-authored children's books that reached publication and led, indirectly, to the ALA's creation of the Coretta Scott King and Pura Belpré Awards for children's books by authors and illustrators of color (Schwebel 15–16). Nevertheless, children's literature remained disconcertingly White, and the newly-created prizes never achieved the attention or economic impact of the Newbery. Fifty years after the inception of the CIBC contest, the We Need Diverse Books movement took up the cause.[15] WNDB's Walter

Dean Myers Award, inaugurated in 2016, recognizes "diverse authors (or co-authors) whose works feature diverse main characters and address diversity in a meaningful way," with "diverse" defined as "one or more of the following: a person of color, Native American, LGBTQIA, a person with a disability, and/or a member of a marginalized religious or cultural minority in the United States" ("Walter"). WNDB's attention to the diversity of both characters and authors links it to the Own Voices movement that emerged on its heels. Own Voices advocates for books written by members of the "marginalized communit[ies]" depicted (Gómez); as such, it represents resistance to the trend of White authorship and biases in prizing throughout much of the Newbery's history.

The advocacy work of the CIBC, WNDB, and associated movements shifted norms within the ALA and ultimately (if unevenly), within the Newbery establishment—witness the 2018 award season, when the Newbery Medal and all three Newbery Honors went to authors of color. The Newbery originated as a close partnership between publishers and children's librarians when the youth publishing industry was young, but over the decades, librarians' influence over which books were published and which became bestsellers waned. Today, we see children's librarians once again marshalling their power as book award judges to bend the publishing industry toward their values. By selecting more Newbery and other book award titles that feature underrepresented communities, librarians are working to bring the We Need Diverse Books movement to bear on the industry, influencing both current sales and future book contracts.

Yet even as books by more diverse authors claim the coveted prize, the Newbery casts a long shadow. Concerns about Newbery texts being an out-of-touch choice of elitist and/or racist adults endure, especially as the disjunction between a persistently White Medal canon and an increasingly diverse youth readership grows deeper every year. At the Newbery centennial, the Medal books of the early- to mid-twentieth century might appear less-than-attractive objects of study. Because these texts played such important roles in shaping and documenting the contours of American children's literature, however, all Newbery books warrant serious reconsideration at this juncture. *Dust Off the Gold Medal* attends to their overlooked history, shedding light on both the hidden elements of diversity apparent in these texts and the way that the books respond—sometimes in quite subtle ways—to contemporaneous concerns around race, class, gender, disability, and nationalism.

Each of this volume's fourteen chapters discusses an understudied Newbery Medal book. Collectively, the chapters trace major themes, topics, and trends in American children's literature of the past century. They analyze representations of a range of social and cultural identities (African American, Asian American, Jewish, Muslim, Hindu, rural, disabled) while exploring a diversity of genres (the sea story, animal story, and sports story; mystery, legend, and biography; verse novel, poetry, and illustrated text; historical fiction and young adult novel). Chapters utilize different critical approaches but all are historically grounded, linking to the historical context of their publication and prizing and addressing, where relevant, the way members of the Newbery Award Selection Committee were influenced by contemporaneous social, political, and literary trends. Every decade of the Newbery's first century is represented, with particular attention to Newbery titles from the 1920s through 1940s, an area of significant critical neglect.

Our volume begins with the third book ever to win the Newbery: Charles Boardman Hawes's largely forgotten *The Dark Frigate* (1923; 1924 Newbery Medal). Paul Ringel argues that the prizing of this pirate adventure elucidates the evolution of US children's literature at a moment when its guardianship was shifting from the male editors of genteel magazines to the "bookwomen," whose worldview was more "cosmopolitan, literary, and (for its time) progressive." Ringel characterizes Hawes's Newbery as a strategic choice. An adventure tale that shared much in common with the mass-market serial fiction the Newbery stood against, *The Dark Frigate* bridged divides between the popular and the literary. Moreover, it was unabashedly male. By prizing this and other 1920s texts that largely reinforced existing social hierarchies, Ringel claims, female librarians were able to gain legitimacy as the arbiters of taste for American youth.

The focus on male-authored adventure tales continues in the two subsequent chapters. Dhan Gopal Mukerji's *Gay-Neck: The Story of a Pigeon* (1927; 1928 Newbery Medal), Poushali Bhadury argues, both punches up and punches down as it tracks the whereabouts of a Brahmin narrator, tribal (Santal) bird handler, and carrier pigeon during World War I. Readers see an Indian landscape where British rule is most visible in its absence—a defiant anticolonialist vision. Yet even as the novel counters Western ideas about an "untamed" India, it reinforces the social hierarchies of the subcontinent through its essentialized depictions of characters who differ from the elite author and narrator in caste, ethnicity, race, and religion. Unlike *Gay-Neck*, Eric P. Kelly's historical novel *The Trumpeter of Krakow* (1928; 1929 Newbery Medal) represents the more typical tradition of "foreign background stories" written by American authors (Viguers 444). Published in the early years of Poland's national independence (and subsequently reissued and promoted during the Cold War), the novel is a decidedly American retelling of a legend of medieval Poland—a work that Kenneth Kidd reads as "a case study in the ethics of writing historical fiction and especially historical fiction about other nations."

Though most often awarded to a novel, the Newbery Medal's first winner was a nonfiction work, Hendrik Willem Van Loon's *The Story of*

*Mankind* (1921; 1922 Newbery Medal) and in its early decades, the Newbery recognized a pair of biographies. Anne K. Phillips and Gregory Eiselein's chapter on *Invincible Louisa* (1933; 1934 Newbery Medal) highlights the Newbery establishment's turn to both female authors and American actors in the years leading up to World War II. It argues that Cornelia Meigs's study of Louisa May Alcott—the first biography to win Newbery gold—reflected "feminist persistence and optimism" during the Great Depression and anticipated later trends in Alcott scholarship, including exploration of the complex relationship between Louisa and her transcendentalist father, Bronson Alcott. Continuing the focus on American biography—and noting a wartime turn toward masculine subjects—Beverly Lyon Clark's chapter on *Daniel Boone* (1939; 1940 Newbery Medal) explores the most disparaged of Newbery winners, the one title that as of the centennial is out of print. Clark argues that James Daugherty's self-illustrated, "romantic" biography presents a muscular, masculine, jingoistic story about "freedom" that resonated for many at the start of World War II but whose racist, mythic narrative now both offends modern sensibilities and departs from adult ideas about the way youth biographies should present complex historical figures.

The 1940s saw Newbery recognition for children's books that addressed or reworked classic texts for adults. Based on author Armstrong Sperry's work as an ethnographer, *Call it Courage* (1940; 1941 Newbery Medal) draws on both South Pacific legends and adventure stories by Western writers like Jack London, Herman Melville, and Robert Louis Stevenson. Situating *Call it Courage* in a tradition of "cannibal talk" that stretches back to antiquity and forward to the 2016 Disney film *Moana*, Mary K. Bercaw Edwards demonstrates how Sperry's Newbery winner projects violence onto the ethnographic Other. Our third Newbery winner from the 1940s also grapples with race, Otherness, and literary heritage. Megan L. Musgrave demonstrates how author Marguerite Henry and illustrator Wesley Dennis condemn both animal cruelty and racism in *King of the Wind* (1948; 1949 Newbery Medal). Musgrave also makes a compelling case for Henry's novel as a rewriting of French author Eugène Sue's serialized *The Godolphin Arabian* (1839). Delineating the changes Henry made to adapt the story for young readers, Musgrave examines how the popularity of the horse story genre helped convince US publishers of the goldmine children's books represented during the postwar baby boom.

The Newbery's gaze remained focused on the past in our 1950s Newbery selection. Anna Lockhart argues that Meindert DeJong's *The Wheel on the School* (1954; 1955 Newbery Medal) was old-fashioned from the moment of its publication. She explores two strands of nostalgia associated with DeJong's novel, that of an immigrant author remembering his happy childhood in Holland, and that of a Newbery Award Selection Committee reading DeJong's story during an anxious

Cold War moment. Already a powerful American symbol by the 1950s, the little red schoolhouse—and DeJong's rural one-room school—contrasted sharply with contemporary fears *for* children's safety and *about* children's performance against the backdrop of Soviet ascendancy. Far from DeJong's charming Dutch village and progressive primary school, our Newbery pick for the 1960s takes us to New York City, where fourteen-year-old Dave shares urban adventures with his adopted cat. A first-person, slang-filled account of father-son struggles and awkward blind dates, Emily Neville's *It's Like This, Cat* (1963; 1964 Newbery Medal) is "perhaps the first true example of young adult fiction." Kathleen T. Horning and Jocelyn Van Tuyl conjecture that *Cat*'s Newbery win may have had a paradoxical effect, making the book less popular with teens and leading scholars to overlook the novel's contributions to the emerging young adult genre.

With the arrival of the 1970s, we begin to see the Civil Rights Movement's influence on the Newbery Award Selection Committee. We turn to two diverging treatments of disability prized during a key decade for disability rights: Betsy Byars's contemporary realist novel *The Summer of the Swans* (1970; 1971 Newbery Medal) and Ellen Raskin's puzzle mystery *The Westing Game* (1978; 1979 Newbery Medal). The first features a search for a child with an intellectual disability who becomes lost in the woods; the second involves a quest for an inheritance. Both the search and the quest, Sara K. Day and Paige Gray argue in their chapter, foreground themes of vision and visibility, thereby engaging with the metaphorical invisibility of disability. The 1970s—and second-wave feminism—also saw the emergence of the women's poetry movement. Donelle Ruwe situates Nancy Willard's *A Visit to William Blake's Inn: Poems for Innocent and Experienced Travelers* (1981; 1982 Newbery Medal) within the context of that movement—which happened to coincide with William Blake's entry into the canon of British Romantic poetry. With her fantastical take on Blakean lyricism, Ruwe argues, Willard joined "a long line of prominent women writers who reimagined Blake—an obscure and difficult author—as a children's poet."

An expansive view of what children can understand and care about informs E. L. Konigsburg's second Newbery-winning novel, *The View from Saturday* (1996; 1997 Newbery Medal)—the tale of an Academic Bowl team comprising "one Jew, one half-Jew, a WASP, and an Indian" (Konigsburg 22). Adrienne Kertzer unpacks Konigsburg's humorous critique of "the institutional language of diversity," demonstrating how the novelist pairs satire with a nuanced and original exploration of identity, community, and courtesy. Our next Newbery book surprises in a different way, by placing a Japanese American family in the Deep South of postwar America. Giselle Liza Anatol argues that Cynthia Kadohata's *Kira-Kira* (2004; 2005 Newbery Medal), often read as assimilationist, is anything but. Rather, the trauma of Japanese/American evacuation and incarceration haunts the text. And the book's Georgia setting, associated as it is with chattel slavery and Indian removal, only accentuates racism's spectral presence.

The prizing of Kwame Alexander's *The Crossover* (2014; 2015 Newbery Medal) brought a welcome departure in Newbery history: an Own Voices verse novel that grapples with systemic racism in the contemporary era. Rachel L. Rickard Rebellino and Rebekah May Degener argue that the novel has been frequently misunderstood, labeled a book for reluctant readers and dismissed as juvenile in its aesthetics. Instead, they argue, *The Crossover*'s use of hip-hop techniques yields an "argument rooted in the politics of literacy" and honors the lived experience of Black boyhood.

This volume's fresh take on critically neglected Newbery books is especially compelling because the Award is still vigorous at one hundred. The institutions associated with the Newbery's founding and early promotion—public libraries, book publishers, book review journals, children's bookstores—have faced considerable challenges as late twentieth-/early twenty-first-century technology and consumer behavior have upended every aspect of the book business, from production to purchasing, circulation, and readership. Yet the Newbery, the most prestigious of US children's literature's prizes, is thriving. Medal-winning books remain influential as a canon, and the annual announcement of Newbery gold continues to generate excitement. The attention is due, in large part, to the Award's acknowledged influence: even those who are unenthusiastic about its history recognize its importance and value, and are committed to change. The essays collected here are both an homage to this enduring institution and an outcome of the contributors' collective ambivalence about its legacy. They invite increased critical attention to the Newbery as it enters its second century.

## Notes

1 In recent decades, a Newbery win has brought, at minimum, a sales increase of several hundred percent in the months immediately after the Medal announcement; the more important figure often remains long-term sales (Cockcroft).

2 Some early committee votes and correspondence are also missing, but since the Newbery papers were not deposited into a collection managed by a professional archives staff until 1973, it is unsurprising that documents were sporadically misplaced. Among the missing are those associated with the decision to award the Medal to Ann Nolan Clark's *Secret of the Andes* (1952; 1953 Newbery Medal) and designate E. B. White's *Charlotte's Web* the first runner-up. (Honor Books were known as runners-up before 1971).

3 The chairman of the Newbery Award Selection Committee of 1954, which ultimately chose Joseph Krumgold's *...And Now Miguel* (1953; 1954 Newbery Medal), asked Frederic Melcher, "Does the medal have to be given each year?" (Darrah). Anita Silvey wrote, "When I asked former ALSC

judges about their choices, they all offered the same rationale: the committees work very hard—and if their top picks aren't exciting, that means there were 'no good books' to choose from that year" (Silvey 40).

4 *School Library Journal* "Heavy Medal" is edited by librarians who themselves have served on the Newbery or other Youth Media Award committees; however, participation in most mock Newbery forums is less exclusive, including child readers, teachers, and public librarians.

5 In the second half of the 2010s, graphic narratives captured two Newbery Honors, Cece Bell's *El Deafo* (2014; 2015 Newbery Honor) and Victoria Jamieson's *Roller Girl* (2015; 2016 Newbery Honor), and the Newbery Award itself, Jerry Craft's *New Kid* (2019; 2020 Newbery Medal).

6 Because children's literature has historically been excluded from the scholarly category of Literature (a designation reserved for adult texts) and because writing for children is always associated with pedagogy, children's literature is considered middlebrow at best—even when it aspires to highbrow status, eschewing popular taste. Kidd explains this tension as it relates to the Newbery: "prizing ... has middlebrow as well as highbrow features and effects; it encourages both the making and unmaking of canons, underwrites but also undercuts faith in popularity" (166).

7 Golden Age texts—those from the second half of the nineteenth century, when most major writers wrote for both children and adults (Clark 48), through World War I—are commonly analyzed in scholarly journals outside the field of children's literature, with articles on Alcott, Carroll, Kipling, and Twain featured in periodicals devoted to general literary studies, comparative literature, Victorian literature, and women's studies.

8 *Children's Literature*, the oldest American scholarly journal in the field, published an article on Jean Craighead George's *Julie of the Wolves* (1972; 1973 Newbery Medal) in 1974, the third year of the journal's existence (Stott). But this is the exception to the rule; even as the journal's focus shifted toward contemporary children's literature, Newbery titles received scant attention.

9 Eight of the highly studied Newberys are in the *Publishers Weekly* top 100, including three in the top 20: *Island of the Blue Dolphins* by Scott O'Dell (1960; 1961 Newbery Medal) is #6, *A Wrinkle in Time* by Madeleine L'Engle (1962; 1963 Newbery Medal) is #11, and *Johnny Tremain* (1943; 1944 Newbery Medal) is #16 (Roback and Turvey).

10 In 1919, 433 new children's books were published in the United States. In 2016, newly published children's titles numbered more than 27,000 and young adult titles nearly 5,000 (Marcus 104; Barr 313).

11 When the ALA changed the name of its lifetime achievement award from the Laura Ingalls Wilder Award to the Children's Literature Legacy Award in 2018, it simultaneously altered the selection criteria. The award now recognizes recipients for their "significant and lasting contribution to children's literature *through books that demonstrate integrity and respect for all children's lives and experiences*" (ALSC 1, new criteria italicized). These updated criteria, with their social dimension, stand in contrast to the Newbery, which continues to recognize literary distinction alone.

12 In her landmark 1965 essay "The All-White World of Children's Books," Nancy Larrick noted the scarcity of characters of color in all children's books—Newbery and Caldecott winners and non-winners alike.

13 White author Elizabeth Yates's Newbery novel *Amos Fortune, Free Man* (1950; 1951 Newbery Medal) presents Christianity as salvation, even justifying slavery. White novelist William H. Armstrong's *Sounder* (1969; 1960

Newbery Medal) implicitly argues for moving out of one's community through literacy and upward mobility (Schwebel 113–114).

14 As Kidd has argued, the Newbery Honor Books became a "safely contained" way to engage "with the vexing theme of Americanness," relegating diversity to a kind of shadow canon (177).

15 While the Council on Interracial Books for Children's *Bulletin* had limited distribution in certain parts of the country, WNDB exploded on social media, where it was available to all and generated additional user content.

## Works Cited

Association for Library Service to Children (ALSC) Awards Program Review Task Force. "ALSC Awards Program Review Task Force Recommendation: Laura Ingalls Wilder Award." *American Library Association.* 15 May 2018. Web. 7 July 2018.

Association for Library Service to Children. "John Newbery Award Committee Manual." Oct. 2009. *American Library Association.* Aug. 2012. Web. 23 July 2018.

Barr, Catherine, ed. *Library and Book Trade Almanac.* 62nd ed. Medford, NJ: Information Today, Inc., 2017. Print.

Bittner, Robert, and Michelle Superle. "The Last Bastion of Aesthetics? Formalism and the Rhetoric of Excellence in Children's Literary Awards." *Prizing Children's Literature: The Cultural Politics of Children's Book Awards.* Ed. Kenneth B. Kidd and Joseph T. Thomas, Jr. New York: Routledge, 2017. 73–86. Print.

Butler, Francelia. "The Editor's High Chair." *Children's Literature* 1 (1972): 7–8. *Project Muse.* Web. 20 July 2018.

Clark, Beverly Lyon. *Kiddie Lit: The Cultural Construction of Children's Literature in America.* Baltimore: Johns Hopkins UP, 2003. Print.

Cockcroft, Marlaina. "Caldecott and Newbery Medal Wins Bring Instant Boost to Book Sales." *School Library Journal.* 10 Feb. 2018. Web. 20 July 2018.

Darrah, Jane. Letter to Frederic G. Melcher. 13 Nov. 1954. Records Series 24/42/5, Box 1, Folder 1. *American Library Association Archives.* Urbana-Champaign, IL: University of Illinois Archives.

Eddy, Jacalyn. *Bookwomen: Creating an Empire in Children's Book Publishing, 1919–1939.* 1st ed. Madison: U of Wisconsin P, 2006. Print.

English, James F. *The Economy of Prestige: Prizes, Awards, and the Circulation of Cultural Value.* Cambridge: Harvard UP, 2005. Print.

Garrison, Dee. *Apostles of Culture: The Public Librarian and American Society, 1876–1920.* New York: The Free Press, 1979. Print.

Gómez, Sarah Hannah. "Six YA Titles that Epitomize #OwnVoices." *School Library Journal.* 25 Apr. 2017. Web. 21 June 2018.

Graff, E. J. "A Gold Star for Tedium: Do the Newbery Medal-Winning Children's Books Really Have to be So Dreary?" *Salon.* 26 Jan. 2001. Web. 11 June 2018.

Horning, Kathleen T. "Secrecy and the Newbery Medal." *Horn Book Magazine* 87.4 (July/Aug. 2011): 60–70. Print.

Kidd, Kenneth B. "Prizing Children's Literature: The Case of Newbery Gold." *Children's Literature* 35 (2007): 166–190. *Project Muse.* Web. 13 June 2018.

Kidd, Kenneth B., and Joseph T. Thomas, Jr. *Prizing Children's Literature: The Cultural Politics of Children's Book Awards*. New York: Routledge, 2017. Print.

Konigsburg, E. L. *The View from Saturday*. New York: Atheneum Books for Young Readers-Simon and Schuster Children's Publishing Division, 1996. Print.

Larrick, Nancy. "The All-White World of Children's Books." *Saturday Review* 11 Sep. 1965: 63–65; 84–85. Print.

Lundin, Anne. *Constructing the Canon of Children's Literature: Beyond Library Walls and Ivory Towers*. New York: Routledge, 2004. Print.

Marcus, Leonard S. *Minders of Make-Believe: Idealists, Entrepreneurs, and the Shaping of American Children's Literature*. Boston: Houghton Mifflin, 2008. Print.

Maughan, Shannon. "And the Winner Is...." *Publishers Weekly* 258.49 (2011): 24–29. *Education Full Text*. Web. 19 Jan. 2021.

Miller, Bonnie J. F. "What Color is Gold? Twenty-One Years of Same-Race Authors and Protagonists in the Newbery Medal." *Journal of Youth Service in Libraries* 12.1 (1998): 34–39 *ERIC*. Web. 20 June 2018.

Rivera, Edward. "Children's Book Publishing in the US." IBIS World Industry Report OD4394. *IBISWorld*, Dec. 2017. Web. 20 July 2018.

Roback, Diane, ed., and Debbie Hochman Turvey, comp. "All-Time Bestselling Children's Books." *Publishers Weekly*, 17 Dec. 2001. Web. 19 Jan. 2021.

Schwebel, Sara L. *Child-Sized History: Fictions of the Past in U.S. Classrooms*. Nashville: Vanderbilt UP, 2011.

Silvey, Anita. "Has the Newbery Lost Its Way?" *School Library Journal*. 54.10 (2008): 38–41. *Academic Search Complete*. Web. 10 June 2018.

Stott, Jon C. "Jean George's Arctic Pastoral: A Reading of *Julie of the Wolves*." *Children's Literature* 3 (1974): 131–139. *Project Muse*. Web. 19 Jan. 2021.

Viguers, Ruth Hill. "Part Four: The Golden Age, 1920–1950." *A Critical History of Children's Literature: A Survey of Children's Books in English from Earliest Times to the Present*. Ed. Cornelia Meigs, Elizabeth Nesbitt, Anne Eaton, and Ruth Hill Viguers. Illus. Vera Bock. New York: Macmillan, 1953. 425–603. Print.

"Walter Awards." *We Need Diverse Books*. We Need Diverse Books, 2021. Web. 9 May 2021.

# 1 *The Dark Frigate* (1924) and the Use of Masculinity in Early Newbery Culture

*Paul Ringel*

Charles Boardman Hawes's Newbery Award-winning novel *The Dark Frigate* (1923; 1924 Newbery Medal) is an adventure tale set in seventeenth-century England and populated with pirates, sailors, and soldiers. Hawes borrows heavily from nineteenth-century nautical and juvenile formulas but adds elements of moral complexity and poignancy uncommon in this genre of children's fiction. The book has ardent supporters: in 1962, the University of Wisconsin's School of Education honored *The Dark Frigate* with its Lewis Carroll Shelf Award, given annually from 1958 through 1979 to books "worthy to sit on the same shelf" with *Alice's Adventures in Wonderland* and *Through the Looking-Glass*. (Other awardees that year included C. S. Lewis' *The Lion, The Witch, and the Wardrobe*, A. A. Milne's collections of Christopher Robin poems, and Mark Twain's *Adventures of Huckleberry Finn*) (Bartell 159). In his 1971 introduction to the novel, celebrated fantasy writer and 1969 Newbery winner Lloyd Alexander raved about its "artistic honesty about life and people" in comparison to the bland sweetness (he called it "synthetic strawberry juice") of other children's books of its time (Alexander xii). Yet *The Dark Frigate* has not sustained an audience; in 1957, Newbery historian Irene Smith ranked it as one of the winners "lowest in popularity" among young readers, and today it—like most Newbery winners of the 1920s—remains largely ignored (Smith 89).

Ironically, the 1924 selection of Hawes's posthumous novel (he died of spinal meningitis at the age of thirty-four, just before *The Dark Frigate* was released) appears to have sparked dissension because some Newbery voters perceived it as more commercial than literary. Members of the American Library Association (ALA) generally did not favor adventure stories, and Hawes held none of the professional credentials as a scholar or journalist that burnished the reputations of other winners of this era. Yet his win marked the second time in three years that Newbery voters honored this former writer for *The Youth's Companion*, the nation's bestselling children's magazine. (Hawes's previous novel, *The Great Quest: A Romance of 1826*, was runner-up for the inaugural medal in 1922). It was also the

DOI: 10.4324/9780367337223-1-2

second year in a row that voters seemed to prioritize young readers' approval over critical acclaim. When *The Voyages of Doctor Dolittle* received the prize in 1923, the Book Evaluation Committee of the ALA's Children's Division reported that "the method of award of the Newbery Medal does not seem satisfactory. We do not believe that a popular vote of the Section can be depended upon to select the most distinguished contribution for the year and think another method should be devised" (Smith 52). Following the announcement of *The Dark Frigate's* victory at the 1924 ALA conference, attendees voted to remove the power to choose future Newbery winners from the organization's entire membership, delegating it to a special executive committee controlled by officers of the Children's Librarian Section.

These disputes over commerce and quality were familiar within the American children's literature industry, but the post-World War I tumult that birthed the Newbery Award reinvigorated and changed them. Production of children's books skyrocketed during the 1920s, and the children's magazines and specialty publishing houses that had served as gatekeepers for the field for two generations lost influence. With prefabricated series fiction from publishers like the Stratemeyer Syndicate dominating the marketplace, ideals for balancing sales, entertainment, art, and education in children's books were more unclear than at any time since the Civil War (Ringel 194–197). Children's authors and librarians sought new methods and forums for resisting this accelerating trend toward standardization, and the ALA became a central vehicle for these efforts through the creation of Children's Book Week in 1919 and the Newbery Medal in 1922.

These changes created new and unstable connections like the one between Hawes and the ALA. *The Dark Frigate* emerged from the same socially conservative, mass-market, male-dominated tradition within the industry that produced series like the Stratemeyer books; though Hawes sought to modernize it through his novels, he retained a perspective of the outside world as a dangerous place that derived from the tradition's evangelical origins. Most ALA librarians, in contrast, were women who embraced a more cosmopolitan, literary, and (for its time) progressive heritage that used children's literature to promote life's possibilities rather than its hazards. This vision was feminized in its validation of nontraditional roles for girls and women as characters, authors, editors, and critics, and for over half a century the ALA's predominantly female membership (particularly within the emerging specialty field of children's librarianship) had persistently and vigorously opposed elements of popular fiction that they perceived as formulaic, immoral, and condescending to young readers.

The backlash against the ALA popular vote for *The Dark Frigate* as a Newbery Medalist was consistent with the well-established strategy of prominent female librarians, but the limited impact of that dustup illuminates how postwar culture reformulated those longstanding divides during the Newbery's early years. The change in voting procedures did not immediately result in a dramatic shift in the type of books selected. Every author the ALA honored during the 1920s was male. Those men, including Hawes, mostly displayed a literary ambition and fascination with other cultures previously associated with the progressive tradition. They also maintained a patronizing perspective toward those cultures—and toward women—that was consonant with the opposing, mass-market heritage. Indeed, the defining trend for the Newbery Award during its formative decade was not a resurgent focus on literary quality; it was the ALA's persistent willingness to subsume its feminized, progressive legacy. This practice was short-lived—every winner of the 1930s was female—but *The Dark Frigate* exemplifies how the industry's emerging female leaders initially felt the need to use traditionally masculine stories to institutionalize their prize and themselves as principal arbiters of American children's literature.

*The Dark Frigate* is a story about men. Philip Marsham, Hawes's young protagonist, is the son of an aristocratically-born ship captain who severed his family connections to pursue a nautical career. Philip follows his father's seafaring path after a shipwreck leaves him orphaned (there is no mention of his mother). The story begins with him recovering from an illness at the tavern of his late father's fiancée. After his careless use of a gun destroys the bar, a still-weakened Philip runs away and begins a tramp across southern England. A Scottish blacksmith nurses him back to health, and an English nobleman inspires his admiration: Philip "watched him until he had fixed in his mind every line of his tall, broad figure, every gesture of his hand and every toss of his head" (56). He meets two "shipwrecked mariners" who bring him to the port town of Biddeford and procure him a position on *The Rose of Devon*, a frigate undertaking a fishing voyage to the North Atlantic (26). His seafaring skills quickly earn him a promotion, but the *Rose* descends into chaos when his companions seize the ship, murdering the captain. Forced to join their crew, Philip gets captured while trying to escape and is branded a pirate by the Royal Navy. After exoneration at trial, he returns to the admired nobleman and fights at his side in the English Civil Wars of the 1660s. The novel ends with Philip sailing alone for Barbados, once again on the *Rose*.

Critics of the time recognized that Hawes's male-centered narrative (the female characters are minor and stereotypical—the heartless widow, the unfaithful maid, the vicious crone, the spirited nobleman's daughter) owed literary debts to the sea stories of James Fenimore Cooper, Richard Henry Dana, and especially Robert Louis Stevenson ("Novel Prize" SC14). These reviewers overlooked his less celebrated sources: nineteenth-century serial fiction for boys, and particularly two generations of stories produced by Hawes's former employer, *The Youth's*

*Companion. The Dark Frigate*'s plot, centered on a young man's unrealistic adventures and accomplishments, followed a template marketed by authors from William Taylor Adams (writing under the pseudonym Oliver Optic) in the 1850s through Edward Stratemeyer in the 1910s. It also retained the moralistic adventure formula the *Companion* had developed over the previous half-century.

Editor Daniel Sharp Ford had grown the *Companion* from a failing regional publication into the highest-circulating magazine in the country (with an audience of half a million weekly purchasers) for much of the 1880s and 1890s. The specific messages of *Companion* boys' fiction shifted with the culture but the structure remained consistent. The protagonist is a young man who leaves home and enters the primary commercial culture of his day; in the seventeenth-century English setting of *The Dark Frigate*, that meant the shipping industry. As he learns independence, he encounters a variety of older male role models: some are good (the blacksmith who offers hospitality, the nobleman who demonstrates leadership), others are bad (the "mariners" who are actually murderous pirates). The bad role models are powerful and entice the young man to adopt their immoral ways. He either does so, which causes his destruction, or resists (as Philip does) and emerges victorious following a tremendous struggle.

The adherence of *The Dark Frigate* (indeed, all three of Hawes's novels) to this formula reveals his work's foundation in the mass-market masculine tradition within the American children's publishing industry. Born from recurring evangelical revivals in the United States between the 1820s and 1850s, this tradition balanced a fear of the moral and physical dangers that rapidly-expanding urban commercial cultures created for American children with a need to control young people's participation in those cultures (Ringel 17–21, 67–71). After the Civil War, entrepreneurs like Ford and dime novel publisher Erastus Beadle developed a commercial strategy for achieving that balance; they produced sensational, nationalistic stories about and targeted toward boys and young men, and legitimized those narratives as cautionary tales that highlighted the consequences of misbehavior in an urbanizing, industrializing society. By the time Hawes joined the *Companion* in 1912, this strategy had spawned a subindustry of popular adventure stories ranging from cheaply produced books and magazines from Street & Smith Publications to Stratemeyer's more expensive and somewhat more reputable series novels.

Almost from the outset, these books in *The Dark Frigate*'s lineage generated opposition from female writers, critics, and librarians. Initially, these women expressed concerns about the social dangers of the genre's unrealistic sensationalism, particularly when stories exaggerated children's opportunities for quick and dramatic economic success. At an 1879 ALA conference on "Fiction in Libraries and the Reading of

Children," Kate Gannett Wells claimed that "many a boy's rash venture in cattle ranches, or uneasiness in the harness of a slight but regular salary, is owing to books that fed early feeble indications of a tendency to future evil" (Wells 325). In the Books for the Young reports delivered to the ALA during the 1880s, trailblazing librarians such as Caroline Hewins singled out Oliver Optic books as particularly harmful because they delivered "false views" of what boys could expect from life (McDowell 21).

By the 1910s the particular concern about unrealistic books largely had faded among librarians and critics (even as Franklin Mathiews, chief librarian of the Boy Scouts of America and a pivotal figure in the professional community that created the Newbery Award, attempted to revitalize it through his sensationalized 1914 article about the dangers of series fiction, "Blowing Out the Boy's Brains"). Yet national leaders of the emerging and predominantly female community of children's librarians continued to criticize these formulaic stories, shifting their focus from the genre's distortion of reality to its disrespect toward children and their intellectual development. Anne Carroll Moore, head of the children's division at the New York Public Library and a leading figure in the ALA, derided series books as "trash," and she and other librarians regularly purged them from their institutions' collections (Marcus 105; Connelly 205).

These generations of conflict over stories like *The Dark Frigate* derived from a philosophical and professional divide among producers and critics of children's literature about how to market books and magazines to young readers in the late-nineteenth- and early-twentieth-century United States. Evangelicals and their commercial descendants' exhortations against danger reflected an original belief in human depravity; the outside world was a dangerous place, and only strict adherence to orthodox theology and (in later stories) a commitment to American exceptionalism could protect children from spiritual and earthly perils. Conversely, women working within the industry inclined toward more liberal Protestant beliefs that emphasized young people's inherent virtue. This confidence generated an optimistic, cosmopolitan tradition; whereas the *Companion* and its ilk published mostly contemporary American adventure stories and realistic fiction set in small towns, liberal magazines and publishers offered historical fiction, fairy tales, and domestic stories in settings from New England to India. The contrast extended into ideas about framing children's development; while conservative publications tended to portray coming of age as an individualistic endeavor (Tompkins 161; Cawelti 40), their more liberal competitors presented the process of earning independence and authority predominantly within the context of family and community. Conclusions offered in community-centered stories were not always progressive, but the settings provided greater opportunities for female authors and for the introduction of female characters, both of which were largely excluded from adventure genres during this period.

When Hawes joined the *Companion* in 1912, the diminishing concerns about sensationalism in children's literature were—despite the ALA's efforts—helping to mitigate the divide between these traditions. Liberal magazines were producing adventure serials featuring improbable characters such as boy railroad detectives, and the *Companion* was publishing the types of community-centered fiction about school and sports that it had criticized in previous decades. This shift reflected both generational change—longtime magazine editors like Ford and *St. Nicholas*'s Mary Mapes Dodge died at the turn of the twentieth century, and their publications were slipping from their dominant roles as industry gatekeepers—and a changing attitude toward child consumers in genteel American culture. Direct marketing to children, fueled by expanding toy sections in department stores and the success of products generated from the 1900 bestseller *The Wonderful Wizard of Oz*, was becoming more common and reputable (Leach 85–91). Children's magazines began publishing advertisements that spoke directly to young consumers, and *St. Nicholas* even ran an advertising competition in which readers produced copy and illustrations for the magazine's sponsors (Garvey 158–170).

Hawes's early *Companion* stories did not reflect these changes. Situated mostly in the back of the magazine, they reinforced the magazine's traditional anti-modern messages. These stories belong to a genre literary critics describe as regionalist or local color. Set in rural northern New England, they offer no identifiable time period or references to nearby industrializing cities. They focus mostly on a taciturn older man named Mr. Ballin and his aging dog Major, who participate in traditional activities such as hunting, fishing, and bartering among neighbors. The unhurried nature of interactions in these stories facilitates the triumph of virtue; over time, repeated personal engagements help Ballin end a feud with an old friend and even learn to trust outsiders like the itinerant Jewish peddler who periodically visits the community. These stories affirm Richard Brodhead and Amy Kaplan's arguments that regional fiction served the purpose of presenting "vernacular cultures as enclaves of tradition insulated from larger cultural contact" and as "separate spaces … serving to erase the more explosive social conflicts of class, race, and gender made contiguous by urban life" (Brodhead 121; Kaplan 242).

Near the end of his *Companion* tenure, Hawes shifted into the adventure genre in which he worked for the rest of his career. Indeed, "Son of a Gentleman Born," his final serial for the magazine, established the template for Hawes's three subsequent novels: a young man at sea becomes ensnared in the immoral activities of a powerful older man and has to extricate himself from the threat of imprisonment or death.

Yet this contemporary story also retained the *Companion*'s provincial, anti-urban perspective. When the young orphaned hero Denny Grigsby escapes from his employer's coastal New England smuggling activities, he finds refuge on the Rhode Island farm of a benevolent mentor. At the end of the story, with his mentor's guidance, Denny turns himself in to the authorities and assists in the capture of his former employer. Through this process, he is reunited with long-lost wealthy relatives and inherits the family fortune. He uses this money to pay off his mentor's farm, where he returns to live in rural serenity.

Only when Hawes left the *Companion* in 1919 for a position as associate editor of *The Open Road* magazine, where all three of his novels first appeared as serials, did his approach begin to change.[1] In this new venue, his stories maintained the *Companion*'s basic template, but he experimented with narrative structure, global rather than regional settings, and issues of race and power that previous generations of children's authors had largely avoided. These shifts aligned his post-*Companion* books with the other Newbery winners of the 1920s: seven of those eight winners were set outside the United States, and all of them addressed issues of race, ethnicity, and religion, predominantly from the perspective of White Protestant men.

This pattern of cosmopolitanism emerged from the reorganization occurring within the post-World War I children's literature industry. Production of new American children's books more than doubled from 433 in 1919 to 931 in 1929, and the total number of children's books printed in the United States nearly tripled from twelve to thirty-one million over the same period. Major American publishers created juvenile divisions within their companies for the first time (Marcus 104). Amidst this dramatic expansion, the direction of the field remained confusing. A clear divide was emerging between juvenile and adult books; eminent authors of previous generations like Mark Twain and Edith Wharton had regularly published books and magazine stories for children, but leading postwar writers mostly eschewed opportunities to engage this audience (Clark 16, 48). In part because of this divide, longstanding children's periodicals like the *Companion* and *St. Nicholas* lost circulation and power during the 1920s. Series books, particularly those produced by the Stratemeyer Syndicate, stepped into this vacuum, but writers who generated those volumes ceded creative control and even authorship to the publisher. For ambitious authors like Hawes who continued to seek opportunities in the juvenile field, established forums for achieving success were dissipating even as the market expanded.

Emerging venues for publishing and evaluating children's literature were increasingly controlled by a new generation of "bookwomen." In the nineteenth century, female editors like *St. Nicholas*'s Mary Mapes Dodge had been an anomaly, but during the 1910s and 1920s a cadre of women achieved management positions as librarians, editors, and heads of publishers' new juvenile divisions (Eddy 3). These women shaped the field for the next half-century and transformed production and oversight of children's literature into predominantly "women's work." But during these early years their standing was insecure, and their need to establish themselves as the industry's new caretakers of quality and respectability was acute (Eddy 6).

Aspiring authors and bookwomen converged through the ALA's postwar effort to revitalize and redefine standards of quality for American children's literature. The organization's two major endeavors, Children's Book Week (which began in 1919) and the Newbery Medal (which debuted in 1922) reflected its blending of the industry's literary traditions. The first Book Week was produced by Mathiews, the Boy Scout librarian; Moore, an early leader of the bookwomen; and Frederic Melcher, the co-editor of *Publishers Weekly* magazine who was raised on both the *Companion* and *St. Nicholas* (Smith 13). Melcher subsequently conceived and named the Newbery Award, which during the 1920s further intertwined the ambitions of predominantly female librarians with socially conservative male authors.

This trend began with the inaugural award, which also illuminated institutional reasons for the librarians' choices. The 1922 winner, Hendrik Willem Van Loon's five-hundred-page, ostensibly global history *The Story of Mankind*, presented an argument of evolution from African savagery to European civilization that was standard for its time. The tome was already a commercial and critical success, and Van Loon was a budding celebrity thanks to his own public relations skills (which included lobbying ALA members during the Newbery voting period) as well as those of his influential publisher, Horace Liveright. Awarding its first medal to *The Story of Mankind* earned the ALA substantial media attention and strengthened its bonds with the literary establishment (Smith 45; Marcus 88; Elleman 13). The next year, ALA voters shifted their focus toward appealing to young readers' tastes, and in doing so engendered controversy within the organization. Their second award went to Hugh Lofting's *The Voyages of Doctor Dolittle*, a sequel to Lofting's popular 1920 children's novel *The Story of Doctor Dolittle*.[2] Though the series eventually ran to fourteen books, Lofting's stories about a man who talks to animals received few other critical plaudits during or since their publication (Elick 323–324). The 1924 medalist, *The Dark Frigate*, offered a compromise between the Newbery's first two winners. It was more intentionally literary than *Dolittle*, and more attentive to young readers' interests than *The Story of Mankind*. Indeed, Hawes's final novel culminated his fitful post-*Companion* efforts to merge literary and popular fiction by elevating the adventure story above its nineteenth-century formulas.

That process began with Hawes's 1920 debut novel *The Mutineers*, which builds upon a familiar plot: young protagonist Benjamin Lathrop gets entangled in the machinations of the mutinous officer known only as Kipping, and upstanding ship's officer Roger Hamlin protects and mentors him while battling the mutineers for control of the ship. Hawes introduces changes to the template established by *The Youth's Companion*, shifting from the contemporary settings the magazine favored to a global voyage begun in 1809 and eliminating the *Companion*'s longstanding contrast between dangerous urban and virtuous rural cultures. Instead, the distinction between good and evil in his novels becomes class-based; *The Mutineers* introduces Hawes's new pattern of immoral common men clashing with righteous, educated elites.

Hawes's next novel, *The Great Quest* (1922), was a distant runner-up for the inaugural Newbery Award (Marcus 88). Yet in comparison to the subsequent *Dark Frigate*, its literary elements are underdeveloped. *Quest*'s setting and plot are similar to *The Mutineers*; an evil common man's machinations place a youth in danger on an international sea voyage (in this case on a slave trading ship), and the youth's protector comes from the social elite (a mysterious clerk who turns out to be a former lieutenant of Napoleon's). Yet throughout the novel Hawes hints at larger ambitions that he never realizes. In the opening chapter, Joe Woods describes his upcoming story as the "wildest, maddest adventure that I ever heard outside the pages of fiction," suggesting an attempt at metanarrative that does not reappear (6). Gleazen is mysterious and promisingly menacing during the novel's first half but dissipates into a one-dimensional violent slave trader. Hawes also experiments with a fevered style of language reminiscent of Joseph Conrad when the travelers reach West Africa, but the frightening atmosphere of those chapters has no sustained impact on the story.

In *The Dark Frigate*, Hawes's literary and commercial efforts converge more effectively. The Newbery winner is subtle and thoughtful where *The Great Quest* was showy and vacuous. For example, whereas his previous two novels include dramatic examples of racial tension, *Frigate* includes almost no Black characters and no discussion of race; however, slavery is the unspoken evil at the heart of Hawes's complex examination of power.[3] The plot is formulaic, yet small diversions from established story structures raise sophisticated questions about causation and personal moral responsibility. Hawes's final novel was not a literary masterpiece, but it reflected a significant maturation in the quality of his work.

The central event of *The Dark Frigate* is young protagonist Philip Marsham's voyage on the *Rose of Devon*, which originally sails from England in pursuit of North Atlantic cod. When the unrevealed pirate Tom Jordan gets rescued from a shipwreck, he suggests that the captain instead sail south, where the potential for riches is more extensive. Slavery is never named in this or any other conversation in the book, but slaves and the products they generated were integral to mid-seventeenth century Atlantic commerce. Philip does not comment on pirate Jordan's suggestion, yet when he departs England at the end of the novel, he books passage to Barbados, an island that was one of the most prosperous and violent models of the slave economy during that period. Clearly, the young protagonist holds no moral objection to the slave trade.

The choice to resettle in Barbados also reflects Philip's admiration for aristocracy and his antipathy toward the reformist and democratizing movements occurring in seventeenth-century England. Though his father turned away from the aristocracy to go to sea, Philip idolizes Sir John Bristol, a wealthy, ostentatious, domineering man whose presumed superiority allows him to treat all of his underlings in a rough but generally fair manner. His other role model is Captain Candle, the master of *The Rose of Devon*, whose food and drink on the ship are far superior to his men's, and who emerges to confront the pirates "in a rich waist with broad cuffs ... his hair new oiled with jessamine butter, and gallant bows at his knees"; in the accompanying illustration, the captain is described as having "the manner of a king on a small island" (opposite 70).[4]

In contrast, the pirate Jordan espouses egalitarian sentiments; after the mutiny, he placates the remaining crew members by telling them that "one man is as good as another and any man may rub his shoulder with mine" and by sharing with the crew Captain Candle's lavish provisions (the narrator expresses disapproval of this choice, commenting that "matters are in a sad way in a ship when the master feasts the men") (121).[5] Following his exoneration, Philip fights under Sir John for the Royalists in the English Civil War. When Sir John dies in battle and the Puritans win the Civil War, Philip determines that "the old order is changing and I would go abroad," but not to "the colonies" where "as many psalms are whined in Boston and New England as in all the conventicles in London." He chooses Barbados because the new master of the *Rose of Devon* tells him "there you'll find men to your own taste"; English landowners on this island were among the wealthiest and most conservative settlers of North America, and they lacked the crusading piety of their Puritan contemporaries (246–247).

The choice to honor such antidemocratic values through an early modern English hero (it seems impossible to imagine the same beliefs vested in an American protagonist) aligned Hawes with his fellow 1920s Newbery winners, whose books presented a cosmopolitan array of ideological perspectives as long as they remained within the spectrum of (mostly) White men. His more radical literary choice within *The Dark Frigate* was to largely eliminate moral consequences from the protagonist's storyline. This decision was the culmination of Hawes's gradual move away from the nineteenth-century American children's book industry tradition of presenting good and bad outcomes as the product of

*There leaned against the rail a single man, of an age in the middle-thirties, with a keen, strong face and the manner of a king on a small island*

*Figure 1.1* The captain of the *Rose of Devon*.

Source: *The Dark Frigate*, by Charles Boardman Hawes, with illustrations by Anton Otto Fischer (The Atlantic Monthly Press, 1923), opposite page 70.

individuals' choices. *The Mutineers* mostly adheres to this tradition, while *The Great Quest* challenges unmitigated evil with a central character whose motivations are legitimate but whose values are problematic. In *The Dark Frigate*, Hawes prevents readers from making any clear assessment of Philip's virtue by placing the character in a culture that prioritizes maintenance of social order over individuals' freedom to shape their own destinies.

The absence of moral causation in Philip's story is foregrounded in the narrator's discussion of the young man's choices throughout *The Dark Frigate*. While Benjamin Lathrop in *The Mutineers* leaves home in romantic pursuit of "a world of commerce bright with adventure" and Joe Woods in *The Great Quest* is driven by the well-established *Companion* trope of economic compulsion (he has to go to sea to protect his financial inheritance), the motivations behind Philip's choices are consistently unclear (*Mutineers* 3). Hawes initially presents him as a mischievous boy who "tak[es] to books with ill grace" and runs away from school to join his father at sea (*Dark Frigate* 1–2). After his father's death, he is left with a woman who has no inclination to care for him, but the event that instigates his departure is his own misdeed of accidentally damaging her tavern with a gunshot.

Sick and alone, Philip sets out walking across southern England with no clear plan and eventually drifts into the company of two drunken sailors. The narrator raises the question of why the boy stays with these men, who turn out to be the pirate Tom Jordan and his henchman Martin, and never provides a clear answer. He suggests that "they had journeyed together thus far" and that Philip was "too easygoing to part company with his companion," but continues to question the wisdom of this choice throughout the story (58, 60). Even when Philip is on trial for piracy, he refuses to testify against the pirates, a decision that the narrator describes as "very wrong," but also one that sparks Jordan to admit Philip's innocence in court, a move that finally exonerates the innocent young man (225). This moment of testimony illuminates the complexity of the world Hawes has created. Traditionally, children's books present characters' loyalty as a positive choice, but the dissonance between the narrator's explicit criticism of his protagonist's behavior and the positive outcome created by this decision serves as Hawes's most direct challenge to the long-promoted link between conduct and consequences that was foundational to nineteenth-century American children's literature.

Hawes's resistance to traditional ideas of moral causality aligns with the unsentimental worldview that he presents in his novels. Each of these books features dangerous circumstances and violent acts that occur without reason or justification. Kipping's motivations for instigating an uprising in *The Mutineers* are never explained. In *The Great Quest*, Hawes's novel that adheres most closely to nineteenth-century structures and values, the previous bad acts that create the threat for the protagonist are not his own but his uncle's. In *The Dark Frigate*, Hawes commits most fully to this vision of an amoral universe. The pivotal event in the novel happens by chance; Tom Jordan and his men come aboard the *Rose of Devon* (where they will lead a mutiny) only because the *Rose* happens to cross paths with their shipwrecked vessel. In the novel's concluding chapters, Hawes's narrator explicitly signals his literary ambition—and his shedding of the formal restrictions of the author's *Companion* past—when he refuses to provide closure for his audience. The narrator tells readers "if this were a mere story to while away an idle hour, I, the scribe, would tie neatly every knot and leave no Irish pennants hanging from my work. But life, alas, is no pattern drawn to scale. The many interweaving threads are caught up in strange tangles" (231). Thus, when Philip returns to visit the blacksmith who nursed him back to health, the man has disappeared. In contrast to Hawes's earlier *Companion* story "Son of a Gentleman Born," the long-lost wealthy relatives do not surface at the end of the novel. Philip's choice near the beginning of the story not to reveal himself to his wealthy grandparents cannot be revisited, because they have died by the time he is released from prison; the narrator never discloses whether they even knew of his existence. He returns to Sir John's estate following his exoneration in part to fulfill his promise to marry the housemaid Nell Entick; he finds her married to another man, yet "she cast Phil such a glance that he knew, maid or matron, she would philander still" (236).

This unromantic perspective is central to what Lloyd Alexander later adored about *The Dark Frigate*. In his 1971 introduction to the novel, he celebrates Hawes's "hard-edged view of the world," and says that "he asked for no easy answers; in *The Dark Frigate*, there are none." From "this view of the world as a rather hard place to live in," he writes, emerges "an impression of surprising, almost startling, modernity." Alexander also praises Hawes's prose, calling him a "serious craftsman" who "writes with love and respect for language ... a controlled-vocabulary devotee might be driven to fits at the nautical terms and some of the archaism in the dialogue. The reader, I think, will relish them" (Alexander ix–xii). Contemporary readers often find this expansive range of language distracting and self-consciously difficult; for Alexander, who wrote during a time when much of the children's book industry had aligned itself with a reading pedagogy that favored simpler, familiar language, the complexity of Hawes's prose further marked him as a serious and praiseworthy children's novelist.

Some Newbery voters clearly agreed with the view Alexander would later express. Lillian Smith, chair of the Children's Librarian Section for the 1924 ALA conference, pronounced that Hawes's novels "reach the highest standards attained by any adventure book in recent years" ("Children's Librarian's Section"). Unlike for previous years, though, neither the total number nor the percentage of votes *The Dark Frigate* received is preserved in the archives, and the ALA announced no runners-up. Nor does the minimal record of debate among the sixty-seven members of the Children's Section present at the 1924 ALA conference (who constituted approximately one-third of the Section's total membership) illuminate their reasons for voting to change the award's voting procedures for subsequent years. The only additional information about that year in Newbery history is Smith's account that the audience was "deeply moved" by the acceptance speech delivered by Hawes's widow (Smith 109).

Despite Smith's statements about Hawes's writing (which were made in the presence of the writer's widow), the juxtaposition of his award and the change in voting read as an implicit condemnation of *The Dark Frigate*'s quality by leaders of the ALA. The organization's leaders may have been reacting to the combination of Hawes's disfavored genre (Smith's celebration of the novel implicitly disparages adventure stories) and his lack of professional qualifications; one more adventure novel, *The Trumpeter of Krakow*, would capture the Newbery in the 1920s, but it was authored by Eric P. Kelly, a college professor and crusading journalist.

Yet for the rest of the decade, the newly created selection committee did not significantly deviate from the voting pattern established by the ALA's general population. The next five Newbery-winning books all shared with Lofting and Hawes's novels a cosmopolitanism that aligned with children's librarians' traditional tastes. They also maintained these authors' nostalgia. *Shen of the Sea* and *Tales from Silver Lands* present foreign cultures through a lens of primitivism; *Smoky the Cowhorse* offers a wistful perspective on the disappearance of the Old West; and *Gay-Neck* honors the story of a carrier pigeon. These choices may seem anachronistic with the decade of flappers and Model Ts, but they align with a conservative backlash against modern society that also surged in the United States during these years. This resistance particularly solidified around the perspective of race and Otherness; thus, the implicit message of White supremacy that lurks throughout the 1920s Newbery winners makes sense for a decade during which the Ku Klux Klan was reinvigorated (particularly in northern cities) and an anti-foreign sentiment led Congress to dramatically restrict the number of immigrants who could enter the United States.

Even within its feminized progressive tradition, American children's literature had rarely operated on the ideological vanguard on issues of race, but ALA members had advocated for half a century on behalf of female authors and modern, urban cultures that created new opportunities for young people. Thus, the ALA's primary ideological transition during the 1920s did not occur after the voting reconfiguration that followed *The Dark Frigate*'s victory. Instead, it began with the launch of the Newbery Award, or perhaps after the initial publicity-driven choice of *The Story of Mankind*, when the librarians broke from two generations of professional precedent and began to favor books that marginalized women and leaned away from modern contemporary ideas.

The pattern began to change in 1930, when Rachel Field became the first woman to win the Newbery Award. Her novel *Hitty: Her First Hundred Years* shared the cosmopolitan and racist characteristics of previous winners, but launched a run of ten consecutive medals for female-authored books, many of which also featured girl protagonists. This reorientation, like the previous turn to male authors, was a product of its historical moment. By the turn of the decade, the onset of the Great Depression had weakened conservative movements in the United States, and Americans struggling with instability in their own lives preferred domestic stories about ordinary people and communities rather than tales of individualistic exploits in distant times and places (Dickstein 523). Under these circumstances, with the Newbery well-established and the field of children's literature becoming "library-dominated," according to publishers, the prize committee began to choose books that were more consonant with the ALA's ideological heritage (Marcus 120).

The short-lived practice of honoring exclusively masculine stories that mostly celebrated existing social hierarchies helped to establish the Newbery Award and institutionalize its sponsoring organization as primary arbiters of quality in the field of American children's literature. Hawes's legacy was much shorter and less powerful. His early death and the resurgent ideological divide within American children's literature during the 1930s left his books in a commercial and literary no-man's land; they were not attached to a popular series, and by the 1950s their genre of historical adventure fiction fell out of favor with librarians, editors, and the readers they guided.[6] Though the novel deserves further scholarly attention, a popular revival of *The Dark Frigate* nearly a century after its debut seems unlikely; who would advocate for it? For now, the book remains an important reminder that standards of quality in children's literature, as in any field, are historicized. Indeed, so too are the standard bearers. The story of *The Dark Frigate* (both within and beyond the pages of Hawes's narrative) affirms that the Newbery Award, which has defined careers in the publishing industry for a century, is an artifact of a precise historical moment: the post-World War I decade when publishers, authors, and librarians converged in a struggle to redefine what modern, consumer-driven American children should read.

## Notes

1 *The Open Road* was a Boston-based magazine devoted, according to its November 1919 debut issue, "exclusively to the varied interests of older boys in America" ("The Open Road" 3). The magazine particularly encouraged boys to embrace outdoor physical activities from athletics to camping and hiking.

2 The ALA would not honor another sequel until Lloyd Alexander's *The High King* in 1969.
3 In *The Mutineers*, Hawes relies on the stereotype of the noble savage. The ship's African American cook and a Javanese chief assume pivotal roles in saving the hero even though the former was "as black as the bottom of his iron pot" and has a "frown, engraved deeply in his low forehead, [that] might have marked him in my eyes as the villain of some melodrama of the sea," and the latter was a "wild, tall man, naked except for a pair of short breeches, a girdle, and a red handkerchief on his head" (8, 167). In *The Great Quest*, interracial encounters are merely a temporary gauntlet the protagonist must survive to earn his manhood in the form of his inheritance and his wife. Black characters encountered in Cuba and West Africa are frightening but abstract figures whose identifying traits are superstition, cowardice, and violence. Protagonist Joe marries the daughter of a missionary in West Africa, but displays no empathy for victims of the slave trade. He describes Africans as "grotesque," "absurd," and "heathen" (180, 192).
4 Miller and Field identify the illustrator of the first edition (unnamed in the text) as Anton Otto Fischer (28).
5 Hawes's interpretation of pirates anticipates the scholarship of historians like Marcus Rediker, who argued that a "rough, improvised, but effective egalitarianism that placed authority in the collective hands of the crew" was institutionalized as the social order aboard eighteenth-century pirate ships (67–68).
6 Smith noted in 1957 that five of the twelve least popular Newbery winners to that time were historical fiction, and most of those books were adventure stories (89).

## Works Cited


Alexander, Lloyd. Introduction. *The Dark Frigate*. By Charles Boardman Hawes. Boston: Little, Brown, 1971. Print.

Bartell, Joyce. "The Lewis Carroll Shelf Award." *Elementary English* 36 (Mar. 1959): 159–166. *JSTOR*. Web. 24 Aug. 2020.

Brodhead, Richard H. *Culture of Letters: Scenes of Reading and Writing in Nineteenth-Century America*. Chicago: U of Chicago P, 1993. Print.

Cawelti, John. *Adventure, Mystery, and Romance: Formula Stories as Art and Popular Culture*. Chicago: U of Chicago P, 1976. Print.

"Children's Librarian Section." *Bulletin of the American Library Association* 18 (Aug. 1924): 303. *Google Books*. Web. 24 Aug. 2020.

Chrisman, Arthur Bowie. *Shen of the Sea: Chinese Stories for Children*. New York: E. P. Dutton & Co., 1925. Print.

Connelly, Mark. *The Hardy Boys Mysteries, 1927–1979: A Cultural and Literary History*. Jefferson, NC: McFarland, 2008. Print.

Dickstein, Morris. *Dancing in the Dark: A Cultural History of the Great Depression*. New York: W. W. Norton, 2009. Print.

Elick, Catherine L. "Anxieties of an Animal Rights Activist: The Pressures of Modernity in Hugh Lofting's Doctor Dolittle Series." *Children's Literature Association Quarterly* 32.4 (Winter 2007): 323–339. *Project Muse*. Web. 24 Aug. 2020.

Elleman, Barbara. "The John Newbery Medal: The First Decade." *The Newbery and Caldecott Awards: A Guide to The Medal and Honor Books*. Chicago: American Library Association, 2007. *Google Books*. Web. 24 Aug. 2020.

Field, Rachel, *Hitty: Her First Hundred Years*. 1929. New York: Aladdin Paperbacks, 1998. Print.

Finger, Charles J. *Tales from Silver Lands*. New York: Doubleday, 1924. Print.

Garvey, Ellen Gruber. "The *St. Nicholas* Advertising Competition: Training the Magazine Reader." St. Nicholas *and Mary Mapes Dodge: The Legacy of a Children's Magazine Editor*. Ed. Susan R. Gannon, Suzanne Rahn, and Ruth Anne Thompson. Jefferson, NC: McFarland, 2004. 158–170. Print.

Hawes, Charles Boardman. *The Dark Frigate*. Boston: Little, Brown and Company, 1923. Print.

Hawes, Charles Boardman. *The Great Quest*. Boston: The Atlantic Monthly Press, 1921. *Project Gutenberg*. Web. 24 Aug. 2020.

Hawes, Charles Boardman. *The Mutineers*. Boston: The Atlantic Monthly Press, 1920. *Project Gutenberg*. Web. 24 Aug. 2020.

Hawes, Charles Boardman. "Son of a Gentleman Born." *Youth's Companion* 11 Dec. (1919): 703. *Google Books*. Web. 24 Aug. 2020.

Kaplan, Amy. "Nation, Region, and Empire." *The Columbia History of the American Novel*. New York: Columbia UP, 1991. 240–266. Print.

Kelly, Eric P. *The Trumpeter of Krakow*. New York: Macmillan, 1928. Print.

Kidd, Kenneth B. "Prizing Children's Literature: The Case of Newbery Gold." *Children's Literature* 35 (2007): 166–190. *Project Muse*. Web. 24 Aug. 2020.

Lofting, Hugh. *The Story of Doctor Dolittle*. New York: Frederick A. Stokes Company, 1922. Web. 24 Aug. 2020.

Lofting, Hugh. *The Voyages of Doctor Dolittle*. Philadelphia: J. B. Lippincott Company, 1922. Print.

Marcus, Leonard S. *Minders of Make-Believe: Idealists, Entrepreneurs, and the Shaping of American Children's Literature*. Boston: Houghton Mifflin, 2008. Print.

Mathiews, Franklin K. "Blowing Out the Boy's Brains." *Outlook* (18 Nov. 1914): 652–654. Rpt. in *Pennsylvania Library Notes* 7.6 (Apr. 1915): 140–145. *Internet Archive*. Web. 18 Jan. 2021.

McDowell, Kate. "Which Truth, What Fiction? Librarians' Book Recommendations for Children, 1876–1890." *Education and the Culture of Print in Modern America*. Ed. Adam R. Nelson and John L. Rudolph. Madison: U of Wisconsin P, 2010. 15–35. Print.

Miller, Bertha Mahony, and Elinor Whitney Field, eds. *Newbery Medal Books: 1922–1955, with their Authors' Acceptance Papers & Related Material chiefly from the* Horn Book Magazine. Boston: The Horn Book, 1955. Print.

"Novel Prize is Awarded to Farmer." *Washington Post* 4 Jan. 1925: SC14. Web. 24 Aug. 2020.

Rediker, Marcus. *Outlaws of the Atlantic: Sailors, Pirates, and Motley Crews in the Age of Sail*. Boston: Beacon Press, 2014. Print.

Ringel, Paul B. *Commercializing Childhood: Children's Magazines, Urban Gentility, and the Ideal of the Child Consumer in the United States, 1823–1918*. Amherst: U of Massachusetts P, 2015. Print.

Smith, Irene. *A History of the Newbery and Caldecott Medals*. New York: The Viking Press, 1957. Print.

"The Open Road: The Quality Magazine for Older Boys." *The Open Road* (Nov. 1919): 3. *Google Books*. Web. 24 Aug. 2020.

Tompkins, Jane. *Sensational Designs: The Cultural Work of American Fiction, 1790–1860*. New York: Oxford UP, 1986. Print.

Van Loon, Hendrik Willem. *The Story of Mankind*. New York: Boni and Liveright, 1921. Print.

Wells, Kate Gannett. "Responsibility of Parents in the Selection of Reading for the Young." *Library Journal* 4 (Sept.-Oct. 1879): 325–330. *Google Books*. Web. 24 Aug. 2020.

Westman, Karin E. "Beyond Periodization: Children's Literature, Genre, and Remediating Literary History." *Children's Literature Association Quarterly* 38.4 (Winter 2013): 464–469. *Project Muse*. Web. 24 Aug. 2020.

# 2 Punching Up, Punching Down

## Anticolonial Resistance and Brahmanical Ideologies in *Gay-Neck: The Story of a Pigeon* (1928)

*Poushali Bhadury*

Dhan Gopal Mukerji, a celebrated children's writer and author of the Newbery-winning *Gay-Neck: The Story of a Pigeon* (1927; 1928 Newbery Medal), occupies a notable place in Asian American history for his early contributions to American life and letters as a "literary missionary" from India (Chang 17). Critics have pointed out Mukerji's status as "the first author of Asian Indian ancestry who successfully wrote for American audiences about Indian life," and opined that "Mukerji remains the best interpreter of the East that Western children have had" (Chang 1; H. J. B. W. 129). While the latter claim—from a 1938 book review of *Gay-Neck*—is fairly dated and hyperbolic, it does gesture towards the remarkable figure Mukerji presented as an active Asian public intellectual in early-twentieth-century America. A prolific author who also undertook highly popular lecture tours across the US and boasted a wide slate of friends among contemporary authors, artists, and philosophers, Mukerji sought to bridge the seemingly vast divide between "East" and "West."[1] At the time of its publication, his Newbery novel *Gay-Neck* served as a significant cultural conduit, acquainting its predominantly American readership with a distinctly South Asian sensibility. The book has since fallen into obscurity—a Newbery that is dutifully shelved but rarely circulates—but warrants new critical scrutiny, especially because of its unlikely inclusion in the all-White pantheon of the Newbery's early decades.

Mukerji, an immigrant from India, was the first non-White author to win the Newbery Medal.[2] This recognition was a rarity at a time when American children's publishing was entirely dominated by White authors. At the 1928 Newbery ceremony, in fact, Mukerji was forced to take part in a humiliating charade: he "had to be kept hidden behind a stand of trees on the hotel grounds prior to the announcement" of *Gay-Neck*'s win; "apparently, the presence of an East Indian man in a crowd of mostly white librarians meeting in French Lick, Indiana, would have

DOI: 10.4324/9780367337223-2-3

been a dead giveaway" (Horning 64). This anecdote highlights the overwhelming Whiteness not only of early Newbery-winning authors but also of the literary establishment more broadly. To put *Gay-Neck*'s exceptional Newbery Medal win in context, it is essential to point out that it has taken over ninety years for another Indian American author to be similarly feted: Veera Hiranandani's *The Night Diary* (2018; 2019 Newbery Honor), depicting the 1947 Indian Partition through the eyes of a young girl, marks only the second time to date that an author of South Asian descent has been recognized by the Newbery Award Selection Committee—this despite the significant demographic growth of South Asians in the United States, particularly since the passage of the Immigration and Nationality Act of 1965.

*Gay-Neck*'s 1928 Newbery win ensured that Mukerji's novel has continuously featured in histories of children's literature, first as a quaint anomaly and more recently as an early example of what is now called an Own Voices story. The increased public interest in and advocacy around diverse topics and diverse authors in youth literature, as evidenced by the popular We Need Diverse Books and Own Voices movements, has brought renewed attention to *Gay-Neck*. But despite a burgeoning interest in issues of author identity—and despite Mukerji's unique place in Newbery history—there has been little scholarship on his oeuvre. Emphasizing the 1928 Newbery winner's present-day relevance, this essay identifies *Gay-Neck*'s relationship to issues of social and political resistance in the British colonial period during which it is set, while infusing the historical analysis with contemporary critiques of the oppressive casteist and racist ideologies which the novel showcases in a positive manner.[3]

## The Life and Times of Dhan Gopal Mukerji and *Gay-Neck*

Born in 1890 in Tamluk, a village near Calcutta, Dhan Gopal Mukerji was educated in English-language missionary schools before attending the University of Calcutta. He subsequently enrolled in the University of Tokyo in 1909, then moved from Japan to the US in 1910, less than a decade before the racist Immigration Act of 1917 barred South Asian immigrants from entering the US.[4] Landing in California, he worked blue-collar jobs washing dishes and harvesting crops, later attended classes at the University of California, Berkeley, and finally graduated with a bachelor's degree from Stanford University in 1914, before commencing a prolific publishing career. But that career was cut short when Mukerji took his own life in July 1936. His suicide at the age of forty-six shocked his friends and followers all over the world, who mourned the loss of a gifted writer and orator.

Mukerji's literary output was exceedingly diverse: his oeuvre includes poems, plays, biographies of Indian saints, translations of Sanskrit epics and Indian folklore, autobiographical works, nonfiction on philosophy and Hinduism, and fiction for adults, as well as several short stories and novels for children. Although Mukerji received early critical acclaim for autobiographical works like *Caste and Outcast* (1923) and *My Brother's Face* (1924), which introduced American audiences to Indian ways of life as well as Hindu religious and philosophical thought, his writing for children brought him even greater recognition and critical appreciation during his lifetime. His long-time publisher E. P. Dutton (also Rudyard Kipling's US publisher) brought out the popular titles *Kari the Elephant* (1922), *Jungle Beasts and Men* (1923), and *Hari the Jungle Lad* (1924), which received positive reviews and were commercially successful. However, it is *Gay-Neck: The Story of a Pigeon* that has since emerged as Mukerji's abiding legacy, better known than any of his other books. After being awarded the Newbery Medal in 1928, *Gay-Neck*'s cultural cachet expanded.

Perhaps the most compelling acknowledgment of Mukerji's influence on American children's literature is the *Horn Book Magazine*'s July/August 1937 issue; appearing a year after Mukerji's death, it was "published in special honor of Dhan Gopal Mukerji" (Mahony 197). A substantial section of the issue focuses on Mukerji's literary significance, including an editorial, excerpts from Mukerji's own works, and tribute essays. "American children have found in Dhan Gopal Mukerji an interpreter after their own hearts," wrote children's author and educator Elizabeth Seeger (200), pointing once again to Mukerji's commonly perceived status as an "interpreter of the East." As it is today, *Horn Book* was one of the most important serial publications devoted to children's literature in the US: it served a crucial curatorial function and arbitrated "taste" when it came to books for the young. For the magazine to dedicate an issue to Mukerji's memory and memorialize his death was unique; no non-White author had previously been the recipient of such an honor.

Recent years have seen a resurgence of interest in *Gay-Neck*, thanks in part to Hachette India's 2016 reissue of Mukerji's four most popular novels for children. Feature articles by literature scholar Oindrila Mukherjee and journalists Lakshmi Gandhi and Pooja Makhijani in US and Indian media publications have reintroduced the "forgotten" *Gay-Neck* to a modern audience. All three of these pieces focus on the significance of the Newbery Award; indeed, the novel's unusual Newbery Medal win still provides the main lens through which critics approach Mukerji's work today. Locating *Gay-Neck* within the cultural matrices of its publication, Makhijani attributes Mukerji's "unlikely success" to the collision of numerous personal and historical forces including "Mukerji's prodigious talent, U.S. immigration policy, and seismic events such as world war and decolonization on the Indian subcontinent" (Makhijani). *Gay-Neck*'s prizing and reception bear ample witness to these fraught sociocultural forces. A closer look at the text, moreover, reveals how Mukerji presents, via spiritual revelations and political vision, a manifesto of peace in a divided, war-torn world.

## *Gay-Neck* in the Twenty-First Century

Based on Mukerji's own childhood experience raising and training some forty pigeons (Mukerji, "Fruits" 60), *Gay-Neck*—the name is a rough translation of the Bengali-language name *Chitra-griva* or "iridescence-throated," referring to the pigeon's shimmering, many-hued throat[5]—follows a Hindu upper-caste adolescent boy as he trains Gay-Neck both in Calcutta and in the forests of the Himalayan mountains. The pigeon's handler, Ghond, is their constant companion, especially during their wilderness sojourns. The beginning of the novel focuses on Gay-Neck's experiences learning to navigate unfamiliar and often dangerous territory, evading lethal avian predators like hawks, and refining his homing instincts. The second half of the novel takes an abrupt, almost dizzying turn, however. It depicts a drastic change of setting, as Gay-Neck and Ghond are drafted to fight in Flanders Fields as part of the Bengal regiment for the British troops in World War I. *Gay-Neck* presents a study in contrasts as it navigates effortlessly between urban environments and Himalayan landscapes, India and France, depictions of wartime and meditations on peace and healing. Most strikingly, perhaps, the novel shifts between two narrators: a teenage boy whom this essay identifies as the primary or human narrator, and the carrier pigeon who narrates some of the novel's most violent incidents, be they avian combat or wartime adventures.[6] Although the pigeon is a secondary narrator, he is decidedly the protagonist of the novel, and this chapter refers to him as such.

*Gay-Neck*'s legacy in the twenty-first century is mixed. To the reader familiar with the history of the Indian Freedom Movement that culminated during the middle of the twentieth century, Mukerji's novel packs a subtly subversive punch, de facto erasing British presence from the colonial Indian geographies it presents to its American child audience. Presenting the pristine beauty of the Himalayan landscape allows characters to move through a landscape that is depicted as largely free of the intrusive British presence. Unlike conventional Western accounts of "untamed" Indian spaces and wildlife, however, these subversive portrayals are laden with meaning and spiritual significance. Mukerji highlights the country's innate strengths, focusing on its verdant landscapes, cultural riches, and profound philosophical ideals such as nonviolence. The narrator's status as an upper-class colonial subject who can afford the expensive hobby of pigeon-rearing provides a stark contrast to the common Western idea of uneducated, impoverished Indian subjects who were the supposed beneficiaries of the "civilizing mission" of the British empire.

During the second half of the novel, which depicts Ghond and Gay-Neck's active military service in France during World War I, the empire is visible.[7] But Mukerji reminds Western readers of India's (and by extension, all British colonies') contributions to the Great War effort, something that has largely been erased in the Western imaginary. These representational choices reflect Mukerji's anti-British stance; we may read this as a colonial subject "punching up" at his British colonial masters, refusing to acknowledge their superiority and instead highlighting Indian achievements on and off the battlefield, in and beyond India.

However, while the novel captures Mukerji's anticolonial sympathies, *Gay-Neck* also exposes the author's own social and political biases. Mukerji's status as a highly educated, high-caste Brahmin hailing from an affluent Calcutta family is mirrored in the unnamed adolescent boy who is the novel's primary narrator.[8] Because most of the novel is presented from this upper-caste teenager's perspective, readers receive a deeply prejudiced account of the hierarchies of Indian society, divided along the lines of caste affiliation, ethnicity, race, religion, and diet. Characters like Ghond the hunter, hailing from the Santal tribe, as well as the Buddhist monks in Himalayan monasteries, are essentialized; Mukerji's casteist and racist depictions expose fault-lines of biases within majoritarian Brahmanical perspectives in India. This representation of minorities within *Gay-Neck* is deeply problematic. Given the renewed interest in the novel as an Own Voices text, an analysis of the insidious ways in which Mukerji presents a homogenized, Brahmanical idea of India, negating the tremendous cultural, linguistic, and ethnic diversity that is a hallmark of the country, is essential.

## "Translating" India: Colonial Landscapes Without the Colonizers

Mukerji was a canny writer who successfully "translated" a specific brand of Indian-ness that his Western audience could appreciate. To do so, he drew liberally on both Indian and British traditions. In the Western imagination, India has historically been associated with its rich and diverse jungles, flora, and fauna; this trope is well-established through colonial representations of India and its "wild" inhabitants. These specific representations are, of course, ideologically loaded. At first glance, Mukerji may seem to have fallen into the trap of self-exoticization, both in his writing and on his lecture tours. As Seeger put it, "however he might adapt himself, wherever he went he was India made visible and audible" (204). Nevertheless, it is possible to read

Mukerji's focus on the subcontinental flora and fauna through a subversive lens. Mukerji's oeuvre incorporates and works against existing stereotypical ideas of India. This was part of the author's commitment to bringing more knowledge and awareness about Hindu religious and cultural practices to Western audiences through his writings and lecture tours in his capacity as "literary missionary"—an endeavor that brought him critical and commercial success in the US.

Even as Mukerji was shrewdly propagating a well-worn idea of India, following an apparently familiar script, his representation upset the status quo in noteworthy ways. Specifically, Mukerji's anti-British stance seeps in through the negative spaces in *Gay-Neck*: the silences and omissions regarding India's colonial masters—who are simply not mentioned—speak volumes. To be sure, the novel features few human characters in the first place, but those it does portray are native to the land, such as the Buddhist monks in the lamasery who offer spiritual guidance and healing from trauma in the aftermath of the Great War. Notably, this strategy also allowed Mukerji to move past common Western perceptions of India as a country of people living in desperate poverty, and focus instead on more privileged sections of Indian society. In depictions of urban spaces like Calcutta, the attention is on the rich North Calcutta *babu* (members of the Bengali genteel class). The narrative is focused on the minutiae of their sport: pigeon- rearing, training, and competitions, all in privileged spaces. The British are nowhere to be seen, their existence entirely ignored.

For an author who espoused strong anti-British sentiments—and whose older brother, Jadu Gopal Mukerji, was a jailed anticolonial freedom fighter—the refusal to address the British presence in India while simultaneously extolling the spiritual wonders of the country is a decidedly political move.[9] His young American readers would get to know the myriad natural wonders and cultural traditions of the Indian subcontinent, but not its political subjugation under the British Raj. This anti-colonial bent, as well as the deep focus on Indian civilization and mysticism, ensures that Mukerji's work is situated ideologically opposite to the civilizing mission implicit in popular texts by writers like Rudyard Kipling, whose colonial representations of India were brimful of imperialist messages.

What sets *Gay-Neck* apart from common Western depictions of Indian jungles and their abundant wildlife? Mukerji's novel takes a tried-and-tested formula and changes it in key ways. A carrier pigeon—an urban, highly domesticated animal—makes an exceptional protagonist in a genre rife with depictions of tropical animals like tigers, elephants, peacocks, and cheetahs. By contrast to typical imperialist depictions of Indian fauna, Mukerji introduces his readers to both urban and rural spaces, with populations of birds, beasts, and insects existing within their own particular ecosystems.[10] Mary Gray, reviewing *Gay-Neck* in

*The Saturday Review of Literature* in 1927, remarks on how "fresh" the material is, adding: "We had heard from Kipling and others a good deal of the habits of elephants, but we do not remember any previous animal story books about pigeons, with the exception of 'Chico,'" Lucy M. Blanchard's 1922 novel about a World War I carrier pigeon (qtd. in Senick 131).[11]

Perhaps most important, the representational trope of associating India almost solely with her wildlife and her jungles is overturned in Mukerji's hands.[12] Well aware of colonial stereotypes about India as a dangerous tropical country in need of "taming" by her White political overlords, Mukerji gave an entirely different meaning to the abundance of natural life in the subcontinent in *Gay-Neck* and other children's books such as *Kari the Elephant* and *Hari the Jungle Lad.*

Some background about Mukerji's literary influences is useful at this point. In *Gay-Neck*'s dedication note addressed to the Sanskrit scholar Suresh Chandra Banerji, Mukerji writes, "Many hunters, poets like yourself, and books in many languages have helped me to write *Gay-Neck*" (n. pag.). While Mukerji does not mention specific texts by name in this dedication, he wrote elsewhere about his inspirations, including works of world literature such as *Aesop's Fables*, which often feature anthropomorphized animals as protagonists and incorporate specific morals in each story (Mukerji, "Fruits" 62). Well-read as he was, Mukerji would also have been acquainted with popular colonial works focusing on India, such as Kipling's *The Jungle Book* and the insistent descriptions of "exotic" Indian forests in popular British children's magazines like the *Boy's Own Paper* (1879–1967). Texts like these, with their Orientalized view of the subcontinent, were chiefly responsible for creating the Western "idea of India." Mukerji was deeply invested in subverting these distorted representations of his beloved country.

Mukerji drew on the indigenous literary traditions of his homeland to do so, and these influences on *Gay-Neck* are readily apparent to informed readers. Those familiar with classics of Indian literature will be struck by Mukerji's clear homage to ancient Sanskrit lyric poems like Kalidasa's *Meghadutam* (*The Cloud Messenger*), which is famous for providing aerial views of the Indian subcontinent, through the eyes of a cloud carrying a message from an exiled *yaksha* (nature spirit) to his wife in the mythical Mount Kailash in the Himalayas. This lyric poem gave rise to the genre of the *sandesha kavya* or messenger poems. The similarities with Gay-Neck, a messenger pigeon providing lyrical descriptions of Himalayan landscapes from a unique aerial perspective while ferrying messages of peace and non-violence, are all too evident.

Other local literary inspirations include early Sanskrit texts like the *Panchatantra*, the *Kathasaritsagara* and the *Betal Panchabinsati*, or religious parables like those featured in the *Hitopodesha* and the Buddhist *Jataka Tales*. These texts are part of India's ancient mythological and folk heritage—they often feature fables about the lives of animals, as well as tales about talking animals, gods, spirits, and trickster figures of all kinds. Arising from oral storytelling traditions spanning the Indian subcontinent, these stories—much like *Gay-Neck*—usually include clearly delineated moral messages for their intended audience.[13] In other words, the focus on animal stories is a far older Indian tradition, and has a very different didactic import, than the ideologically loaded colonial representations of Indian wildlife with which Western readers are typically familiar.

In *Gay-Neck*, we see a synthesis of such diverse literary influences—told from an Indian perspective.[14] Unlike British colonial accounts of India, *Gay-Neck* presents no "wild" land, full of fierce beasts of prey, that need to be killed, "tamed," and "civilized"; instead, readers encounter a land brimming with spiritual resonance, where the animals can communicate. Crucially, both Gay-Neck and his handlers speak in terms of the necessity for profound harmony with the world, nature, and its elements. This message holds complex associations. On the one hand, this ideal might evoke stereotypes about "the East"; on the other, the heartfelt call for harmony would have resonated profoundly less than a decade after the ravages of World War I.

Though not explicitly framed as religious, *Gay-Neck* evokes spirituality through its appeals for peaceful coexistence, its awe-inspiring descriptions of the environmental wonders of the Himalayas, and its reverential treatment of Hindu and Buddhist beliefs. Mukerji's religious beliefs are further revealed in the sequel *Ghond the Hunter*, which leans more heavily into Hinduism. *Ghond* introduces young Western readers to specific aspects of the Hindu religion while presenting a highly biased, laudatory view of the supposedly fluid caste system. Mukerji was an ardent follower of the Ramakrishna order of monks in India, and his writings are clearly influenced in large part by the idea of immanent divinity as preached by them (Chang 21–24). Moreover, *Gay-Neck*'s narrator evinces "a kind of awe-struck wonder at the landscape that becomes blatantly spiritual at times" (Mukherjee). *Gay-Neck* displays a pantheistic sensibility, where characters like the Buddhist lamas (monks) preach that the souls of all living beings are interconnected, and where Gay-Neck and Ghond are healed from battle-induced trauma by meditating on "Infinite Compassion" (171). In the novel, Mukerji's India features a primeval landscape with its "unexplored and untrodden" Himalayan mountain ranges and peaks; the narrator speaks of their "inviolate sanctity" as a "perpetual symbol of divinity," ventriloquizing Mukerji's spiritual proclivities in the process (35).[15] In other words, unlike colonial British accounts of Indian spaces, Mukerji imbues his lyrical descriptions of South Asian geographies, wildernesses and their animal inhabitants with meaning, significance, and spiritual purpose. The established narrative tropes that equated India primarily with its animals and jungles would be familiar to *Gay-Neck*'s child readers, but the import of such formulaic representations is turned on its head when Mukerji endows the spaces and creatures with the spirituality of his homeland.

At the same time, *Gay-Neck*'s depictions of "Eastern" religions and mysticism are often highly essentialized. Mukerji was an extremely learned commentator on Hindu philosophy. But the problem arises when he conflates all communities, religions and spiritual practices of Eastern cultures in one indistinguishable mass, instead of highlighting distinct traditions of each—whether of his own volition (for the benefit of child readers or non-Indian readers more generally) or at the behest of his American publisher.[16] In *Gay-Neck*'s essentialized depictions, the specific tenets of Hinduism and Buddhism (even in cases of core concepts such as non-violence) become melded into a vague, exoticized idea of "Eastern spiritual practice," playing to the starkly Orientalist fantasies of the West.

## Representations of War and Non-Violence as Anticolonial Resistance

One of *Gay-Neck*'s central occupations is violence: in what contexts one may face it (whether as pigeon or human), how one copes when plunged in the thick of it, and most importantly perhaps, the lasting psychological damage of such violence and the means to recover from the terror it generates. For a pigeon especially, life is one long sequence of evading deadly predators like hawks, eagles, *baz* (buzzards), and owls, and in the first half of the book, Mukerji provides several accounts of Gay-Neck's bravery and the strategies employed to survive continual avian attacks. The second part of the novel takes an unexpected detour. Far from the pristine, idyllic wildernesses of the Himalayas, readers are plunged instead into the bloody, war-torn fields of World War I France. There, Gay-Neck (accompanied by his handler, Ghond) provides invaluable service as a messenger pigeon carrying coded missives for the British forces as part of the Bengal regiment in France. This kind of literary representation of *desi* (South Asian) soldiers who comprised the largest volunteer army from Britain's imperial dominions during the Great War is extremely rare.[17] History has largely forgotten the contributions of the 1.3 million Indian soldiers who fought in World War I, including the approximately 70,000 that died while fighting overseas.[18]

Ghond and Gay-Neck serve from September 1914 until they are discharged from duty in February 1915, after the latter is seriously injured. Even in this European wartime setting, Mukerji adheres to the highly political depictive strategies he adopted in the first half of the novel. For instance, in his descriptions of the battlefield and barracks, Mukerji largely excludes any mention of British troops; instead the focus is entirely on the sepoys of the Bengal regiment, including the "Indian warriors from Calcutta," and the daunting enemies they fight (134). Moreover, the shift in narrative voices from human to pigeon allows Mukerji to incorporate implicit critiques of the British Commander-in-Chief who *is* mentioned (141): what would be inadmissible from a human narrator is perhaps more acceptable when a pigeon is the one sharing such unflattering views.

Continuing his focus on animals, Mukerji shares views of the bloody battlefield through Gay-Neck's eyes. We are told about the local animals that suffered during this human war—the natural inhabitants of the land forced to flee or die while men battled each other. Because he is unfamiliar with gunfire, cannons, artillery fire, poison gas, and fighter planes, Gay-Neck "translates" these violent horrors into familiar animal analogies. Thus, he describes guns as "pups" and "metal dogs barking and belching out death" (134, 132); fighter planes as "vast eagles roaring and growling like trumpeting elephants" (133); and "turbaned men from India [who] crawled like little insects" (134). The conversations of the sepoys under the cover of incessant gunfire become "the whisper of a lazy breeze in the grass"; by contrast, gunfire sounds like "the laughter of a hyena" and fighter planes emit a "tiger-roar" (134, 139). Through this device, Mukerji renders his fraught descriptions of war a bit more palatable for child readers.

Furthermore, reversing the colonial gaze and describing deadly European wars via animal metaphors allowed Mukerji to critique Eurocentric representations of India's "wildness" in a more unambiguous fashion. The implication is stark: Europeans are no more "civilized" than Indians are, and representational tropes are always double-edged. When the Empire writes back from the periphery, the view of the "center" is often unflattering, eradicating any notions of superiority that the British exercised over their imperial dominions. Moreover, Gay-Neck and Ghond's presence in France suggests that despite the might of the British empire, that imperial power could not defeat its enemies without the active support of its colonies. Ghond and Gay-Neck sustain heavy injuries—both psychological and physical—during their months on the Western Front, and the novel highlights their exceptional bravery and the sacrifices they make while fighting for a king and country not their own. This is, in turn, an implicit comment on the colonial situation, for Ghond and Gay-Neck would not have gone to war in Europe were it not for the British domination of India.

*Gay-Neck* is rife with depictions of warfare, whether on the human battlefield or in the numerous midair avian battles. These violent encounters traumatize both Gay-Neck and Ghond, inducing what we now call post-traumatic stress disorder. With Ghond and Gay-Neck's eventual healing at the hands of Buddhist monks in Sikkim, Mukerji embeds the novel with a powerful anti-war message. The last part of the narrative is about finding one's way home, surmounting all possible obstacles, and embracing the message of peace and non-violence among all living creatures. Mukerji does descend into somewhat hackneyed accounts of the Buddhist philosophy of non-violence as he describes how Gay-Neck is released from his crippling fear and shell-shock by his young master's extensive meditation and healing chants. Nevertheless, the novel's ending provides a balm of sorts to the scenes of extreme violence depicted earlier in the narrative. Mukerji was stridently anti-war, as seen in letters to friends (Chang 11), and he wrote elsewhere that a deep desire for establishing international cooperation and harmony lay behind his writings: "I hold that until a nation appreciates the common culture of another nation it will not be able to understand the value of international peace. We need peace between nations because peace alone can augment the forces of true culture" (Mukerji, "Fruits" 64). This message of peace and international cooperation would have resonated with many American readers in the 1920s, who, following the carnage of World War I, witnessed the establishment of the League of Nations and the rise of peace movements throughout much of the Western world.

## Brahmanical Hegemony and the Idea of the "East"

While *Gay-Neck* was subversive in how it overturned clichéd Western depictions of Indian spaces and cultures, the text is also laden with regressive and knotty representational issues. Mukerji's unique position as a "literary missionary" writing about Indian life and spirituality for a Western audience means that readers view India solely from his specific vantage point. This has consequences, especially with respect to issues of region, religion, and caste. India is a country of incredible regional diversity of languages, cultures, food habits, and social customs. But in Mukerji's writings more broadly, and in *Gay-Neck* most specifically, the myriad complexities of Indian lives and customs are largely flattened into the image of a homogeneous, indivisible Hindu nation; other religions such as Islam, Jainism, or Sikhism are cropped out of the picture. Chang points out that one of Mukerji's central tenets was that "the East should learn activity and science from the West, whereas the West should learn 'repose and meditation' from the East" (18). This "East" that Mukerji refers to is often a highly Orientalized space, where entire regions, communities, and philosophies are portrayed as one. Perhaps this was for the sake of simplifying the stories he wrote for his primarily American audience—and a child audience at that—but this sort of flattening is ideologically problematic, especially given Mukerji's status as an upper-class, upper-caste Hindu Brahmin man.

Casteism is rife at every level of Indian society, even in present-day India, and has been recognized by the eminent early-twentieth-century activist Bhimrao Ramji Ambedkar as a deeply ingrained social evil leading to systemic human rights abuses for India's significant Dalit (lower-caste, formerly called "Untouchable") populations over the centuries (Ambedkar). Mukerji, while espousing the glories of Hindu religious and spiritual traditions, glosses over his human narrator's status at the top of the Hindu caste hierarchy, reflecting his pervasive caste bias. For instance, the wealthy, high-caste narrator of *Gay-Neck* speaks admiringly of his friend Radja, a Brahmin priest whose family members have been priests of the village of Ghatsila "for ten centuries" (120). He praises Radja for his impeccable caste pedigree and considers it indicative of a superior moral quality.

This is in direct contrast to Ghond the hunter, a member of the indigenous Santal tribe who is depicted along the lines of the "noble savage" archetype. While *Gay-Neck* does not specifically mention Ghond's tribal affiliation, the 1928 sequel *Ghond the Hunter* identifies his ethnicity. Mukerji dedicates *Ghond* to "the memory of Pradhan the Santal, the original of Ghond" (n. pag.). In *Gay-Neck*, readers learn that Ghond hails from a remote village tribe, and is extremely poor and uneducated. He also exists in the narrative primarily to serve his young upper-caste master, both as his mentor and his manservant. In *Ghond the Hunter,* Mukerji specifies that although a Santal, Ghond is Hindu; moreover, he is a Kshatriya: he belongs to the warrior caste and has been formally initiated into his caste identity by a Brahmin priest. Despite being a supposedly upper-caste Hindu, Ghond's status would be very different from that of the adolescent narrator, since Ghond is a Santal by ethnicity. Hindus from tribal populations such as the Santals—who were mostly converted from their indigenous animist religion—did not enjoy the same status as higher-caste Hindus from mainstream Indian societies, whether rural or urban. As the 1921 Census of India explains, the census category of "Brahmanic Hindus" includes both "the recognized Hindu castes" and "a large passive and acquiescent mass of functional and tribal castes, who are excluded from all the religious exercises and denied all the social privileges of Hinduism" (113).

While Ghond is praised in *Gay-Neck* for his hunting skills and unrivalled knowledge about animals, his Santal identity is nowhere mentioned, even in a narrative rife with casteist depictions of his character. Santals are not vegetarian as a rule; as a hunter-gatherer tribe, their sustenance is primarily derived from the forest, and their diet incorporates meat (beef, pork, and various insects). However, Ghond, despite being a hunter, is portrayed as a vegetarian (171). This discrepancy makes sense only because the omnivorous eating habits of tribal communities are abhorrent to traditional vegetarian Brahmins with their strict notions of "purity" and "cleanliness." Brahmanical hegemonic beliefs equate vegetarianism with moral purity; by making Ghond a vegetarian, Mukerji takes away a crucial component of his ethnic identity and "purifies" him enough to associate closely with his

Brahmin master, as it were. In this way, Mukerji replicates the representational strategies seen in some colonial texts, where the indigenous characters identified as "good" or "noble" are those who conform to what the colonizer values.

Another blatant instance of the caste politics in *Gay-Neck* appears when Ghond travels to Marseilles as Gay-Neck's handler: "Ghond and not I went to the front ... for I was under age and ineligible for any kind of service" (131). Subsequently, Gay-Neck takes over the narration and refers to the "black water" they had to cross to get to France (132). While the significance of this remark would not have been clear to Mukerji's Western audiences, presumably unfamiliar with the minutiae of Hindu taboos, a reader aware of Hindu rituals would instantly comprehend the real reason why Ghond, the Santal manservant, travels to France instead of Gay-Neck's upper-caste teenage owner. "Black water" here is a literal translation of the term "*kala pani*"; this is significant because Hindus, especially those from higher castes, were strictly forbidden to travel across oceans or seas. A Hindu crossing the forbidden "black water" was effectively excommunicated from his caste and his religion, and as a practicing Hindu, this would have applied to Ghond as well. The privileged narrator would not have taken the drastic step of crossing the water and losing his religion, as it were, but Mukerji has no trouble sending the poor tribal manservant on his behalf. This textual detail encapsulates *Gay-Neck*'s casteism and classist tendencies in one neat package.

Moreover, *Gay-Neck* presents highly racist views of people from the mountainous northeastern parts of the Indian subcontinent. The Buddhist lamasery that occupies such an important space in *Gay-Neck* is inhabited by wise lamas who teach Ghond, the teen narrator, and Gay-Neck about peace and non-violence, healing their traumatic fears. The descriptions of the lamas are supremely Orientalized, using tropes commonly associated with East Asian peoples: the Himalayan Buddhist monks are depicted as mystical practitioners who can "read [the] thoughts" of both people and animals through powers acquired during decades of prayer and meditation (54–55). Moreover, both the human and avian narrators use racist descriptors: the boy describes a Buddhist lama with "almond-shaped eyes," and both narrators refer to men encountered in the Himalayas as "flat-faced" and "yellow" (175, 54, 90). There is a very clear division between "Indians" and "mountain folk, who loo[k] much like Chinese" and who are treated as exotic curiosities (37); additionally, hill tribes of different regions in Sikkim and other northeastern Himalayan regions are conflated into one indistinguishable mass of "yellow" people.

While Mukerji critiques the British colonial presence by refusing to feature colonial oppressors in the novel, he seems to be oblivious to the fact that, to those of other castes and ethnicities, upper-caste Brahmins such as the narrator, Radja, and Mukerji himself were equally cruel oppressors. In effect, Mukerji is "punching down" at these Others just as much as he "punches up" at the British oppressors. His subversive critiques—by omission—of the British Raj were timely and necessary, and remain relevant today. Sadly, the novel's less admirable stances—the markedly casteist and classist sympathies it evinces—remain equally timely. Take Mukerji's casteist representation of the Santal hunter Ghond, whom he portrays as a vegetarian in keeping with Brahmin values. Hindu nationalists in present-day India would enact a similar change by force: indeed, India has recently seen the rise of a kind of vegetarian tyranny, with beef consumption used as a justification for enacting deadly violence upon Dalits and Muslims (Editorial Board).[19]

This chapter's critique of casteism and racism in *Gay-Neck* points directly to a key aspect of the novel's continued relevance. With the resurgence of interest in diverse books, Mukerji's novel has attracted renewed interest as an early, noteworthy Own Voices text. However, there can be a tendency, when reading an Own Voices author, to accept a text uncritically as an authentic representation of a given cultural group, without interrogating the nuances of the representational politics at play. *Gay-Neck* offers an exceptionally important anticolonial meditation, and it richly merits increased attention. However, if the novel is going to be excavated and reintroduced, as Mukherjee and Makhijani have done in their excellent but overwhelmingly laudatory feature articles, it is essential to show readers the ways in which a work like this can also be harmful. This is especially crucial given the majoritarian political rule of India's right-wing Hindu nationalist Bharatiya Janata Party since 2014. I contend that publishing the century-old novels *Gay-Neck* and *Ghond the Hunter* with no critical or contextual framework, as Hachette India did in 2016, was an act of editorial irresponsibility given the country's current political climate. As we analyze and celebrate Own Voices literature, then, let us do so with contextual awareness and a critical mindset. This is a key lesson to be taken from reading *Gay-Neck* in the twenty-first century.

## Notes

1 The luminaries in Mukerji's close social circle ranged from contemporary poets, scholars, actors, and artists to philosophers and civil rights leaders—even Jawaharlal Nehru, who would become the first Prime Minister of independent India in 1947 (Chang 13–14, 18–19).

2 Mukerji was not the first immigrant author to win: the inaugural Newbery went to *The Story of Mankind* (1921; 1922 Newbery Medal) by Dutch-born Hendrik Willem Van Loon.

3 India's caste system divides Hindus into four main categories: Brahmins (the priestly caste), Kshatriyas (the warrior caste), Vaishyas (the mercantile caste), and the lower-caste Shudras (formerly known as Untouchables and now often called Dalits). Brahmins, at the top of the caste hierarchy, wield the

greatest social power and authority. Casteism in India is comparable to racism in the United States and elsewhere.

4 The Immigration Act of 1917 followed in the wake of previous anti-Asian immigration laws such as the Chinese Exclusion Act of 1882. The 1917 Act is emblematic of a pattern of racist laws and judgments, such as the landmark 1923 US Supreme Court case *United States v. Bhagat Singh Thind*, which ruled that Indian immigrants were not eligible for naturalization or citizenship, and that previous citizenship granted by lower courts would be overturned, due to Indians' status as non-Whites. Such anti-immigration and anti-naturalization measures effectively put a stop to South Asian immigration to the United States for the next several decades, until the Immigration and Nationality Act of 1965 ended the immigration quotas articulated in the National Origins Formula (in place since the Emergency Quota Act of 1921), thus reversing earlier bans on South Asians entering the United States.

5 This translation has perhaps not aged well, as Americans' use of the term "gay" has shifted away from its earlier meaning of "colorful" to a term broadly denoting queer identity. Since the late twentieth century, it has also sometimes been used by children or teens as a general pejorative. As a result, the novel's title now seems awkward, and may make the book unappealing to young readers.

6 In sections where Gay-Neck takes over the narration, readers are invited to use "the grammar of fancy and the dictionary of imagination" to see the world through an avian perspective (74).

7 Naturally, the portions of the narrative devoted to the war make reference to the British (97, 149). Significantly, the British domination of India subsequently becomes visible in the narrative, as if a switch had been flipped by this incursion into war: after Ghond and Gay-Neck return from Europe, the narrator finally acknowledges the colonial presence in his homeland, noting that the "British Government forbids the use of firearms to the common people of India" (180).

8 As a person born into a Bengali Brahmin family, I share Mukerji's caste and ethnic background, and hence his upper-caste privilege within Indian society. I share this information in the interest of transparency and accountability, since this essay critiques Mukerji's casteist stance.

9 Associated with national organizations like the Samiti Movement, Jugantar Party, and the Indian National Congress, Jadu Gopal Mukerji was imprisoned on several occasions by the British for his revolutionary activities (Mukerji, *Caste* 258n5).

10 Mukerji's specificity of detail is remarkable—he mentions existing place names like Dentam, Singalila, Ghatsila, Sikkim, and Himalayan peaks like Makalu, Everest, and Kanchenjungha, as well as recurring lists of the species of flora and fauna his human and pigeon narrators encounter.

11 Blanchard's *Chico: The Story of a Homing Pigeon* is set in Italy, and features a conventional human narrator.

12 The focus on animals and jungles was in evidence in Mukerji's own life as well. In her essay on Mukerji's legacy, Seeger mentions that while talking to his son's American schoolmates, "no matter what subject he may have started with, he ended invariably in the Indian jungle where his listeners most wanted him to take them" (203).

13 Mukerji actively espoused the value of the morals in such traditional Indian stories, and declared, "behind each one of my books the reader will discover a moral. I believe that there is no point in writing for the young, if one has no ethical convictions to set forth before them" ("Fruits" 61).

14 Mukerji was a pioneer in this sense: his autobiography *Caste and Outcast* was "the first widely read book on India ... written by an Indian" for US readers, Chang notes, and "reviewers immediately appreciated this significance" (17). I contend that the same holds true for *Gay-Neck* in terms of its Western child audiences, especially in light of its heightened fame following the Newbery Medal win.

15 It was not until 29 May 1953 that Tenzing Norgay and Edmund Hillary first climbed Mount Everest. In Mukerji's lifetime, most of the towering Himalayan peaks he mentions, such as Kanchenjunga and Makalu along with Everest, remained "inviolate."

16 Mukerji gave the impression that editorial pressure influenced the narrative of his memoir *Cast and Outcaste* (1923): he maintained that publisher E. P. Dutton encouraged him to spin his immigration story into "a Horatio Alger-like account because it resonated with the reassuring and familiar narrative of America as the land of opportunity for the entire world" (Chang 5).

17 The only other notable work by an Indian author about the ravages of the Great War on ordinary Indians is Mulk Raj Anand's *Across the Black Waters* (1939).

18 Recent scholarship has begun to recover this largely ignored history. See Shrabani Basu's *For King and Another Country: Indian Soldiers on the Western Front 1914–1918* (2016), David Omissi's *Indian Voices of the Great War* (1999), and David Olusoga's *The World's War: Forgotten Soldiers of Empire* (2014). Santanu Das also has a series of excellent articles on India's World War I engagements at the British Library's online digitized collections of censored mail from contemporary war correspondence. The 1920 memorial in northern France's Neuve Chapelle was the only postwar European historical monument of note acknowledging Indians who died in World War I. The 2015 National Memorial Arboretum in Straffordshire, funded in large part by British Sikhs, honors the 130,000 Sikh soldiers who fought in the Great War.

19 Following the election of Hindu nationalist Prime Minister Narendra Modi in 2014, prohibitions on the slaughter and consumption of beef were instated or tightened in some Indian states. In 2015, a mob murdered a Muslim man just outside the Indian capital New Delhi because it was rumored that he had eaten beef (Raj). This murder was part of a recent spate of Hindu supremacist violence enacted by so-called "cow vigilantes."

## Works Cited

Ambedkar, B[himrao]. R[amji]. "Annihilation of Caste." 1936. *The Essential Writings of B. R. Ambedkar*. Ed. Valerian Rodrigues. New Delhi: Oxford UP, 2002. 263–305. *HathiTrust*. Web. 12 Jan. 2021.

*Census of India 1921*. Vol. 1, Part 1. Calcutta: Superintendent Government Printing, India, 1924. *HathiTrust*. Web. 10 Jan. 2021.

Chang, Gordon H. "Introduction: The Life and Death of Dhan Gopal Mukerji." *Caste and Outcast*. By Dhan Gopal Mukerji. Ed. Gordon H. Chang, Purnima Mankekar, and Akhil Gupta. Stanford: Stanford UP, 2002. 1–40. Print.

Editorial Board. "Modi and India's Dalits." *The New York Times* 3 Aug. 2016: n. pag. Web. 10 Jan. 2021.

Gandhi, Lakshmi. "Remembering the First Indian-American Children's Book to Win the Newbery." *NBC News*. NBC Universal, 30 June 2017. Web. 8 May. 2021.

H. J. B. W. Rev. of *Gay-Neck*, by Dhan Gopal Mukerji. *Junior Bookshelf* 2.8 (May 1938): 129–131. *HathiTrust*. Web. 12 Jan. 2021.

Horning, Kathleen T. "Secrecy and the Newbery Medal." *The Horn Book Magazine* 87.4 (July/Aug. 2011): 60–70. *Gale Literature Resource Center*. Web. 5 Jan. 2021.

Mahony, Bertha E., ed. *The Horn Book Magazine* 3.4 (July/Aug. 1937): 197–256. *HathiTrust*. Web. 12 Jan. 2021.

Makhijani, Pooja. "What a Forgotten Kids' Book Reveals About U.S. Publishing." *The Atlantic* 3 Oct. 2017. Web. 10 Feb. 2018.

Mukerji, Dhan Gopal. *Caste and Outcast*. 1923. Ed. Gordon H. Chang, Purnima Mankekar, and Akhil Gupta. Stanford: Stanford UP, 2002. Print.

Mukerji, Dhan Gopal. "Fruits from the Living Tree." *Bunny, Hound and Clown*. New York: E. P. Dutton & Company, 1931. 11–17. Rpt. in Bertha Mahony Miller and Elinor Whitney Field, eds. *Newbery Medal Books: 1922–1955 with their Authors' Acceptance Papers & Related Material chiefly from the* Horn Book Magazine. Boston: The Horn Book, 1955. 59–64. Print.

Mukerji, Dhan Gopal. *Gay-Neck: The Story of a Pigeon*. 1927. New York: E. P. Dutton, 1954. Print.

Mukerji, Dhan Gopal. *Gay-Neck, the Story of a Pigeon & Ghond, The Hunter*. 1927, 1928. Gurugram: Hachette India, 2016. Print.

Mukerji, Dhan Gopal. *Ghond the Hunter*. 1928. New York: E. P. Dutton, 1936. Print.

Mukherjee, Oindrila. "'Gay Neck': The Forgotten Book by an Indian that Won America's Top Children's Literature Prize." *Scroll.in*. Scroll Media Inc., 12 June 2015. Web. 13 Feb. 2018.

Raj, Suhasini. "Mob in India Kills Muslim Man Over Rumors of Cow Slaughter." *The New York Times* 30 Sept. 2015: A10. Web. 10 Jan. 2021.

Seeger, Elizabeth. "Dhan Mukerji and His Books." *The Horn Book Magazine* 13.4 (July/Aug. 1937): 199–205. Print.

Senick, Gerard J., ed. "Dhan Gopal Mukerji: 1890–1936." *Children's Literature Review*. Vol. 10. New York: Gale, 1986. 127–136. Print.

# 3 Sounding the Broken Note

## *The Trumpeter of Krakow* (1929) and Polish History

*Kenneth B. Kidd*

Eric Philbrook Kelly's historical novel *The Trumpeter of Krakow* (1928; 1929 Newbery Medal) makes for an interesting case study in the motivations, ethics, and impacts of award-winning historical fiction about non-American history and culture.[1] Formally and ideologically, *Trumpeter* is a flawed but intriguing book, written out of Kelly's deep and admirable involvement with Poland. It was apparently the first English-language children's title about Poland to appear, and it remains one of the few such titles not about the Holocaust.[2] Kelly composed *Trumpeter* between two world wars and with Poland newly affirmed as a nation, via the Treaty of Versailles, comprised of areas previously part of Germany, Russia, and Austro-Hungary. An English teacher and journalist, Kelly undertook war relief work in Poland in World War I and became a lifelong advocate of Polish independence. Like other Medal authors of what children's literature specialist Ruth Hill Viguers calls "foreign background stories," popular in this period, Kelly loved his adopted country and did everything he could to paint it in a positive light, while never losing sight of American interests (444).

Kelly registers no discomfort with his status as an American writing about a Central European nation with its own languages and customs. He certainly does not use *Trumpeter* to defamiliarize American or Western culture, as literary critic Tim Morris claims for Elizabeth Foreman Lewis in her roughly contemporaneous novel set in China, *Young Fu of the Upper Yangtze* (1932; 1933 Newbery Medal).[3] Rather, Kelly seeks to frame Polish history in the context of both American exceptionalism and Christianity. His vision of Poland is also a vision *for* Poland, one of proud independence modeled on American nationhood and positioned against the twin dangers of Russia and Germany. In her analysis of a later Medal title, Elizabeth George Speare's *The Witch of Blackbird Pond* (1958; 1959 Newbery Medal), children's literature scholar Sara Schwebel reminds us that historical fiction tends to reflect both the historical past it takes for subject matter and the historical moment of its own creation, "as well as beliefs and attitudes in the present in which it is read" (213). *Trumpeter* comments obliquely on

DOI: 10.4324/9780367337223-3-4

1920s global politics and in particular the situation of Poland in its story of fifteenth-century Krakow. In the process, Kelly appeals to—and accidentally helps to reinvent—a native legend about a Krakow Trumpeter that ostensibly symbolizes Polish national heritage but clearly reflects America's own self-image. Kelly's book was written for American readers, but in a curious turn of events it became influential in Poland, not as a children's book but rather as a source text for the Trumpeter legend.

As a work of historical fiction, *Trumpeter* is ostensibly grounded in the great Krakow fire of 1462, in which much of the city was destroyed.[4] In Kelly's version, the fire results from an act of alchemy gone bad. But the book's greater commitment is to the legend of the Krakow Trumpeter, which blends the historical past with the present and minimizes the Otherness of Poland for American readers. Kelly explains in a prologue that the person selected as the Trumpeter of Krakow plays a five-note anthem called the Heynal (Polish: *Hejnal mariaki*, "Saint Mary's dawn") every hour out of each window in the tallest tower of the Church of Our Lady Mary. The Trumpeter keeps time but also serves as a lookout, watching for dangers such as fire or invasion. The Heynal ends on a broken note, Kelly explains, because in 1241 the Trumpeter stayed at his post during an invasion but was killed before he could finish the piece.[5] It's unclear, however, if this event actually happened. And while the Heynal seems to end abruptly, it doesn't necessarily conclude on a "broken note," much less one that commemorates the death of the martyred Trumpeter. Even so, Kelly fashions a story of adventure and heroism around that legend of the broken note, a legend now famous in Poland.[6] The Heynal is a national tradition, still played hourly out of the Church of Our Lady Mary. The noon performance is even broadcast on Polish national radio, a tradition dating to 1927, the year before *Trumpeter* appeared.

In Kelly's novel, which begins in 1461, the Charnetski family—Pan ("Sir") Andrew, his unnamed wife, and their fifteen-year-old son Joseph—flee their Ukrainian estate after being attacked by Tartars, led by Bogdan the Terrible (or Peter of the Button Face), in the employ of Russia's Ivan the Great. Assuming new identities, the Charnetskis find accommodation and some safety in Krakow, although Peter hunts them. The Trumpeter position has just opened up, and Pan Andrew undertakes the role. Fifteen-year-old Joseph learns the Heynal to help his father with the night watch. One night, Peter attacks them inside the tower, and Joseph plays the Heynal *beyond* the broken note, alerting others to the danger. Peter does not know the tradition and is caught unawares in turn. While neither Joseph nor Andrew is injured in the attack, the episode is designed to recall the originating incident of the broken note legend.

In his prologue, and citing no sources and giving no explanation of how he heard of the legend, Kelly draws a heroic sketch of the Trumpeter killed by a Tartar arrow in 1241, imagining him as a "young man, perhaps nineteen or twenty" who praises God that his mother and sister are safe and then reflects on "what a sweet thing life is." "And then it came to him," Kelly continues, "young as he was, that he was part of the glorious company of Polish men that was fighting for all Christendom against brutal and savage invaders" (5). He intuits that his "bravery was to descend as a heritage to the people to whom he belonged, and was to become a part of their spirit, their courage, their power of everlasting" (5). That young man dies, but the Heynal tradition continues, such that two centuries later another young man (with the help of his father) takes up the trumpet and saves the day in Kelly's novel.[7]

*Trumpeter* found immediate success in America before becoming largely forgotten; its career in Poland followed the opposite trajectory. When *Trumpeter* won the Medal in 1929, librarian Alice M. Jordan, long-time head of children's work at Boston Public Library, predicted that it was "bound to rouse cordiality for a people whose passion for a national life has survived generations of exile" (105). At almost a century's distance, however, it seems that *Trumpeter* has had more lasting influence in Poland, where it is now widely credited as a source for the Trumpeter legend, especially in tourist materials such as Krakow guidebooks. Granted, some of these materials target English-speaking visitors, but Polish historians and critics also cite (apparently without reading) Kelly's book. In the States, Kelly was considered an effective spokesman for Poland, while in Poland he was never well-known and/or quickly forgotten. His Newbery-winning *Trumpeter* has never been translated into Polish. Yet the novel enjoys a strange afterlife as a basis for Krakow history, even though—perhaps because?—it was never translated.

## Literary Alchemy: A 1920s Portrait of 1460s Krakow

In 1918, after a decade in newspaper journalism, Kelly volunteered to work with the French welfare organization Les Foyers du Soldat in Quentin, France. In 1919, Kelly (in the company of two thousand Polish soldiers) was sent to the Warsaw area in the newly recognized state of Poland, to help with war relief efforts. During the 1919–1920 Polish-Soviet War, he was posted at Chelm. He studied the language and fell in love with Poland and its people. In 1921, Kelly returned to the United States and began writing about his experiences abroad. He was hired as an English professor by Dartmouth College, his alma mater. Kelly returned to Poland in 1925 as the first American exchange scholar sponsored by New York's Kosciuszko Foundation; he went again in 1930 and

1931, publishing two more Polish-themed children's novels in the wake of *Trumpeter*: *The Blacksmith of Vilno* (1930) and *The Golden Star of Halicz* (1931). Kelly later worked for the US State Department providing humanitarian aid to Polish refugees in Mexico.

At the time of *Trumpeter*'s publication, Poland had only been an independent country for a decade, Polish forces having stopped the advance of the Bolshevik army into central Europe in 1920, after having repulsed Russian, German, and Austrian occupation just two years earlier. Under the leadership of Chief of State Jozef Pilsudski, Poland repelled both German and Russian imperialism by pushing successfully into western Ukraine. The Red Army launched a counter-offensive, and eventually a cease-fire was declared and the Treaty of Riga signed in March 1921, dividing the Ukrainian territories between Soviet Russia and Poland. Poland faced dramatic challenges in the early 1920s, including economic instability and the lack of infrastructure resulting from more than a century of foreign rule. Poland was a republic until 1926, when its first president was assassinated, at which point Pilsudski staged a coup d'état. By 1930 Poland was a dictatorship. Even so, it was slowly beginning to rebuild its economy, developing industries such as mining and steel and building a new port on the Baltic Sea. Its status as a nation was hard-fought and precarious.

Kelly knew Poland's situation firsthand. He was there during and after the Polish-Soviet War, involved with relief efforts. *Trumpeter* emerged out of that experience. Rather than write about the contemporary moment, however, Kelly tells the story of Poland's struggle for autonomy by returning to an earlier historical moment in which eastern forces were pushing west across Ukraine and into Poland. *Trumpeter* takes place during what's known as the Jagiellonian period (after the founder of the royal dynasty), which saw Poland in possession of Hungary and (later) Prussia. By 1526 Jagiellonian rule extended from the Baltic to the Black Sea and encompassed Poles, Lithuanians, Latvians, Estonians, Germans, Ukrainians, Belarusians, and Tartars. The period saw advances in Polish government and law, and Poland became an eastern center for Renaissance ideas and culture. In the 1460s Poland was a major force in Europe, with Krakow assuming a critical role due to its location along the continental trade routes. Writing in the 1920s, as Poland struggled to survive, Kelly emphasizes the longer arc of Polish identity, offering hope for the future by emphasizing the glories of the past.

*Trumpeter* stresses both the durability and the precariousness of Krakow, which stands for Poland at large. The Charnetskis come to Krakow after Button-Face Peter and his forces attack and burn their estate in Ukraine. Kelly does not comment on the Charnetskis' presence in Ukraine, something his readers might have questioned at the time of publication, Poland having recently seized parts of Ukraine. Instead, he focuses on Krakow as the symbolic heart of Poland. Kelly's Krakow is bustling, cosmopolitan, and diverse. Entering the city, Joseph marvels at the many languages and dialects he hears and the many ethnicities of people he sees. On display also are "curiosities in dress" and all sorts of merchandise. "Everywhere could be heard the cries of vendors shouting or singing their wares or professions, the flower girls, the knife sharpener, the baker's boy, and the butcher's apprentice. '*Co brakuje, co brakuje*?' they all shouted in a chorus. 'What do you lack? What do you lack?'" (23). Joseph also sees prisoners in iron collars and worse; the narrator intones that life "was a precarious thing in many ways in those days" (23). Kelly portrays Krakow as a lively and exciting, if also dangerous, place.

But if Kelly's Krakow features people with different religious and cultural outlooks, it is also decidedly Christian and Anglophone-Western in bias. Kelly's characters tend to be either really good or really evil—along racist-nationalist lines. Kelly creates two villains in his novel: Peter of the Button Face, the Tartar in the employ of the Russians, and Johann Tring, a greedy German alchemy student. Both have evil faces. Peter's "dark, oval, wicked face" gives "the effect of a monkey rather than a man," disfigured by the "scar of the button plague that is so common in the lands east of the Volga, or even the Dnieper, and marks the bearer as a Tartar or a Cossack or a Mongol" (12). As for Tring, "it was not that the face was distorted, indeed it was not.... But the nose was thin and mean, the mouth was small and smug, and out of the eyes came a look that signified an utterly selfish spirit behind them" (63). Such racist physiognomy has lost favor and presents an obstacle for contemporary readers.

These offensive descriptions of Peter and Johann, however, serve an additional purpose in the book: they express Kelly's selective sympathy for Poland's ongoing struggle with two world powers with expansionist agendas in the 1920s, the Soviet Union and Germany. Tring represents the German threat to Polish stability, soon to be very significant indeed, while Peter represents the Russian threat (he acts on behalf of the Tsar) as well as anxiety about invaders from the east (mostly Turks and Mongols). Kelly writes in his prologue that "the name 'Tartar' was one that froze folks' blood in their veins" (1). "The Tartars came through the world like a horde of wild beasts," he continues. "Brave they were as lions, courageous they were as great dogs, but they had hearts of stone and knew not mercy, nor pity, nor tenderness, nor God" (2). Given these remarks, we shouldn't be surprised by Peter's characterization. While Poland does have a history of persecution by the Germans and Russians, and while Kelly isn't wrong to encourage sympathy for such, we should remember that Poland of 1462 was itself an imperial power of sorts. Unless readers know this history, they might think of Poland in twentieth-century terms, as a nation that suffered under German and then Soviet rule. Kelly's villains speak as much to the moment of the book's 1920s composition as to the fifteenth-century history the book dramatizes.

The same is true of the alchemy plot, which functions to accentuate the racial and national Otherness of the villains against the Polish identity of the protagonists. The devastating Krakow fire of 1462 was not started by an alchemic experiment gone wrong, as far as we know. But it is true that medieval Poland, like much of Europe, was preoccupied with (if also fearful about) the practice of alchemy, a mix of science, philosophy, and mysticism. Alchemy was a precursor to modern chemistry, and one famous Polish alchemist working in the sixteenth century, Michael Sendivogius, anticipated the discovery of the element oxygen. In *Trumpeter* alchemy represents some of the scientific and philosophical ambitions of the early Renaissance, but it also serves as a metaphor for the ills of personal greed versus national (and specifically Polish) pride. Early in the book, we learn that the Charnetski family has long been safeguarding for the Polish crown a precious jewel known as the "Great Tarnov Crystal." It's unclear under what circumstances and with what expectations they were assigned this role. They were hiding the Crystal in their Ukrainian estate, which prompted the raid by Peter of the Button Face. The family comes to Krakow not only to escape Peter but to return the Crystal to King Kasimir Jagiello. This mission sets them apart from the rabble. Their material circumstances greatly reduced, they nonetheless carry the Crystal in their fancy wagon with "two horses instead of the usual one" and a shaft pole "stouter than those of the other wagons." They are "better dressed than the peasants and seemed somehow not like the actual workers of the soil" (9). They are not in Krakow for mere trade, in short; they serve a higher purpose. This plot contrivance makes crystal clear that the Charnetskis are Polish insiders, their Ukrainian heritage notwithstanding, which means also that they can be entrusted with that other sacred Polish symbol, the Heynal.

The Crystal is actually the famed Philosopher's Stone of alchemic legend, first described in Alexandrian and Arabian texts and believed to hold the secret of transmuting baser elements into gold as well as the power to grant immortality. Stories of the Stone are typically cautionary tales against greed and manipulation, however, as the Stone tends to reflect, amplify, and distort the desires of the user.[8] Midway through *Trumpeter* Peter tries to steal the Crystal on behalf of Ivan the Great, and in the confusion the Crystal temporarily winds up in the hands of an alchemist named Kreutz. The Charnetskis are befriended by Kreutz when they arrive in Krakow, and live in an apartment occupied by Kreutz and his niece Elzbietka. Kreutz is a good man and earnest alchemist, but the Crystal's temptations are just too strong. Not only does Kreutz fail to return the Crystal to the Charnetskis; he secretly uses it in his alchemy. Kreutz is already under the sway of the power-hungry German student, Johann Tring. Tring puts Kreutz in a hypnotic trance to discover the secret of making gold. Feverishly they follow a formula "revealed" by the Crystal that is mostly nonsense and highly combustible, resulting not in gold but in an explosion in the lab.

Disaster erupts in the form of a fire that devours a third of Krakow. Not long after, the Crystal is recovered and finally taken to the king, but at the last minute, Kreutz seizes the Crystal and pitches it into the Vistula River. All agree the Crystal is better off lost.

Kelly warns against alchemy even as *Trumpeter* itself might be described as a work of alchemy, aiming to transmute the "baser" elements of history and myth into historical fiction (if not a Newbery gold-medal-winning children's book—that Kelly could not have foreseen). Kelly uses the alchemy plot to caution readers against not only the menace of presumptively evil outsiders like Peter and Tring but also the harm that even well-meaning insiders can do if misguided or manipulated. The accompanying Heynal plot, meanwhile, consolidates Polish identity around and through the Charnetskis and their successful safeguarding of a precious heritage, far more important than a precious object.

## Non-Translation and the Trumpeter Legend

*Trumpeter* was allegedly an accidental children's book. Louise Seaman Bechtel, the pioneering Macmillan editor who published *Trumpeter,* reports that Kelly initially set out to write a history of Poland and instead wrote a historical novel for children (Bechtel x). Bechtel implies that for Kelly, nonfiction wouldn't suffice, so strong was his passion—that is, Kelly *had* to write a novel, and a children's novel at that.[9] Of course, the shift into children's literature might well have been tactical, given the contemporary currency of foreign background stories in American children's literature. Kelly himself never mentions any change in plans. In any case, the book was published to great fanfare in America—literally. It won the Medal, and Kelly went on tour with a silver trumpet borrowed from Krakow's Church of Our Lady Mary itself. The trumpet was first blown in America at the 1928 Children's Book Week meeting of the New York Public Library. "The tune rang forth," Bechtel would later recall, "loud and spine-chilling. It was a great moment!" (viii). The trumpet then "traveled all over America for a year, was shown in bookshops, and was blown in schools and libraries," and "of course it rang out over the American Library Association meeting" at which Kelly made his Medal acceptance speech (Bechtel viii–ix). Keep in mind that *The Horn Book* launched just a few years before, in 1924, to "blow the horn for fine books for boys and girls," as the magazine's co-founder and pioneering children's bookseller Bertha Mahony (later Bertha Mahony Miller) explains in the inaugural volume. That volume's cover featured a reproduction from Randolph Caldecott's *The Three Jovial Huntsmen,* featuring said huntsmen blowing horns, "so full of exuberant joy for the hunt that they can't blow hard enough" (Mahony). Kelly's trumpet isn't a horn, but *Trumpeter* must have appealed to exuberant hunters of good children's books.

In her foreword to the 1966 reissue of the novel,[10] titled "A Trumpet for the Trumpeter," Bechtel claims that Kelly's book "won immediate critical praise. Boys and girls were as keen about it as reviewers; it was the sort of book to pass on as a special discovery ... within a few months of its publication," she continues, "one library wrote me that copy after copy had been 'worn to shreds' on its shelves" (viii).[11] In Poland, she claims, the book was welcomed as "a symbol of new understanding and friendship between Poles and the valiant American people" (viii). But there's no evidence of such a welcome. It wasn't translated into Polish when it first appeared, although to be fair, most of the children's books that were translated by that point were classics like *Pinocchio* and *Anne of Green Gables* (Czernow and Michulka 92). No Medal title had in fact been translated at the time of *Trumpeter*'s publication. Lofting's *The Voyages of Doctor Dolittle* (1922; 1923 Newbery Medal) was the first Medal title to appear in Polish, in 1936. Kelly's novel was not translated in 1966, despite the reissue and Bechtel's trumpeting on behalf of Kelly. And it's *still* not translated, which seems curious given it's the only Medal title about Poland and the fact that at least twenty Medal winners have been translated into Polish thus far, including the first two Newberys and *Young Fu of the Upper Yangtze*.[12] How to explain the non-translation across almost one hundred years?

*Trumpeter* runs counter to trends in Polish children's literature in the 1920s, in particular the emphasis on modern life and the expectation that children's books be relatively "free from prejudices and national complexes" (Czernow and Michulka 86). It arguably shares more with nineteenth-century Polish children's literature, which strove to preserve Polish language and history.[13] In fact, what probably appealed to the Newbery committee about *Trumpeter* was just what the Polish advocates for children's literature rejected: a romanticized version of Polish history and the particular theatricality of the legend. A little later, the book was decidedly out of step with the post-World War II Polish literature of socialism and social realism, expected to be "thoroughly devoid of mystical motifs" (Czernow and Michulka 88). According to Czernow's working data, only two of the twenty Medal titles translated into Polish were translated during the Soviet occupation: Scott O'Dell's *Island of the Blue Dolphins* (1960; 1961 Newbery Medal), translated in 1976, and Katherine Paterson's *Bridge to Terabithia* (1983; 1984 Newbery Medal), translated in 1984 ("Newbery Medal in Polish Translation"). Two were translated in the 1930s and all the others since 1991. It's not surprising that *Trumpeter* didn't appeal to cultural authorities in the period of Soviet occupation given its pro-Christian and pro-Western message.

It's possible that *Trumpeter* remains untranslated because it's serving another purpose, namely cultural tourism. If the book has no life as children's literature in Poland, it seems to have contributed to Polish mythmaking. The novel is ostensibly the first written "account" of the martyred Trumpeter and the broken note. As a consequence, *Trumpeter* is generally taken as a legitimate source for the story rather than a creative and perhaps embellished interpretation of such. Writing for the Polish American Historical Association (PAHA) website, Maja Trochimczyk contests Kelly's version of the legend of the broken note, however, noting that the earliest written mention of the Heynal appears in civic pay records from 1392. Here Trochimczyk seems to be drawing from Polish musician and historian Jerzy Dobrzycki, who underscores that there's no historical proof of the Trumpeter legend, both generally and as recounted by Kelly. As noted earlier, the Heynal seems to end abruptly, which supports the notion of a "broken note." Nearly all discussions of the legend (with or without reference to Kelly) refer to Dobrzycki's text, a history of Polish music as yet unavailable in English. Another historical source often cited is Ludwik Ancyzc's 1861 version of the legend, which likewise describes the trumpeter sentry and the invading Tartars without mentioning a martyred trumpeter. Trumpet calls were often used in medieval cities to signal the opening and closing of city entrances, and Krakow originally had four such gates. There is some speculation that the broken note (or abrupt ending) was designed to allow a second trumpeter to take up the Heynal and thereby signal the opening or closing of a gate. To make matters more complicated, a Trumpeter of Krakow was recorded as having died from a heart condition while playing the Heynal in 1901, leading some to consider the legend a modern invention (Kępa). In any case, according to Trochimczyk, the Heynal "has sounded daily since 1810, and the performances were institutionalized in 1873 when the professional Fire Brigade was created and the firemen were given the task of playing the Heynal." Professional musicians have since taken over.

In 2018, Polish commentator Marek Kępa published an online article about the Trumpeter legend, confirming that "this highly popular legend—known to pretty much every Pole—is said to have first been put into writing by a foreigner," namely Kelly. Kępa goes on to speculate that the American connection "leads some to believe that the legend is actually a fake," pointing to a skeptical piece by historian Michal Rozek who postulates that the story was likely a prank played on Kelly by a native.[14] "In this version of events," continues Kępa, "the false tale gained momentum when the American turned it into his successful historical novel," which in turn established the tale as a "popular domestic legend." But Kępa also thinks that the Trumpeter legend could be both legitimate and locally sourced, noting another or at least overlapping version of the legend set in distant Samarkand, Uzebekistan. Kępa is finally agnostic on the legend's historical basis and Kelly's role in its promulgation, shifting focus to the work of modern-day Trumpeters and to recent special performances of the Heynal. And indeed, the tradition of the Heynal has worked to consolidate more than undermine Kelly's version of the legend, especially in tourist materials as well as some histories of Polish music and culture.[15]

References to the Trumpeter legend seem to be on the uptick in the wake of accelerated Krakow tourism. As economist and cultural geographer Monika A. Murzyn reports, the Krakow heritage industry has a long history but intensified after the end of Communist rule in Poland in 1989, with the medieval core of the city highlighted in guidebooks and brochures, and with special focus on significant buildings like St. Mary's. The historic Cloth Hall building in the Main Square sells many heritage products, including toy dragons and other merchandise inspired by the legend of the Wawel dragon (also mentioned in *Trumpeter*). Visitors can enjoy folk music and dance as well as traditional gingerbread cookies in the shape of Krakow's most famous monuments, St. Mary's Church included. "Moreover," Murzyn continues, "those who would like to remember that they have listened to the trumpet call from St. Mary's church, a custom existing since the Middle Ages, may buy a 'Trumpet Call Listener's Certificate'" (172). Murzyn too provides a footnote on the Trumpeter story and she also references Kelly's text, reinforcing the impression that *Trumpeter* is a trustworthy historical account. In another scholarly history of Krakow's cultural heritage industry, published in 2016 by the Historical Museum of the City of Krakow, historian and curator Katarzyna Winiarczyk speculates more usefully that the Heynal was long "a symbol of the city and Polishness in general" but became the "tourist showcase of Krakow"—a way to attract tourists—in the interwar period (84–86).[16] Winiarcyzk also credits Kelly's as the first written account. Print and online travel guides to Krakow often mention the legend of the broken note and sometimes also Kelly; they do not raise the question of historical authenticity or mull over the ethics of cultural outsiders writing Polish history. In his *Pocket Kraków* (part of the Lonely Planet series pitched to English-speaking travelers) for instance, Mark Baker acknowledges Kelly as a source for the legend but shrugs away the possible complication, writing "Never mind—Krakovians have embraced this tradition with gusto" (51). Travel writer Joseph Francis takes much the same stance, acknowledging Kelly's novel as a source but concluding "whether the product of later literature or a city's long held homage to a brave trumpeter that once saved its skin, the [Heynal] remains one of the most iconic features of Krakow life." In his self-published *The Krakow Legends*, available online, Polish writer Jaroslaw Skora not only echoes but also expands upon Kelly's version of the legend, reproducing Kelly's racism in describing the Tartars as "slant-eyed invaders" (20).[17] Polish commentators like Murzyn who do acknowledge Kelly's role in promoting (if not fabricating) the legend don't seem any more concerned about the possibility of cultural contamination or theft. Kępa does the most to acknowledge the complexities, citing Rozek, but he is more interested in what the story does for Polish tourism and specifically for the Krakow heritage industry. Whatever its origins or authenticity, the attitude seems to run, the story helps Krakow. Likely *Trumpeter* has succeeded as a source text more than a work of historical fiction in Poland because it was written by a foreigner and never translated; that is, the vagueness of the legend's basis is bound up with the book's obscurity and even inaccessibility.

## A Trumpet for *Trumpeter*?

Kelly contributed significant service to Poland in his physical person and as a writer. *Trumpeter* itself is noteworthy for drawing the attention of American readers to Poland and Polish history, and at a critical historical moment. Despite some pacing problems and loose plot threads,[18] the book has its positive points. The story is engaging and even exciting at times. From a contemporary perspective, however, the book's ideological problems are significant, in particular the demonization of non-Poles as well as the very limited attention given to female characters.[19] If the young reader is expected to identify with Joseph, Kelly himself seems to identify with Pan Andrew, the outsider made insider who helps save the day. And Bechtel seems to have recognized that identification in her 1966 signal-boosting effort.

Making matters worse is the way Kelly talked about his identification with Poland, an identification that sounds more like a claim to ownership. In a note composed for a 1955 compilation of Medal materials, Kelly explains that the "subject matter of the *Trumpeter* had launched me into the destiny of a new nation, I was one with those who were building Poland into a very miracle of a nation" ("Autobiographical Note" 67). His much earlier Medal acceptance speech, titled "The City that Sings," is (to put it bluntly) cringeworthy. It begins: "I don't know if you call it song exactly, but it's a kind of vibration that issues from this city of Krakow that arouses a very tumult in my heart" (70). Polish people, he explains, "start me vibrating with the most exquisite pleasure, and the world suddenly ceases to become a place of masks and manners and takes on color and life and rainbow radiancy" ("City" 70). Kelly traces his identification with Poland to his childhood encounter with "a page in a magazine where a picture of the old Wawel in Krakow was shown. *It was somehow mine* and I knew that in some past day I had walked along that winding road by the river with the old walls of Krakus [Mound] looming over my head" (70; italics for emphasis).[20] When he finally makes it to Krakow, he is ecstatic, especially upon first hearing the Heynal: "I can't describe my emotions. I was so happy I wanted to scream aloud. I wanted to sing and dance and stand on my head. My heart started to beat, gently but without speed, and seemed to be throwing off sparks of fire" ("City" 71). We shouldn't fault Kelly for his passion, but this kind of published comments and his general lack of critical self-awareness compound the ideological problems of the book.

*Trumpeter* is valuable, finally, not as an exceptional children's book worthy of broader circulation but rather as a case study in the ethics of writing historical fiction and especially historical fiction about other nations. Its odd reception history also raises the intriguing question of how other Medal books set outside the United States have or have not circulated in those countries, and what significance any such circulation might have. If this particular text is any indication, the production and subsequent value of Newbery gold has undertones of alchemy—undertaken in earnest, seemingly successful sometimes, but subject to human failing and leading to unpredictable (if not fiery) outcomes.

## Notes

I am very grateful to Anna Czernow for help with translations and for information concerning Newbery Medal title translations to date (see note 7). Thanks also to Justyna Deszcz-Tryhubcza, Marek Kępa, Corinne Matthews, and Doroto Michulka for their research assistance, and to the editors of this volume for their patience and great feedback.

1 If *Trumpeter* seems less familiar than other Newbery titles, that's partly due to its age: it was published at the end of the Medal's first decade. Even so, we shouldn't exaggerate its obscurity, since even the most neglected title benefits from its Medal status. WorldCat reports that 111 editions of *Trumpeter*, in five languages, appeared between 1928 and 2017, and that copies are held by 5,109 WorldCat libraries worldwide. Moreover, the book still appears on lists of recommended reading, especially at Christian academies.

2 A 1971 survey by Polish-American educator and librarian Anne Pellowski lists twenty-six English-language titles about Poland for children published to that point, beginning with *Trumpeter* and including Kelly's informational *The Land and People of Poland* (1964). Nearly all the titles on Pellowski's list were published in the 1960s.

3 "Much of *Young Fu*," Morris writes, "is taken up with perceiving Americans through Chinese eyes, and letting Chinese bewilderment at American customs teach American readers about cultural differences." While Lewis was a missionary as well as a teacher, *Young Fu* doesn't simply affirm American and/or Christian values, Morris avers; it also respects the specificity and sometimes superiority of Chinese culture.

4 Although his characters are mostly made up, Kelly does include as a minor character the Polish theologian and philosopher Saint John Cantius (1390–1473), referred to elsewhere and in Kelly's texts as "the good Jan Kanty."

5 In his endnotes, Kelly appends a translation of the Trumpeter's oath, citing as his source the *Iuramenta* or Book of Oaths, held in the Old Archives of the City of Krakow.

6 In another chapter in this volume, Paul Ringel suggests that Charles Boardman Hawes's *The Dark Frigate* (1923; 1924 Newbery Medal) follows a narrative template for sensational, unrealistic adventure tales standardized in *Youth's Companion* and observable also in series fiction. I would argue

that *Trumpeter* also follows that template, which gives priority to setting and action over character development.

7 Ostensibly focusing on its teenage protagonist Joseph, *Trumpeter* does not offer much of a coming-of-age story in which character transformation embodies a broader historical evolution of the nation, as happens in Speare's novel (see Schwebel).

8 Readers may recall *Harry Potter and the Philosopher's Stone* (1997), which has not one but two dangerous magical objects (the Stone and the Mirror of Erised).

9 Kreutz's niece Elzbietka remarks in *Trumpeter* that "If I were a poet, I should not think of writing in an old language that no one speaks except a few scholars. I would write of Poland and its flowers; I would write of the trumpeter in the tower and the blue sky" (101).

10 This Cold War-era reissue of *Trumpeter* boasts new artwork as well as a new foreword, with Janina Domanska's half-page illustrations (resembling medieval woodcuts) replacing Angela Pruszynska's original illustrations (adapted from fifteenth- and sixteenth-century architectural models).

11 Contrary to Bechtel's claim, Norma Schlager finds that it was one of the five least circulated Newbery titles through 1973. For more on the mixed reception of the book and Newbery books more generally, see Leal and Chamberlain-Solecki; Patterson; Petitt; Smith. No wonder Bechtel's 1966 foreword reads like a defense, insisting that the book "has won a place among the best-loved adventure stories of our time" and that it "must hold its readers engrossed, for it has overcome that strange name on the cover, 'Krakow,' a city by no means well known to tourists and before 1928 never used in a book for boys and girls" (vii).

12 Many of the Newbery winners translated into Polish are titles that are particularly popular with children. Translated titles include: *The Story of Mankind* (1921; 1922 Newbery Medal); *The Voyages of Doctor Dolittle* (1922; 1923 Newbery Medal); *Young Fu of the Upper Yangtze* (1932; 1933 Newbery Medal); *Rabbit Hill* (1944; 1945 Newbery Medal); *Island of the Blue Dolphins* (1960; 1961 Newbery Medal); *A Wrinkle in Time* (1962; 1963 Newbery Medal); *From the Mixed-Up Files of Mrs. Basil E. Frankweiler* (1967; 1968 Newbery Medal); *The Grey King* (1975; 1976 Newbery Medal); *Bridge to Terabithia* (1977; Newbery Medal 1978); *Sarah, Plain and Tall* (1985; 1986 Newbery Medal); *Number the Stars* (1989; Newbery Medal 1990); *The Giver* (1993; 1994 Newbery Medal); *Walk Two Moons* (1994; 1995 Newbery Medal); *Holes* (1998; 1999 Newbery Medal); *The Tale of Desperaux* (2003; 2004 Newbery Medal); *Kira-Kira* (2004; 2005 Newbery Medal); *The Graveyard Book* (2008; 2009 Newbery Medal); *When You Reach Me* (2009; 2010 Newbery Medal); *The One and Only Ivan* (2012; Newbery Medal 2013); and *The Girl Who Drank the Moon* (2016; 2017 Newbery Medal). Czernow clarifies that twenty is a working number as it's possible others were also translated. "We are still finding books we had no idea were translated before World War II," she writes, due to a "period of harsh censorship (1949–1956)" (Czernow, "Newbery").

13 That project of preservation sometimes involved the translation of European materials into a distinctly Polish idiom. When Poland regained independence in 1917, the focus in the literature shifted toward the development of child readers as citizens, albeit with some debate about how best to achieve such. Opinion varied on how Polish-centric the cultivation of child readers should be, with some arguing for a nationalistic approach bordering on isolationism (Czernow and Michulka 86). Unfortunately, both Poland's independence and Polish children's literature were halted by World War II. As Matthews notes,

scholars offer sometimes competing claims about the situation of Polish children's literature in the Communist period, with Marek Oziewicz proposing an undercurrent of subversive writing and Monika Woźniak emphasizing the effects of censorship (Matthews 3). In the last two decades or so, Polish publishing houses have published more original work by Polish authors for children, including speculative fiction (Matthews 10).

14 With regard to the Rozek source, Kępa clarifies in an email to the author that he had cited an interview in a Krakow University student magazine that is no longer available, but points out that the same account is offered in Rozek's 1991 *Mistycyny Kraków*, available in Polish only.

15 Don L. Smithers references it in *The Music and History of the Baroque Trumpet before 1721*, for instance. Both oral and written accounts of the legend persist and are mutually reinforcing.

16 Czernow observes that "tourist showcase" is the closest English translation for "turystyczna wizytówka," but underscores that the phrase carries no negative meaning for Winiarczyk or more generally ("Re: Eric Kelly's *The Trumpeter of Krakow*").

17 An English-language brochure picked up by Matthews on site, Zbigniew Iwanski's *The Legends of Cracow*, includes the story of the Trumpeter as one of ten legends of the city but offers no sources for that story.

18 Kelly tends to interrupt action scenes with tedious asides. When Krakow is ablaze, for example, Kelly halts the story to explain the municipal division of medieval Krakow into quarters with designated quartermasters.

19 Elzbietka plays only a minor role, and Joseph's mother doesn't even get a name; she is just Joseph's mother or Pan Andrew's wife.

20 Kelly links this memory to the dreamy fantasies of Kenneth Grahame and Lewis Carroll. "Alice went through a looking glass into a dream world," he writes, "but she had often wondered about the glass before she found her opportunity to enter it. And as soon as she entered that Looking Glass Land, something in her began to sing, and sings as well in every child or grownup that reads the book" ("City" 70).

## Works Cited

Baker, Mark. *Pocket Kraków*. 2nd ed. N.p.: Lonely Planet Publications, 2016. Print.

Bechtel, Louise Seaman. "A Trumpet for the Trumpeter." *The Trumpeter of Krakow*. Ed. Eric P. Kelly. New York: Simon & Schuster, 1966. vii–x. Print.

Czernow, Anna Maria, and Dorota Michulka. "Historical Twists and Turns in the Polish Canon of Children's Literature." *Canon Constitution and Canon Change in Children's Literature*. Ed. Bettina Kümmerling-Meibauer and Anja Müller. New York: Routledge, 2017. 85–102. Print.

Czernow, Anna. "Newbery Medal in Polish Translation." Message to Kenneth Kidd. Sept. 2019. E-mail.

Czernow, Anna. "Re: Eric Kelly's *The Trumpeter of Krakow*." Message to Kenneth Kidd. Sept. 2019. E-mail.

Deszcz-Tryhubcza, Justyna. "ODP: question about Eric Kelly's *The Trumpeter of Krakow*." Message to Kenneth Kidd. 13 Feb. 2019. E-mail.

Dobrzycki, Jerzy. *Hejnał Krakowski*. Krakow: PWN, 1983. Print.

Francis, Joseph. "The Amazing Story Behind Krakow's Bugle Call." *Culture Trip*. Web. 4 Aug. 2020.

Gillespie, Cindy S., Janet L. Powell, Nancy E. Clements, and Rebecca A. Swearingen, "A Look at the Newbery Medal Books from a Multicultural Perspective." *The Reading Teacher* 48.1 (1994): 40–50. Print.

Iwanski, Zbigniew. *The Legends of Cracow*. Illus. Anna Kaszuba-Debska. Trans. Antonio Lloyd-Jones. Krakow: Wydawnictwo WAM, 2014. Print.

Jordan, Alice M. "Children's Books as Good Will Messengers." *The Elementary English Review* 6.4 (1929): 104–106. Print.

Kelly, Eric P. "Autobiographical Note." *Newbery Medal Books: 1922–1955, with their Authors' Acceptance Papers & Related Material chiefly from the* Horn Book Magazine. Ed. Bertha Mahony Miller and Elinor Whitney Field. Boston: The Horn Book, 1955. 67–69. Print.

Kelly, Eric P. "The City That Sings." *Newbery Medal Books: 1922–1955, with their Authors' Acceptance Papers & Related Material chiefly from the* Horn Book Magazine. Ed. Bertha Mahony Miller and Elinor Whitney Field. Boston: The Horn Book, 1955. 70–73. Print.

Kelly, Eric P. *The Trumpeter of Krakow*. Illus. Angela Pruszynska. New York: Macmillan, 1928.

Kępa, Marek. "Re: the Hejnal Call of Kraków." Message to Kenneth Kidd. 24 Apr. 2019. E-mail.

Kępa, Marek. "The Hejnal Trumpet Call of Kraków: Fact vs. Fiction." *Culture.pl*. Web. 30 Apr. 2018.

Leal, Dorothy J., and Julie Chamberlain-Solecki. "A Newbery Medal-Winning Combination: High Student Interest Plus Appropriate Readability Levels." *The Reading Teacher* 51.8 (1998): 712–715. Print.

Mahony, Bertha E. "Editorial, First Issue, 1924." *The Horn Book Magazine*. Web. 20 July 2018.

Matthews, Corinne. *Polish Children's Literature*. Gainesville, FL: U of Florida, 2018. Seminar essay.

Michulka, Dorota. "ODP: question about Eric Kelly's *The Trumpeter of Krakow*." Message to Kenneth Kidd. 4 Mar. 2019. E-mail.

Murzyn, Monika. "New Interpretations and Commercialisation of Heritage in Krakow After 1989." *Practical Aspects of Cultural Heritage—Presentation, Revaluation, Development*. Ed. Sebastian Schröder-Esch. Weimar, Germany: Bauhaus-Universität Weimar, 2006. 167–188. Print.

Oziewicz, Marek. "Children's Literature in Eastern Europe: Trends, Themes and Authors Since the Sixties." *Bologna: Fifty Years of Children's Literature from Around the World*. Ed. Giorgia Gilli. Bologna, Italy: Bononia UP, 2013. 263–273. Print.

Patterson, Emma L. "The Junior Novels and How They Grew." *The English Journal* 45.7 (1956): 381–387, 405. Print.

Pellowski, Anne. "Books on Poland for Children." *Polish American Studies* 28.2 (1971): 66–70. Print.

Peterson, Linda Kauffman, and Marilyn Leathers Solt. *Newbery and Caldecott Medal and Honor Books: An Annotated Bibliography*. Boston: G. K. Hall, 1982. Print.

Petitt, Dorothy. "A Search for Self-Definition: The Picture of Life in the Novel for the Adolescent." *The English Journal* 49.9 (1960): 616–620, 625–626. Print.

Ratcheva-Stratevia, Lilia. "Earth Hanging in Infinity: Janusz Korczak's *King Matt the First*." *Beyond Babar: The European Tradition in Children's Literature*. Ed. Sandra L. Beckett and Maria Nikolajeva. Lanham, MD: The Scarecrow Press, 2006. 1–20. Print.

Schlager, Norma. "Predicting Children's Choices in Literature: A Developmental Approach." *Children's Literature in Education* 9.3 (1978): 136–142. Print.

Schwebel, Sara L. "Historical Fiction and the Classroom: History and Myth in Elizabeth George Speare's *The Witch of Blackbird Pond*." *Children's Literature in Education* 34.3 (2003): 195–218. Print.

Skora, Jaroslaw. *The Krakow Legends*. N.p.: n.p., 2011. Kindle file.

Smith, Irene. *A History of the Newbery and Caldecott Models*. New York: Viking Press, 1957. Print.

Smithers, Don L. *The Music and History of the Baroque Trumpet before 1721*. London: J. M. Dent, 1973. 130–131. Print.

Trochimczyk, Maja. "On Hejnal Mariacki and the Soundscape of Krakow." *Polish American Historical Association (PAHA) News*. Web. 4 Aug. 2020.

Viguers, Ruth Hill. "Part Four: The Golden Age, 1920–1950." *A Critical History of Children's Literature: A Survey of Children's Books in English from Earliest Times to the Present*. Ed. Cornelia Meigs, Elizabeth Nesbitt, Anne Eaton, and Ruth Hill Viguers. Illus. Vera Bock. New York: Macmillan, 1953. 425–603. Print.

Winiarczyk, Katarzyna. "Czymże więc jest czas (miejski)? Opis badań fenomenu czasu miejskiego w Muzeum Historycznym Miasta Krakowa." *Niematerialne Dziedzictwo Miasta: Muzealizacja, Ochrona, Edukacja*. Ed. Magdalena Kwiecinska. Krakow: Muzeum Historyczne Miasta Krakowa, 2016. 76–89. Print.

Woźniak, Monika. "Where (and When) Do You Live, Cinderella?: Cultural Shifts in Polish Translations and Adaptations of Charles Perrault's Fairy Tales." *Textual Transformations in Children's Literature: Adaptations, Translations, Reconsiderations*. Ed. Benjamin Lefebvre. New York: Routledge, 2013. 87–100. Print.

# 4 Invincible Nina

## Louisa May Alcott and the Depression-Era Feminism of *Invincible Louisa* (1934)

*Anne K. Phillips and Gregory Eiselein*

Cornelia Meigs's biography of Louisa May Alcott, *Invincible Louisa* (1933; 1934 Newbery Medal), written at the centenary of Alcott's birth, remains under-appreciated but significant in US literary history. Initially published by Little, Brown and Company of Boston in May of 1933, the book was reprinted numerous times throughout the twentieth century and eventually re-issued as a Scholastic paperback. The first biography to win the Newbery Medal, *Invincible Louisa* occupies an important position within the history of US children's literature. Building on Ednah Dow Cheney's *Louisa May Alcott: Her Life, Letters, and Journals* (1889), a collection of biographical documents loaned by Alcott's sister Anna, some of which subsequently were lost or destroyed, and moving beyond Belle Moses's 1909 repackaging of Cheney's work, Meigs's biography examined a range of published, archival, and oral sources. It offered for the first time genuine interpretive insight into the complicated influence of Bronson and Abigail Alcott on their daughter's writings and the complex dynamics of the Alcott family, as well as insightful analysis of Alcott's fiction. In these and other significant ways, it anticipated the work of Alcott scholars who followed in her footsteps.

Drawing on a decades-long immersion in Alcott's work and on her own experience as a successful young adult author, Meigs captured her subject's determined optimism and reflected the values of her own era's foremost (and predominantly female) editors and librarians. Indeed, *Invincible Louisa* tells us as much about the 1930s as it does Alcott's era. The poverty that shaped the Alcotts' existence and the national crises that affected Alcott's work mirror the international economic calamities and precariousness of Meigs's own era. Effectively establishing these connections, Meigs makes the Alcotts' story into her readers' stories. While not often read now by children for pleasure, Meigs's book served as a revealing expression of feminist persistence and optimism in the era between first-wave and second-wave feminism, a period defined by world war and global economic crisis.

The key factors that played a role in the selection of *Invincible Louisa* as the 1934 Newbery Medalist include developing trends in the Newbery

DOI: 10.4324/9780367337223-4-5

selection process, Meigs's position within the burgeoning field of children's literature, and the enduring popularity of Meigs's subject. In the Newbery's first eight years, librarians Mara Houdyshell and Janice Kirkland note, "all of the awards went to books that were male-linked through authors, characters, or both" (254). Although in the ensuing ten years awards went to female authors, the increasingly female profession of children's librarianship clamored not only for women authors but also for female protagonists to win the field's most distinguished award. In an unsolicited letter to a Newbery committee member in November 1933, librarian Edna Miriam Hoopes wrote to support Meigs's protagonist: "May I cast a vote for *Invincible Louisa* by Cornelia Meigs for the Newberry [sic] Medal 1933? ... [T]he last two medals were given for books about boys and now comes a lively girl to claim our attention." Adult professionals invested in the Newbery selection process were eager for female representation and parity among authors and protagonists.[1]

Having recognized a series of works with international subjects, Newbery committees were also urged to celebrate distinctly American topics. As Sophie L. Goldsmith wrote in an early history of the Newbery Medal published in *The Bookman*, "it seems not too much to hope that future selections may alight on books which give children conceptions of their own country as unmistakably native in flavor as does much adult fiction" (313–314). Preference for US subjects aligned with publishers' desires to expand their catalogs of US authors and works. Delineating the trajectory of Macmillan's Louise Seaman, the first editor to head an American juvenile book department, Gary Schmidt notes that she "set out to develop an American children's literature not to supplant but to go along with her European 'classics.' ... In her fifteen-year tenure at Macmillan she published over five hundred children's books, increasing the size of the children's catalog from thirty to eighty pages. But it was her American authors who shone: she would publish three of the first Newbery Honor Books named at the inception of the award" (xii). Among those authors was Cornelia Meigs, who began publishing with Macmillan in 1915.[2]

From the start of her career, Meigs showcased US youth, settings, history, and grit. Several of her works focused on America's shipping industry, including *The Trade Wind* (1927) and *Clearing Weather* (1928); she celebrated US technological development in works such as *The Wonderful Locomotive* (1928). While often associated with "olden days" New England tales (Anderson 128), not all of her publications were set in New England. *Swift Rivers*, a Newbery runner-up for 1933, traces a youth's quest to float Minnesota timber to St. Louis. *The Windy Hill* (1921), Meigs's first Newbery runner-up, is particularly attentive to what it means to be American. The novel traces a dispute between relatives over the family's land, as three adolescent cousins work together to understand and heal this schism. Throughout the novel, one of their fathers shares a series of stories (in an embedded tale technique often used by Meigs) about the land and its inhabitants, including a Native tribe's first contact with European colonists, early-nineteenth-century Americans' experiences with European blockades during the War of 1812, and mid-nineteenth-century Easterners' participation in the California Gold Rush. In each, brothers turn against brothers or elders and later regret it. Summarizing *The Windy Hill* in their study of Newbery Medalists and Honor Books, children's literature scholars Linda Peterson and Marilyn Solt dismiss the novel as "contrived" and "inferior to her many volumes of historical fiction" (15). However, the novel is consistent with Meigs's overarching attention to US history, and the embedded stories, which Peterson and Solt find digressive, are central to the meaning of the work. In them, Meigs celebrates not only "the courage of those white men who crossed the stormy Atlantic in their little vessels to explore an unknown continent" (45) but also, in the Native American Nashola, "that born leadership that makes real men see through the long-established doubts and terrors of their race ... who can go forward through shadowy perils to the clear light of knowledge and success" (46). Native and White North Americans, through generations, may embody this heroism and vision, but they also often harbor a bellicosity that results in conflict. Meigs's representations of Native peoples in *The Windy Hill* and other works, while characteristic of the period in which she published, are problematic for twenty-first-century readers. As Schmidt acknowledges, Meigs's *The Willow Whistle* (1931), while containing a US setting and emphasizing inclusiveness, highlights Native Americans' "wild" nature and infantilizes them (72).

Beyond Meigs's investment in American subjects, what else might have prompted the Newbery committee to select resoundingly *Invincible Louisa* for the Newbery Medal in 1934, bestowing upon it eleven first-place and four second-place among fifteen total votes? Letters submitted by members of that committee acknowledge that Meigs, who had been in contention for the award several times, particularly deserved to win. Their comments allude to her publication history, her accolades, including three Newbery runner-up designations as well as the Beacon Hill Book Shelf prize awarded by Little, Brown and Company in 1927 for *The Trade Wind*, and the evident respect accorded by earlier Newbery selection committees. Alluding to the reception of *Swift Rivers* in the previous year's deliberations, 1933 Newbery committee chairman Della McGregor wrote:

> Last year, for example, the East felt very strongly in regard to Cornelia Meigs and there was a general feeling and much gossip from the beginning there that the award was practically assured her book. The Middle West and Central States felt that it did not give an authentic enough picture of the early days in the Wisconsin

> lumbering camps to warrant Newbery distinction even though it was the best piece of writing Miss Meigs had done since *Master Simon's Garden.*

To some extent, then, previous deliberations continued to influence the 1934 negotiations. Moreover, committee members wrote ballot comments knowing that Meigs was the frontrunner. Librarian Rosemary Earnshaw Livsey commented, "I wish I could honestly cast my vote for the Invincible Louisa, as it seems to be the choice of so many."

Those members who did not issue first-place votes for *Invincible Louisa* offered rationales for their selections. Livsey felt that it seemed more appropriate for older readers, echoing concerns about the committee's privileging of works for middle and high school audiences.[3] Other committee members suggested that the popularity of Meigs's biography stemmed from the success of RKO's 1933 feature film of *Little Women* starring Katharine Hepburn. Others, such as librarian Zella Spence, asserted that the subject itself was highly engaging: "it is not quite such a difficult thing to write an interesting biography of Louisa Alcott as it is to write an original story of the Civil War such as Elsie Singmaster has written. Louisa Alcott was an intensely interesting person herself, and her life furnishes material for an absorbing book." For these voters, Alcott's enduring popularity diminished Meigs's own literary achievement.

Nonetheless, more than two-thirds of the 1934 Newbery committee preferred Meigs's work. Librarian Vera Winifred Schott alluded to the criteria for the award, noting that "[t]he book has an appeal to wide age group [sic], it has high literary merit; and its author has long been a contributor to the field of children's literature." Others addressed the originality of its genre: "I should like … 'Invincible Louisa' considered not only because of the book and the distinguished work Miss Meigs has done previously also, but that another type—biography—should be considered as well. Hers is certainly an outstanding contribution," wrote Louisa Singley. Writing for the *Bulletin of the American Library Association* in 1934, librarian, children's literature translator, and Newbery committee chair Siri Andrews addressed genre as a central reason for its selection: "this award recognizes the value of biography which presents to boys and girls a glowing portrait of real and admirable people … *Invincible Louisa* gives us a fresh view of one of the most widely known and read of all American writers for children" (408). Reporting the "decidedly" pro-Meigs vote in a May 1934 letter to Frederic G. Melcher, co-editor of *Publishers Weekly,* originator of Children's Book Week, and founder of the Newbery Medal, Andrews added, "I am glad Miss Meigs is to have the recognition which children's librarians have long felt was due her." In this context, her selection as the medalist might serve as a kind of lifetime achievement award, an honor "due her" for a consistently excellent body of work.

Beyond her work's literary merit, it is important to acknowledge that Meigs was well connected within children's literature and enjoyed proximity to the field's most prominent leaders. These figures, whom Jacclyn Eddy calls "the bookwomen," were at the center of American children's literature, including Seaman at Macmillan, where Meigs published several works, but also New York Public Library figurehead Anne Carroll Moore. Of the same generation as other bookwomen like Bertha Mahoney and May Massee, Meigs fostered relationships with most of these significant figures. Indeed, although Meigs is not among the half dozen professionals profiled at length by Eddy in *Bookwomen: Creating an Empire in Children's Book Publishing, 1919–1939*, she was a bookwoman in her own right, representing an authorial contribution that rounded out the others' accomplishments. Eddy observes, "Most of the six [leading] bookwomen were native New Englanders, born between 1870 and 1894 and raised in relatively affluent circumstances. They shared similar recollections of childhood literacy and began their professional lives in other fields, primarily teaching" (11). Born in Illinois in 1884 and raised in Iowa, Cornelia Meigs, known as Nina to friends and family, came from New England stock and traced her American lineage to her great-grandfather, Commodore John Rogers, and she spent many summers on her grandfather's Vermont farm (Roberts 45). After graduating from Bryn Mawr in 1907, Meigs worked as a schoolteacher while becoming an author. She corresponded with Moore as early as 1919 about the danger of commercializing children's literature (Eddy 96) and developed friendships with other leading figures. When Seaman married Edwin Bechtel in 1929, Meigs teased that "everyone was involved in 'the great question' of whether she would give up her career" (qtd. in Eddy 137). Meigs's affinities for the bookwomen may have stemmed from friendship, but their support also fostered her professional development. As Leonard Marcus has established, these leaders in the field acclaimed Meigs early and often: "Meigs wrote 'with distinction from an unusual background,' noted Anne Carroll Moore, conferring her blessing on a rising star with one Newbery Honor already in her quiver" (96–97). This circle of influential women—"noted for its homogeneity, a 'closed world' that virtually always agreed about what constituted 'good' reading and, in fact, constituted a 'metaphorical matriarchy'" (Eddy 11)—helped advance Meigs's career trajectory. Fittingly, Meigs pays tribute to "Miss Moore," among other bookwomen and librarians, throughout the first half of her Newbery acceptance speech ("Acceptance" 123).

That Meigs won the Newbery not for one of her historical fiction novels but for her biography of Alcott suggests that subject, genre, and authorial cachet had aligned in a persuasive way. Spence emphasized in her ballot that Meigs, and the other top nominees, "have, to my way of thinking, given us their best, so far, in these three books." The quality that put *Invincible Louisa* over the top may have been the biographer's deep affinity for her subject and that subject's enduring fame. More than forty years after her death, Alcott remained popular, as Beverly Lyon Clark demonstrates in *The Afterlife of "Little Women."* In 1927, *Little Women* "was still the book requested most by teenage girls in the New York Public Library" (Clark 50); moreover, "in 1922 *Little Women* led the list of twenty-five books ... recommended by a joint meeting of the America Library Association and the National Education Association for use in the first through eighth grades. This list, and *Little Women*'s position on it, was widely reported across the country in both newspapers and professional journals. At least one journalist suggested that the report had renewed interest in Alcott" (51). Many bookwomen grew up reading and retained deep connections to Alcott's books. As Eddy reports, "we are left with images of the sentimental Moore, reverently placing lilacs beneath the picture of Louisa May Alcott in an exhibit for the children's room" (42). Other librarians shared Moore's enthusiasm for Alcott and her works, and it was evident to them that Alcott deserved greater acclaim. In Hoopes's letter to the Newbery committee, she affirmed the appropriateness of honoring Alcott through *Invincible Louisa*: "The fact that L.M.A. can never achieve the medal, even posthumously and that the reasons for giving the medal are so closely allied with the motives of Miss Alcott that to honor her through the pen of Miss Meigs would seem a nice thing to do." Meigs herself embraced this perspective in her acceptance speech, graciously noting,

> what you have done today is, in effect, to bestow the Newbery Award upon Louisa Alcott. She has deserved it for a very long time. I think my publishers cannot object to this division of the honors, for we are both, as it were, daughters of the same house. If I could stretch my voice across the years, I would say, "Louisa, this medal is yours," and I do assure that Louisa and I both thank you from the bottom of our hearts. ("Acceptance" 124)

In awarding the Newbery Medal to *Invincible Louisa*, committee personnel, bookwomen, librarians, editors, and others could glory in Alcott's triumph.

In the early 1930s, other cultural currents that enhanced the reception of Meigs's biography were also in motion. 1932 was the centennial of Alcott's birth, an occasion that engendered new tributes, editions, and analyses.[4] Meigs herself later reflected: "It was a most fortunate chance that when in 1932 Louisa Alcott's publishers made ready to bring out a new life of her, there were a few of her friends and relatives left who could still remember her" ("Introduction to the Alcott Centennial Edition" 536), among them the widow of Alcott's nephew Fred Pratt. Having been hired in 1932 as an instructor of English at Bryn Mawr,

Meigs must also have found the biography a happy concordance of personal nostalgia for a favorite author and a research opportunity appropriate to her academic position. Raised with Alcott's writings and Cheney's biographical collection, Meigs featured in her fiction relationships and situations that evoked material reminiscent of the Alcott family's dynamics. In *The Pool of Stars* (1919), for instance, Miranda Reynolds is the daughter of an impractical but prescient inventor, a gifted thinker who has devoted years to an invention that has not yet come to fruition. Encountering him for the first time, the protagonist, Betsy, recalls that she "had heard her own father speak of him as quite a famous person, a scientist of long standing reputation" (9). Later, a family member accuses Miranda's father of failing to support her: "Have you stopped, ever, to think of how she works and saves and pinches, how she toils in that garden and fattens miserable fowls for the market so that you can go on with this game of yours?" (141). Meigs's depiction of Miranda's steadfast support for her father, despite his inability to contribute or even attend to the family's financial situation, anticipates the representation in *Invincible Louisa* of Bronson Alcott's evolving philosophical theories and his ensuing inability/refusal to provide for his family. As Mr. Reynolds is respected for his brilliance, so Bronson is praised by figures such as Ralph Waldo Emerson. At the same time, Meigs sympathetically represents the way that Bronson's wife Abigail and his daughters support him, despite his failings. In earlier fictional efforts, then, Meigs draws from her own favorite childhood reading and re-processes that reading with the expertise born from her authorial experience.

*Invincible Louisa* highlighted Meigs's precise if sometimes nostalgic historical imagination and her considerable skill as an historian. As Elizabeth Janeway later noted in *The New York Times Book Review*, Meigs's volume provides an "excellent" picture of "that vanished New England culture" (46) of the mid-nineteenth century. With careful attention to historical documents and to the larger historical context that shaped Alcott's life and career, Meigs illustrates vividly how the world of the antebellum North shaped Alcott's childhood, identity, and young adulthood. Although Meigs was carefully attuned to the world of the nineteenth century, the power of her biography stems from the purposeful way that she arranges events and images from the past to sustain and encourage both child and adult readers. Written during the nadir of the Great Depression and released in May 1933, the year the unemployment rate in the US peaked at 25 percent and gross national product had dropped 50 percent from its 1929 level (Kennedy 163), *Invincible Louisa* is a book about poverty and adversity, about acknowledging staggering challenges and learning to confront them.

Chapter III, "Running in the Wind," particularly captures the Depression-era cultural work of *Invincible Louisa*. Of the ten chapters that make up *Invincible Louisa*, it covers the shortest period of time, just seven months from June 1843, when the Alcotts arrive at Fruitlands, until January 1844, when they depart following the utopian community's dissolution. In the chapter's opening paragraphs, Meigs evokes hope and energy. The old house they are moving into is "now, suddenly, full of life and bustle" (*Invincible Louisa* 51). From Louisa's point of view, the move is the start of a "great adventure," and this new home is "a glorious playground" (51). The "unbroken fields, sloping to the river" (51) offer Louisa unbounded freedom.

When the Fruitlands experiment slides into catastrophe, Meigs refrains from blaming Bronson Alcott and instead historically contextualizes. She begins not by absolving Bronson but reflecting on his pragmatic daring to test his ideas: "Bronson and his friends, wise in some ways, mistaken in others, had the courage to find out, by the only possible means, where they were right and where they were wrong. There is only one method of testing a system of living; that is by living it" (54). Instead of accounting where the Fruitlanders had gone wrong or right, Meigs detours into a brief historical account of the Transatlantic North in the early 1840s: "The year 1843 was at the end of a period very like that which has become all too familiar to us ninety years later. Long wars, involving both Europe and America, had brought their slowly arriving results of poverty, unemployment, and bewildered suffering. Something was very wrong with the world" (54). Meigs explicitly parallels this period with her readers' own Depression-era moment, and the similarities are striking. The financial crisis of late 1839 did not lead to a quick recovery, as had happened in the financial panic of 1837. Instead, October 1839 marked the beginning of a prolonged and severe economic downturn, often described as a "depression," marked by numerous bank failures, extensive loan defaults, and a period of crushing deflation (Gallman 12; Howe 505). Moreover, these economic struggles fueled numerous attempts at social, economic, and political reform of the period, just as they had during Franklin Roosevelt's New Deal.

For Meigs then, this world of poverty and suffering is precisely the context for understanding Louisa's early life and the efforts of Bronson and others to find a better, more equitable, less cruel way to live on the planet: "Here and there, a few were trying to organize totally new schemes of living" (54). Acknowledging the crushing poverty that shaped the Alcotts' existence, she resists seeing their poverty as simply the result of Bronson's egotism, idealism, or foolishness, instead situating their struggles within the national and international crises that shaped Alcott's life and work.

It is also this context that Meigs uses to help her readers make sense of the suffering and economic adversity they and their families and communities were facing in 1933. As the title *Invincible Louisa* suggests, the recurring theme of the biography is Louisa's unconquerable determination to survive and thrive. Recounting Fruitlands' demise and the housing insecurity and near destitution it would bring to the Alcott family, Meigs portrays Louisa's perspective on the experience as both a victory and the beginning of a new set of "real adventures" (72). Toward the end of the communal experiment, one of the Fruitlands founders, the English Transcendentalist Charles Lane, had advocated joining the nearby Shaker Community and adopting its celibate, communal way of life, which rejected the nuclear family. He urged Bronson to join him, though Abigail and the girls were strongly opposed to this suggestion. In the biography, when Lane departs for the Shakers and Bronson and Abigail decline to join him, instead leaving Fruitlands together, it is a victory for Louisa, Abigail, and even Bronson.

Although Louisa's father is often portrayed as an abject failure during the dissolution of Fruitlands, and as depressed and passive during and after the experience, Meigs suggests that fundamentally Bronson was standing up for his most original and powerful and deepest convictions: "He maintained that children had minds and hearts and spirits of their own, and should have a voice in what was decided concerning them. It was a portentous moment in the history of them all, when he finally acted upon that belief" (69). Meigs represents Bronson, at the nadir of his career, with his family in economic and existential crisis, as staying true to himself, his values and beliefs, and his family and children, although subsequent paragraphs suggest that the experience has "shattered him" (70). Abigail, however, remains for Meigs an "unbroken spirit" (70), while Louisa focuses on the positive: "They were together at least, and, as long as she lived, she was going to battle against anything that might try to separate them. People who loved one another must stand together" (72). Meigs's protagonist is ready to do battle and succeed, despite adversity: "Louisa Alcott, as she trudged away over the snow, had set her face determinedly toward the real adventures of life" (72).

It is not only at Fruitlands, however, where Meigs provides readers with opportunity to identify not only with Louisa's hardships, which are typically economic or economically related, but also with her indomitable efforts to meet and overcome those challenges and, along the way, to relish "the adventure" (a word Meigs uses repeatedly to describe Louisa's experience of the events in her life). In Chapter IV, Meigs emphasizes the family's housing insecurity—"in the first twenty-eight years of Louisa's life, this household was to achieve the record of twenty-nine moves" (73). In Chapter V, Meigs presents the years from 1857 to 1862, when the US experienced two major recessions (the devastating Panic of 1857 and the milder secession recession of 1860–1861 [see McPherson 189–191, 253]), as the darkest, unhappiest period of Alcott's life. Although beginning to earn "small sums, here and there" (105) from her published work, she faces professional "discouragement" (106) and finds herself often drawn into teaching, work she does not enjoy.

Political antagonism in the US is rising to new heights over slavery, and the antislavery Alcotts feel intensely those tensions: "The feeling against slavery, long held in check, was now rolling up into a tremendous wave" (111). Louisa's sister Elizabeth dies in 1858, and her mentor and inspiration, Theodore Parker, follows in 1860 (Meigs erroneously records it as "the next year" [119]). Her oldest sister, Anna, becomes engaged to John Bridge Pratt in 1858 and marries him in 1860, which, as readers of *Little Women* know, causes Louisa much sadness: "why, oh, why should families have to separate? She lamented continually and bitterly, although not in Anna's hearing" (Meigs 122). Moreover, as Meigs acknowledges, the often-idealized Orchard House had become not a comfort for the ailing Elizabeth, as intended, but instead an unwanted economic encumbrance: "Louisa had a burden of debt to carry now, a sordid addition to her weight of grief" (120). This is a dark period in Louisa's life, which Meigs highlights and links closely to Louisa's and her family's difficult economic situation: "At no time in her life had she ever fallen so low in spirits as now. She was discontented with her old, drudging ways of making a living; she was lonely, sad, and unbelievably disheartened.... She did not want to go on living in a world where everything was so hard. She trudged here and there looking for employment and did not find it" (125). Like many in Meigs's intended audience, Louisa endures yet another economic downturn, worrying about the looming threat of war, while dealing with the separations from loved ones that life brings.

Throughout these hardships, however, invincible Nina Meigs continues to highlight Louisa's resilience, determination, and survival. Delineating Louisa's horrific experience as a domestic servant, Meigs conveys that Louisa found triumph in helping to support her family: "Louisa was exultant over one thing. Her own family needed money sorely and she had earned it for them!" (97). When Louisa is discouraged by her inability to find non-degrading work, Meigs emphasizes her indomitable will: "'There is work for me to do and I will find it,' she told herself fiercely, and in that very challenge overthrew something of her discouragement" (126). Likewise, Meigs refuses to see Louisa's pain or any of the family's hardships as simply private agony but rather as part of a larger pattern of social suffering related to economic volatility and war. As the Civil War approaches and as Louisa remains grieving and without steady income, Meigs continues to portray Louisa as a fighter: "She was restless and unstrung; for not only had unsettling changes come about in her own family but the shadow of an enormous change was reaching over the whole country. No one could doubt now that there was going to be a war. And, as Louisa often said darkly to herself, 'I'm a fighting May'" (130).

The reference to her mother's family denotes where not only Louisa but also Meigs locates the source for this intrepid behavior. Meigs was writing in a time between two great feminist reform eras, the women's suffrage movement that culminated in the US in the right to vote in 1920 and second-wave feminism that began in the 1960s. In *Invincible Louisa*, she pioneers the kind of feminist scholarship that would flourish later in the century, in part by drawing attention to the powerful women of earlier eras, women in the domestic sphere, those in the public and professional sphere, and those who managed to make an impact in the home and in work outside the home. We see this in her portrayal of Alcott's "tremendously important" Aunt Hancock (31), a great-grand aunt on her mother's side, as "a spirited wife" who "lived to a great age and was the grand figure of the whole family relationship" (32). An embodiment of the "peppery" Mays (34), Aunt Hancock inspires Alcott's "inflammable" behavior throughout her life. Perhaps even more importantly, Meigs represents Abigail Alcott as Louisa's chief model of invincibility. For instance, when Bronson comes home with only one dollar from his Western speaking tour, the focus is on Abigail's abiding love, as other biographers have conveyed, but Nina makes her steadfast resolve even more explicit and admirable by explicitly stating that Louisa "knew very clearly how her mother had hoped, what were the things she might have said; ... knew what courage was behind those words of approval and affection" (102). Other strong women also play key roles throughout Meigs's narrative, as in the depiction of Elizabeth Peabody's collaborations with Bronson in his school (22, 29) or in their cousin Elizabeth Wells's recurring interventions to assist Louisa and her sisters in making their way through the world (103, 108, 110, 122, 136, 209). When Louisa decides to join the Union effort in the Civil War as a nurse, Meigs emphasizes again how Louisa ascribes her decisiveness and courage in the face of danger and suffering specifically to her mother's family: "'The blood of the Mays is up,' she announced" (137).

From the depression of the 1840s to the wartime of the 1860s, Meigs effectively casts the Alcotts' story as her readers' stories, especially during the Civil War period. As she notes, "Louisa did what most other women do in wartime, she agonized, worked, worried, exulted, and worked again" (133). Delineating Louisa's nursing experiences, Meigs effectively shifts focus from Louisa's own suffering to her witnessing of others' suffering and pain. The chapter devoted to this experience is named after a soldier, "Kit" (Chapter VI, 138–164), who saves a twelve-year-old drummer boy named Billy. The event recounted is a brief scene from *Hospital Sketches* (1863), where Alcott comforts a sobbing boy who has awakened from a dream about the man who saved him: "I dreamed Kit was here, and when I waked up he wasn't" (Alcott, *Hospital* [1869] 47).[5] Meigs imaginatively develops this episode into the four-page heart of her chapter on Alcott's Civil War experiences. It is an interesting authorial choice to focus on a figure three times removed. Kit is a figure in a story told by Billy to Alcott and now recounted and expanded in Meigs's biography. We are thus receiving Meigs's perception of what Alcott felt about Billy's agony over Kit's death. Given Nina's larger cultural project to provide her young readers with a way to reflect empathetically on adversity amidst their own challenges and discover how to learn resilience in the face of those struggles, this decision is an attempt to witness the horrors of war not objectively or from a distance but from the perspective of a child, Billy. Meigs makes the most of Alcott's already poignant account, in which Billy blames himself for Kit's death: "Oh! if I'd only been as thin when Kit carried me as I am now, maybe he wouldn't have died; but I was heavy, he was hurt worser than we knew, and so it killed him; and I didn't see him, to say good bye" (47–48). Alcott's own spare account ends with her failure to console the distraught boy. Meigs, like Alcott, asks her readers to confront not only the fact of death and dying in the Civil War but also to imagine how it felt for a child to lose someone. Meigs is asking us to witness not just the suffering and deaths of the Civil War soldiers (like Kit), but also the pain of those who experience that loss (like Billy) and those who witness both (like Alcott).

What Meigs amplifies most in this episode is the resilience and courage it takes to move forward in the middle of such tragedy. Though "at her wit's end" (Alcott, *Hospital* [1869] 48), Alcott continues to move, to attend to the other wounded and dying. Interestingly, Meigs rewrites Billy's story to highlight *his* strength amid adversity: "Kit had – had gone. Billy would have cried out in anguish, but soldiers did not do that. He was one of the regiment; he must take this blow without whimpering. He did" (Meigs, *Invincible* 146). Billy's dream "betrayed him" temporarily (146), and Louisa arrives to console. In Meigs's version, with her emphasis on facing even extreme adversity with courage, Louisa's consolations are effective: "For a whole hour she listened and comforted. At last he was cheered and quieted" (147). Her strength gives him strength and comfort. Nevertheless, to make this point, which is consistent with the cultural work she imagines for the biography, Meigs fails to add what Alcott later admits: Billy actually returned to his inconsolable crying "more piteously than before" (Alcott, *Hospital* [1869] 48). Though this omission perhaps reveals how Meigs may not have always been faithful to her sources, it also highlights how important she felt it was to offer examples of childhood resilience and endurance to her readers, even in the hardest times.

Nina Meigs was, in the early 1930s, writing for the young people of a nation in distress. Yet her most powerful impact on US culture might not have been to show readers how to be invincible like Louisa. Instead, the more enduring influence of *Invincible Louisa* may have been on the emerging field of children's literature as an academic discipline and on subsequent critical and biographical study of Alcott. In an era before children's literature was considered a legitimate academic field, in the era of "children's books" before even such texts are recognized as children's *literature* (Lundin 143), Meigs and her Alcott biography, her first non-fiction book and one of her earliest publications while working as an instructor at the prestigious women's college Bryn Mawr, establishes Alcott as an original and vitally important children's author. The chief merits of Alcott's novel *Little Women* (1868–1869) are, according to Meigs, its originality and its realism. She calls the book a "completely fresh story" and something "of a kind different from anything they [its first child readers] had read before, a book just about themselves" (206). For Meigs, the academic and the author of children's books, "The real power of the book, however, centers about Jo" (208), and it is Alcott's faithfulness to life and to her experience that make Jo such an important literary achievement: "She was Louisa to the life. ... Her picture of Jo is the farthest thing removed from flattery. She has told frankly every drawback in her appearance and nature.... Yet Jo is lovable beyond words and more real than any of the others" (208–209). Verisimilitude clearly plays a role in what Meigs sees as Alcott's defining accomplishment as a writer, her ability to connect with young readers: "she sees things through their eyes" (227). This ability to see the world through the eyes of children and to portray what they see (as opposed to what they ought to see or what might be best for them to see) is, for Meigs, Alcott's unique contribution to the development of children's literature.

Meigs puts decidedly less emphasis on Alcott's life following the publication and successes of *Little Women* in 1868–1869, when Alcott was thirty-five to thirty-six years old. The final two decades of Alcott's life occupy just twenty-seven pages or about ten percent of the total volume. This decision makes sense in terms of Meigs's emphasis on documenting Louisa's invincibility for a young audience. With the publication of *Little Women*, the financial hardships of Louisa and her family disappeared ("there would never again be want and anxiety" [233]), making the final two decades of her life and her ongoing literary and financial successes a "Happy Ending" (Chapter X), a final reward for her refusal to give up in the face of adversity. Nevertheless, even though Meigs treats the last third of Alcott's life as dénouement to a life of struggle, her key goal is to recognize that Alcott's efforts established her as a nearly legendary American writer for children. Accordingly, in the 1950s, as children's books finally became children's literature, Meigs and her co-authors produced their enormously important *Critical History of Children's Literature*, considered by all account "the first survey of American children's literature" (Lundin 136). In it, Alcott would play a critical role in the co-authors' vision of this field and its significance.

*Invincible Louisa* would also exert significant influence on subsequent Alcott biographies, though it was rarely cited by scholars or other biographers.[6] This omission may be related to its fame as a children's book rather than as an adult work of scholarship. Whatever the case, Nina Meigs's work would exert palpable influence on subsequent biographers. Her complex, sympathetic, and historically contextualized portrait of Bronson Alcott, for instance, resonates with John Matteson's own nuanced and insightful examination of Louisa and Bronson in his Pulitzer-Prize-winning biography, *Eden's Outcasts: The Story of Louisa May Alcott and her Father* (2007). While Eve LaPlante casts her attention to Abigail May Alcott as something of a neglected novelty in her 2012 *Marmee and Louisa: The Untold Story of Louisa May Alcott and Her Mother*, Meigs also saw Louisa's mother as both her greatest champion and as her source and role model for the determination and resilience that define Meigs's version of Louisa. Although underserved by existing critical conversations about children's biography and children's literature, *Invincible Louisa* is both a significant moment in the history of children's literature and a key milestone in the development of Alcott studies.

## Notes

The authors thank Kristen Emig for her research contributions to this article.

1 For more about the gender patterns of Newbery recipients, see Kidd and Smith.
2 Although Meigs published many of her early works with Macmillan, *Invincible Louisa* was published by Little, Brown—the company that bought Roberts Brothers, the primary publisher of Alcott's juvenile works.
3 For instance, in 1946, Leo R. Miller argued, "Of the twenty-three books selected by the award committee through 1944 … only two are shown by the present data to be at the elementary-school level" (398).
4 For specific lists of representative tributes, see Alberghene and Clark (388–389, 402–403) and Clark (237–240).
5 In the 1869 edition of *Hospital Sketches,* which Meigs uses, the boy is known as Billy, though he is named Teddy in the 1863 edition.
6 Two notable exceptions include Shealy (158) and Clark (111–112).

## Works Cited

Alberghene, Janice M., and Beverly Lyon Clark, eds. Little Women *and the Feminist Imagination: Criticism, Controversy, Personal Essays*. New York: Garland, 1999. Print.

Alcott, Louisa May. *Little Women*. Ed. Anne K. Phillips and Gregory Eiselein. New York: Norton, 2004. Print.

Alcott, Louisa May. *Hospital Sketches*. Boston: James Redpath, 1863. *HathiTrust*. Web. 27 Aug. 2020.

Alcott, Louisa May. *Hospital Sketches and Camp and Fireside Stories*. Boston: Roberts Brothers, 1869. Print.

Anderson, Celia Catlett. "Meigs, Cornelia (Lynde)." *American Women Writers: A Critical Reference Guide from Colonial Times to the Present*. Ed. Lina Mainiero. 4 vols. New York: Ungar, 1981. 3: 128–129. Print.

Andrews, Siri. Letter to Frederic G. Melcher. 7 May 1934. Records Series 24/2/6, Box 2, Folder 7. American Library Association Archives. Urbana-Champaign, IL: University of Illinois Archives.

Cheney, Ednah D. *Louisa May Alcott: Her Life, Letters, and Journals*. Boston: Roberts Brothers, 1889. Print.

Clark, Beverly Lyon. *The Afterlife of "Little Women."* Baltimore: Johns Hopkins UP, 2014. Print.

Eddy, Jacalyn. *Bookwomen: Creating an Empire in Children's Book Publishing, 1919–1939*. U of Wisconsin P, 2006. Print.

Gallman, Robert E. "Economic Growth and Structural Change in the Long Nineteenth Century." *The Cambridge Economic History of the United States*. Ed. Stanley L. Engerman and Robert E. Gallman. 3 vols. New York: Cambridge UP, 1996–2000. 2: 1–56. Print.

Goldsmith, Sophie L. "Ten Years of the Newbery Medal." *The Bookman* 74 (Nov. 1931): 308–316. Print.

Hoopes, Edna Miriam. Letter to Della McGregor. 14 Nov. 1933. 1–2. Records Series 24/2/6, Box 2, Folder 7. American Library Association Archives. Urbana-Champaign, IL: University of Illinois Archives.

Houdyshell, Mara L., and Janice J. Kirkland. "Heroines in Newbery Medal Award Winners: Seventy-Five Years of Change." *Journal of Youth Services in Libraries* 11.3 (1998): 252–262. Print.

Howe, Daniel Walker. *What Hath God Wrought: The Transformation of America, 1815–1848*. New York: Oxford UP, 2007. Print.

Janeway, Elizabeth. Rev. of *Invincible Louisa: The Story of the Author of* Little Women, by Cornelia Meigs. *The New York Times Book Review* 29 Sept. 1968: 46. Print.

Kennedy, David M. *Freedom from Fear: The American People in Depression and War, 1929–1945*. New York: Oxford UP, 1999. Print.

Kidd, Kenneth B. "Prizing Children's Literature: The Case of Newbery Gold." *Children's Literature* 35 (2007): 166–190. Print.

Livsey, Rosemary Earnshaw. Letter to Siri Andrews. 10 Apr. 1934. Records Series 24/2/6, Box 2, Folder 7. American Library Association Archives. Urbana-Champaign, IL: University of Illinois Archives.

Lundin, Anne H. *Constructing the Canon of Children's Literature: Beyond Library Walls and Ivory Towers*. New York: Routledge, 2004. Print.

Marcus, Leonard. *Minders of Make-Believe: Idealists, Entrepreneurs, and the Shaping of American Children's Literature*. Boston: Houghton Mifflin, 2008. Print.

McGregor, Della. Letter to Siri Andrews. 30 Dec. 1933. 1–4. Records Series 24/2/6, Box 2, Folder 7. American Library Association Archives. Urbana-Champaign, IL: University of Illinois Archives.

McPherson, James M. *Battle Cry of Freedom: The Civil War Era*. New York: Oxford UP, 1989. Print.

Meigs, Cornelia. "Acceptance Paper." *Newbery Medal Books: 1922–1955, with their Authors' Acceptance Papers & Related Material chiefly from the* Horn

Book Magazine. Ed. Bertha Mahony Miller and Elinor Whitney Field. Boston: The Horn Book, 1955: 122–124. Print.

Meigs, Cornelia. *Clearing Weather*. Boston: Little, Brown, 1928. Print.

Meigs, Cornelia. *Invincible Louisa: The Story of the Author of* Little Women. Boston: Little, Brown, 1933. Print.

Meigs, Cornelia. *The Pool of Stars*. New York: Macmillan, 1919. Print.

Meigs, Cornelia. *The Windy Hill*. New York: Macmillan, 1921. Print.

Miller, Leo R. "Reading-Grade Placement of the First Twenty-Three Books Awarded the John Newbery Prize." *Elementary School Journal* 46.7 (1946): 394–399. Print.

Moses, Belle. *Louisa May Alcott, Dreamer and Worker: A Story of Achievement*. New York: Appleton, 1909. *HathiTrust*. Web. 16 Jan. 2019.

Peterson, Linda Kauffman, and Marilyn Leathers Solt. *Newbery and Caldecott Medal and Honor Books: An Annotated Bibliography*. Boston: G. K. Hall, 1982. Print.

Pratt, Anna B. "A Foreword by Meg." *Comic Tragedies: Written by 'Jo' and 'Meg' and Acted by the 'Little Women.'*" Boston: Roberts Brothers, 1893: 7–13. Print.

Schmidt, Gary D. *Making Americans: Children's Literature from 1930 to 1960*. Iowa City: U of Iowa P, 2013. Print.

Schott, Vera Winifred. Letter to Siri Andrews. 5 Feb. 1934. Records Series 24/2/6, Box 2, Folder 7. American Library Association Archives. Urbana-Champaign, IL: University of Illinois Archives.

Shealy, Daniel. "Prospects for the Study of Louisa May Alcott." *Resources for American Literary Study* 24 (1998): 157–176. Print.

Singley, Louisa. Letter to Siri Andrews. 14 Feb. 1934. Records Series 24/2/6, Box 2, Folder 7. American Library Association Archives. Urbana-Champaign, IL: University of Illinois Archives.

Smith, Irene. *A History of the Newbery and Caldecott Medals*. New York: Viking, 1957. Print.

Spence, Zella. Letter. [No addressee, no date.] Records Series 24/2/6, Box 2, Folder 7. American Library Association Archives. Urbana-Champaign, IL: University of Illinois Archives.

# 5 The Most Scorned of the Newbery Medalists?: *Daniel Boone* (1940)

*Beverly Lyon Clark*

"Hands down the worst Newbery winner out there," claims Goodreads commentator Sandy D. This judgment captures the tenor of most recent responses to James Daugherty's *Daniel Boone* (1939; 1940 Newbery Medal). The book had a "fair and steady popularity" into the 1950s (I. Smith, *History* 89) and was reprinted into the 1960s. Even the educator Nancy Larrick called it "a magnificent biography" in 1960 (*Teacher's* 58), five years before her stunning indictment of racial imbalance in children's literature, "The All-White World of Children's Books." *Daniel Boone* was out of print by 1982 (Peterson and Solt 73) and is out of print now. For it is arguably the most scorned of the Newbery Medalists. And rightly so. The muscular and energetic illustrations are no longer generally appealing. Nor is the gushing style. More significantly, the portrayals of American Indians offend Indigenous and modern non-Indigenous sensibilities. Published at a moment of national threat, prizing a masculine Americanness, *Daniel Boone* has received little scholarly attention and now lingers in libraries primarily in Newbery collections—thanks to its illustrations, style, and racism.

Why exactly did the book win a Newbery? In the history of the Medalists, Daugherty marks a gender turning point: much as 1930 ended a spate of male winners, his 1940 award ended a decade of female winners. In June 1939 the author Howard Pease, speaking to the Institute on Library Work with Children, had critiqued the femininity of recent Newbery Medalists, labeling the "world of children's books ... a completely feminine world" with respect to editors, reviewers, booksellers, and librarians (5). He called for "a better balance" to offset "the strictly feminine values of the poetic, the quaint, the fragile, the beautiful" (11); he called for more realism, more that was American, more attention to the present (even if he did find the frontier strongly American). He called for less "tender-minded censorship" (13). He called, in short, for more men. Several days later, at the larger conference of the American Library Association (ALA), the 1939 Newbery Medal winner was announced, another female winner.

DOI: 10.4324/9780367337223-5-6

Participants in the preconference Institute took note of Pease's "audacious masculine challenge," his "challenging bomb" to the presumed "female autocracy," which generated a "barrage of vehement defense" (Sayers 167; Nolte 588). Even a non-children's librarian later reported, "[T]he accusation was hurled by an author that the Children's book world is a feminine world" (Stephens 11). In July, Frederic Melcher, who had inaugurated the Newbery Medal, reported on Pease's plaint in *Publishers Weekly*, titling his editorial, "Men Wanted?" In October and November, the male editor of an education journal echoed Pease by calling for less "faded prettiness" in the Medalists, more of "the stuff that quickens the pulse of young people," less of what could be regarded as "sissy" (Certain, "What" 247; Certain, "Open" 283). The following April he quoted responses to these editorials: Lesley Newton, the chair of the all-female 1940 Newbery-Caldecott Selection Committee, temporized, "It is perhaps unfortunate that so many of the books chosen recently have been feminine in appeal" but added that "there are little girl children, too"; her vice chair, Irene Smith, admitted, "As I wrote Mr. Melcher, this year's committee will seek earnestly for *literary masculinity*" (qtd. in Certain, "Newbery" 161, 162).[1] In early 1940, *Daniel Boone* apparently did not require the usual multiple balloting but was chosen as the Medalist on the first ballot (Breed 725). Here was an answer to Pease's complaint: a book by a man, about a man, focused on adventurous exploration, with a good measure of pulse-quickening fighting thrown in.

Pease's broadside continued to echo in the minds of librarians into the 1950s (see Sauer 53; Breed 725; I. Smith, *History* 83). James English has pointed to the ways that controversy and scandal in prize-giving can publicize and otherwise support the aims of the prize givers (187–246). Although the controversy that Pease incited seems not to have had much impact beyond the children's book world, it created shock waves in that world and seems to have influenced at least some of the prize choices.

The prizing of *Daniel Boone* was timely in other ways as well. Its subject, an eighteenth-century frontiersman credited with opening the so-called wilderness (Kentucky) to White settlement, is an historical figure who acquired mythic status even in his own lifetime. And Americanness such as his was already central to the Newbery Medal: as Kenneth Kidd has argued, even when the award went to a work set in another country or in an Indigenous culture, it "affirm[ed] WASP American society precisely by depicting other cultures as exotic, primitive, and 'historical'" (176–77). *Daniel Boone* both depicted a WASP figure and set up a contrast with Indigenous cultures. But celebrating America was even more vital in 1939, and not just because Daugherty's Boone and his family embodied a version of the self-reliance called for in the hardscrabble Depression. For World War II broke out in Europe that year, with Germany invading Poland in September.[2] That month

Anne Carroll Moore declared that "freedom [was] at a crossroads"—in the context of reviewing *Daniel Boone* ("Three" 293). She went on to call Daugherty's work "the most important book of the year," praising the way it captured "the zest for a free life" ("Three" 294). Moore may not have been a member of the 1940 committee, but she was the most influential children's librarian in the mid-twentieth century, someone whose pronouncements carried great weight (see Clark, *Kiddie Lit* 70). A couple of months later the committee member Irene Smith called *Daniel Boone* "a great book," one that "reaches back to the freedom, stillness, and danger of the untrod forests, beyond the borders of settlement" ("1939" 839). Again, freedom.

It's noteworthy too that the book is self-illustrated—one of fourteen such Newbery Medalists, nine of them winning between 1938 and 1952. Why that surfeit during those years? Especially why then given that in 1938 the committee had started awarding the Caldecott Medal for the "most distinguished" picture book, so that one might expect that books with outstanding illustrations would be siphoned off to that Medal? Since at least 1978, Newbery criteria have specified that the Medal is for text and not images (see Peterson and Solt 399), but during the first decade and a half of the Caldecott, the sorting for the two medals was not yet complete, and, indeed, it was during this time that the picture book as we now know it was being defined (see op de Beeck xix). Midcentury Newbery Medals tended to favor authors who were also distinguished illustrators: five of this period's nine self-illustrating Newbery Medal-winning authors also created art that won a Caldecott Medal or runner-up recognition. Including Daugherty, whose *Andy and the Lion* had been a runner-up for the 1939 Caldecott. Indeed, many subsequent readers have been more enthusiastic about it than about the 1939 Medalist, Thomas Handforth's *Mei Li*. Both Newbery and Caldecott Medals are supposed to recognize a specific work, not an author's full oeuvre, but at the very least, knowledge of a writer's earlier work is likely to set up expectations, to frame a committee member's response.[3] The recognition of *Daniel Boone* may thus have been partly acknowledging Daugherty's previous work.

Moreover, it's hard to read the book and ignore the images. The theorist W. J. T. Mitchell points to "the inextricable weaving together of representation and discourse, the imbrication of visual and verbal experience" when words and images are conjoined (83). They're not as tightly interwoven in *Daniel Boone* as they are in *Andy and the Lion*, but the illustrations do refract and parallel the text, both embodying "the same gusto and dash and enjoyment of significant detail, the same passion for movement, color and structural unity" (Ward 184).[4] Furthermore, as Leonard Marcus has noted, illustrations "traffic to some degree in unnameable objects, states and feelings" (17). It's hard simply to turn off the affect. The lithographs in *Daniel Boone*, which appear at most page turns, are in black, sienna, and—what else—hunter green. The muted colors slightly counterbalance the destabilizing and energizing of Daugherty's frequent diagonals (often provided by the rifles that figures conveniently carry) and depictions of bodies in motion. His representational images, arguably influenced by the depiction of movement in Futurism, are busy, crowded, energetic, dynamic, muscular; as critics have said of his other visual works, his "trademark lines" are "coiling and curvy" and convey an "explosive sense of movement" (op de Beeck 198; Lawton 3). His images even "straggl[e] in fluid lines a little beyond any given space without wandering out of the picture" (Titzell 2073).

Daugherty had previously illustrated another Boone biography, a 1926 reissue of Stewart Edward White's 1922 *Daniel Boone: Wilderness Scout*. The figures in this earlier book may be just as muscular as those in the later one, but many of the earlier images are allegorical, with captions like "Vision," "Effort," or "Defence." The images aspire, in many ways, to high art, as befits a painter and muralist described as "one of America's first avant-garde painters," one of "America's pioneer modernists" (Levin 24; "Out" 88). The stunning double-page frontispiece, captioned "The Wilderness Road," resembles a mural, with its fourteen vibrant human figures rising from a gray-bearded elder in the lower left to a pioneer madonna and child framed by the nimbus of a covered wagon. Moore had been so enthusiastic about these early illustrations that, while dismissing White's text as "lack[ing] the spark of life," she claimed that, next to Carl Sandburg's *Abraham Lincoln*, "Mr. Daugherty's pictures stand out as the richest imaginative contribution to the reading and study of American history which has been made in my time" ("Seeing" VII: 8). The illustrations in the Newbery-winning biography are less allegorical; almost all directly represent scenes or actions in the text, from the image of Boone's parents bending over and playing with a lusty baby in a cradle, heading the first chapter, through full-page images of, say, an unperturbed Boone surrounded by four American Indians at a moment of capture, to a half-page chapter head that shows an aged Boone kneeling with his dog and rifle and displaying on his palm the silver half-dollar that was all he had left after finally paying off his debts in Kentucky.

As for literary merit, the style in *Daniel Boone* is spiced with the vernacular ("swingling," "blab school," "shindig") but is also lyrical, even florid, with its alliteration and lists, its occasional inverted word order and its additive, paratactic syntax. "Over the Ohio valley," Daugherty intones, "linger the long shadows of Logan and Cornstalk and Dragging Canoe, of old Oconatosta, of Atta Culla Culla, and Moluntha and Black Fish" (39). His cadences are Whitmanesque, old-fashioned, almost Biblical, unlike in such other works as *Andy and the Lion*. And he glories in figurative language: the pioneers who traveled the Wilderness Road, for example, peopled "a rough and violent saga full of lights and shadows, sweet and bitter as the wild persimmon, rough and tough as the shag-barked hickories, fierce and tender as the tall waving corn of the valleys" (52). Or more grandiloquently:

> Next day the clear-shining sun rose over the vast land like high-calling trumpets of glory. The splendor and the brightness came upon his spirit like the rushing of mighty wings, and the voice of mighty thunderings: "Enter into a promised land such as no man has known, a new born creation all your own; drink deep, O Daniel, of the mysterious wine of the wilderness." (34)

Daugherty's contemporaries praised his "backwoods vernacular" and "lovely phrases," his "tangy, eloquent" and "singing, muscular" prose (Buell 10; Ulrich 24; I. Smith, "1939" 839). But the style hasn't worn well. In one of the few contemporary demurrals, Katharine Sergeant White wrote that the pictures were "distinguished" but the text a little less so "because of occasional lapses into forced folksiness and grandiloquent cliché" (78). Modern readers, raised on her husband's *Elements of Style*, would agree.

With respect to the rest of the verbal content, Daugherty portrays not so much the Scouting Boone popular in the 1910s and 1920s as a distinctly patriotic one. Where Stewart White had hailed Boone as "the great Scout," Daugherty keeps invoking "democracy" and "America," "dream" and "independence," "wild" and "joy" and "free." An early poem in the text acknowledges his debt to Whitman's vision of America: "Rise up, you lanky sons of democracy," Daugherty urges, going on to envision "generations marching on to higher freedoms /.../ Chanting: Democracy, here we come" (7). Daugherty also exalts America with religious language, his Kentucky both Eden and the Promised Land (see Schmidt 41–42). In accepting the Newbery Medal, he celebrated, in his own words, "the nation composed of all nations marching on the long, rough road to freedom," also an Americanness that could withstand the rising tide in Germany, at this time "when subtle propaganda more deadly than bombs is trying to undermine the walls of our faith" (Daugherty, "Acceptance" 187, 185). Faith and America.

Furthermore, "the pursuit of biography," Nigel Hamilton has argued, "is integral to the Western concept of individuality and the ideals of democracy" (2). American biographies for the young are especially likely to promote liberal individualism, historical progress, and freedom (see VanderHaagen 60–69). The educator Charlotte Huck shed light on early-twentieth-century norms for juvenile biographies when she contrasted them with those prevalent in 1979. Both older and newer biographies should offer children "a fast-moving narrative," she argued, but older ones were likely to stress role modeling, to avoid unsavory details, and not to acknowledge primary sources; she prevaricated on whether it was still acceptable to include invented dialogue (551–553). *Daniel Boone* fits the older norms: Huck called it "outstanding for its time" and noted, "Daugherty did not write objective biography. He rendered events as he interpreted them, in a poem of praise to the pioneers" (78, 563).[5] In the later words of a member of the 1940 committee, children like to read biographies about "those about whom there is a story to tell; into whose lives is woven the colorful thread of adventure and romance" (L. Smith 187).

Like other Boone biographers for the young, before and since, Daugherty participates in a romantic tradition of biography, not the realist tradition that emerged at the turn of the twentieth century in biographies targeting adults (see Faragher 346–348). The sources Daugherty draws on include not just historical records but also legends, yet without any hedging as to veracity—as when relating that Boone carved "D. BOON cilled a bar" on a tree or that he escaped from Indians by swinging on a grapevine (36, 74). Several commentators have reported that when growing up in the Midwest, Daugherty had listened to tales of the frontiersman told by his grandfather (e.g., Kemp and Kemp 6). The image is no doubt meant to evoke warm and child-friendly storytelling, but it also weakens claims to historical reliability. While Daugherty does mention some historical records in the text, he does not provide the fuller sourcing and the list for "further reading" that authors of juvenile non-fiction now proffer. Moreover, some of his sources have now been debunked; for example, he quotes Audubon regarding an apocryphal encounter with an aged Boone (see R. Taylor 533). From the perspective of a twenty-first-century reader, the book is "a mixed bag of historical anecdotes masquerading as serious biography by an armchair biographer" (Plume45).

Like Stewart White and most of the more than a hundred other authors of juvenile books about Boone, Daugherty is, however, firmly committed to role modeling. Indeed, one reviewer, someone who had chaired the previous year's Newbery-Caldecott Medal Selection Committee, called *Daniel Boone* "an ideal book to stir the imagination of youth to a realization of what one man's courage and faith and loyalty could achieve, then and now" (G. English 13).

So, of course, Daugherty minimizes Boone's potential weaknesses. He does briefly address the court-martial at which the frontiersman was acquitted and Boone's being robbed of twenty thousand dollars that he'd been entrusted with, quoting a letter of support from one of those whose money was lost. Fair enough. But it's more difficult to excuse Boone's fecklessness with respect to legal land holdings, hard though Daugherty tries by criticizing claim jumpers and dismissing legal formalities. Another challenge is how to address Boone's recurring problems with debt, something useful to note if one wants to laud his eventually discharging those debts. Daugherty simply has Boone decide, rather suddenly, to pay off his previously unmentioned debts in the Kentucky that he has long since left—and suggests that these were merely to "old friends who had lent him money and forgotten or merchants who had advanced him supplies for which he had never turned in barter or skins" (93). Daugherty concludes by having Boone assert, "No one can say when I am gone that Boone was a dishonest man" (93). The assertion diverts us from an alternate message: that Boone was not exactly thrifty.

Speaking of dishonesty, though—Daugherty minimizes Boone's willingness to lie, his willingness to deceive the Shawnee who captured him, for instance, whether his initial "apparent friendliness made the Indians feel that he was really glad to be captured," or he is later "pretending he was happy and satisfied" as an adopted Shawnee and would gladly persuade the inhabitants of Boonesborough to surrender (32, 56). Boone likewise deceives the British to whom the Shawnee bring him, telling "of his fictitious plan to capture Boonesborough in the spring" (56). "Fictitious," mind you, not "devious" or "lying" or "deceitful." Of course, some consider lying acceptable when feuding or warring, but I'd argue that it's at least morally ambiguous. Moreover, historians have claimed that Boone "loved the Indians" (Faragher 362, ventriloquizing Boone), that perhaps he considered remaining with the Shawnee—but Daugherty and other juvenile biographers ignore such a possibility. In any case, lack of thriftiness, of attention to the law, and of honesty are not necessarily desirable traits in a moral exemplar, so children's biographers routinely occlude them.

Furthermore, the biographer of Boone has to navigate around a central contradiction: as the scholar Henry Nash Smith has queried, "Which was the real Boone—the standard-bearer of civilization and refinement, or the child of nature who fled into the wilderness before the advance of settlement?" (55). How does the frontiersman embody both the dream of freeing oneself from civilization and that of being its beachhead? Daugherty attempts to resolve the issue partly through Boone's wife Rebecca. He invokes her name more than, say, White does, and he accords some attention to the role of frontier women who "fought as boldly as their men in desperate singled-handed combat with ax and knife and rifle" (74). And he uses Rebecca to inject local color—she speaks in Irish brogue when he pretends to quote her. But also she represents an insistent resistance to Daniel's urge to set off on yet another venture, perhaps partly constraining him with his Sunday homespun, which "fitted too tight for action" (73)—so that's how the British once caught him; it was her fault. She is, in any case, the representative of civilization, while Daniel constantly itches for more "elbow room."[6]

The contrary urges to flee and to settle are likewise resolved, in part, by slippages in the equivocal trope of freedom, variously individualized and nationalized, variously associated with the so-called wilderness and Native Americans and with the White enclaves. In his preface, Daugherty describes Boone lyrically as "a free singing rider in a lost dream" (6). For this frontiersman didn't go on to gain any dream of personal wealth but sought an ever-receding freedom not associated with the White communities. Yet early on, when first settling in the Yadkin valley of North Carolina, Boone and his family look "forward with joy to taking up again the free peaceful life in the quiet valley" (25). Freedom is associated with settlement here. But still Boone listens to hunters engage in "tall talk of the free life among the Indians beyond the mountains" (28). He then, hunting alone in the forests beyond those mountains, feels a "new sense of freedom and power": "He was the only freeman in all the western world, like Man himself in the Beginning of Things" (34). So is it "among the Indians" that one accesses "the free life," or is it as a solitary individual, "the only freeman?" Slippages in freedom can erase the Indians. Back among his countrymen, Boone relays "the call of the golden West forever saying: 'More freedom and good fortune across the mountains...'" (37). Freedom is in the woods, possibly among American Indians, but not when they capture Boone and he ponders—and makes—"a dash for freedom" (56). So much for "the free life among the Indians." Instead, it's White communities that are becoming associated with freedom, as the colonies are "fighting for independence" from England (46). As Boone's life trajectory intersected with the American Revolution, and "Boone's story [became] the story of a whole people," with "all their ranging freedom and mortal bondages" (52), the tenor of freedom shifted. At his death, Boone is memorialized as a trailblazer for "a free people marching on" (95). The freedom from civilization, as "the only freeman in all the western world," has become the "ranging freedom" of the "free people" of the new nation.

Yet such freedom and its blithe assumption of the march of Manifest Destiny does violence to the Shawnee. Daugherty's narrative is not more racist than contemporary narratives by other Whites. At least he avoided the tired stereotype, recycled twice by Stewart White, that Indians dashed out children's brains, preferably against a tree. Yet for all that Daugherty may have been relatively progressive—he's praised, for instance, in the radical *New Masses* (H. Taylor 23, 24; see also Mickenberg 351–352n43)—he does resort to stereotypes.[7]

Consider, again, his illustrations. The artist Norman Kent has noted that Daugherty's "exaggerations and distortions make his graphic intentions very clear" (17). Indeed, too clear. His Shawnee and other American Indians are only somewhat more angular than the Whites but their facial features are stern and stereotypical. As for his choice of scenes, Daugherty favors Native Americans lurking in sinister ambush or attacking or capturing Whites, often with Natives surrounding or menacingly towering over their adversaries. Even when Daugherty seems to be trying to create a benign image, to accompany a stereotypically noble speech on the doomed race, the dominant Native figure is defiant and menacing.

The image is allegorical, unlike most of the images in the book, as the figure protectively straddles a Native woman embracing a fallen youth and, with shield held high, ineffectively fends off a Bible, a bottle, and a gunshot. Then again, defiance can be empowering, and the image offers a visual counterpoint to the resignation that Daugherty foregrounds in the quoted speech. Still, unlike for the Whites that he illustrates, there are no calm or joyous hunting or family scenes, no scenes of the Shawnee town or village life that Boone observed. Of course, any such sympathetic depictions might make it harder to accept that Whites were simply laying claim to a pristine wilderness, might "raise the possibility that Europeans invaded and conquered and pillaged heavily populated, developed real estate" (P. Smith 51).

In the verbal text, the early mentions of Native Americans are neutral to presumably positive: North Carolina "Indians" may be "friendly," which is to say that they do not impede Whites' encroachment but "barter and visit and depart," and Seminoles are "friendly" too, for without their aid Boone and his companions "would have starved" in "the dismal swamp" on one of Boone's expeditions (15, 26). Daugherty does have the grace to say that, at the Cumberland Gap, Boone and his companions witness beautiful country "that few white men had ever seen" (30). Many contemporary White writers would have inappropriately omitted the descriptor "white." And when Colonel Henderson wants to buy the land that will become Kentucky from the Cherokee, Daugherty notes that, "although they had no papers to prove it, [the Cherokee] had possessed the land from immemorial time" (42), which reveals Daugherty's limited perspective in that the Cherokee and other Native peoples didn't see themselves as possessing the land in the European sense. Most often in the text Native Americans are "Indians," which was a relatively neutral term in the thirties. But the terms "savages" and "redskins" and "varmints" recur. Whites may sometimes be "wild" and "whooping" (66). But it's "whooping Indians" who "broke from ambush tomahawking and scalping the white men running for the river" (78)—to add more stereotypes to the mix. Elsewhere the "warriors" are idle as the "bronze squaws" work, war chants are "shrill," dancing entails "wild frenzies," "chiefs" are "iron-faced," and Indians "on the warpath" are "fierce" and "ghastly" and "fearsome," whereas those that are not have "buried the war hatchet" (56, 60, 22, 43). Before they head to the "Happy Hunting Grounds" (79), of course. Stereotypes run rampant, so thoroughly intertwined into the text and illustrations that they can't just be edited out, the book then republished, whitewashed.

Another kind of stereotyping appears in Daugherty's misunderstanding of Native kinship. When the captured Boone is brought to the British fort at Detroit, Daugherty tells us that the captor "insisted that Boone was his personal property and he was not for sale" (56).

*Figure 5.1* Noble or savage?

Source: *Daniel Boone*, written and illustrated by James Daugherty (Viking, 1939), page 41.

Daugherty has made no mention by this point that Boone has been adopted by the Shawnee and that perhaps this political and affective connection was a reason he was not "for sale."[8] Only a couple of paragraphs later does Daugherty claim that the Shawnee "had washed away [Boone's] white blood in the river, pulled out half his hair, and painted him with strange symbols that meant he was the adopted son of the chief Black Fish" (56). The use of the past perfect leaves the timing of the adoption vague, but mentioning the ceremony only after the trip to Detroit allows Daugherty to finesse the issue of whether Boone was by then a family and tribal member instead of a possession. Moreover, the phrasing in the delayed announcement—"strange symbols that meant he was the adopted son"—signal that it's the Shawnee that construe Boone as adopted, not necessarily Boone himself or Daugherty. Only much later, when Boone is telling tales to his grandchildren, for instance, does Daugherty refer to Blackfish (as his name is commonly written) as Boone's "Indian father" (94). Daugherty allows the threat of a family connection (what if such a "real" American became a "real" Indian, not just an honorary one?) to emerge only in retrospect, an admission that is nostalgically safe once physical threat has disappeared.

Two striking extended quotations in Daugherty's text also color his portrayal of Native Americans. Joe Sutliff Sanders has explored how hedging, the presence of a visible narrator, and certain uses of para-textual materials can question the authority often granted to nonfictional texts and thus foster critical engagement by the modern child reader. Sanders endorses books that show "a multiplicity of ideas rather than a monologue dedicated to one idea" (67). By including quotations Daugherty does allow for some multivocality, but his framing attempts to corral them to support a single, blindered vision.

Early on, following mention of the burning of Indian towns by a militia to which Boone was attached, Daugherty gratuitously tosses in "an account of the destruction of an Indian village" (24). Historians have noted that, despite fighting American Indians, the Quaker-born Boone "never became an Indian hater"; indeed, in later life he frequently visited with his Shawnee captors, who became "his second family," and he is reported as saying that Indians "have always been kinder to me than the whites" (Faragher 23, 300). As for Daugherty's account of destruction, it derives not from sources about Boone but from the autobiography of Davy Crockett. According to the quoted anecdote, after forty-six "warriors" retreat into a house, the narrator and his companions shoot a "squaw" who has loosed an arrow, hitting her at least twenty times, shoot down others "like dogs," and burn down the house and the men inside. A boy who'd been shot was "so near the burning house that the grease was stewing out of him"; he makes no noise and asks for no quarter, yet that makes him not brave but "sullen" (25). Daugherty offers no further comment. The anecdote may be more graphic than others in the book, but the stance does not differ significantly from his dominant one.

Yet subsequently Daugherty inserts a quotation with a different import, probably as a gesture of respect: the "noble" speech to which I've alluded. In it the Seneca Red Jacket (Sagoyewatha) testifies that Whites called his people brothers but wanted ever more land, hired "Indians ... to fight against Indians," and furthered the destruction by bringing "strong liquor among us"; he pointedly goes on to ask the missionary to whom he is speaking, "If there is but one religion, why do you white people differ so much about it?" (40). Daugherty attempts to give some voice to an American Indian, but the written texts of such solemn speeches were translated and redacted by Whites and at least subtly shaped by them. In the case of this 1805 speech, the missionary who was addressed kept a journal of his travels but did not record the speech; the first redaction apparently appeared in 1809 but lacked the customary documentation of naming the source or the interpreter, and its dating of the speech is inconsistent with other evidence of the missionary's whereabouts at the time (Densmore 64–68). Furthermore, the 1937 source that Daugherty cites (Beston 238–39) omits almost half of the earliest recorded version, and Daugherty omits almost half of that. Still, few accounts of Boone even attempt to include a Native voice, especially narratives written in and before the mid-twentieth century. Daugherty counterbalances the tenor of most of the book, outlining some Whites' reprehensible motivations and actions, and especially noting Red Jacket's resistance to Christianity, a resistance that potentially undermines some of the religiosity of the book's hosanna to American progress.

Nevertheless, Daugherty vitiates the power of the speech in the way that he frames it. He opens its chapter with a sentence I've already cited, the one that begins, "Over the Ohio valley linger the long shadows of Logan and Cornstalk" (39). The lingering shadows conjure a nostalgic retrospection, as does the archaic inversion of word order and the heightened, alliterative style. It's also safe to refer to these leaders as "[t]he wise old prophet-chiefs" since they "saw their destiny in the sky; they knew their fate was the doom of the buffalo" (39)—thus the stereotypical disappearing Indian, reading the signs of nature. Then, as if invoking the scene that the earlier graphic quotation described, "[a]mid their burning villages and the awful butcheries and sickening betrayals of friends and foes, they met the personal tragedy of violent death with a serene indifference" (39). Okay, it's clear whose villages are burning, but whose butcheries? whose betrayals? The attribution is conveniently vague. And "serene indifference"? True, the indifference is not "sullen," but it's still a stereotype, this time invoking both stoicism and lack of feeling. Daugherty also calls the speech a testament to "the last tribes driven like mists down the mountain valleys before the brightness of the pale-faced gods" (39)—the Whites' gods driving out the tribes? or the Whites themselves as gods? (The language is misty, like its referent.) He attenuates the power of this voice that he sees as doomed to disappear—gaining, in effect, what Philip Deloria has described as a modernist's/anti-modernist's "access to an authenticity that became legitimate only when one could not gain access" (120). The disappeared Indian whom Daugherty ventriloquizes offers some resistance to the rest of the text but ultimately authenticates the America that the author celebrates.

Later, in concluding *Daniel Boone*, Daugherty again tries to accord respect, hinting at an equal footing: Boone and such "solemn chieftains" as Blackfish and Cornstalk "had fought it out man to man. They had been great enemies and he, too, was a disinherited son of Kentucky" (93). Man to man, yes, in part, although the phrasing occludes the more systematic exterminations, the various deceptions—in which Boone himself participated—and the trail of broken treaties. The individualism fostered in biographies, and especially those about Boone, minimizes the communal, societal, and federal implications. Instead—single combat. And as for Boone's being disinherited, it was just he and his constantly migrating family that had felt the need to leave Kentucky, not entire peoples forced out of their homelands.

Ultimately, Daugherty's biography raises questions. He does offer a glimpse of multiple perspectives. He even provides a rather visible narrator, one whose inflated style may have seemed simply celebratory in 1939 but now seems artificial and draws attention to the author's shaping presence. As does the muscular style of the illustrations. But Daugherty doesn't question his sources; he doesn't distinguish between historical record and legend. It may be that a biography is always "an illusion, a fiction in the guise of fact" (Fisher 302). But Daugherty's biography of Boone is particularly fictive, especially by current norms, and more obviously so because his guiding principles, his construction of Americanness, is at odds with most current constructions of what it means to be American, occluding those who are Black, Indigenous, and people of color. In life and legend, as John Mack Faragher has argued, Boone "stands for some of the things that Americans feel are most important about themselves—the central significance of the frontier in their history, a fantasy of wanderlust yet a commitment to family, a love and admiration of nature coupled with an almost desperate desire for development and material advancement" (351)—which I'd augment by specifying the racializing that talk of the frontier engenders and that always underlies conceptualizations of America. Faragher adds, "By considering Daniel Boone's life and legend, Americans have always sought to learn something of themselves" (351). The prizing of this life, by Daugherty, teaches us—Whites especially—truths about ourselves, truths that we no longer wish to hear.

## Notes

1 For additional contemporary response, see Ulrich 24; Lambeck 2135; Lesser et al. 190. For more on the gender controversy, see Jenkins and Horning.

2 Certainly that year's Caldecott Medal, decided by the same committee, went to another very American work, Ingri and Edgar Parin d'Aulaire's *Abraham Lincoln*. Bechtel also sees social changes in the 1930s as inviting "the advent of the American folk hero," which "stood for the American working man" (249).

3 J. English notes the "tension between the prestige of a particular contemporary work and the prestige of all the past works by its author" in prize giving (58). And two members of the 1939 Newbery-Caldecott Medal Selection Committee had served on the 1940 committee.
4 For discussion of the relationships between words and images in illustrated books, as opposed to picture books, see Clark, *Afterlife* 190–92.
5 This praise disappears in later editions of her text.
6 In what is now the standard scholarly biography, Faragher notes that the frequent claim that Boone said he was seeking "elbow room" originates from an unreliable nineteenth-century source (326).
7 For insights on judging stereotypes, see, e.g., Seale, Slapin, and Gonzales; and Reese. With respect to Daugherty's book, Sieruta has pointed to the tomahawks, guns, and knives—and generally negative portrayals of Native Americans—in what is "probably nobody's favorite Newbery" (n. pag.).
8 For discussion of the Indigenous non-nuclear-family kinship system as organizing its politics, not just its intimacies, see, e.g., Rifkin. Daugherty's treatment of the pioneer nuclear family as particularly American is part of what blinds him to the power and meaning of Indigenous kinship. For recent juvenile fiction that treats adoption in ways that reflect Indigenous mores, see, e.g., Louise Erdrich's *The Porcupine Year* (2008) and Joseph Bruchac's *The Winter People* (2002).

## Works Cited

Bechtel, Louise Seaman. "Books on the Ladder of Time." *Books in Search of Children: Speeches and Essays*. Ed. Virginia Haviland. New York: Macmillan, 1969. Print.

Beston, Henry, ed. *American Memory: Being a Mirror of the Stirring and Picturesque Past of Americans and the American Nation*. New York: Farrar, 1937. *Internet Archive*. Web. 30 July 2020.

Breed, Clara E. "The Newbery Medal: A Plea for Understanding." *Wilson Library Bulletin* 16.9 (May 1942): 724–725. Print.

Buell, Ellen Lewis. Rev. of *Daniel Boone*, by James Daugherty. *New York Times Book Review* 12 Nov. 1939: 10. *ProQuest*. Web. 30 July 2020.

Certain, C. C. "The Newbery Award: Open Forum." *Elementary English Review* 17.4 (Apr. 1940): 160–162. *JSTOR*. Web. 5 Mar. 2018.

Certain, C. C. "Open Forum on the Newbery Award." Editorial. *Elementary English Review* 16.7 (Nov. 1939): 283. *JSTOR*. Web. 5 Mar. 2018.

Certain, C. C. "What Are Little Boys Made Of?" Editorial. *Elementary English Review* 16.6 (Oct. 1939): 247. *JSTOR*. Web. 5 Mar. 2018.

Clark, Beverly Lyon. *The Afterlife of "Little Women."* Baltimore: Johns Hopkins UP, 2014. Print.

Clark, Beverly Lyon. *Kiddie Lit: The Cultural Construction of Children's Literature in America*. Baltimore: Johns Hopkins UP, 2003. Print.

Daugherty, James. "Acceptance Paper: Children's Books in a Democracy." *Newbery Medal Books: 1922–1955, with their Authors' Acceptance Papers & Related Material chiefly from the* Horn Book Magazine. Ed. Bertha Mahony Miller and Elinor Whitney Field. Boston: The Horn Book, 1955. 185–191. Print.

Daugherty, James. *Daniel Boone*. Illus. James Daugherty. New York: The Viking Press, 1939. Print.

Deloria, Philip J. *Playing Indian*. New Haven: Yale UP, 1998. Print.

Densmore, Christopher. *Red Jacket: Iroquois Diplomat and Orator*. Syracuse: Syracuse UP, 1999. Print.

English, Gladys. "Quality in Children's Books." *Western Journal of Education* 46 (Oct. 1940): 12–13. *Internet Archive*. Web. Mar. 2018.

English, James F. *The Economy of Prestige: Prizes, Awards, and the Circulation of Cultural Value*. Cambridge: Harvard UP, 2005. *ProQuest Ebook Central*. Web. 20 July 2020.

Faragher, John Mack. *Daniel Boone: The Life and Legend of an American Pioneer*. New York: Holt, 1992. Print.

Fisher, Margery. *Matters of Fact: Aspects of Non-fiction for Children*. New York: Crowell, 1972. Print.

Hamilton, Nigel. *Biography: A Brief History*. Cambridge: Harvard UP, 2007. *ProQuest Ebook Central*. Web. 30 July 2020.

Horning, Kathleen T. "The Search for Distinguished." *Horn Book Magazine* 88.4 (July/Aug. 2012): 59–68. *Academic OneFile*. Web. 2 Mar. 2018.

Huck, Charlotte S. *Children's Literature in the Elementary School*. 3rd ed., updated. New York: Holt, 1979. Print.

Jenkins, Christine A. "Women of ALA Youth Services and Professional Jurisdiction: Of Nightingales, Newberies, Realism, and the Right Books, 1937–1945." *Library Trends* 44.4 (Spring 1996): 813+. *Academic OneFile*. Web. 2 Mar. 2018.

Kemp, Edward, and Elaine Kemp. "James Henry Daugherty." *Imprint: Oregon* 2 (Fall 1975): 6–9. Microform.

Kent, Norman. "James Daugherty, Buckskin Illustrator." *American Artist* 9.3 (Mar. 1945): 16–20. EBSCOhost. Web. 12 Apr. 2021.

Kidd, Kenneth B. "Prizing Children's Literature: The Case of Newbery Gold." *Children's Literature* 35 (2007): 166–190. *Project Muse*. Web. 2 Mar. 2018.

Lambeck, Frederick. "James Daugherty and His America." *Publishers Weekly* 137.22 (1940): 2135–2136. *Readers' Guide Retrospective*: *1890–1982* (H. W. Wilson). Web. 18 Apr. 2021.

Larrick, Nancy. "The All-White World of Children's Books." *Saturday Review* 11 Sept. 1965: 63–65, 84–85. Print.

Larrick, Nancy. *A Teacher's Guide to Children's Books*. London: Merrill, 1960. *Internet Archive*. Web. 12 Apr. 2021.

Lawton, Rebecca E. "Heroic America: James Daugherty's Mural Drawings from the 1930s." *Traditional Fine Arts Organization*. Excerpted from *Heroic America: James Daugherty's Mural Drawings from the 1930s*. Poughkeepsie: Frances Lehman Loeb Art Center, 1998. *Resource Library*, 23 June 2005. Web. 30 July 2020.

Lesser, Margaret, et al. "Mr. Melcher's Address." Section for Library Work with Children. *ALA Bulletin* 34.7 (Aug. 1940): 189–191. *JSTOR*. Web. 6 Aug. 2018.

Levin, Gail. "James Daugherty: Early Modernist and Simultaneist." *Whitney Review* (1976/1977): 24–27. Print.

Marcus, Leonard S. "Life Drawings: Some Notes on Children's Picture Book Biographies." *The Lion and the Unicorn* 4.1 (1980): 15–31. *Project Muse*. Web. 30 July 2020.

Melcher, Frederic G. "Men Wanted?" *Publishers Weekly* 136.1 (1939): 7. *Readers' Guide Retrospective: 1890–1982* (H. W. Wilson). Web. 18 Apr. 2021.

Mickenberg, Julia. *Learning from the Left: Children's Literature, the Cold War, and Radical Politics in the United States*. New York: Oxford UP, 2006. Print.

Mitchell, W. J. T. *Picture Theory: Essays on Verbal and Visual Representation*. Chicago: U of Chicago P, 1994. Print.

Moore, Anne Carroll. "Seeing Daniel Boone with James Daugherty." *New York Herald Tribune Books* 31 Oct. 1926: VII: 8. Microform.

Moore, Anne Carroll. "The Three Owls' Notebook." *Horn Book Magazine* (Sept./Oct. 1939): 293–295. Print.

Nolte, Claire. "The Sayers Institute." *Library Journal* 64.14 (Aug. 1939): 588–591. Microform.

op de Beeck, Nathalie. *Suspended Animation: Children's Picture Books and the Fairy Tale of Modernity*. Minneapolis: U of Minnesota P, 2010. Print.

"Out There in the Universe." Rev. of an exhibition. *Newsweek*, 1 Nov. 1965: 88. Microform.

Pease, Howard. "Children's Books Today: One Man's View." *Proceedings of the Institute on Library Work with Children (June 15–17, 1939)*. Berkeley: School of Librarianship, U of California, 1939. 5–16. Print.

Peterson, Linda Kauffman, and Marilyn Leathers Solt. *Newbery and Caldecott Medal and Honor Books: An Annotated Bibliography*. Boston: Hall, 1982. Print.

Plume45. "Disinherited Son of Kentucky." Customer Review of James Daugherty's Daniel Boone. *Amazon.com*, 6 June 2013. Rpt. as Gale. "Disinherited Son of Kentucky." *Goodreads.com*, 6 June 2013. Web. 31 July 2020.

Reese, Debbie. *American Indians in Children's Literature*. Blog. Web. 31 July 2020.

Rifkin, Mark. *When Did Indians Become Straight? Kinship, the History of Sexuality, and Native Sovereignty*. New York: Oxford UP, 2011. Print.

Sanders, Joe Sutliff. *A Literature of Questions: Nonfiction for the Critical Child*. Minneapolis: U of Minnesota P, 2018. Print.

Sandy, D. Community Review of James Daugherty's *Daniel Boone*. *Goodreads*, 4 Oct. 2008. Web. 31 July 2020.

Sauer, Julia L. "Making the World Safe for the Janey Larkins." *Library Journal* 66.2 (1941): 49–53. Microform.

Sayers, Frances Clarke. Closing Remarks. *Proceedings of the Institute on Library Work with Children (June 15–17, 1939)*. Berkeley: School of Librarianship, U of California, 1939. 167. Print.

Schmidt, Gary D. *Making Americans: Children's Literature from 1930 to 1960*. Iowa City: U of Iowa P, 2013. *Project Muse*. Web. 30 July 2020.

Seale, Doris, Beverly Slapin, and Rosemary Gonzales. "How to Tell the Difference: A Guide for Evaluating Children's Books for Anti-Indian Bias." 2000. *Oyate*. Web. 31 July 2020.

Sieruta, Peter D. "The Mural in the Gym." *Collecting Children's Books*, 3 Nov. 2009. Blog. Web. 31 July 2020.

Smith, Henry Nash. *Virgin Land: The American West as Symbol and Myth*. 1950. Cambridge: Harvard UP, 1978. *ACLS Humanities E-Book*. Web. 30 July 2020.

Smith, Irene. "1939 Variety for Children's Book Shelves: A Public Library Selection for the Nine to Twelve-Year-Olds." *Library Journal* 1 Nov. 1939: 839+. Microform.

Smith, Irene. *A History of the Newbery and Caldecott Medals*. 1957. New York: Viking, 1963. Print.

Smith, Lillian H. *The Unreluctant Years: A Critical Approach to Children's Literature*. Chicago: American Library Association, 1953. Print.

Smith, Paul Chaat. *Everything You Know about Indians Is Wrong*. Minneapolis: U of Minnesota P, 2009. Print.

Stephens, Eleanor. "Gunpowder Women of the A.L.A." *California Library Association Bulletin* 1.1 (Sept. 1939): 9–13. Print.

Taylor, Harry. "What Shall My Child Read?" *New Masses* 11 Aug. 1942: 22–24. *The Unz Review*. Web. 22 June 2018.

Taylor, Richard. "Daniel Boone as American Icon: A Literary View." *Register of the Kentucky Historical Society* 102.4 (Autumn 2004): 512–533. *JSTOR*. Web. 30 July 2020.

Titzell, Joseph. "James Daugherty, American." *Publishers Weekly* 116.17 (1929): 2073–2076. *Readers' Guide Retrospective: 1890–1982* (H. W. Wilson). Web. 18 Apr. 2021.

Ulrich, Katharine. "Biographies for Boys and Girls." *Saturday Review of Literature* 18 Nov. 1939: 24. Print.

VanderHaagen, Sara C. *Children's Biographies of African American Women: Rhetoric, Public Memory, and Agency*. Columbia: U of South Carolina P, 2018. Print.

Ward, Lynd. "Biographical Note: James Daugherty." *Newbery Medal Books: 1922–1955, with their Authors' Acceptance Papers & Related Material chiefly from the* Horn Book Magazine. Ed. Bertha Mahony Miller and Elinor Whitney Field. Boston: The Horn Book, 1955. 178–184. Print.

White, Katharine Sergeant Angell. Rev. of *Daniel Boone*, by James Daugherty. *The New Yorker* 25 Nov. 1939: 78. Microform.

White, Stewart Edward. *Daniel Boone: Wilderness Scout*. 1922. Illus. James Daugherty. New York: Garden City Pub., [1926]. Print.

# 6 In the Tradition of Cannibal Talk

## *Call It Courage* (1941)

*Mary K. Bercaw Edwards*

Armstrong Sperry's adventure novel *Call It Courage* (1940; 1941 Newbery Medal) is the story of a South Pacific island boy who faces his fear of the ocean by venturing out on it alone. Stranded on an isolated island after a storm, young Mafatu uses traditional skills to survive as he builds a canoe to carry him home. He escapes from the island just ahead of cannibals who chase after him and returns to his family in triumph. It is the kind of thrilling tale found in the sensational novels that the Newbery establishment disparaged, but Sperry's lush language and lovely illustrations help distinguish his book from that tradition and were two of the prime reasons he won the award.[1] Praised at the time for its wide appeal, read-aloud potential, and "distinguished" design ("Heroic" 76), *Call It Courage* has been translated into many languages, including, in 1965, Samoan.[2] For American readers, the novel's South Pacific setting may have contributed to its appeal given that World War II was fought, in part, in the Pacific.[3] But the book's popularity waned toward the end of the twentieth century, as questions of cultural appropriation—and distortion—arose.

As an ethnographer in the South Pacific in the early 1920s, Sperry was steeped in South Pacific myths and legends and in the rhetorical practice of descriptive, observational writing. Having read Herman Melville, Robert Louis Stevenson, and Jack London as a child, Sperry was immersed in South Pacific literature and lore, which is characterized by exaggeration and the blurring of fact and fiction. Under the influence of these traditions, he rhetorically frames *Call It Courage* as a myth, though it is not an authentic legend, and he casts his 1941 Newbery acceptance speech as truth, though it, too, is a self-created story. This essay examines the cultural work the book performs—work echoed by Sperry's subsequent Newbery acceptance speech—and highlights the way the truth claims of both the novel and speech obscure that work.

Though it is presented as a retelling of a traditional tale, *Call It Courage* is informed more by the Western literary canon than by indigenous legends. More specifically, the novel is part of a long trajectory of cannibal talk that stretches from *The Histories of Herodotus* (circa

DOI: 10.4324/9780367337223-6-7

440 BCE), a foundational text in Western literature, forward to Disney's widely popular animated feature *Moana* (2016). This essay unearths the underpinnings of cannibal talk in *Call It Courage*, comparing the novel's style and moral stance to those of its literary forebears, and follows its influence forward into more recent youth literature and media.

## South Pacific Travels and the Making of a Myth

Armstrong Sperry's life-long interest in the sea was inspired by the tales of his mariner great-grandfather, Captain Sereno Armstrong. Born in New Haven, Connecticut in 1892, the younger Sperry showed early talent as an artist. He studied at the Art Students League of New York intermittently between 1915 and 1923 and also briefly attended the Yale School of Art. On his first voyage to the South Pacific, between October 1920 and May 1921, Sperry sketched during stops in Tahiti, Raiatea, Bora Bora, New Zealand, Australia, the Fiji Islands, and Hawai'i (Burns). The paintings that resulted were exhibited at the Art Centre in New York and reviewed in the *New York Times* ("Art"); they also served as inspiration for his later illustrations in *Call It Courage*.

The book's artwork—which includes woodcut-style illustrations and a first-edition binding made to resemble tapa, the cloth made from soaking and pounding bark—is one of the most beloved elements of the novel and may have helped it to secure the Newbery, as more than half the award winners between 1938 and 1952 were self-illustrated.

Sperry returned from his first journey with more than an art portfolio: he had also learned to speak Tahitian "fairly well" (qtd. in Krauss 84). This newly acquired skill led directly to his second South Pacific voyage, further inspiration for *Call It Courage*. Through a relative, Sperry was introduced to Kenneth Emory, an important early Pacific ethnographer. Emory spoke Hawaiian and wished to learn Tahitian, so the two men "exchanged lessons," fueling each other's "enthusiasm" to "return among the islands" (qtd. in Krauss 84). Their dream to travel together came true when both joined the 1924 *Kaimiloa* Expedition. Organized by the American businessman Medford R. Kellum and the Bernice Pauahi Bishop Museum in Honolulu, this scientific expedition to the remote islands of the South Pacific included a zoologist, botanist, and ethnographer as well as an assistant for each. Emory was appointed ethnographer; as assistant, he selected Sperry. They sailed aboard a four-masted cargo schooner that had been converted to a luxury yacht and renamed the *Kaimiloa*, or "long search." The vessel was outfitted to carry the Kellum family, several guests, and the six scientists on a three-year voyage.[4] Shortly after departure from Honolulu on 9 November 1924, however, the relationship between Kellum and the scientists, including Emory and Sperry, grew fraught. Kellum was uninterested in the islands the scientists wanted to visit and impatient with their work

*Figure 6.1* Mafatu alone in a vast sea.

Source: *Call It Courage*, written and illustrated by Armstrong Sperry (Macmillan Publishing Company, 1940), page 25.

ashore. Soon he barely spoke to them. By the end of 1924, the situation was untenable. The scientists disembarked at Papeete, Tahiti, on 1 January 1925, less than two months after the voyage began.

The excitement generated by the *Kaimiloa* Expedition, its extensive media coverage (Gill; White), and the fact that even today, nearly a century later, it has a place of honor on the Bishop Museum Wikipedia page and the Tahitian Historical Society website seem disproportional to its less than two months' duration. Yet it mirrors the extravagance and intrigue of the expedition's aims. The ethnographic work engendered in Sperry an abiding interest in Polynesian legend. Emory believed, correctly, that many ancient songs, myths, and genealogies were being lost under colonial French rule, which introduced European diseases and effected the conversion of much of the population to Christianity. During their two months on the *Kaimiloa* and in the five months in French Polynesia that followed, Emory and Sperry recorded songs and myths on wax cylinders and primitive movie film, now preserved in the Bishop Museum.

In line with other novelists writing about the South Pacific, Sperry spun mythic tales about his travels. His 1941 Newbery acceptance speech provides one example. In his remarks, Sperry credits his time in French Polynesia, especially Bora Bora, as his inspiration for *Call It Courage*, but he muddies the facts.[5] During his 1925 visit, Sperry was on Bora Bora a total of seventeen days (Krauss 124, 131),[6] which he lengthens to "almost a year" ("Acceptance" 206). He tells a vivid story of coming alone to Bora Bora aboard a copra schooner, the *Tiaré Taporo*, in July of 1925 ("Acceptance" 200), but we know that Sperry was not alone nor was he in Bora Bora at that time. Moreover, Sperry claims he lived ashore with Opu Nui, "the Tavana Rahi, the Great Chief of Bora Bora" ("Acceptance" 201), although there is no evidence that such a man existed. Yet critics have relied unquestioningly on Sperry's Newbery acceptance speech, accepting it as literally true.[7] It is only Clive Barnes who calls the story "almost certainly apocryphal" (135).[8]

Barnes is right to be skeptical, for exaggeration and the intertwining of fiction and reality are common to those who write about the South Pacific and especially to those Sperry names in the speech: Melville, Stevenson, and London. In places, Sperry seems to be borrowing directly from these literary forebears, as in "The Charge of the Tiger Shark," a story published shortly after his 1926 return to New York from Tahiti. It begins like a straightforward account of Sperry's experiences: in November 1924, he states, "the Bishop Museum of Honolulu invited me to join an expedition to the South Seas" ("Tiger Shark"). It transforms, however, into a grisly tale of friendship where fact and fiction meld. Sperry describes how he is fishing with a Tahitian companion, Terii, when their canoe is capsized by a tiger shark.[9] Terii swims in front of Sperry to save his friend's life. Only after both men are pulled from the water by other fishermen does Sperry realize what has happened: "Terii, my friend Terii, who had put himself between me and death, lay at my feet in a pool of blood on the floor of the canoe. I saw the [sic] both his hands were gone at the wrists" ("Tiger Shark"). Sperry constructs the story as if it actually happened to him, but it is instead a borrowing from London's "The Heathen" (1910).[10] Also a tale of friendship, "The Heathen" ends with the Tahitian Otoo thrusting himself between his friend Charley and a shark. "The next instant he broke surface," Charley narrates: "Both hands were off at the wrist, the stumps spouting blood" ("Heathen" 1517). In borrowing from London, Sperry may have sought to depict the kind of adventure he "knew" (from his readings) to be typical of the South Pacific.

South Seas writers also share in common with contemporary ethnographers a longing for stasis. In his 1941 Newbery speech, Sperry states that the people of Bora Bora have become degenerate since his first visit. The culprit is the vanilla bean. Driven by Prohibition in the United States, the demand for the island's vanilla as a flavoring for soda skyrocketed in the 1920s.[11] Sperry claims that the other Tahitian islands suffered a blight from which Bora Bora was spared, creating great wealth for the islanders. He deplores this wealth and the crime it engenders. But then Bora Bora is hit by a destructive hurricane and the islanders recover their old ways. "The people of Bora Bora had won a great victory," Sperry observes, "a victory not so much over elemental disaster as a personal victory over themselves" ("Acceptance" 206). By emphasizing self-transformation, Sperry's interpretation echoes the narrative arc of *Call It Courage*, where Mafatu vanquishes his fears and emerges as a hero. But there is another, unspoken message here: the islanders have strayed from an Edenic state, and their return to that state is desirable. Sperry gives expression to the Western fantasy of "unspoiled" exotic spaces and peoples.[12] His statement also exemplifies the way Sperry bends the truth about events and his own proximity to them. The dramatic narrative of a blight destroying the vanilla crop everywhere in the Tahitian islands except Bora Bora seems to be fictional; vanilla production waxed throughout French Polynesia until 1929. A terrible cyclone did strike the Tahitian islands on 31 December 1925, and Bora Bora was especially hard hit (d'Aubert and Nunn). But Sperry was long gone, having left the island on 6 April and departed Tahiti for New York on 2 June 1925.

The event "just missed"—not observed, but confidently reported—is a staple of these travel narratives and particularly so where cannibalism is concerned. In a mixture of unsubstantiated hearsay and minute detail, Stevenson writes of an event that occurred in the Marquesas "two or three years ago" when the body of a "wretch who had offended" the islanders "was accordingly divided; and every man retired to his own house to consummate the rite in secret, carrying his proportion of the dreadful meat in a Swedish match-box" (101). Stevenson narrates this story as fact but he did not observe it; instead, as with so many accounts of South Pacific cannibalism, it supposedly occurred just before he arrived. As with the Edenic fantasy that underlies Sperry's account of Bora Bora, writers' (and readers') investment in cannibal stories speaks to Westerners' assumptions about the South Pacific and the role they need the Other to fulfill. These desires and presuppositions have been cultivated by a long ethnographic and literary tradition.

## *Call It Courage* and Cannibal Talk

Sperry sets *Call It Courage* on Hikueru, a coral atoll in the Tuamotu islands, not Bora Bora, the island he so often referred to as the source of his inspiration. Because of their remote location in the very center of the South Pacific Ocean, roughly 1,400 miles south of the Equator, the Tuamotus were far less visited than other South Pacific island groups. Emory and Sperry had hoped to go to the Tuamotus to record oral histories and ancient lore, first as a part of the *Kaimiloa* Expedition and later on their own, but never succeeded. Yet Sperry claims that *Call It Courage* is based on Hikueru lore; his ethnographic desire unfulfilled, he "visits" the island narratively in his fiction.

Sperry presents his novel as a retelling of a folk story he calls "Mafatu, the Boy Who Was Afraid."[13] By opening with a narrative device that mirrors those used in the legends narrated to Emory and Sperry, *Call It Courage* makes a claim of authenticity: "It happened many years ago, before the traders and missionaries first came into the South Seas, while the Polynesians were still great in numbers and fierce of heart. But even today the people of Hikueru sing this story in their chants and tell it over the evening fires" (7). In the story, when Mafatu was three, he and his mother were swept out to sea clinging to the mast of their capsized canoe. Encircled by sharks, they barely made it to a coral outcropping, where Mafatu's mother died. Ever since, Mafatu has been afraid of the sea. Taunted by peers for his lack of courage, Mafatu, now fifteen, sails off to an unknown island with only his dog and an albatross with deformed feet for company. There he discovers evidence of the dreaded "eaters-of-men." Mafatu acquires courage as he fights and kills a hammerhead shark, wild boar, and octopus, before escaping from the cannibals and returning home.

The story of Mafatu is presented as a Polynesian myth, but just beneath the surface is something very familiar: projections of its Western author's knowledge, beliefs, and judgments. Mafatu's perception of the idol he encounters on the far side of the island, for example, is oddly monotheistic: "on top of this pyramid [Mafatu saw] a grotesque idol, hideously ugly"; he "felt that he was stifling. His heart pounded. A *marae*—a Sacred Place" (46). A boy raised on Hikueru would hardly have been disconcerted by such sights; marae and idols were common throughout the Tuamotus. Later, when the eaters-of-men return to the marae, Mafatu describes them with the Western term "savages" (82).

His attitude toward the ocean is also oddly Western. Mafatu's goal is to conquer the sea, whose ocean currents he views as "mysterious" (21). But as a child of maritime people who navigated from island to island, ancestral knowledge of the waters was his birthright: "the *Ara Moana*, Paths of the Sea, as the Ancients called them ... were the ocean currents that had carried the Polynesian navigators from island to island in the childhood of the world" (21–22). A myth of Polynesia may be speaking to us, but it is in a Western voice. And that Western perspective points toward the book's imperialist underpinnings. As Barnes has argued, Sperry perpetuates "outmoded imperialist, ethnocentric, and/or masculinist attitudes.... *Call It Courage* is a regenerated imperial Robinsonade [a survival tale on the model of Defoe] in the guise of a traditional indigenous tale" (Barnes 120–121).

This Western perspective is further demonstrated by the way *Call It Courage* fits into a long literary tradition of cannibal talk.[14] Until the fifteenth century, eaters of human flesh were called "anthropophagi," a term derived from ancient Greek, and conceptualized as exotic Others, beyond the boundaries of the known world. Drawing on this framework, European explorers brought back from their travels tales of anthropophagi, as well as people with faces in the middle of their stomachs, men with dogs' heads, and Amazons. The word *cannibal*, coined in the fifteenth century, derives from the Spanish pronunciation of Carib, the Native people Christopher Columbus encountered on his 1492 voyage. By the time Columbus sailed, the ancient Roman and Greek texts that helped to shape the Renaissance, including natural histories that mentioned human oddities, had been invested with an aura of unquestionable authority; Columbus and his contemporaries were therefore primed to find anthropophagi in the spaces to which they traveled. Columbus first met the Arawak, whom he deemed gentle and peaceful, and from them heard of the Carib, their enemies. The Arawak depiction of their rivals, as interpreted by Columbus, sounds Greco-Roman: "far from there were men with one eye, and others with dogs' noses who ate men, and ... when they took a man, they cut off his head and drank his blood and castrated him" (Columbus 52). Had Columbus encountered the Carib first, he might have viewed the Arawak as savage and inhuman. Yet with remarkable tenacity, Columbus's portrayal of the Carib as fierce and heartless flesh-eaters has lasted for over five hundred years, as seen, for example, at the beginning of the feature film *Pirates of the Caribbean: Dead Man's Chest* (2006), in which Johnny Depp is about to be eaten by Caribs.

In part as a means to justify violence against the racial and ethnic Others encountered, Westerners described the Native people they met as "cannibals"—savages who violated central norms of humanity. Cannibalism, like incest or necrophilia, is the boundary beyond which we cannot stray and remain fully human. Those who do eat people are monstrous: animals, savages, witches, non-humans. The term "cannibal" has been applied to almost all peoples at one time or another. As the borders of the world known to Europeans were pushed back, the identification of the anthropophagi, or man-eaters, changed. What remains consistent is that those labeled cannibals were on the fringes of the world known to those doing the labeling. In the mid-nineteenth century, the accusation of cannibalism was centered in the South Pacific; today it centers on the island of New Guinea. Early European explorers expected to find cannibals in the South Pacific, and they were simultaneously attracted to and repelled by that notion—as were the readers of their narratives. The discourse of cannibalism that pervaded both accounts of early contact and later writing, whether fiction or nonfiction, is consistently exaggerated. For one human being to eat another is so unthinkable and repulsive that the talk about it must be extravagant. Absurdity, black humor, intimations that something is too horrible to describe, and an atmosphere of foreboding are characteristic.

## Horror and Morality in the Cannibal Encounter

Sperry absorbed the literary tradition of cannibalism from his childhood reading of Melville and the "South Sea stories of Stevenson and Jack London" ("Acceptance" 199), works that foreground the fear of eaters-of-men. In *Call It Courage*, Sperry evokes this fear much as Melville does in *Typee* (1846), the fictional story of Tommo, an American sailor who deserts his whaleship and lives among the cannibals of Nuku Hiva in the Marquesas Islands. Both Melville and Sperry use intense sensory experiences to convey their protagonists' fear and horror. In *Typee*, the dread of being eaten culminates towards the end of the book when Tommo's "eyes fell upon the disordered members of a human skeleton, the bones still fresh with moisture, and with particles of flesh clinging to them here and there! ... All that night I lay awake" (*Typee* 238). Tommo never actually witnesses cannibalism, but his mind is so suffused with its horrors that just the sight of a dead enemy soldier is enough to terrify him. Likewise, Mafatu is terrified by the mere sight of a dark island in the distance—one that might potentially be inhabited by "savage tribes" (40).

In nineteenth-century travel narratives, in the fictional works modeled on them, and in Sperry, for whom they were source texts, the people who inhabit these dark islands are so dehumanized that they become caricatures. All of these works traffic in the kind of intense fear elicited by horror films and stories—often using similar techniques to achieve their effects.[15] In *Typee*, for example, Mow-Mow functions like a horror film character. Tommo feels Mow-Mow's presence before he sees him, adding to the dread of the situation. Tommo is being pressed backwards by his companion "when I felt a heavy hand laid upon my shoulder, and turning round, encountered the bulky form of Mow-Mow, a one-eyed chief" (*Typee* 236). He appears like a specter, a felt presence, before Tommo is presented with the horror of his corporeal being. Similarly, in *Call It Courage*, ominous sights and sounds lead up to the final encounter. In these texts and their predecessors, the tension that arises has racist undertones. Before he sees the eaters-of-men, Mafatu comes upon the place where they worship, topped by a massive idol surrounded by bones "too large for dogs, too large for pigs" (46). When Mafatu realizes that they are human bones, his "heart congealed" (46). Later, it is primarily sound that triggers a sensation of horror. He is awakened before dawn by the terrifying sound of drums: "Thump—thump THUMP! Thump—thump THUMP!" (79). The noise renders him immobile: "He crouched there listening, unable for the moment to make a single movement" (80). When the eaters-of-men come into his vision, they look as savage as he had imagined: "figures as black as night's own face, darting, shifting, bounding toward the sky" (82). Even upon sight, they are not fully human but faceless, black figures with zigzags of paint streaking their bodies (82). It is these figures' blackness—a contrast to the lighter brown skin of Mafatu and his kinsmen—that most specifically associates them with cannibals (Barnes 130).

The identity of the cannibals in *Call It Courage* is never revealed, but contextual cues suggest they are from Fiji. Throughout the early nineteenth century, the words *cannibal* and *Fiji* were coupled and associated with blackness. As one example among many, an 1848 article on the Irish famine published in *Littell's Living Age* discusses being driven by deep hunger to survival cannibalism, then adds: "Such a man, placed in a position where the only food was human flesh, would have made his experiment a habit, and would have enjoyed his cannibal meals with as much relish as a chief of the Feejee Islands" (G. A. H.).[16] Melville, too, equates Fijians with cannibalism throughout *Moby-Dick* (1851), for example describing the killer whale as "very savage—a sort of Feegee fish" (143). Sperry had visited Fiji on his first trip to the South Pacific, and while the dark islands of the eaters-of-men in *Call It Courage* do not correlate with any specific archipelago, the inhabitants' darker skin, described by Sperry as "black," suggests Fiji.[17] So, too, does the landscape. Both Fiji and the dark islands of the eaters-of-men are tall and mountainous. Moreover, Sperry calls his fictionalized version of Fiji "Smoking Islands" (40). The smoky quality of the islands may be a result of rain clouds that (as on Fiji) encircle their mountain peaks, but the term also suggests human sacrifice and the fires of Hell. By contrast, Mafatu's native Hikueru is a coral atoll, low, flat, covered with white sand, and bathed in sunlight. On dark, rain-shrouded islands, blood sacrifice and the consumption of human flesh seem more plausible than on sun-soaked coral. The fear of cannibalism is most readily evoked by the juxtaposition of dark islands and dark-skinned men.

In South Seas stories, encounters with the cannibal Other often reveal the subject's own violence. This involves a second type of horror: not the heart-pounding cinematic kind, but a moral repulsion that can lead to a questioning of values and assumptions. In the dramatic climaxes of both *Typee* and *Call It Courage*, the protagonist is moved to violence, though Sperry ultimately forecloses the difficult moral questions Melville raises in *Typee*.

In their conclusions, Sperry and Melville make strikingly similar use of the hair's-breadth escape plot device. Both Mafatu and Tommo flee in small boats pursued by cannibals. Mafatu leaps into his canoe, followed closely by "the eaters-of-men ... with death in their hearts" (86). When the cannibals close in, Mafatu commits an act of violence upon them. "Now [the eaters-of-men] were swimming. One of them, in the lead, reached to lay hold of the outrigger. His black hand clutched the *purau* pole. The canoe slacked. Mafatu could see the gleam of bared teeth. The boy lifted the paddle and cracked it down" (84). In *Typee*, Tommo inflicts a more appalling and visceral violence on his pursuers: "Even at the moment I felt horror at the act I was about to commit; but it was no time for pity or compunction, and with a true aim, and exerting all my strength, I dashed the boat-hook at [Mow-Mow]. It struck him just below the throat, and forced him downwards" (*Typee* 252). Unlike Mafatu, who is presented as courageously responding to his pursuers' aggression, Tommo feels momentary "horror" at his own actions.

At the same time, Melville's narrative justifies Tommo's violence by dehumanizing Mow-Mow, the man he attacks. Mow-Mow's cheek, Melville tells us, "had been pierced by the point of a spear, and the wound imparted a still more frightful expression to his hideously tattooed face, already deformed by the loss of an eye" (*Typee* 236). Melville depicts Mow-Mow's face as a caricature that is almost unrecognizable as human. Tommo's perception of Mow-Mow's lack of humanity allows him to commit such violence against him. But there is also a dark humor in the horror associated with Mow-Mow's face. Mow-Mow's dreadfulness is over the top: not only does he have only one eye, his face is also "hideously tattooed" and to top it off his cheek has been impaled by a spear (236). Unlike Melville, Sperry treats the danger of the eaters-of-men with total seriousness. They are pure evil. There is no possibility of humor in their portrayal and no moral condemnation of Mafatu's response to them.

Tommo's and Mafatu's dramatic, violent escapes point toward a shared device in Sperry's and Melville's novels: that of inviting readers to define existential concepts. In *Call It Courage*, Sperry conflates Mafatu's escape with courage. One of the subtexts of the work, as made explicit in its title, is Sperry's asking the reader to define courage. Melville, too, subtextually requests a definition, but his is that of savagery. Tommo's violence against Mow-Mow and his companions' subsequent mauling of the islander's wrists raise questions: Who is the greater savage? How do we define savagery—and by extension, cannibalism? Ishmael, the narrator of *Moby-Dick*, decouples cannibalism from race when he asks: "Cannibals? who is not a cannibal?" (300). Sperry, however, does not interrogate savagery. Tommo "felt horror at the act" of violence he commits on Mow-Mow (*Typee* 252), but Mafatu feels no such qualms. *Call It Courage*, unlike Melville's writing, is aimed at children and therefore shuns moral ambiguity. But Sperry's moral stance may have as much to do with his historical moment as with his intended audience. Mafatu's character, a young man who acquires courage and perceives the world as starkly divided between good and evil, resonated in 1940 on the eve of the United States's entry into World War II, when so many young people left to fight the very embodiment of evil in Hitler and the Nazis. In this context, Sperry's narrative arc—in which Mafatu goes from being weak and afraid to becoming fierce, brave, and "manly"—made for a most timely take on cannibal talk.

## Sperry's Posterity: Cannibals for Kids

The tradition of cannibal talk in which *Call It Courage* participates extends not only backward but also forward to more recent books and films for children. In Maurice Sendak's *Where the Wild Things Are* (1963), Max is sent to bed when he tells his mother he'll eat her up. Later, it is Sendak's titular beasts who want to "eat" the protagonist "up." Max's violent impulses are thus externalized—much as Westerners externalize their own violence by claiming that the non-Western Others whom they encounter are the violent ones. Sendak's wild things were inspired by his relatives who had escaped the Holocaust: "they were unkempt. Their teeth were horrifying.... And they'd pick you up and hug you and kiss you. 'Aggghh. Oh, we could eat you up,' they'd say. And we knew they would eat anything. Anything" ("Yiddish"). By making the figurative expression "we could eat you up" literal, Sendak humorously turns doting relatives into beasts. Max tames the wild things, symbolically taming his strong emotions in the process. At the same time, the adult Sendak may be grappling with his own childhood cruelty: as a boy, he laughed at the refugee relatives whose foreignness made them into "wild things" ("Yiddish").

Sendak loved Melville's works. I have long argued that *Where the Wild Things Are* is a retelling of Melville's *Typee*. Similar to Max, Tommo enters a fraught Eden, where the joyful present is underlaid with the fear of cannibalism. When Tommo stumbles upon evidence of cannibalism and wants to leave, the Typees attempt to prevent his departure. Sendak's words ring true: "Oh please don't go—we'll eat you up—we love you so!" (31).

While Sendak set *Where the Wild Things Are* in a geographically nonspecific fantasy world, other works for children took up the themes of *Call It Courage* within a South Pacific setting. Eight years after Sperry's novel, Astrid Lindgren completed her Pippi Longstocking trilogy with *Pippi in the South Seas* (published in Sweden in 1948, in the United Kingdom in 1957, and in the United States in 1959). The novel is founded on imperialist logic, with Pippi's father becoming king of a South Pacific island. In the 1959 American edition, as in the original Swedish, Pippi's father rules over "Kurrekurredutt Island," whose inhabitants are called "Kurrekurredutts," an untranslatable nonsense word (59, 70).[18] Though there is no reference to cannibalism in Lindgren's original text, the idea was introduced by the 1957 UK translation, which calls the isle "Canny Canny Island" and its inhabitants "Canny Cannibals" (Lindgren [2002] 58, 60).[19] For British translator Marianne Turner (Berry 133), the South Seas setting seems to have conjured up cannibals even though none are present in Lindgren's Swedish text.

Most recently, the cannibal trope has been revived and reimagined by Disney's 2016 animated movie *Moana*, which makes an island, rather than its inhabitants, serve as antagonist, while transferring the role of cannibal from human to non-human characters. Like Mafatu in *Call It Courage*, Disney's Moana is the eldest child of a chief. Both protagonists leave the protection of their home islands, cross the reef, and set out across the ocean: Mafatu to find courage and Moana to find the heart of Te Fiti, the Creator of Life, in order to save her people from ecological disaster. Both succeed and return in triumph. But the novel and the animated feature have very different takes on Polynesian mythology. The word "Moana," which the Disney film co-opts for its female lead, translates as ocean, so perhaps it's not surprising that the name appears in so many stories set in the South Pacific. In *Pippi in the South Seas*, for instance, a "pretty little girl called Moana" becomes Pippi's friend on the island of Kurrekurredutt (Lindgren [1959] 76). Unlike the Moanas imagined by Disney and Lindgren—young, female, and human—Sperry's Moana is male and malicious. Moana is the "Sea God" (9) who killed Mafatu's mother: "The boy seemed to hear Moana saying: 'Someday, someday, Mafatu, I will claim you'" (48). At the novel's end, however, Mafatu has triumphed over both the god Moana and his own fear of the sea (92–93).

In *Call It Courage*, the god Moana is set in contrast to Maui, the "God of the Fishermen" (24), who serves as Mafatu's protector. The film *Moana* diverges from Sperry's book in making Maui a trickster. Sperry and Disney draw on competing Polynesian traditions: in Tahitian mythology, Maui is a wise man or prophet, whereas in Maori mythology, he is a trickster. Unlike Sperry's Sea God, Disney's trickster Maui is not a fearsome enemy but a companion to the young protagonist. Together,

Moana and Maui tame the wrath of the volcanic island Te Ka. Significantly, the danger that centers on dark, smoking islands in both *Call It Courage* and *Moana* has shifted from a human threat—Mafatu has been taught to fear the "Smoking Islands," the "dark islands of the eaters-of-men" (40)—to a geographical one: in *Moana*, it is the island itself that is dangerous. Awareness and sensibilities had changed a great deal in the seventy-five years between Sperry's novel and *Moana*, and the shift to Te Ka as antagonist seems a way to avoid the racial stereotypes surrounding the dark eaters-of-men in *Call It Courage*.

In the made-for-television film "Call It Courage" (1973), directed and produced by Roy Disney, Sperry's eaters-of-men are dubbed *Maoka*, a Tahitian word meaning "sufficiently baked, cooked" (Andrews and Andrews 79). The term eaters-of-men is never used; they are now headhunters.[20] By the 2016 film *Moana*, cannibals have evolved into anthropomorphized coconuts called Kakamora.[21] Such villains suggest a comic reversal, as it is humans who eat coconuts. Modern-day sensibilities preclude the depiction of human cannibals—at least for children—so Disney has made coconuts and the island of Te Ka into "cannibalistic" figures. Such displacement answers the critiques leveled at *Pippi in the South Seas*—not to mention the biases implicit in *Call It Courage*.

In *Call It Courage*, Sperry tells a story that is transcendent and eternal: that of a boy's acquisition of courage. Indeed, the text feels deeply familiar (and perhaps even formulaic) because it draws on so many Anglo-American literary influences, including Melville, Stevenson, and London. This familiarity may well have been an attraction for the Newbery committee gathered in the shadow of world war. Moreover, the novel's connection to canonical authors renders it a kind of "junior" classic, conferring prestige on both the text and the body of midcentury American children's literature. But that deep connection to literary forebears comes at a cost. *Call It Courage* emerges from a long, fraught tradition of cannibal talk—and from a history of ethnography that, however well intentioned, was part of colonialism's machinery. Sperry's work as an ethnographer in the early twentieth century presupposes his construction of characters as "primitives" who, in their stark Otherness, may engage in cannibalism.[22] Given this, *Call It Courage* cannot escape the wrenching questions its context raises: questions of identity, power, race, and violence towards those who are different from us.

## Notes

1 Numerous reviewers and critics mention Sperry's language and illustrations (Patee 590; Follett 2464; Miller and Field 193; McGrath 723).

2 Sperry wrote that of all the translations, the one "that has pleased me most has been Samoan. For then it seemed that Mafatu, who had paddled his

canoe around the world so to speak, had returned at last to Polynesia where he belonged. The circle was complete" (Letter to Haviland).

3 In 1942, the US would establish a naval base and fueling station on Bora Bora, the island that Sperry claims "had a definite part to play in the making of" *Call It Courage* ("Acceptance" 199).

4 The author has a personal, if distant, connection to the story as she became acquainted with Medford Kellum, Jr. and his wife, the former Gladys Laughlin, decades after the *Kaimiloa* expedition when, at age sixteen, she and her family began a 3-1/2-year circumnavigation of the globe aboard a thirty-eight-foot sail boat. They visited the island of Moorea, sixteen miles west of Tahiti, where they anchored off the home of the Kellums, then an elderly couple. (When anchored at Bora Bora in 1972, the author also witnessed the filming of *Call It Courage* for Disney's made-for-TV movie.)

5 Sperry visited the island, located 170 miles northwest of Tahiti, twice, first at some point during his 1920–1921 sketching excursion and later when he traveled there with Emory.

6 He arrived in Bora Bora on 12 March and departed on 6 April 1925, but he spent the eight days from 17–25 March on the tiny island of Maupiti.

7 See Patee, Montgomery, Miller and Field, Barrett, Bostrom, and op de Beeck.

8 This chapter and Barnes's essay were in development simultaneously.

9 Here the story plays liberally with the facts. Sperry did know a man by the name of Terii, but he was an acquaintance met on Bora Bora, not a close friend on Tahiti (Krauss 126). And while Sperry asserts that Terii vacated his home so that Sperry would have a place to stay, Sperry actually lodged at a rooming house with Emory (Krauss 117).

10 Kellum's descendants claim that Kellum "became immortalized" in "The Charge of the Tiger Shark," which "was based on Sperry's experiences as a member of the *Kaimiloa* crew" (Guma-Diaz).

11 There was an "upward surge" in the price of vanilla in 1924 (Thompson and Adloff 128). Vanilla growers "have been through a boom and bust cycle of production, which at times offered the islands excellent revenues" (Ecott 169).

12 To a great extent, the feeling of a lost Eden stems from the Western voyager's own subjective experience, as Stevenson states in a passage that Sperry quotes (or rather misquotes) in his 1926 *New York Herald Tribune* article about Bora Bora and Prohibition ("Volstead" 8). "The first experience can never be repeated," Stevenson says at the beginning of *In the South Seas* (1896), his account of his voyage through the South Pacific on the 95-foot schooner *Casco*: "The first love, the first sunrise, the first South Sea island, are memories apart, and touched a virginity of sense" (Stevenson 2).

13 "Mafatu" translates as "heart (of men only)"; the *fatu* translates as "core" or "pip," which is appropriate for a young boy (Andrews and Andrews 74).

14 See Arens, Barker et al., and Obeyesekere.

15 These same techniques have an earlier history in adventure stories like Defoe's *Robinson Crusoe* (1719) and such ephemeral pieces as dime novels and comics. The influence of *Crusoe* on *Call It Courage* is obvious: both detail the means by which a lone protagonist survives on an island and both involve the discovery that the far side of that island is the site of unspeakable cannibal rites (Defoe 152; Sperry 46).

16 Another example of the coupling of cannibal with Fiji occurs in Mary Wallis's narrative *Life in Feejee: Five Years Among the Cannibals* (1851). Wallis, the wife of an island trader, never actually witnesses cannibalism, but she earnestly believes it to exist, especially in Fiji. In the early nineteenth-century imagination, Fiji is the central location of cannibalism. Wallis's

narrative purports to be true, but it is riddled with the extravagant language of cannibal talk.

17 The geography is not exact. Sperry places the island of the eaters-of-men south and west of Hikueru whereas Fiji is west, but not south, of the Tuamotus; moreover, at a distance of over 2,800 miles, it would have been much too far for Mafatu to paddle.

18 My thanks to Göran Buckhorn, former editor of *Mystic Seaport Magazine* and a native Swedish speaker, for answering questions about the translation of "Kurrekurredutt."

19 When Puffin published the Pippi trilogy in paperback in the 1970s, editor Kaye Webb questioned the appropriateness of the cannibal references in the UK translation, but no changes were made. In 1990, Oxford University Press proposed "some 'tasteful' editing" to suit modern sensibilities, but Lindgren refused. After the author's death in 2002, her literary estate authorized updates to the UK translation, which now refers to "natives" rather than "cannibals" (Berry 137–139).

20 *Call It Courage* was filmed on location on Tahiti and Bora Bora in 1972, incorporating indigenous languages and local actors. In this regard, it echoes the filming of the 1961 Newbery Medal winner *Island of the Blue Dolphins*, produced by Universal Pictures in 1964. Both Sperry's and Scott O'Dell's stories, which draw on field work conducted by anthropologists, bear markers of the ethnographic gaze. See Schwebel 55–63.

21 Doug Herman, Senior Geographer at the National Museum of the American Indian, points out that "in fact, the Kakamora have actual cultural roots: they are a legendary, short-statured people of the Solomon Islands" (Herman).

22 Michael A. Elliott traces the intersections between ethnographic writing and mid-nineteenth-century literature, using Melville's *Typee* as case study (492).

## Works Cited

Andrews, Edmund, and Irene D. Andrews. *A Comparative Dictionary of the Tahitian Language*. Chicago: The Chicago Academy of Sciences, 1944. Print.

Arens, William. *The Man-Eating Myth: Anthropology and Anthropophagy*. New York: Oxford UP, 1979. Print.

"Art: The December Exhibitions." *New York Times* 18 Dec. 1921: 79. Print.

Barker, Francis, Peter Hulme, and Margaret Iversen, eds. *Cannibalism and the Colonial World*. Cambridge: Cambridge UP, 1998. Print.

Barnes, Clive. "*Call It Courage* and the Survival of the Imperial Robinsonade." *Didactics and the Modern Robinsonade: New Paradigms for Young Readers*. Ed. Ian Kinane. Liverpool: Liverpool UP, 2019. 119–138. Print.

Barrett, Robert R. "To Bora-Bora and Back Again: The Story of Armstrong W. Sperry." *Burroughs Bulletin* 11 NS (July 1992): 3–8. *Armstrong Sperry*, 3 April 2009. Web. 30 July 2020.

Berry, Charlotte. "Pippi and the Dreaming Spires: Nordic Children's Literature and Oxford University Press." *True North: Literary Translation in the Nordic Countries*. Ed. B. J. Epstein. Newcastle Upon Tyne: Cambridge Scholars Publishing, 2014. 130–148. Print.

Bostrom, Kathleen Long. "1941: Armstrong Sperry." *Winning Authors: Profiles of the Newbery Medalists*. Westport, CT: Greenwood, 2003. 63–65. Print.

Burns, Margo. "The True Biographical Facts." *Armstrong Sperry: Recipient of the Newbery Medal, 1941. Armstrong Sperry*, 3 Apr. 2009. Web. 22 May 2020.

*Call It Courage*. Dir. Roy Disney. Perf. Evan Temarii and Don Ho. Walt Disney Pictures, 1973. DVD.

Columbus, Christopher. *The Journal of Christopher Columbus*. Trans. Cecil Jane. New York: Bramhall House, 1960. Print.

d'Aubert, AnaMaria, and Patrick D. Nunn. *Furious Winds and Parched Islands: Tropical Cylclones (1558–1970) and Droughts (1722–1987) in the Pacific*. Bloomington, IN: Xlibris Corporation, 2012. N. pag. Print.

Defoe, Daniel. *Robinson Crusoe*. 1719. New York: Modern Library, 2001. Print.

Ecott, Tim. *Vanilla: Travels in Search of the Ice Cream Orchid*. New York: Grove Press, 2004. Print.

Elliott, Michael A. "Other Times: Herman Melville, Lewis Henry Morgan, and Ethnographic Writing in the Antebellum United States." *After the Cultural Turn*. Spec. issue of *Criticism* 49.4 (Fall 2007): 481–503. Print.

Follett, Helen. "Armstrong Sperry and his Work." *Publishers Weekly* 139.25 (1941): 2462–2464. *Readers' Guide Retrospective: 1890–1892* (H. W. Wilson). Web. 30 July 2020.

G. A. H. "Article 3." *Littell's Living Age* 19 Feb. 1848: 355. Print.

Gill, Lorin Tarr. "Cruising Among the Polynesian Atolls." *Pacific Motor Boat* (Oct. 1925). Tahitian Historical Society. Web. 17 Jan. 2021.

Guma-Diaz, Marie. "A Famous Spanish Mission-Style House, Owned by the Kellum Family for Nearly Seven Decades, Has Gone on the Market." *Miami Herald* 1 May 2007. Web. 20 Jan. 2019.

Herman, Doug. "How the Story of 'Moana' and Maui Holds Up Against Cultural Truths." *Smithsonian.com*. Smithsonian Institution. 2 Dec. 2016. Web. 20 Jan. 2019.

"Heroic Legend." Rev. of *Call It Courage*, by Armstrong Sperry. *The New York Times* 24 Mar. 1940: 76. Web. 23 May 2020.

Krauss, Bob. *Keneti: South Seas Adventures of Kenneth Emory*. Honolulu: U of Hawaii P, 1988. Print.

Lindgren, Astrid. *Pippi in the South Seas*. Trans. Gerry Bothmer. Illus. Louis S. Glanzman. New York: Viking, 1959. Print.

Lindgren, Astrid. *Pippi in the South Seas*. Trans. Marianne Turner. Illus. Tony Ross. 1957. Oxford: Oxford UP, 2002. Print.

London, Jack. "The Heathen." 1910. *The Complete Short Stories of Jack London*. Vol. 2. Stanford: Stanford UP, 1993. 1501–1518. Print.

McGrath, Joan. "Sperry, Armstrong." *Twentieth-Century Children's Writers*. 2nd ed. Ed. D. L. Kirkpatrick. New York: St. Martin's Press, 1983. 722–723. Print.

Melville, Herman. *Moby-Dick*. 1851. *The Writings of Herman Melville*. Vol. 6. Evanston: Northwestern UP, 1988. Print.

Melville, Herman. *Typee*. 1846. *The Writings of Herman Melville*. Vol. 1. Evanston: Northwestern UP, 1968. Print.

Miller, Bertha Mahony, and Elinor Whitney Field. "The Newbery Award 1941." *Newbery Medal Books: 1922–1955, with their Authors' Acceptance Papers & Related Material chiefly from the* Horn Book Magazine. Ed. Bertha Mahony Miller and Elinor Whitney Field. Boston: Horn Book, 1955. 192–207. Print.

*Moana*. Dir. Ron Clements and John Musker. Perf. Auli'i Cravalho, Dwayne Johnson, and Rachel House. Walt Disney Animation Studios, 2016. DVD.

Montgomery, Elizabeth Rider. "The Blessing of the Hurricane: *Call It Courage*—Sperry, 1940." *The Story Behind Modern Books*. New York: Dodd, Mead, & Co., 1949. 136–141. *Armstrong Sperry*, 3 Apr. 2009. Web. 30 July 2020.

Obeyesekere, Gananath. *Cannibal Talk: The Man-Eating Myth and Human Sacrifice in the South Seas*. Berkeley: U of California P, 2005. Print.

op de Beeck, Nathalie. *Suspended Animation: Children's Picture Books and the Fairy Tale of Modernity*. Minneapolis: U of Minnesota P, 2010. Print.

Patee, Doris S. "Armstrong Sperry, 1940 Newbery Winner." *The Library Journal* 66 (July 1941): 589–590. Print.

Schwebel, Sara L., ed. *Island of the Blue Dolphins: The Complete Reader's Edition*. Oakland: U of California P, 2016. Print.

Sendak, Maurice. *Where the Wild Things Are*. 1963. New York: HarperTrophy, 1984. Print.

Sperry, Armstrong. "Acceptance Paper." 1941. *Newbery Medal Books: 1922–1955, with their Authors' Acceptance Papers & Related Material chiefly from the* Horn Book Magazine. Ed. Bertha Mahony Miller and Elinor Whitney Field. Boston: Horn Book, 1955. 199–207. Print.

Sperry, Armstrong. *Call It Courage*. New York: Macmillan, 1940. Print.

Sperry, Armstrong. "The Charge of the Tiger Shark." *The World Magazine* 7 Feb. 1926: 7. *Armstrong Sperry*, n.d. Web. 20 Jan. 2019.

Sperry, Armstrong. "Letter to Virginia Haviland (11 Dec. 1972)." *Armstrong Sperry*, 3 Apr. 2009. Web. 30 Sep. 2019.

Sperry, Armstrong. "What Volstead Did for a South Sea Isle." *New York Herald Tribune Magazine* 28 Mar. 1926: 8–9. Print.

Stevenson, Robert Louis. *In the South Seas*. New York: Charles Scribner's Sons, 1896. Print.

Thompson, Virginia, and Richard Adloff. *The French Pacific Islands*. Berkeley: U of California P, 1971. Print.

White, Tom. "A Modern Motor Adventure Ship." *Motor Boating* 40.4 (Oct. 1927): 38–39, 138, 140, 142. Print.

"The Wild Things were my Yiddish Relatives." *The Jewish Chronicle*. 3 Dec. 2009. Web. 10 June 2020.

# 7 Of Sultans, Studs, and Stable Boys

## Equine and Literary Lineage in *King of the Wind* (1949)

*Megan L. Musgrave*

By the time Marguerite Henry won the Newbery for *King of the Wind* (1948; Newbery Medal 1949), she had already established a reputation as a writer of excellent and popular horse stories for children. She had won accolades for *Justin Morgan Had a Horse* (1945; 1946 Newbery runner-up) and for *Misty of Chincoteague* (1947; 1948 Newbery runner-up). She may have finally earned Newbery gold for her consistent favor among critics and her contributions to the horse story genre as a driver of the children's book market. That influence endures today, as Henry's horse novels continue to be read and marketed in both original and adapted form.[1] The slim body of scholarship on *King of the Wind* previously focused on how the novel fits within Henry's expansive oeuvre; more recently, cultural studies scholar Dawn Heinecken has offered a posthumanist reading of the novel.[2] What has not been explored is the book's relationship to its source text, the 1839 French novel *The Godolphin Arabian* by Eugène Sue. Reading *King of the Wind* against its literary predecessor casts doubt upon the originality of the 1949 Newbery Award winner, raising questions about what Henry's Newbery win means for the history of the award. This essay offers a comparative analysis of the two texts in order to expand understanding of audience and expectations for children's books in the 1940s.

### The Horse and His Boy

*King of the Wind* is the story of a horse called Sham and his bond with Agba, the voiceless Moroccan stable boy who attends him. Born in the stables of a Moroccan sultan, Sham is sent as a gift to the King of France. But Sham does not allow the young king—or anyone but Agba—to ride him easily, so no owner keeps him for long. Sham is first sold off to a carter who cruelly mistreats him, then purchased by a benevolent English Quaker who witnesses this abuse; from there he is transferred to England, sold to an innkeeper, and finally purchased by the Earl of Godolphin, in whose stables he will sire an illustrious line of racing champions. The horse known as the Godolphin Arabian was a legend in

DOI: 10.4324/9780367337223-7-8

the annals of horse breeding long before Henry captured his story for children. The reasons for this are two: first, the facts about the horse's life, as detailed in the horse breeding records Sue used as the basis for his original novel, follow a Romantic storyline in which the horse figures as a Byronic hero complete with mysterious origins, surly attitude, and an ability to threaten the virtue of purebred females (mares, in this case).[3] Second, his legacy is unimpeachable: he is widely acknowledged as one of the three founding sires of what is now known as the Thoroughbred, the primary breed used in the sport of horse racing.[4]

*King of the Wind* opens in 1920, with racing phenomenon Man o' War's last, triumphant race. This dramatic victory sets up the novel proper as an explanation of how the winner's ancestry contributed to his phenomenal success. Just as Man o' War, Seabiscuit, and so many other famous Thoroughbred racehorses are descendants of the Godolphin Arabian known as Sham,[5] critics generally assume that *King of the Wind* and the horse story itself are literary descendants of Anna Sewell's seminal 1877 animal rights novel, *Black Beauty*.[6] Protest literature like *Black Beauty* cultivates empathy in order to inspire reader action. Thus, Sewell condemns animal cruelty by representing working horses as noble, enslaved creatures.[7] Henry similarly denounces cruelty toward animals, and links this critique to a censure of racism, by representing as noble an abused stallion and his ill-treated Moroccan stable boy. However, *Black Beauty* is not, as many critics have assumed, the sole literary progenitor of *King of the Wind*. Sue's *The Godolphin Arabian* precedes *Black Beauty* by more than thirty years, and it employs many of the same tropes for which Sewell's book is notable. A socialist, animal rights activist, and equestrian, Sue emphasizes political themes in a number of his novels; however, *The Godolphin Arabian* is the only one specifically focused on animal rights.[8] Yet Sue's narrative lacks the coherence of Henry's. Perhaps because *The Godolphin Arabian* was initially serialized, its central purpose seems to wander: from denouncing animal cruelty in the beginning, it drifts toward an unexpected capitalist coda that advocates for change in French horse breeding practices in order to produce more winning racehorses.[9]

Setting aside the novels' diverging conclusions, the events of Henry's and Sue's texts are, scene for scene, nearly identical. The similarities are so numerous, in fact, that their differences usefully illuminate the strategies Henry used to adapt this story for young twentieth-century readers. The novels' opening pages differ starkly in tone. Sue's novel opens with the story's most disturbing scene: the moment when the horse is beaten to his knees in a Paris street by his cruel owner. By contrast, Henry frames her novel with Man o' War's 1920 racing triumph, thereby emphasizing victory and connecting Sham's story to recent events: horse racing was a wildly popular mainstream American sport in the 1940s, and Man o' War was a household name. From there, the two texts' narrative structures diverge significantly. Sue's novel is marked by frequent flashbacks and leaps forward in time, all with the effect of amplifying the pathos, suspense, and drama of Scham's story.[10] Henry simplifies the chronology, going back in time to the birth of Man o' War's ancestor Sham, then relating Sham's life story via a straightforward linear narrative. This may suggest the author's belief that young readers would have trouble following a storyline as unpredictable as Sue's. It also reflects her conviction that a connection to present-day popular culture would help young readers feel the story's relevance: if she "could make children understand that this hero of theirs [Man o' War] was a direct descendant of the Godolphin Arabian," Henry knew, "history ... would quicken to life" ("Acceptance" 330).

The most significant alteration in Henry's juvenilization of *The Godolphin Arabian* is the transformation of Agba, who is thirty years old at the outset of Sue's novel, into a child protagonist with whom young readers can identify. Sue's Agba is a flat, underdeveloped character who exists primarily in service to the horse's story.[11] Henry, by contrast, emphasizes the joint coming of age of horse and boy. Through this conjoined origin story, Henry positions readers to sympathize with both the orphaned horse of noble ancestry and the orphaned Moroccan stable boy who is Sham's lifelong caregiver and companion. Agba, the human protagonist with whom Henry invites readers to sympathize, is Other in multiple ways: a child in an adult world; a mute in a society that communicates verbally; a dark-skinned Muslim in a predominantly White, Christian Europe. His distance from Henry's readers—Agba lives in eighteenth-century Morocco and Europe—presents a type of Otherness frequently honored in Newbery's early decades: as Kenneth Kidd has observed, early Newbery committees evinced a predilection for "cultural other[s]" who were "safely removed across time and/or space" (177).

Another significant difference between Sue's text and Henry's concerns the treatment of Islam. Sue's depiction of Agba relies heavily on stereotypes. The French author alludes to Agba's Islamic faith in passing but characterizes him as guided by superstition, whereas Henry illustrates how Islamic practice informs Agba's daily life. Henry's central narrative opens before the horse is born, at the royal stables of Sultan Mulai Ishmael[12] during "the sacred month of Ramadan when, day after day, all faithful Mohammedans neither eat nor drink from before sunrise until the moment after sunset" (19).[13] But the Sultan in whose stables Agba works misinterprets the Islamic law governing this sacred practice: he requires both his human and his animal subjects to fast during Ramadan.[14] In this way, Henry suggests that the Sultan's interpretation of the law is extreme and misinformed, but it also provides the catalyst for her story. When the fasting mare dies after giving birth, newborn Sham is orphaned, and Agba is positioned to become a parent to the foal just as readers are positioned to lay the blame for the death of his mother at the despotic Sultan's feet.

Sue does not detail Agba's religious practice, so that Agba's prevailing characteristic—his superstitiousness—is conflated for the reader with Islam.[15] Henry, on the other hand, uses Agba's religion as an opportunity to introduce readers to some of the basic practices of Islam in a respectful and informative manner, in keeping with the Newbery's educational mission (Kidd 174). After Sham's mother dies, Agba discovers that he can keep the foal alive by feeding it camel's milk and honey. Agba marks the occasion by offering a prayer of thanksgiving, "carefully spreading his mantle to kneel on, and facing the eastern sky that showed itself through the round window at the back of the stall. After touching his head to the mantle, he formed the words with his lips, 'Allhouakibar! God most great!' Then he rose, stretched his arms upward, his palms to the heavens, and made his own private prayer for Sham's welfare" (42). Henry presents the ritual in an abbreviated form; for instance, she does not describe the preparatory ritual cleansing, nor does she detail all of the stages of the prayer practice. Yet the detail that is provided—Agba prepares a clean space, using his mantle for lack of a prayer rug, and prostrates himself to the east as he offers his prayer—is an effective means of communicating to Western readers Agba's proper practice of Islam.[16]

The discovery that prompts Agba's prayer of thanksgiving—the revelation that he can keep the foal alive by bottle-feeding it—signals Agba's assumption of a parental role.[17] To an enslaved orphan who has little agency or protection, taking total responsibility for nurturing the foal is empowering. He declares himself the colt's father: "I will be a father to you, Sham, and when you are grown the multitudes will bow before you. And you will be King of the Wind" (41). Meanwhile, the narrator designates Agba as the foal's mother: the other yearlings run "to their mothers when … hungry or in trouble. But Sham's mother was a slim brown horseboy" (44). Gender is immaterial: Agba is both mother and father to Sham. So, too, is species immaterial, so strong is the bond between boy and horse. The message is one of connection, rather than difference.

## Critiquing Racism and Xenophobia

Nevertheless, Agba lives in a world where his differences from the majority single him out for abuse—especially after he and Sham arrive in Europe. Both Sue and Henry acknowledge that Agba's dark skin and foreign origins are cause for discrimination by the French and British people he encounters. Sue's characters frequently insult Agba with racist epithets like "blackamoor"(25) and animalistic terms like "monkey" (21), but the author invariably condemns this kind of language by characterizing the abusive characters as ignoble.[18] The "old horseboy" who calls Agba a "black bird of ill omen," for example, is labeled an "old churl" (53–54). The most offensive bigot, the cruel cartman who mistreats both Sham and Agba, is a "brute" (23).[19] Sue expresses his negative judgment of racist language both through a narrative intervention—he states that "the carter *vulgarly*" calls Agba a "blackamoor" (25; italics for emphasis)—and by having a more humane character pointedly correct the cartman. The English Quaker Jethro Coke, who observes the carter abusing Sham and engages him in conversation about the horse's faithful attendant, asks: "who is this man whom I imagine is an African, and whom thou callest the blackamoor?" (20).

Henry characterizes abusive characters in a similar way, though the offensive language in her novel is milder and less frequent. In addition to the cartman taken from Sue, Henry adds a new character, Mistress Williams, the wife of an English innkeeper who briefly becomes Sham's owner. Significantly, Henry shifts the focus from racism to xenophobia, with Mistress Williams refusing to house "that varmint-in-a-hood!" (105). Whereas Sue has the Quaker Coke model appropriate language (using "African" instead of "blackamoor"), Henry more explicitly guides her readers to be outraged at Mistress Williams's offensive language by demonstrating that it is evidence of her own inadequacies. Henry is careful to articulate "the truth of the matter," namely that "Agba's deep, searching eyes, his soft, pattering footsteps, his flowing mantle and quiet ways, were so foreign to [Mistress Williams's] own coarseness that she felt ill at ease in his presence" (105). The narrator's judgment of the woman's "coarseness" is further confirmed by the transcription of her dialectal speech—"Get'im outa here! 'E gives me the creeps!" (105). Henry makes it clear that the innkeeper's wife is a coarse person of low character, despite the title "Mistress Williams" that marks her relative superiority in the social hierarchy. In so doing, Henry overturns the notion that it is reasonable to cast Agba as a "varmint."[20]

Where *King of the Wind* does address race, I argue, it does so primarily through the illustrations by Wesley Dennis that accompany Henry's text. Henry and Dennis had a long, productive working relationship, collaborating on some twenty books, and it was in fact Dennis who suggested the story of the Godolphin Arabian to Henry (Henry, "Acceptance" 327). Dennis's images underscore the deep connection between Agba and Sham and also—in the case of several full-color illustrations—celebrate Agba's brown skin in gorgeous tones.[21] This is especially apparent in the images of Agba riding on Sham at a gallop, a repeating visual trope throughout the novel.

In the black and white vignette illustration that opens Chapter 6 (45), Dennis seamlessly blends horse and boy into a single being. Agba's body

*Figure 7.1* Agba and Sham racing the other horseboys.

Source: *King of the Wind*, by Marguerite Henry, with illustrations by Wesley Dennis (Rand McNally & Company, 1948), page 45.

and costume are intertwined into Sham's streaming mane in a way that makes it difficult to differentiate where one ends and the other begins. In the full-color variation of this illustration captured in the end sheets of the first edition, boy and horse are virtually the same shade of golden brown, and their limbs are similarly long and lanky. Agba's brown leg and bare foot blend perfectly into the horse's flank, and the boy's entire body lays so flat upon the horse's neck and back that they appear to be a single creature. Characteristic of Dennis and Henry's famously harmonious collaboration, the synergy of text and image reflects the synergy between boy and horse.[22] From a posthumanist perspective, the fusion of boy and horse enhances both: together, they are something more than the sum of their parts.

Dennis's illustrations appear even more profound when set against the cultural landscape of the midcentury United States. When Henry introduced her mute, dark-skinned protagonist to American readers in 1948, "cowboy and Indian" movies were at the height of their popularity. These entertainments often constructed Native Americans as barely-verbal sidekicks, a stereotype exemplified by Tonto from *The Lone Ranger* radio and television programs. Compared to the White titular hero, Tonto had darker skin, "rode a darker horse," and "had much less vocabulary" (Deloria 200). Though Agba originated in a nineteenth-century French novel, Henry's sympathetic, triumphant portrayal of her nonverbal, non-White hero subverts racial stereotypes of 1940s America.

## An Equine Love Triangle

The deep bond between Sham and Agba takes on new resonances when the pair encounters Sham's "love interest," the white mare Roxana. As a matter of historical record, Sham was eventually bought by the Earl of Godolphin, a notable breeder of racehorses in eighteenth-century England. It is also a matter of record that after his arrival at the Earl's stables at Gog Magog, the horse disrupted the Earl's plans to mate a mare named Roxana with another resident stallion, Hobgoblin. Numerous historical sources corroborate that Sham did indeed "attract the attention of the most beautiful Arabian mare, one who had resisted all advances until then" and that the stallion "allegedly bit and killed the intended sire, a lackluster rival, before leaping upon the beauty named Roxana, who seemed to return his interest: a fervent start to a glittering career as a stud and foundation sire" (Raulff 151). In both *The Godolphin Arabian* and *King of the Wind*, the racial implications of this moment are clear. Roxana is "'exquisitely made'" and pure white, shining like "a white marble in the sun" (Henry 138) and Sham is a diminutive brown Moroccan stallion with no paper pedigree. In both versions, Agba clears the way for Sham to usurp Hobgoblin's claim to Roxana by releasing Sham from his stall.

Sue's characterization of the mare Roxana, and both the stallions' and the human men's reactions to her, is highly sexualized. Roxana arrives at the Earl of Godolphin's stables covered in her travel robes and a hood that leaves only her eyes visible. Sue compares the men's excitement over the mare to "*the same great and provoking desire* that a cavalier experiences when, at a ball, he meets two large and sparkling eyes dazzling him through an immoveable mask, and when at each motion of a lovely foot the black satin domino moves in graceful wave" (90; italics for emphasis). Sue even puts Lord Godolphin in the position of worrying over how best to remove the robe covering the mare's body before the other men: should he "enjoy their surprise and gradually increasing delight as her beauties should be gradually developed to their charmed eyes," or should he "display her at once, radiant with all her unfolded charms, like another Venus Aphrodite?" (90). In these moments, the wealthy horse breeders' excitement over Roxana is surely related to the money she will generate from producing perfect progeny; yet the writer does not hesitate to depict her as a prostitute for sale.[23] The female is depicted as an object of men's sexual pleasure and a source of potential economic benefit.[24]

Though not motivated by financial gain, Sue's Agba, too, "become[s] desperately smitten by Roxana" (97). A mature man in the French novel, Agba experiences a "deep but inexplicable sensation," a "feeling of ecstasy" when he looks upon the mare (90). This pleasure is purely aesthetic, Sue specifies—and yet, it is the prime motivation for Agba's decision to release Scham from the stable to breed with Roxana. Upon learning that Scham is to be used as a teaser—before Hobgoblin approaches, Scham will be presented to Roxana to see if she behaves receptively—Agba is "overcome" with "bitter jealousy" (95, 91). "Substituting Scham's instincts for his own" (97), Agba "begin[s] to … desire [Roxana] for Scham with an ardour which hardly fell short of passion" (90–91). Thus, the stallion becomes the stable hand's sexual proxy.

Sue's oddly sexy depiction of Roxana is echoed by the horse herself when she hears Scham call to her with an "impassioned neigh" (93). Roxana's response is unquestionably described in terms of sexual arousal: "She stood motionless and quivering; her breathing became hasty and short; her large sides heaved up and down convulsively" (93). Given his highly sexualized representation of the mare, it is then surprising that Sue puritanically codes the language of her mating with Scham. After Scham escapes from his stall and conquers the rival Hobgoblin, Sue only describes Scham's "resounding neigh as the song of triumph," the answering call of "Roxana, the conqueror's prize!" and, "the consequences of Scham's victory"—a cryptic allusion to the later discovery that Scham has impregnated Roxana (102). A wide section break marked by asterisks in the text leaves readers space to imagine this much-anticipated consummation between Roxana and her unsanctioned mate.

Henry, writing for children, downplays the frank sexuality of Sue's novel. Surprisingly, though, her version of the "honeymoon scene" provides young readers with details that Sue leaves to the adult reader's imagination.[25] As in Sue's text, Sham's value as a stud remains known only to Agba; his paper pedigree is lost, and his stature is markedly small compared to what Agba describes as the enormous, "coarsely made" English racehorses populating the Earl's stables (133). But Lady Roxana presents him with his opportunity to prove his genetic superiority. When Agba quietly releases him from his stall, the Arabian charges forth, "challenge[s] the king of Gog Magog," wins the violent battle between stallions (139), and claims the willing Roxana as his own. In Sue's version of the story, Agba prevents Godolphin's men from intervening, in what the French author describes as "revenge" against Hobgoblin (99–100). Henry, by contrast, makes the story about romance. Consequently, while Sue provides no other detail than the mention of each horse's whinny, Henry describes their interlude as one of mutual attraction and affection:

> Suddenly they were together, touching each other with their noses, talking in excited little nickers. Then, manes and tales in flowing motion, they streaked to the far end of the paddock....
>
> Agba wanted to sing for joy. He longed to talk, to laugh, to cry. His hands flew to his throat helplessly. But it was Roxana whose voice substituted for his own. It was her whinny, high and joyful, that said all he wanted to say. (141)

While Sue makes the stallion Scham a proxy lover for Agba, who greatly "admire[s] Roxana" (90), Henry has the mare express what voiceless Agba is unable to verbalize. She makes the scene about Agba's frustration with his communication difficulties rather than about any sexual desire or frustration. This is, of course, a children's novel. And yet adult readers will acknowledge that this is a conjugal scene, complete with mutual touching, excitement, and finally Roxana's "high and joyful" response to their act of consummation (141). Importantly, this is a shared moment of agency for Sham, Agba, and Roxana; it is Roxana who calls to Sham, Agba who sets Sham free, and Sham who claims the lady—to the equal delight of all three.

Moreover, Sham and Roxana's tryst is clearly described and celebrated as an act of joyous equine miscegenation; the golden-brown Moroccan stallion mates with the pure white European mare (though—importantly—she is also a purebred Arabian), to the horror of the assembled nobles and the owner who had planned Roxana's match so carefully. The horses' actions undermine Lord Godolphin's plan to carefully curate the bloodlines of Roxana's future foal.[26] Moreover, the horses' respective colors—brown and gleaming white—can be read as racialized markers, with the prized white mare embodying human constructions of racial superiority. Whether or not they register the implied social critique, readers are invited to applaud Sham and Roxana's union because it is an appealing story of rebellion, of individual greatness just waiting to be discovered, and of romantic pursuit—safely embodied for young readers by horses, not humans.

## One Horse, Two Agendas

Though the incidents of Sue's and Henry's novels track very closely, the authors' agendas diverge. Henry focuses on denouncing animal cruelty and on eliciting her readers' empathy in service to this cause. For Sue the sportsman, an intense preoccupation with Scham's illustrious bloodline sometimes muddies his novel's animal-rights message. This difference is apparent in each author's handling of one of the most iconic scenes in Sham's story: that in which the cartman viciously abuses the stallion in a Paris street.[27] In a grisly passage, Sue recounts how the horse struggles to pull his heavy cart up an icy Paris hill, stumbles and is twice yanked back up, then falls painfully to the ground. Both authors emphasize the horse's anguish and suffering (Sue 10; Henry 92).[28] The most notable difference is that Sue uses impersonal descriptors—"the unfortunate animal," "the horse," and elsewhere in the scene, "the poor creature" (10)—whereas Henry uses Sham's name throughout, thereby inviting her reader to empathize with this horse specifically (92). The empathy that Henry elicits by presenting Sham as a named individual, a fellow-creature, encourages readers to understand that he deserves to avoid mistreatment simply because he is a living being. Moreover, Sham is loved, so harming Sham means harming the sympathetic boy with whom he is so deeply connected. By contrast, Sue shows Agba reflecting that Scham does not deserve his fate because "the fierce descendant of so many illustrious ancestors" is "destined to perpetuate the spotless race of the 'Kings of the Wind'" (29–30). Sue thus positions the reader, following Agba, to abhor the degradation of Scham because it threatens the horse's status as a noble stallion of pure pedigree.

The conclusion of Sham's story presents the point of greatest divergence between the two texts. The historical record confirms that when three of Sham's sons won major races at England's famous Newmarket racetrack, the Godolphin Arabian's value as a stud was established. Sue concludes Scham's story by praising the stallion's role in the "regeneration of [England's] thorough-bred horses" (113). But that is not the end of the book. There follows a kind of coda in which Sue appears to dismiss everything he has written thus far when he invokes "the apparent uselessness of this biographic narrative" (113). In a jarring turn, Sue directly addresses his readers with a plea to change French horse breeding practices, which at the time involved mixing horses of different breeds. He argues that Scham's legacy proves the value of using purebred Arabian stallions instead, "for they demonstrate the undeniable power of pure blood as the means of regenerating bastard races, and thus affect a grave question of agriculture, commerce, and national interest" (113).

Sharing none of these preoccupations, Henry concludes her novel with a scene not found in Sue's text. Following the victories of Sham's offspring at Newmarket, Queen Caroline bestows the Queen's Plate upon Sham and the Earl of Godolphin, anointing the Godolphin stables as the most successful horse breeding operation of the year 1738. In Henry's version, the boy is every bit as important as the stallion, and his effort and dedication matter at least as much as the genetics of the horse.

Henry indicates this by turning her focus from the "Father of the Turf" (171) to the "father" of the horse. Sitting astride Sham, "what a contrast Agba made!" to the trappings of English aristocracy (163). "His feet and legs were bare and he wore his plain mantle. But he sat his horse with such pride that he might have worn ermine" (163). Agba is visibly distinguished by his Moroccan habit, but his pride in his horse

*Figure* 7.2 Agba astride Sham, being presented with the Queen's Plate at Newmarket.

Source: *King of the Wind*, by Marguerite Henry, with illustrations by Wesley Dennis (Rand McNally & Company, 1948), page 168.

transcends the vast racial and class differences between the dark-skinned young man and the fair-skinned Queen of England. Reaching forward to fix one of her own purple plumes in Sham's bridle, the Queen inquires after "the pedigree of this proud sire of three winning horses" (167). Deeply moved, Agba brushes a tear from his cheek and realizes that "he was growing a beard! He was a man!" (169). Agba's acknowledgment of his own coming of age parallels Sham's coming into his own as a sire. It also prompts him to realize that he has fulfilled his long-ago promise: "*I will be a father to you, Sham, and when I am grown I will ride you before the multitudes. And they will bow before you, and you will be King of the Wind*" (169; italics in original). The joint coming-of-age story has reached its end, triumphantly.

The full-color illustration opposite this passage powerfully complements and enhances the text (Henry 168). The focal point of the image is the bright white mantle and turban of Agba, sitting on Sham's bare back in stark contrast to the blurred crowd in the background. Sham and Agba are bathed in beams of sunlight streaming through the clouds, visually referencing an earlier illustration of Sham's birthing stall (33), where Agba first promised to be Sham's father, and to make Sham a King (41). The tone is victorious and subversive; a voiceless, brown-skinned Muslim boy and his North African horse with no affirmation of his pedigree but the achievements of his offspring literally look down upon the Queen of the British Empire. While celebrating Agba and Sham's shared triumph over adversity, the image also holds empowering implications for subaltern subjects of the British crown—and for all marginalized people.

## Prizing *King of the Wind*

This comparative analysis of Henry's and Sue's novels reveals the authors' diverging agendas and the changes Henry made to suit the story to a juvenile audience. It also demonstrates the extent to which *King of the Wind* is a rewriting of *The Godolphin Arabian* and not the type of "individually distinct," "original work" described in the American Library Association (ALA)'s criteria for the Newbery Medal (Association). That being the case, what conclusions can we draw about the Newbery committee's selection of Henry's text in 1949?

First, *King of the Wind* may be an example of a text prized for its popularity among young readers, and thus its contribution to the marketability of children's books.[29] Henry's novel was a bestseller when first released into a crowded field of horse stories. Of the top fifteen children's books listed by the *New York Herald Tribune* for the first three months of 1949, *King of the Wind* was ranked first, and four more were horse stories, including *The Island Stallion* by Walter Farley, the third novel in his Black Stallion series ("What"). At a publishers' forum that year,

Random House President Bennett Cerf emphasized the economic value of children's books by declaring that "Walter Farley's horse books are among the biggest money-makers at Random House" (qtd. in Marcus 180). While Farley's Black Stallion series was wildly popular among young readers, Henry's horse books earned stronger critical praise. Both writers were instrumental in convincing publishers that children's books were a tremendous, untapped market in the postwar baby boom. Indeed, the mid-twentieth-century expansion of the children's book market coincides with the commercial peak of the horse story as a popular genre, one long preoccupied with "the ways in which horses satisfy readers' psychological or emotional needs" (Heinecken 23). For girls, in particular, the horse story has been understood as a means of envisioning oneself as powerful.[30]

These factors together may explain the prizing of a work of genre fiction—a category rarely recognized by the Newbery establishment because such works, while popular, are typically not considered elevating. The issue of genre fiction, moreover, may have been counterbalanced by the fact that *King of the Wind* hews closely to the model of books that the Newbery had previously honored: it is among the realistic "foreign background stories" that came into vogue in the 1920s and that the Newbery committee tended to favor for decades (Viguers 524, 444). With a setting that is both exotic and historically informative, *King of the Wind* managed to be both didactic and popular together. And this may lead to a way to understand the 1949 prizing of a work that is by no means original.

Contemporaneous reviews do not indicate awareness that Henry's novel is a juvenilization of Sue's, although some note familiarity with the Godolphin's story and acknowledge the "impressive list of 'books consulted'" included at the end of Henry's text (Castor). And the busy librarians on the Newbery committee, who pride themselves on reading all possible contenders for the award, undoubtedly lacked the time to follow up on secondary sources mentioned in all eligible books, let alone in the case of *King of the Wind*, whose list of "Books Consulted" includes thirty-five titles (175). A closer look reveals that most of Henry's sources relate to historical background. The only work devoted entirely to Sham's story is *The Godolphin Arabian*, and Henry's text tracks so closely with the plot and incidents of Sue's novel that any reader familiar with *The Godolphin Arabian* would have difficulty claiming *King of the Wind* as a wholly original work. As Sue's novel indicates, however, the eighteenth-century story of the Godolphin Arabian had already been transformed from history to legend by the nineteenth century, and the terms of the Newbery Medal do provide for original retellings of "traditional" stories. Another way of understanding the novel's prizing might be to treat *King of the Wind* as a fictionalized biography (recalling that Sue calls his story a "biographic narrative" [113]). Juvenile biographies of famous men and women, including those from historically underrepresented populations, enjoyed a popular and commercial heyday in the 1950s, with series such as Bobbs-Merrill's "Childhood of Famous Americans" and The Landmark Books circulating widely. In some ways, *King of the Wind* fits within this trend, presenting the case of a "great horse" and his unacknowledged human partner, both of whom helped shape history. One of several novels in which Henry tells the story of a notable historic horse, *King of the Wind* gives readers the historical, didactic, uplifting story of a breed originator—the biography of a true horse-hero that continues to resonate in the twenty-first century.[31]

## Notes

1 In 2015, Simon and Schuster reissued twenty of Henry's horse novels in deluxe hardcover editions. The publisher simultaneously launched *Marguerite Henry's Ponies of Chincoteague*, Catherine Hapka's eight-book series of middle-grade novels spun off from Henry's *Misty of Chincoteague*. This series was preceded by Checkerboard Press's 1988 "King of the Wind Storybooks," Catherine Nichols and Joan K. Nichols's short adaptations of chapters from Henry's novel for second- and third-grade readers.

2 Heinecken argues that Henry's horse stories "function as what [posthumanist theorist Donna] Haraway calls 'contact zones,' spaces enabling cross-species conversation that destabilize boundaries and hierarchies between humans and other animals" (Heinecken 22).

3 Equine historian Ulrich Raulff confirms that the horse's success as a stud simply amplifies the drama of his origin story, not only because there "remains some doubt about his true provenance" but because the story of "his arrival in England has the gloss of a Latin lover and good old-fashioned machismo" (151).

4 The other two founding studs, known as the Darley Arabian and the Byerly Turk, are also the subjects of numerous books, though their origin stories lack the drama of the Godolphin Arabian's tale.

5 Man o' War (1917–1947) and Seabiscuit (1933–1947) are two of the most successful Thoroughbred racehorses in American history.

6 Sentimentally appealing because its narrative point of view is commanded by the suffering titular horse, *Black Beauty* is "not only a crusade against the maltreatment of working horses, but also an acknowledgement of the societal forces that pressure humans into such behaviour" (Kendrick "Riders," 184).

7 *Black Beauty* itself is in close conversation with Harriet Beecher Stowe's antislavery novel *Uncle Tom's Cabin* (1851–1852).

8 Sue wrote *The Godolphin Arabian* in the wake of two significant pieces of legislation concerning animal and human rights in Great Britain, where Sue published translations of his books serially: the Cruel Treatment of Cattle Act of 1822 and the Slavery Abolition Act of 1833. Similar legislation followed in Sue's home country with France's Proclamation of the Abolition of Slavery in 1848 and its first animal welfare act in 1850.

9 Sue's position as a competitive sportsman and founding member of the French Jockey Club, "established with the express aim of improving French bloodstock until it could compete on level terms with its British rivals," explains the agenda expressed in the novel's final pages (de Jonge ix).

10 Throughout this essay, I distinguish between the two versions of the story by using the spelling employed by each author: Sue renders the horse's name *Scham*, while Henry spells it *Sham*.

11 Sue's novel generally lacks character development, and the writing tends to be pedantic, didactic, and repetitive. Needless to say, it was not a prize-winner in its time.

12 Moulay Ismail Ben Sharif was a Sultan of Morocco from 1672 to 1727 (Abun-Nasr 230). It is not likely, however, that Sham was born in his stables. Although Henry designates Morocco as the horse's homeland, equine historians indicate that the horse who became known as the Godolphin Arabian more likely originated from Yemen (Clee 70) or Tunisia (Milner). In Sue's version, the horse is Tunisian, given by the Bey of Tunis to King Louis XV in 1751 (Sue 24).

13 The term "Mohammedan" that Henry uses here would have been common usage during the mid-twentieth century. Later in the century, the term was recognized as offensive due to its emphasis on the worship of a prophet rather than of Allah. The accepted term today is Muslim.

14 Islamic law does not in fact require that all living creatures practice fasting as the Sultan in Henry's tale insists. On the contrary, the compassionate treatment of animals is an important tenet of Islam.

15 While Sue constantly refers to the "superstitious ideas of the Orientals" (27), he does not explore the matter of Agba's Islamic faith beyond his occasional appeal to "the will of the Prophet" (28). In *King of the Wind*, some emphasis on superstition as a thematic structure remains. Rather than praying, the chief groom Signor Achmet reads signs and listens for birdsong to guide his discernment (35). Agba, though depicted as a practicing Muslim, is himself not immune to superstition.

16 The detailed description of Agba's prayer is the novel's only account of his religious practice; nonetheless, it sufficiently solidifies for readers that Islam is an essential component of Agba's identity.

17 In another essay in this volume, Kathleen T. Horning and Jocelyn Van Tuyl examine the parental relationship between a teenage boy and his cat in Emily Neville's *It's Like This, Cat* (1963; 1964 Newbery Medal).

18 Quotations are from the 1845 English translation of *The Godolphin Arabian*. The original French text has abundant racial slurs, though their nuances are sometimes different from those of the English translation.

19 The carter, who actually compares Agba to a monkey, also uses animalistic comparisons to describe his lack of speech: Agba—whom he frequently calls "Dumby"—is "as mute as a mackerel or a horse" (Sue 21, 22). Henry offers a milder version of the carter's animalistic insults, having him yell "You dog!" when Agba gets in the way of his vehicle (Henry 85).

20 It is primarily Agba's "foreign" manner and the "flowing mantle" marking him as Moroccan (Henry 105) that draw censure and even punishment. When Agba scales the wall of the inn to be with Sham, Mistress Williams misinterprets his actions as an attempted theft. A constable promptly takes the boy to Newgate Jail upon spotting his "tell-tale turban hanging over the wall"—a garment that signifies Agba's ethnic Otherness and thus renders him suspect in the eyes of the law (110).

21 Most contemporary paperback editions offer only black and white versions of Dennis's color illustrations.

22 The 1948 *New York Herald Tribune* review of the book is measured in its praise of Henry's "satisfying" writing but lavish in its praise of Dennis's illustrations and the synergy between text and image (P. A. W.).

23 The men are stirred by the horse as by a woman: "The motion of her large haunches, and her nervous and symmetrical legs, gave an elegant undulation to the emblazoned skirts of her housing, just as the Andalusian girl, in walking, gives motion to the folds of her" garments (Sue 89–90).

24 The patriarchal concern with property and bloodlines is further evident in the punishment the horses receive for their unsanctioned encounter: Scham is banished to a farm sixty miles away and Roxana is "treated with the same severity as a young lady of rank who, refusing a noble marriage, sacrifices all for an outlaw" (Sue 103).

25 Concerned that her editor might find the equine love triangle "distasteful to gentle readers," Henry was delighted by the editor's unexpected reaction: "Doesn't this happen too fast? Should there be more time for love-making?" (Henry, "Acceptance" 332).

26 To a breeder like Godolphin, it is Scham's lack of written pedigree that makes him an unacceptable sire.

27 Sue's and Henry's texts both accompany this scene with dramatic illustrations—by Victorian-era illustrator Thomas Onwhyn and Wesley Dennis, respectively—each depicting the noble horse collapsed in his harness in the street. Both texts emphasize the savagery of the cartman, who lashes the horse mercilessly throughout this episode and responds to the horse's collapse by beginning to light a fire under his tail. In both versions, it seems important to the story arc for text and image to convey the depth of the horse's suffering.

28 Throughout her novel, Henry tames the violence that Sue depicts graphically. Sue narrates, in painful detail, the pleasure the innkeeper takes in torturing Scham and the psychological toll this takes on Agba. Henry evokes enough cruelty to provoke outrage in the reader—she makes it clear that the innkeeper is trying to break Sham's spirit through starvation (Henry 107)—but spares young readers the details that render Sue's text deeply disturbing.

29 In a 1957 retrospective on the first thirty-five years of Newbery winners, Irene Smith identifies *King of the Wind* as one of the few Newbery winners she considered truly popular with children (84).

30 Historically, horse stories were commonly structured as coming-of-age narratives for girls, and as such have now been identified as protofeminist fiction, with horses positioned as signifiers of girls' desires and as vehicles for them to become "more fully realized, powerful, and mature" (Heinecken 23). See also Haymonds (52), Kendrick ("Equine"), and Tucker.

31 *Justin Morgan Had a Horse* (1945; 1946 Newbery runner-up) narrates the origins of the Morgan horse breed.

## Works Cited

Abun-Nasr, J. M. *A History of the Maghrib in the Islamic Period*. Cambridge: Cambridge UP, 1987. Print.

Association for Library Service to Children. "Terms & Criteria: John Newbery Medal." *American Library Association*. 1987. ALA, n.d. Web. 14 July 2020.

Castor, Gladys Crofoot. "King of the Wind." *New York Times* 14 Nov. 1948. *Proquest*. Web. 15 Feb. 2019.

Clee, Nicholas. *Eclipse: The Horse That Changed Racing History Forever*. New York: The Overlook Press, 2009. Print.

de Jonge, Alex. Introduction. *The Godolphin Arabian*. By Eugène Sue. Trans. and adapt. Alex de Jonge. Lanham, MD: Derrydale Press, 2004. Print.

Deloria, Vine. *Custer Died for Your Sins: An Indian Manifesto*. 1969. New York: Macmillan, 1988. Print.

Haymonds, Alison. "Rides of Passage." *A Necessary Fantasy? The Heroic Figure in Children's Popular Culture*. Ed. Dudley Jones and Tony Watkins. New York: Garland, 2000. 51–72. *Google Books*. Web. 22 Feb. 2019.

Heinecken, Dawn. "Contact Zones: Humans, Horses, and the Stories of Marguerite Henry." *Children's Literature Association Quarterly* 42.1 (2017): 21–42. Print.

Henry, Marguerite. "Acceptance Paper." *Newbery Medal Books: 1922–1955, with their Authors' Acceptance Papers & Related Material chiefly from the* Horn Book Magazine. Ed. Bertha Mahony Miller and Elinor Whitney Field. Boston: The Horn Book, 1955. 327–334. Print.

Henry, Marguerite. *King of the Wind*. Illus. Wesley Dennis. New York: Rand McNally, 1948. Print.

Kendrick, Jenny. "Riders, Readers, Romance: A Short History of the Pony Story." *Jeunesse: Young People, Texts, Cultures* 1.2 (2009): 183–202. Print.

Kendrick, Jenny. "Equine Fiction Between the Wars and the Woman Who Called Herself 'Golden Gorse.'" *Out of the Attic: Some Neglected Children's Authors of the Twentieth Century*. Ed. Pat Pinsent. Lichfield, UK: Pied Piper, 2006. 5–31. Print.

Kidd, Kenneth B. "Prizing Children's Literature: The Case of Newbery Gold." *Children's Literature* 35 (2007): 166–190. Print.

Marcus, Leonard S. *Minders of Make-Believe: Idealists, Entrepreneurs, and the Shaping of American Children's Literature*. New York: Houghton Mifflin, 2008. Print.

Milner, Mourdant. *The Godolphin Arabian: The Story of the Matchem Line*. London: J. A. Allen, 1990. Print.

P. A. W. "Castaways: King of the Wind." *New York Herald Tribune* 14 Nov. 1948. *Proquest*. Web. 15 Jan. 2019.

Raulff, Ulrich. *Farewell to the Horse: A Cultural History*. Trans. Ruth Ahmedzai Kemp. New York: W. W. Norton, 2018. Print.

Smith, Irene. *A History of the Newbery and Caldecott Medals*. New York: Viking, 1957. *HathiTrust*. Web. 15 June 2020.

Sue, Eugène. *The Godolphin Arabian; or, the History of a Thorough-Bred* (1839). Illus. Thomas Onwhyn. Trans. for *The Sunday Times*. London: Chapman and Elcoate, 1845. *Google Books*. Web. 16 July 2020.

Tucker, Nicholas. *The Child and the Book*. Cambridge: Cambridge UP, 1991. Print.

Viguers, Ruth Hill. "Part Four: The Golden Age, 1920–1950." *A Critical History of Children's Literature: A Survey of Children's Books in English from Earliest Times to the Present*. Ed. Cornelia Meigs, Elizabeth Nesbitt, Anne Eaton, and Ruth Hill Viguers. Illus. Vera Bock. New York: Macmillan, 1953. 425–603. Print.

"What American Children Are Reading." *New York Herald Tribune*. May 8, 1949. *Proquest*. Web. 15 Jan. 2019.

# 8 Double Dutch Nostalgia

## *The Wheel on the School* (1955)

*Anna Lockhart*

A cozily exotic story set in a fishing village in Holland, Meindert DeJong's *The Wheel on the School* (1954; 1955 Newbery Medal) tells the story of students in a one-room schoolhouse who are searching for a wagon wheel to place on their building's roof. The Dutch view storks as a symbol of good luck for the people on whose houses they nest, and wagon wheels affixed to the roofs attract the birds to nest for the spring and summer. As the children leave their classroom to engage with the natural world and diverse members of their community, it becomes clear that they learn more profound lessons through their absorption in the stork project than they would have from any number of books studied at their desks. *The Wheel on the School* already appeared old-fashioned at the moment of its publication, in part because it is steeped in two strains of nostalgia. This essay first examines the novel's own nostalgia—the way its Dutch-born author grapples with his traumatic childhood emigration to the United States through a rosy recreation of his native land. The discussion then turns to the nostalgia of the novel's prizing, arguing that the Newbery committee's elevation of this quaint story represented a national longing for a simpler, less fearful time as Cold War-era anxieties found expression in concerns about education and childhood.

### Meindert DeJong: A Tale of Two Childhoods

A prolific writer for children, Meindert DeJong set most of his novels in either Holland or the American Midwest. This bifurcation speaks to the geographical rift in his childhood.[1] DeJong was born in 1906, in Wierum, Friesland, the inspiration for the fictional Shora of *The Wheel on the School*. He was a sickly child, contracting pneumonia three times by age five (D. DeJong, "Brother" 427). When his third bout brought him near death, the entire town prayed for him (D. DeJong, *Accent* 77). He grew up surrounded by extended family, and sometimes visited relatives in a nearby town that, unlike Wierum, had trees and "storks that nested on wagon wheels placed expressly for them on the roofs of houses" (D. DeJong, *Accent* 98).

DOI: 10.4324/9780367337223-8-9

Childhood in rural Holland had a special intensity, DeJong recalled in his 1955 Newbery acceptance speech. Because all but the wealthiest children ended their schooling and began work at age eleven, there was an "instinctive knowledge that childhood was brief" (M. DeJong, "Acceptance" 437). Before reaching that cusp, however, Meindert embarked on a second, American childhood at age eight when his family emigrated to Grand Rapids, Michigan.[2] Life in the US was cruel. The family's financial security, kin network, and social status evaporated, as did their health: an infant son was born and died, and his mother became incapacitated by chronic health problems. Despite living within an enclave of Dutch immigrants and descendants, the family faced "prejudice" and harsh treatment from their neighbors, authority figures, and other children, who viewed them as greenhorns (Kibler; D. DeJong, *Accent* 224).

Worst of all was school. Public education was academically superior to religious schools (Kibler), and the impoverished DeJongs could ill afford tuition. Nonetheless, the parents enrolled their children in a school supported by their Dutch Christian Reformed Church to protect them from the influences of the "worldly, abysmally sinful country" in which they now lived (D. DeJong, *Accent* 220). As English learners, the children were assumed to be unintelligent. Meindert's older brother, the novelist David Cornel DeJong, recalls the "humiliation" of being put back several grades and seated with the low-achieving pupils placed in the last rows of the room (D. DeJong, *Accent* 221–222). With corporal punishment and bullying added to the academic indignities, the younger DeJongs resorted to truancy, often spending the day hiding in the "nearby city dump" (D. DeJong, *Accent* 225). While cruel behavior from children and teachers was not unknown in Holland, it was balanced by warm tradition—a child's first day of school, for example, was marked by a ritual including eating honey cake fastened to one's arm (D. DeJong, *Accent* 34–37); moreover, in Holland, sectarian schools felt pressure to keep up with the "new methods and experimental ways of teaching" that characterized the innovative public schools. There was little warmth and no such corrective force in the US, where it was assumed that religious schools were not in competition with public ones (D. DeJong, *Accent* 221). Meindert and his brother David eventually graduated from high school and worked their way through the denominational Calvin College. Meindert "hated and dreaded the prospect" of teaching after graduation, but with no other job prospects, he reluctantly accepted a position at a small college in Iowa after earning his bachelor's degree in 1928. He quit after a brief, unhappy teaching stint, vowing never to return to the classroom (D. DeJong, "Brother" 429–430; Kibler).

The years before his harsh classroom experiences—before the rupture of emigration—would stand out in DeJong's memory "as if set in amber" (M. DeJong, "Acceptance" 437). In his many Dutch stories,

DeJong leans into these memories, undoubtedly supplementing them with "family lore" to create a romanticized vision of the Old Country (Kibler). In addition to their "distinctively Dutch" geography and customs (Kibler), the Netherlands novels "have lasting appeal because they present an idealized community" (Hartzell 227). These are all, of course, things DeJong lost as an immigrant. He wrote "no stories about the immigrant period of his life"; instead, literary scholar Myra Kibler maintains, "he developed a sensitivity to the plight of people and animals who are mistreated just because they are different" (Kibler). In the same way, this essay argues, the author's ghastly educational experiences, as both pupil and teacher, may have inspired him to imagine what school should be. Thus, *The Wheel on the School*'s fantasy of an ideal classroom and educator—and of school as an agent for change in the community—represents an indirect way for the author to grapple with his immigrant experience. From an author who had experienced outsider status, then, comes a story focused on community and inclusion; from a former intellectually curious truant comes an idealized teacher who nurtures students' inquisitiveness; from the bullied young immigrant comes a story of children's cooperation and empowerment.

## The Stork Project: Building Community

Having resolved to bring storks to their village, the schoolchildren of Shora set out to find a wheel that could support a nest. They scatter in separate directions, searching village, dike, and countryside, with each individual child's quest detailed in its own chapter. DeJong's friend Judith Hartzell has likened the novel's structure to that of the titular wheel: "It begins with the hub—Lina"—the schoolgirl whose musings about storks launch the entire project. "Like spokes running out toward the rim, the six children go on their separate adventures, and bit by bit, through the children, the whole rim of the village comes into play" (Hartzell 230). In particular, the stork project leads the children to connect with people of various ages, physical abilities, and socioeconomic status, changing the students' perspective on their community entirely.

At the start of the book, the narrator introduces the school-age children of Shora as "important," while reporting that older people are not "too important" and younger children are "not so important either" (1). But as the schoolchildren explore their community this perspective shifts. To begin their quest to learn about storks, students turn to the village elders. The first person Lina asks about the history of storks in Shora is Grandmother Sibble III, the oldest woman in town; she recalls storks nesting on roofs when she was a girl, before a giant storm swept through and stripped away nesting trees. Sibble's memories reveal the scope of the problem, the environmental imbalance that prevents storks from nesting in Shora, and its historical origins. Moreover, Sibble ceases to be "just an old person ... miles of years away" and becomes "a friend, like another girl" (24). The children also gain insights from Douwa, the oldest man in town, who tells them stories about the storm, and later helps uncover a wagon wheel lodged under an upturned boat beached in the long-ago disaster. During the rescue, Douwa calms Lina by telling jokes, and the girl comes to a realization: "I didn't know people were funny when they were old," she ingenuously tells her newfound ninety-three-year-old friend (155). The stork search connects the schoolchildren to the opposite end of the age spectrum as well, their annoying younger siblings, who are humorously presented as the last obstacle for the children's empathy. In the penultimate chapter, "The Tots in the Tower," Lina and Auka's little sister and brother, respectively, climb Shora's clock tower and spot, miles away, a pair of storks who have been caught in the ocean roiled by a storm: they prove the final step to securing storks for the schoolhouse roof.

Also brought into the widening community circle is the impoverished tin man, whose dilapidated wagon jangles between villages in a fruitless effort to earn enough to keep his many children comfortably housed and fed. Once he gets to know the tin man, whose poverty makes him "feel full of lumps and unhappiness" (113), Auka becomes as determined to secure a new wagon wheel for him as he is to obtain a wheel for the storks. He persuades a man in the nearby village of Nes to accept the tin man's broken-down wheel in exchange for the sturdy, gaudily painted wheel he is about to install on his own roof: "the bright paint will keep [storks] away," Auka argues (118). The boy helps an impecunious outsider obtain a measure of financial security, and the good deed circles back: racing toward the dike in his newly repaired wagon, the tin man helps rescue from the incoming tide Lina, Douwa, and the ancient, buried wheel they are bringing up from the sea.

But the real hero of the rescue is Janus, a double amputee. Indeed, the novel's strongest narrative of inclusion centers on the disabled man's reentry into society and his return to the esteem of others.[3] Initially known to the children only as "legless Janus," a curmudgeon who throws rocks at youngsters who attempt to steal cherries from his fiercely barricaded yard, Janus is not only humanized but becomes the children's closest ally. After several boys sneak into his yard in search of a wheel, Janus hears about the project and becomes integral to it, imparting wisdom, encouragement, and guidance. "Janus had become real; he had become a part of their village. He wasn't a fearsome ogre to be hated and outwitted.... Janus had become important, in the same way that old Grandmother Sibble III had become real and important. He had become a friend!" (77). When Lina and Douwa are imperiled by the inrushing tide, it is Janus who engineers and leads their rescue. With the young and old safe, he next secures the much-desired wheel by exploiting his adaptations to his disability: with his wheelchair as a fulcrum, Janus uses his upper-body strength to pry the wheel from the sand (186). Janus's social exclusion definitively ends when the village men affix the secured wheel to the school roof. One villager is irritated by Janus's copious coaching. "If you think you can do it better," he calls down, "you come up here and hold" the wheel yourself (229). Having forgotten about his disability, they "were treating Janus man to man. He was one of them again" (229).

Ultimately, the children's stork project brings marginalized members of Shora into the mainstream. Notably, "the adults who help them are (with the exception of the bright and imaginative teacher) people who normally have little power in the lives of children—legless Janus, old Grandmother Sibble, the indigent tin man, and ancient Douwa" (Hartzell 230–231). The children also grow confident in their own power, individually and collectively, as they test their strength and ingenuity.

Nevertheless, there are limits to the novel's narrative of inclusivity and empowerment—most notably where gender is concerned. Lina, the central character, is almost always referred to as the "only girl" in the school. From early on, her gender keeps her apart from the boys, who exclude her from ditch-jumping. "Girls are no good at jumping. It's a boy's game," says Jella: "girls worry about wet feet and their dresses flying" (10). Later, Jella suggests the boys dig a moat for pickerel, while Lina brings them hot chocolate milk (33). This kind of service task is reinforced by the adult women who bring the men hot coffee when they are working to erect the wagon wheel on the schoolhouse roof (226). Roles are clearly defined in Shora: the fathers are out at sea, the mothers are home raising children and tending house. The sole exception is Janus's wife Jana, who goes out peddling bread, undoubtedly because Janus can no longer earn a living as a fisherman (247). Separate spheres are an ingrained part of Shora's culture. Men and women even sit in separate aisles at the church, a tradition that goes unquestioned. When Janus and Jana attend church together, the latter has to "sit on the women's side of the church," while the children sit in the children's pew on the men's side (202). Though the children, subject to age separation, are exempt from a gender separation, it is assumed that they will inherit it unquestioningly when they grow up. Their temporary freedom from gender segregation lends poignancy to their childhood—much as the prospective of work at age eleven lent intensity to the author's brief childhood in Holland (M. DeJong, "Acceptance" 437).

In the end, Lina distinguishes herself as a brave little girl when she finds the buried wagon wheel and risks drowning to retrieve it. She even removes her cumbersome dress and wooden shoes to more easily negotiate the rescue. But when she catches sight of her mother watching from the dike, she hastily puts her dress back on, fearing her parent's censure. Thus, Lina's movement outside of the confines of gender roles is remarkable, but also contained within her girlhood: she will grow up to be a woman who adheres to tradition. At the end of the book, even the storks that begin to nest on the roof of the school reinforce traditional gender roles in a sweet scene: "The male stepped over and stood above [the female stork] defensively," and she "looked at her lord and master" (296). By taking an example from the natural world (the mated storks) and overlaying it with the human concept of subservience within marriage, the narrative implies that traditional gender roles and hierarchies are natural, even desirable, since the nesting stork pair represents the culmination of the children's quest.

## Nostalgia in the Nuclear Age: Democracy and the One-Room Schoolhouse

The Dutch village setting of *The Wheel on the School*, set "tight against the dike," with just "some houses and a church and a tower," is closely based on DeJong's early-twentieth-century childhood home (1). Yet it is shaped by an adult author who interprets both his personal past and that of his adopted nation from the perspective of a midcentury American. *The Wheel on the School*, then, captures a view of Holland that is both authentically Dutch and distinctly American. Frequent mention of wooden shoes and traditional Dutch foods like "fat balls" render the setting foreign and exotic. Yet the coziness of a tightknit rural community whose members file into church with warming stoves and whose children gather around a solitary teacher in a one-room school is also closely associated, in history and memory, with the American Midwest that became DeJong's second home. Indeed, during the 1950s, an era shadowed by the threat of nuclear war and marked by policies of containment in both domestic and national security (May 13–14), the sentimental image of the one-room schoolhouse crystallized as a potent symbol of safety.

One-teacher schools delivering basic grade-school education—the proverbial little red schoolhouse—were the norm for American children for more than a century. By World War II, however, these small, intensely local schools were rapidly shifting from lived experience to collective memory: in 1913, half of all American schoolchildren attended one-room schools, whereas in 1960 just one percent did (Zimmerman 17, 52). With their dilapidated structures, uncomfortable seating, poorly educated teachers, and unregulated teaching methods, one-room schools were far from ideal. Yet they stood, physically and metaphorically, at the very center of rural communities. Indeed, as the only communal building for miles, schoolhouses served both as the place of youth instruction and as the site of political rallies, voting stations, weddings, picnics, funerals, and dances. When they were replaced by modern, consolidated buildings, the importance of the little red schoolhouse was preserved through transformation into symbol. And just as the red paint of these schoolhouses is more fiction than reality, the schoolhouse as symbol is more a vessel for projected ideas than a reflection of any historical experience (Zimmerman 170).

In the 1950s, a period of rising birthrates, lowering age of first marriage, and sprawling suburbs, children were seen as a bulwark against an uncertain future, and the little red schoolhouse became shorthand for the American democracy they would inherit and protect: its classrooms hummed with the free exchange of ideas and its curricula were rooted in the moral foundations that ensured the republic's ongoing health (Zimmerman 99–100). The Newbery committee's prizing of *The Wheel on the School* in 1955 captures this version of the one-room schoolhouse: DeJong's fictional classroom, though ostensibly in Holland, can be construed as an idealized vision of American democracy at midcentury.

As historian Jonathan Zimmerman argues, American artists, writers, and cartoonists drew on the little red schoolhouse as symbol throughout the twentieth century. And when they did so, they treated it as a "sacred entity" that remained "pure and unspoiled" even when having to contend with corrupting forces including communism, racism, greed, etc. (122). This was true during the era of federally-mandated desegregation when, following the decision of *Brown v. Board of Education* the same year *The Wheel on the School* was published, both segregationists and integrationists tapped the one-room schoolhouse's symbolic weight as a way to talk about the American ideals expressed through the education of the nation's children: opportunity for all, local control, the cultivation of virtue, individual responsibility, the common good, discipline and respect for authority, the responsible execution of the rights of citizenship.

As a site of American nostalgia and a symbol of American democracy, the one-room schoolhouse reads as universal. Yet as Zimmerman notes, Black and Latino populations "rarely indulged in this brand of nostalgia" (52). A long history of inequitable school funding meant that poor children of color attended hazardous, unsanitary rural schools for much longer than White children—and that these schools were segregated. The popularity and pervasiveness, but not the universality, of the one-room school as a site of memory is exemplified in the novels of Laura Ingalls Wilder, which won a series of Newbery runners-up between 1938 and 1944 and which became embedded in popular culture, thanks in part to a long-running television series adaption in the 1970s and 1980s. Wilder's narratives share the domestic, rural charm of *The Wheel on the School* and capture both the symbolic freight and the limitations of the one-room school as symbol. In *Little Town on the Prairie* (1941; 1942 Newbery runner-up), Laura studies for her teaching certificate while attending a school that also hosts evening concerts, spelling bees, and other entertainment—including a minstrel show complete with blackface.[4] In addition to being a site of segregation and racism at home, the little red schoolhouse also came to be a symbol of American imperialism abroad as the United States established school systems in its overseas possessions with greater energy than any other twentieth-century empire.[5] American nostalgia for the "little red schoolhouse," then, can be linked to both Whiteness and cultural imperialism.[6]

*The Wheel on the School* depicts rural schooling in Holland, not the United States, yet it obliquely gestures toward both, revealing the way a treasured American symbol, the one-room schoolhouse, obscures a national history of racism at home and abroad. Lina's composition about storks—the essay that sets the novel's plot in motion—makes clear that she understands the beautiful white birds to be Dutch. But in one of the few lectures the teacher delivers as part of the student-driven stork project, he emphasizes the birds' status as migrants: "Do you know where our storks come from—where they are when they aren't in Holland? Imagine the heart of Africa. The head of a big river deep in Africa.... That's where our storks are now. Right there among the zebras and the herds of gazelles, among the lions and the buffaloes" (36). Africa remains foreign, exotic, and far away to the children of Shora, a provincial, subsistence-based fishing village. And Lina and her classmates appear entirely unaware of the larger forces shaping their identity as (White) Dutch citizens, including the Netherlands' long colonial presence in Africa.[7]

Shora's teacher, an outsider who is never named, does more than introduce surprising information; he also brings unorthodox pedagogical strategies into the classroom. The teacher figures throughout as facilitator rather than authoritative voice, and instead of upholding any local or national agenda, he seeks to follow the children's interests. His students' understanding of themselves and their immediate community is altered as a result. "To start with there was Shora," the novel begins (1), and Shora, a fishing village with its six houses, church, and schoolhouse, seems to be an insular enclave in which nothing much changes. Yet Lina's question about storks disrupts business as usual: the teacher abandons his lesson plans to encourage and nurture student inquiry. First, he asks his students to "think" about storks. Eelka explains that it's hard to think when one knows so little: "I'd be through in a minute" (6). When the students laugh, the teacher clarifies: "We can't think much when we don't know much. But we can wonder! ... For sometimes when we wonder, we can make things begin to happen" (6). With this unconventional prompt, the school becomes an engine of activity and an impetus for change in a small, intensely local community.

The initial response of Shora's children to an invitation to hypothesize and investigate, coupled with an early dismissal, is to play. But as the teacher had anticipated, play leads to insight. After falling into the water when jumping ditches, for example, Eelka looks for a tree on which to hang his wet clothes. Finding none, it occurs to him that the absence of trees might be a deterrent for storks looking for nesting grounds. When students return to school the next day, eager to report on the fruits of their wondering, there is another departure from school-day norms: they skip their usual practice of "singing the old, old song about their country" to focus on the stork project (26). As the students share their hypotheses about Shora's inability to attract storks, the teacher stands at the blackboard to take notes. Traditional order and discipline fade as "the teacher laughed as long and hard as the class" at Eelka's story of falling into the ditch, Lina "frantically waved her hand" and "almost shouted when the teacher did not turn" to her, and Auka *actually* "shouted" in the classroom (29, 30, 31). Only Lina, with rules about appropriate gendered behavior deeply internalized, seems concerned. The teacher, by contrast, is pleased by the excitement and especially with Lina's insistence that the problem of Shora, as far as the storks are concerned, is its sharp roofs. That characterization of the obstacle leads to an actionable plan that doesn't take decades, as planting trees would: "Now we are getting to something that we can do.... We wondered why and we reasoned it out. Now we must do" (34).

The teacher's attempted turn to arithmetic, grammar, and penmanship does not go well, and he demonstrates respect for the children's developmental stages (that is, their inability to delay gratification) by dismissing class an entire hour early. In exchange for the children's promise to give up part of a future Saturday for missed class time, the teacher sends them off in different directions in search of a wagon wheel. By presenting each child's search as a distinct chapter—"Jella and the Farmer," "Eelka and the Ancient Wheel," "Auka and the tin man"—DeJong highlights each child's contribution to the larger project. Readers and characters alike see that each student brings a different, valued skill to the collective, and that each child's individual efforts to secure a wagon wheel simultaneously raise the child's awareness of the needs of the broader society of which they are a part. In other words, even as they gain help from the adults in their community, the schoolchildren give back to those adults, strengthening the fabric of their village and its surrounding farmland in the process.

Each of these elements of the stork project—the inquiry-based learning that is rooted in an authentic question; recognition of the connections between play and discovery; flexible schedules; an emphasis on personal growth; and an understanding, in the words of John Dewey, that education should acknowledge that "a community only existed when its members relied upon and cooperated with one another" (Hartman

15)—is a hallmark of Progressive education, a movement originating in the late nineteenth century that viewed education as the linchpin of democracy. DeJong only briefly worked as a college instructor, and it's unclear how closely he followed contemporary debates around pedagogy—including the Cold War backlash against Progressive education. His depiction of a one-room schoolhouse is clearly an idealized view of what school could be. But whatever the source of his fictional stork project, it corresponds to the ideals of Progressive education (Cuban 43–44).

At the time of DeJong's writing, education was foremost in American minds. A "great appraisal" of education in the 1940s and 1950s put the school and "the innocent child" in focus, "mobilized as a way to regulate society" (Hartman, 1, 8). With the United States vying with the Soviet Union for world dominance, leaders agonized over youth's preparedness, finding it lacking. Calls for academic rigor and achievement (not to mention patriotism) rang through the corridors of power, and the child-centered, flexible, outside-the-box approaches detailed in DeJong's novel were among the first casualties.[8] The seeds of nostalgia for a different, softer, more child-friendly school experience were planted, and would in fact bear fruit in the 1960s, when educationalists again drew on the image of the little red schoolhouse to critique the changes brought about by the post-Sputnik National Defense Education Act of 1958, including a curricular emphasis on science, math, and second language acquisition and an instructional emphasis on memorization, testing, and tracking (Zimmerman 133–134). In this vision, the little red schoolhouse was championed less as a site of American democracy than as a model of Progressive education in action: ungraded classrooms, group learning, and an intimacy of student-teacher relationships that contrasted starkly to the conditions in sprawling, overcrowded postwar schools.

At the time of its publication, readers might also have appreciated the ways in which Shora's children are faced with problems that they can legitimately tackle by working together and drawing on local expertise. The very real dangers they face—storms, tides, near-drownings—might seem "cozy" in comparison to the new, human-made threats of the atomic age. In *Duck and Cover*, the chilling propaganda film created in 1951 and shown in schools throughout the country, a narrator instructs children to be prepared to protect their bodies from "the flash" of the atomic bomb, which might strike at any moment. "There might not be any grownups around when the bomb explodes," a measured narrator explains. "Then, you're on your own" (*Duck*). DeJong's is a world where children can still save themselves and each other and, working together, they can help other people and animals as well. The narrative techniques DeJong uses to build suspense and urgency pit humans against nature in "race the clock" scenarios: the stork migration is ending, so the children must find a wheel quickly; the tide comes in swiftly as Lina and Douwa unearth the ancient wheel, and the children must orchestrate their rescue. The challenges are real but they are always won, with children taking the lead.

## A Newbery Winner by Design—And by Default

Though largely forgotten today, Meindert DeJong achieved unparalleled literary recognition during the mid-twentieth century. Active for over three decades, he authored twenty-seven titles for children, saw his works translated into twenty languages, and became the first American recipient of the Hans Christian Andersen Award, the premier international prize for a body of work for young readers ("Meindert"). He is also among the authors most decorated by the Newbery establishment. Perhaps uncoincidentally in an era in which many prize-winning books were illustrated, DeJong is noted for his collaboration with Maurice Sendak, who was an emerging artist when their association began in 1953. Author and illustrator enjoyed an exceptional synergy, and Sendak illustrated "six of the seven DeJong books that won major awards"—including Newbery winner *The Wheel on the School* and four Newbery runners-up (Hartzell 228).[9] Two of those Newbery runners-up were awarded, in 1954, to the DeJong-Sendak collaborations *Shadrach* and *Hurry Home, Candy*.[10] "Frustrated" that both books fell short of Newbery gold in 1954, DeJong "deliberately set out to win it the next year" (Hartzell 230). He consulted his brother and fellow novelist, David Cornel DeJong. Thinking perhaps of the sensitive, intimate miniature that is 1954 runner-up *Shadrach*, the acutely emotional story of a very young boy and his pet rabbit, David advised his brother: "You're too much inside these kids. Paint a big canvas" (Hartzell 230). Heeding his brother's advice, DeJong created a group of child protagonists in *The Wheel on the School*, and sent them out into the world.

This deliberate bid for the Newbery worked—though in a roundabout way, as behind-the-scenes correspondence reveals. The members of the 1955 American Library Association (ALA) Newbery Award Committee claimed they couldn't identify a deserving winner. On behalf of the committee, Bertha Mahony Miller, the editor of *Horn Book Magazine* and founder of the nation's first children's bookstore, said the group found "good books, yes, but no truly distinguished books!!!" (Miller). Given this, she asked publisher Frederic Melcher, advisor to the committee and the person who had originally proposed the idea of the Newbery Award, whether it was necessary to grant an award that year. Melcher's response is not preserved in the archives, but the committee went ahead with their votes, proposing a broad range of titles ("Nominations"). This is a familiar narrative in Newbery history: both the committee's complaining that no single title rises to the top and the choice to select a previously-recognized author's book.

The selection of *The Wheel on the School* as the winner was a predictable and conservative choice.[11] During the first forty years of Newbery history, novels set in "far away" places were common. Kenneth Kidd has posited that the Newbery's focus on foreign settings could be a way to affirm American WASP society. Stories like *Wheel* allow the reader, and the prize-giver, to elide difficult social issues at home: "Difference is tolerated until it threatens native soil," writes Kidd, "then it must be contained" (179). Published in 1954, the year of the *Brown v. Board of Education* decision, *The Wheel on the School* centers on the project of attracting and welcoming storks from Africa into the insular village school of Shora. The storks' absence is in fact marked as unnatural since Holland has served as the birds' nesting grounds for centuries; they are viewed as quintessentially Dutch. Yet there is some ambivalence expressed, as the teacher associates the storks' other home, Africa, with exoticism and wildness. Nonetheless, the message of the novel is unequivocally about inclusivity and making connections with people who previously seemed like outsiders. This reflects what Kidd has described as the 1950 Newbery books' "anxious insistence on the universality of human experience" (179).

*The Wheel on the School*'s resonance for Cold War readers has not endured; while the title is mentioned in some homeschool reading blogs, it has periodically fallen out of print, despite its Newbery Medal and Sendak illustrations. Even in 1971, when DeJong was still active, critic John Rowe Townsend dismissed him as a "rather old-fashioned writer" (qtd. in Kibler). Yet "old-fashioned" might be exactly what a reader (or a Newbery committee) wants in a moment of cultural anxiety and fear such as the Cold War. Looking past the nostalgia embedded in both the author's craft and the Newbery committee's prizing, we can see ways in which the text was, in fact, forward-thinking. Its acknowledgment of environmental concerns is ahead of its time, as is its engagement with a number of social issues including the idea that disability is socially constructed, the dismissal and neglect of the aged, and the familial stress associated with precarious income (as with the tin man). The novel also anticipates 1960s Progressive educators' critique of Cold War-era education; in challenging post-Sputnik emphases on rigor, achievement, and a frantic pace of competition, the educationalists saw in the one-room schoolhouse a model to emulate. *The Wheel on the School* highlights education's restorative potential, its capacity to address the societal wrongs of neglect and exclusion. And it advances the idea that the purpose of education is to expand lives, not to win a struggle for power or dominance. Today's readers might find that the text resonates even as it pulls in two opposing directions: toward a longing for the "good old golden rule days," as well as toward a future in which children realize their power to enact social change within cohesive, multigenerational communities.

## Notes

1 The sole exception is *The House of Sixty Fathers*, which DeJong drafted while serving with a Chinese-American Air Force unit stationed in China during World War II (Hartzell 232). Inspired by a young Chinese refugee whom DeJong's unit "adopted," this war story was deemed "too realistic and too harsh for a children's book" (Kibler). It was perhaps on the strength of DeJong's 1955 Newbery win that *The House of Sixty Fathers* was published in 1956.

2 The family emigrated in part so that the older DeJong brothers would not be inducted into the army during World War I (Kibler).

3 DeJong's sensitivity to the exclusion of people with disabilities may relate to a relative's experience. Though the author's Uncle Meindert was the eldest son of his generation, he was deaf and nonverbal. As a result, it was DeJong's father who took over the family business in his place when young Meindert's grandfather died (D. DeJong, *Accent* 12).

4 Decades of critical discomfort with the *Little House* books' participation in settler colonialism and racist depictions of non-White characters culminated in the renaming of the American Library Association's Laura Ingalls Wilder Medal to the Children's Literature Legacy Award in 2018.

5 During the era of the US's earliest expansion overseas, the little red schoolhouse figured in political cartoons as shorthand for the transference of American values to colonized peoples. The school buildings erected in the Philippines, Hawaii, Puerto Rico, and elsewhere were not actually painted red or only one room in size (Zimmerman 70–74).

6 Importantly, populations in one-room schoolhouses were far from homogenous, even if White. Language, religion, and cultural practices were recurring sources of tension between immigrant and native-born families and teachers, particularly in the rural Midwest, where one-room schools endured well into the twentieth century.

7 The Netherlands was among the earliest European powers to exploit material and human resources in Africa (Cape Town was founded in 1652 by the Dutch East India Company) and one of the last European countries to abolish slavery; its influence can be seen today among South Africa's Afrikaners, descendants of early settlers.

8 Cold War critiques of Progressive education stemmed from wholescale rejection of a midcentury academic movement in American high schools, the "Life Adjustment Course." This curricular intervention drew on some principles of Progressive education, including child-centeredness, but was fundamentally anti-intellectual (Hartman 56). It had been designed as a solution to the delayed workforce entry and extension of schooling that greatly diversified the population of youth attending secondary school in the United States. The ensuing backlash against Progressive education and the many ideas associated with it—from open classrooms and flexible schedules to student inquiry and experimental learning—meant that Progressive education would not gain traction again until the 1960s.

9 Prizewinning DeJong-Sendak collaborations include Newbery Medal winner *The Wheel on the School*, four Newbery runners-up—*Shadrach*, *Hurry Home, Candy*, *Along Came a Dog*, and *The House of Sixty Fathers*, which also won the Child Study Association of America's Children's Book Award—and *Journey from Peppermint Street*, winner of the first National Book Award for children's literature (Hartzell 228; Kibler).

10 DeJong's editor Ursula Nordstrom, the influential head of Harper & Row's children's division, had written to him the year both books came out, "If

*Shadrach* doesn't win the Newbery surely *Hurry Home Candy* ought to" (Nordstrom 65). In 1954, to a colleague, she lamented: "No, [*Hurry Home, Candy*] did not win the Newbery Medal. It was a strong runner-up but it didn't win. DeJong will win it one of these days, maybe in 1955. (And I'm a Dodger fan, too.)" (Nordstrom 74).

11 Curiously, the Newbery-Caldecott Selection Committee that prized *The Wheel on the School* also named *Wheel on the Chimney*, written by Margaret Wise Brown and illustrated by Tibor Gergely, a Caldecott runner-up. This picture book tells the story of a stork couple that is migrating from Africa in search of a proper roof to nest on. The storks end up settling in Hungary, Gergely's native country, in a similar expression of nostalgia for an Old World tradition.

## Works Cited


Brown, Margaret Wise. *Wheel on the Chimney*. Illus. Tibor Gergely. New York: J. B. Lipincott, 1954. Print.

Cuban, Larry. *How Teachers Taught: Constancy and Change in American Classrooms, 1880–1990*. New York: Teachers College Press, 1993. Print.

DeJong, David Cornel. "My Brother Meindert." *Newbery Medal Books: 1922–1955, with their Authors' Acceptance Papers & Related Material chiefly from the* Horn Book Magazine. Ed. Bertha Mahony Miller and Elinor Whitney Field. Boston: The Horn Book, 1955. 427–433. Print.

DeJong, David Cornel. *With a Dutch Accent: How a Hollander Became an American*. New York: Harper & Brothers Publishers, 1944. Print.

DeJong, Meindert. "Acceptance Paper." *Newbery Medal Books: 1922–1955, with their Authors' Acceptance Papers & Related Material chiefly from the* Horn Book Magazine. Ed. Bertha Mahony Miller and Elinor Whitney Field. Boston: The Horn Book, 1955. 434–439. Print.

DeJong, Meindert. *The Wheel on the School*. Illus. Maurice Sendak. New York: Harper & Row Publishers, 1954. Print.

*Duck and Cover*. Prod. United States Office of Civil Defense and Archer Productions. 1951. Film.

Hartman, Andrew. *Education and the Cold War: The Battle for the American School*. New York: Palgrave Macmillan, 2008. Print.

Hartzell, Judith. "Happy Centennial, Meindert DeJong!" *Horn Book Magazine* 82.28 (Mar./Apr. 2006): 227–233. Print.

Kibler, Myra. "Meindert DeJong." *American Writers for Children Since 1960: Fiction*. Ed. Glenn E. Estes. *Dictionary of Literary Biography* 52. Detroit: Gale Research, 1986. Web. 18 June 2020.

Kidd, Kenneth B. "Prizing Children's Literature: The Case of Newbery Gold." *Children's Literature* 35 (2007): 166–190. *Project Muse*. Web. 12 June 2018.

May, Elaine Tyler. *Homeward Bound: American Families in the Cold War Era*. New York: Basic Books, 1988. Print.

"Meindert DeJong." *Gale Literature: Contemporary Authors*. Detroit: Gale Research, 2004. Web. 18 June 2020.

Miller, Bertha Mahony. Letter to Frederic G. Melcher. 13 Nov. 1954. Record Series 24/42/4, Box 1, Folder 1. American Library Association Archives. Urbana-Champaign, IL: University of Illinois Archives.

"Nominations for 1954 Newbery Award." Record Series 24/42/4, Box 1, Folder 1. American Library Association Archives. University of Illinois Archives, Urbana-Champaign, IL.

Nordstrom, Ursula. *Dear Genius: The Letters of Ursula Nordstrom.* Ed. Leonard S. Marcus. New York: HarperCollins, 1998. Print.

Wilder, Laura Ingalls. *Little Town on the Prairie.* 1941. New York: Harper & Row, 1953. Print.

Zimmerman, Jonathan. *Small Wonder: The Little Red Schoolhouse in History and Memory.* New Haven: Yale UP, 2009. Print.

# 9 Lost Cat

## *It's Like This, Cat* (1964) and the Invention of Young Adult Literature

*Kathleen T. Horning and Jocelyn Van Tuyl*

How did the young adult (YA) novel emerge? With a girl's first romance (Maureen Daly's 1942 "junior novel" *Seventeenth Summer*)? The urban wanderings of a privileged but alienated boy (J. D. Salinger's 1951 novel *The Catcher in the Rye*)? Or with gang rivalries and social inequality (S. E. Hinton's 1967 novel *The Outsiders*)? Critics routinely place the birth of YA in one of these locations (Trites 9). But that narrative leaves out a seminal YA novel: Emily Neville's *It's Like This, Cat* (1963; 1964 Newbery Medal), published four years prior to *The Outsiders*. This essay argues that *Cat* is perhaps the first true example of YA fiction and hypothesizes about why the Newbery winner has failed to garner critical attention for its contributions to the emerging YA genre.

### An Unexpected Win for an Unconventional Book

*It's Like This, Cat* was a dark-horse contender for the Newbery. Though the novel was favorably reviewed upon publication, the influential yet conservative *Horn Book Magazine* didn't review it until after it had won the Newbery Medal (Bird et al. 160–161). But over at *Kirkus*, children's book review editor Lillian N. Gerhardt, who would go on to become editor in chief of *School Library Journal* (*SLJ*), promptly flagged *Cat* as "a potential prize-winning book" ("It's"). This endorsement was a breach of etiquette: *SLJ* editor Pat Allen soon informed Gerhardt that she was "in deep trouble with the grande[s] dames" because mentioning the Newbery Award simply wasn't done.[1] Gerhard was unapologetic: "Not a bit sorry. Now I'm going to go look for the Caldecott," she said (qtd. in Sutton 121).

The impact of Gerhardt's review may never be known; what is known is that the 1964 Newbery-Caldecott selection process did not involve a swift consensus. In late January 1964, a committee of twenty-three librarians from around the country met in a small room in a Chicago hotel to select the Newbery and Caldecott winners from a group of eligible

DOI: 10.4324/9780367337223-9-10

books that had been published in 1963. In those years, the executive board members of the American Library Association (ALA)'s Children's Services Division (now ALSC) were on the committee, with the president-elect serving as chair. In addition to the 1964 Newbery-Caldecott Medal Selection Committee chair, Helen R. Sattley, the roster reads like a who's-who of twentieth-century children's library services leaders, including Augusta Baker, head of children's services at New York Public Library; Sara I. Fenwick, professor at the University of Chicago's library school; Rosemary Livsey, children's services coordinator at Los Angeles Public Library; Marilyn Miller, school library consultant for the state of Kansas; and Spencer Shaw, children's consultant for the Nassau Library System in New York.

There was also an enthusiastic elementary school librarian, Sarah Dickinson, from Washington State, who didn't seem to have heard the admonition to keep all committee proceedings confidential. She went home after the January meetings and wrote up a chatty, detailed account called "I Was There on the 1964 Newbery-Caldecott Awards Committee," which was published in her school library association newsletter. In it, she listed the titles of the twenty-seven Newbery and twelve Caldecott contenders that were still on the table after the first round of eliminations. Sharing this information was a serious breach of confidentiality: even the number of finalists is to be kept secret. So, too, is the number of voting rounds required, but Dickinson revealed that it took five ballots, an "unusually high number," to select the Caldecott winner (6). This lack of consensus is surprising, considering that the 1964 Caldecott went to *Where the Wild Things Are* (1963; 1964 Caldecott Medal), a book widely considered today to be the best picture book of the twentieth century, and definitely the best Caldecott Medal book ever. "The Newbery winner was still more difficult to select," Dickinson continues. Voting continued "until long after midnight and on the ninth ballot the winner came out" (7).

The book that won the Newbery that year, *It's Like This, Cat*, was a first novel by a middle-aged housewife, Emily Cheney Neville. A former journalist, Neville had only just started writing fiction when the youngest of her five children entered kindergarten. When her short story "Cat and I" was published in the *New York Mirror*, she gained enough confidence in her writing to submit it to editor Ursula Nordstrom at Harper & Row. Given its length, she thought it might be the text of a picture book. But the story was written in the voice of a fourteen-year-old boy who was arguing with his father about getting a cat. Not the typical fare for a picture-book story, but Nordstrom obviously saw the potential in Neville and invited her to come in for a meeting.

Nordstrom suggested Neville use the cat story as the basis for a full-length contemporary novel about a boy living in the city. According to Neville, the editor told her, "I'm so sick of [historical novels] starting

'Gold! the cry went up'" ("Emily" 169). Under Nordstrom's direction, she went home and teased it out into the book that became *It's Like This, Cat*. The opening lines were quite a departure from the usual manuscripts Nordstrom was seeing (and dreading): "My father is always talking about how a dog can be very educational for a boy. This is one reason I got a cat" (1).

The story, told in fourteen-year-old Dave Mitchell's comical first-person present-tense voice, takes place over the course of twelve months: the end of a school year, the long summer vacation, and the beginning of his first year in high school. There's not much of a plot; instead, it offers vignettes of his life in New York City, where he lives in a Gramercy Park apartment with his lawyer father, who's "a small guy with very little grey curly hair, so maybe he thinks he's got to roar to make up for not being a big hairy tough guy," and his mother, who is quiet and prone to asthma attacks whenever Dave and his dad get into one of their frequent arguments (1–2). He prefers to hang out with easygoing Kate, the "Crazy ... Cat Woman" a few doors down, who offers Dave a tiger kitten to care for, whom he names Cat (3, 7).

When Cat gets lost, Dave eventually finds him in the basement of a neighboring apartment building, trapped in a stranger's storage locker. Luckily, there is also a thief in the basement who picks the padlock on the locker in order to free Cat, and then helps himself to some of the locker's contents. The thief is a nineteen-year-old NYU dropout named Tom, and he and Dave become friends. There are other friends, too: schoolmates Nick and Ben, and Mary, a girl Dave meets at Coney Island, who shares his love of Harry Belafonte records and whose mother is a free-spirited beatnik, so different from Dave's own parents. His interactions with this cast of characters take him all over New York City, to the Bronx, to Brooklyn, to the Fulton Fish Market, and points in between. Dave travels freely on foot, on his bike, and on the subway when he has enough pocket money for a token. Throughout his journeys, he makes wry observations about the people and places he sees. In a very real sense, New York City is like a character, and whatever the book may lack in plot is more than made up for in setting.[2]

Dave's mobility within the city says a great deal about both his identity and the moment of the book's creation.[3] Dave's freedom to explore indicates that he is no longer a child, but his age does impose some constraints: for example, he is sometimes denied entry to movie theaters, or confined to the under-sixteen seating area (69, 38). His mobility is implicitly a male privilege (Tribunella, "Child" 68): despite her laissez-faire parents, Dave's Coney Island friend Mary travels into Manhattan only with her mother (77, 164). Though sometimes forced to walk for lack of bus fare, he is clearly middle-class (109). And his Whiteness is reflected by the areas he chooses to visit: he explores the Lower East Side, "a real

Jewish neighborhood" (110), and has ethnic White friends (33, 102), but he never interacts with people explicitly identified as African American (Wilkin 79), and the long list of neighborhoods he visits does not include Harlem. Everything about Dave's wanderings marks him as a White, middle-class postwar teenage boy.

And that demographic was, implicitly, the book's target readership. Contemporaneous critics identified *Cat* as "directed especially to a male readership" (Goodwin 449): "11-to-14-year old boys" (Hood 2). Today, ALA's Newbery Medal, for children's literature, and Printz Award, for YA literature, both claim that demographic, but in the 1960s, the YA genre was just emerging. Not until the end of the decade would YA literature be "understood to be a distinct literary genre" (Trites 9) and not until 2000 would the ALA create a separate award for it. Lukewarm or negative reactions to the novel may have stemmed in part from a lack of familiarity with what we now understand as conventions of the genre. To be specific, Neville narrated typical adolescent experiences but told her story in a style that had more in common with "literary" texts for adults than did most youth literature of the day. Neville's stylistic particularities include an episodic structure, "first-person narration, and [an] unresolved plot"—techniques common in "adult fiction" since the 1940s. But a "literary lag" of approximately twenty years separates "the time a storytelling method is generally accepted at the adult reading level and the time it is first employed and finally accepted in books for children," Gerhardt argues ("Argument" 7).[4] *Cat*'s early adoption of these stylistic innovations—particularly the first-person vernacular and decidedly realist approach—in a book for youth may have impressed a Newbery committee looking for distinct and distinguished children's literature.

## "It's Like This": Vernacular Voice and the New Realism

The novel's narrative voice was mentioned in nearly every review in 1963. This unanimous reaction underscores the novelty of Neville's narrative style and suggests that voice was becoming a key factor defining the emerging new literature for teens. Today we are used to first-person, present-tense fiction for children and teens, but in its time, Neville's book was called a "new-style story" and a "rare reading experience" ("It's"). As a first-time author not steeped in the truisms of publishing for children, Neville didn't realize that "it was well accepted that children didn't like books told in the first person," so she "went ahead" with the first-person narration that would become one of *Cat*'s distinguishing features (Neville, "Emily" 169). Neville was apparently also unaware of the bias toward Standard English. The novel's use of slang and vernacular English was striking—so up-to-the-minute that one reviewer felt it necessary to clarify that the "Cat" in the title referred to an actual four-legged animal, lest someone think it a slang word for "person" (Dalgliesh 34). (Fresh and modern at the time, the sixties teen slang is, of course, one of the things that dates the book today.) When reviewers praised the accuracy of the novel's "teenage dialogue and slang," they implied that adolescent readers would be attracted by this feature (Goodwin 449). But in some reviews, that approachability was secondary to a more literary aim: boosting *Cat*'s prestige by comparing its style to both a recent literary sensation, Salinger's *The Catcher in the Rye* (Taylor D20), and to the dean of American vernacular fiction: Neville "knows the language of a New York boy in the same sense that Mark Twain knew the talk of a Mississippi one," claims Gerhardt, and shows equally "complete mastery of the technique" ("It's").

In a novel that stands out because of its distinctive narrative voice, the narrator-protagonist also comments repeatedly on how other people talk, offering a meta-reflection on speech variations and sociolinguistic identity. After Tom picks a lock to rescue Cat, Dave expresses surprise that Tom "didn't really *look* like a burglar. And he didn't talk 'dese and dose.' Maybe real burglars don't all talk that way—only the ones on TV" (16). Dave expects gangster talk; not hearing it, he implicitly registers that Tom's background and social standing are similar to his own. (Dave is college-bound and Tom was, until recently, an undergraduate.) While showing us Dave's sensitivity to language, Neville is also having a joke at the boy's expense, revealing his naive assumptions and uncritical media consumption. But when the narrative turns to a character whose background differs from Dave's, it becomes apparent that the author herself has unquestioningly absorbed stereotypes. Butch, the janitor in Dave's building, "says 'Yas'm' to all ladies," Dave points out (4). Butch is never explicitly identified as Black, but Neville's cringeworthy use of stereotypical, stylized dialect implies that he is African American (Wilkin 79). In an apparent attempt at humor, Neville has Butch drop malapropisms, such as "veteran" for "cat doctor" (71).[5] This kind of gag comes straight out of entertainments like the sitcom *Amos 'n' Andy*, which was playing on reruns at the time of *Cat*'s publication. Whereas Dave interrogates the way popular entertainment has warped his expectations about criminals' speech patterns, Butch's stereotyped language and minstrel-inspired gaffes are embedded in the text without comment. The author's own biased assumptions about African Americans' speech and knowledge go entirely unquestioned in the novel.

The limited knowledge (he can't get the word "veterinarian" right) and caricatured dialogue Neville gives to Butch point toward two potential problems with Dave's narrative voice: naivete and diction. Narrative voice is about more than tone and slang: as the narrator speaks, he reveals things about his knowledge, awareness, and beliefs. But when an adult author adopts the position of an adolescent first-person narrator, there is a disjunction. As literary scholar Mike Cadden argues, "novels constructed by adults to simulate an authentic adolescent's voice are inherently ironic because the so-called adolescent voice is never—and can never be—truly authentic." In attempting to portray the adolescent focalizer's consciousness, the author may intentionally construct a "limited awareness of the world that the novelist knows to be incomplete and insufficient" (146). This narrative move might seem authentic: contemporaneous reviewer Mark Taylor claimed that Dave's "naiveté and one-sided point of view rings true" (D20). But even if this naive and limited viewpoint serves to set up future growth—the realization that robbers don't always talk like TV gangsters, say, or that fathers aren't always bent on making life hard for their sons—it is not entirely authentic: it is, in Cadden's words, an "artful depiction of artlessness" (146).

Another angle from which to question the authenticity of the narrative voice concerns diction. Many contemporary reviewers suggested that Dave Mitchell was pitch-perfect. But just a few years after *It's Like This, Cat*, teenaged author S. E. Hinton became a sensation with her novel *The Outsiders*. Naturally, she was deemed an authority on the literary depiction of the adolescent voice and viewpoint. Writing in the *New York Times* in 1967, Hinton called out adult authors' attempts to render teen vernacular in novels as inauthentic: "The rule is: If you don't say it yourself, don't say it" ("Teen-Agers" BR 14). Like a parent or teacher's failed attempts to seem cool by using teen jargon, Hinton implies, the stylistic borrowing of teen slang actually undercuts a novel's realism.

David C. Davis, a professor of education who did not think *Cat* deserved the Newbery, took a different tack, arguing in a 1964 *Horn Book Magazine* essay called "It's This Way, Kid!" that the novel privileged style over substance. Davis parodied the novel's narrative voice, imagining Dave talking to Frederic Melcher (father of the Newbery and Caldecott awards) about a conversation he had had with his librarian about what makes a good book. It's evident from the following passage that Davis did not think *It's Like This, Cat* was one of them: "Well, you see, it's this way, there are some writers who make you see everyday things. You know, family squabbles, first dates, subway rides ... but after you get through, you've just seen them! Nothing sticks to show new angles. You don't see them in a different way. That's all, you've just seen them—not *inside* them!" (525–526). The way in which Professor Davis used Dave's own voice to critique Neville's book was clever, if a bit mean-spirited, but he clearly missed the subtleties of the story. Dave does indeed come to see his father from a "new angle" when he begins to see him through Tom's eyes. This comes out most clearly in a conversation Dave has with Tom near the end of the book. Pop "just likes to boss everything I do," Dave complains:

"So—he cares."

"Huh." I am not ready to buy this, but then I remember Tom's father, who *doesn't* care. It makes me think.

"Besides," says Tom, "half the reason you and your father are always bickering is that you're so much alike."

"Me? Like *him?*" (173)

The conversation is subtle, but Tom has clearly planted the seed of an idea. Davis, however, does not acknowledge Dave's maturing understanding of the family conflict.

More significantly, Davis failed to see what so many others did when they looked at *It's Like This, Cat*: the birth of modern YA literature in the form of contemporary realism, now so common in YA literature that we forget it was ever new. But in 1963, it was. The story was fresh and honest. And because it was recognized as realistic, it was considered acceptable for a character to disrespect his father and question authority, a departure for a Newbery character. In her Newbery acceptance speech, "Out Where the Real People Are," Emily Neville defended this new genre for teens: "The real world, with its shadings of light and dark, its many-toned colors, is so much more beautiful than the rigid world of good and bad. It is also more confusing. I think the teen-age reader is ready for both" ("Newbery" 135).

One thing everyone agreed on at the time was that *It's Like This, Cat* was a book for teenagers. There was none of the hand-wringing we see today about the Newbery choice being "too old." Instead, there was a tacit understanding that the Newbery audience included teens. There were quite a few articles published in the professional library journals of the time about books for young adults, or "junior novels" as they were often called then. Many, including Ursula Nordstrom, advocated for less romance and more realism in books for teens, using *It's Like This, Cat* as a model work. Writing for the Children's Services Division's *Top of the News* in November 1964, Nordstrom recalled a conversation she had with a librarian who told her she hadn't liked the book because Dave didn't respect his father. Nordstrom wrote: "A teenager, as he lives his own life, is not protected from reality. If books try to protect him from harm, they will supply him only with escape literature, and so deny him a true outlook on the world. And critically speaking, we believe manuscripts from which everything ugly, wicked, and disturbing has been expurgated are usually dull, because they are so unlifelike" (36).

Neville's unflinching adherence to reality made her part of a literary trend, the new contemporary realism that was emerging in the 1960s and 1970s. An early observer of this "admirable" trend was Robert Hood, executive editor of the Boy Scouts of America's *Boys' Life* magazine, whose 1963 review article praised books like *It's Like This, Cat* and *The Loner* (Ester Wier's eventual runner-up for the 1964 Newbery Medal):

"in step with our times, skillfully and subtly written," these recent books "demonstrate a psychological awareness usually found only in adult novels" (2). They feature a "new-style hero"—distinct from the "stereotyped" "hero" of the "old-fashioned junior novel"—a descendant of Salinger's Holden Caulfield who "has trouble adjusting" (2). (In fact, Hood labels this new kind of fiction the "novel of personal adjustment" [2].) Within two years, reviewer Jane Thomas pointed out that this "new kind of straight-talking, sophisticated juvenile fiction is beginning to appear, not only for the teens, but for younger children, too." These novels by writers like Louise Fitzhugh—author of *Harriet the Spy* and *The Long Secret*, both edited by Nordstrom—tackle problems that were previously off-limits in youth literature, doing so with neither "pussyfooting" nor sensationalism. What fueled this trend? Thomas credits Neville's *It's Like This, Cat*, which "boosted this modern school of juvenile fiction by winning the Newbery" (E7).[6]

## Families, Friends, and Felines

While Dave roams widely across the city, *Cat*'s most intense realism surrounds the central domestic conflict: the strained relationship between the fourteen-year-old boy and his "Pop." The subjects of conflict between the teen and his father are classic: hairstyle (Dave's is longish), musical tastes (Dave adores the African American singer and political activist Harry Belafonte), and perceived softness (Dave fails to replicate the paper route and hunting trips of his father's youth).[7] Rebellion against his father's belief that dogs are good for boys is one motivation for Dave's decision to adopt a cat (1). Ironically, though, Cat immediately starts bringing the teen into closer alignment with his father's ideals. After Tom burgles the neighbor's basement, a newspaper describes a person of interest who is clearly Dave, with his "long 'ducktail' haircut" and "heavy black sweater" (18). To avoid recognition, Dave dons a "necktie and suit jacket" and gets a "Butch" haircut—earning Pop's approval for his "Ivy-League disguise" (19). From that point onward, Cat is responsible, if only indirectly, for improvements in the father-son relationship.

It is during an attempt to rescue Cat from a nearby basement that Dave meets nineteen-year-old college dropout Tom—Tom as in tomcat, as children's literature scholar Carolyn T. Kingston points out (152). Tom's father has disappeared, leaving him without financial or social support. It is Dave's father who steps in to help him get a job, recover college credits, and deal with the juvenile justice system after he is caught returning items he had stolen. Dave "learns, by seeing the relationship between his father and his friend, that his father really is a pretty good guy," explain children's literature critics May Hill Arbuthnot and Zena Sutherland, noting that "the experience of seeing one's parents through a friend's eyes is a common one, usually revelatory and seldom touched on in books for young people" (464).[8] Dave's view of his father, colored by the inevitable tensions between teen and parent, gets its first jolt when he hears Tom call his Pop "quite a guy" (83). Deeper shifts come about as he implicitly compares the stability and opportunities he enjoys with Tom's less favorable situation. YA theorist Roberta Trites defines YA literature as fundamentally concerned with power—with the various institutions (school, church, government) and "social constructions" the adolescent must "learn to negotiate," arguing that growth in the YA novel always relates to "what the adolescent [learns] about power" (3, x). Power in *It's Like This, Cat* has a lot to do with family support, financial means, and social capital, and Dave's dawning awareness of what his parents do for him (along with his observation of his Pop's interventions on Tom's behalf) is part of his maturation process.

Dave also grows through the challenges of "parenting" Cat.[9] Significantly, the tiger-striped stray is described as a "father cat" the first time Dave meets him (6). Feline fathers rarely remain with their offspring: they are more like the father who abandoned Tom than Dave's Pop, who is involved and present (perhaps too present for the teenager's tastes). The tomcat's paternity—"your Cat has probably fathered a few dozen kittens by now," Kate informs Dave (68)—forces the teen to make a difficult decision on his pet's behalf. In a tragicomic projection of concerns about his own manhood, Dave anguishes over the decision to neuter his pet after Cat is severely injured in an after-hours fight. Kate provides a clinic address and Dave's mother contributes cash, but the teenager makes the decision and handles all arrangements on his own (Kingston 153). Coming of age in this novel involves taking responsibility for another being and making hard choices on its behalf. This leads to increased understanding: when Pop insists that Dave enroll only in core academic courses for the upcoming school year, the teen grumbles, but Tom reminds him that "your father's the one has to see you get into college or get a job" (173). The experience of "parenting" Cat, combined with his older friend's insights, makes Dave better able to understand the motivation for his own father's parenting decisions.

Another painful decision about a cat's welfare falls not to Dave, but to Kate, his "cat lady" neighbor. When reporters swarm her house for news of an inheritance, one of them steps on a kitten—not just any kitten, but the "adventurous orange kitten" who has charmed Dave, Kate, and the reader for the last several pages—and "a shattering caterwaul goes up" (154). The kitten's injuries are extensive and unsurvivable. "With one violent, merciful stroke Kate finishes it. She picks the limp body up and wraps it neatly in a paper towel and places it in the wastebasket" (154). As Kingston argues, this incident builds on the novel's earlier "tragic moment," Dave's decision to sacrifice "his pet's masculinity" in order to "keep Cat from further suffering" (Kingston 153). The mercy-killing, characterized by the "element of shock" (Kingston 154) and a total lack of sentimentality, alienated some readers. Neville's Newbery acceptance speech quotes a letter from an indignant 10-1/2-year-old who signed herself "an ex-reader, Barbara." "I respect Barbara's position," Neville says: "I killed her kitten, and she hates me." The author goes on to distinguish between child readers like Barbara and her target readership, "twelve- to sixteen-year-olds," who are mature enough to realize that Kate's action is not cruel but "courageous." This difference in understanding warrants a totally different type of fiction, Neville argues: it explains the "difference between a children's tale and a young adult's novel" ("Newbery" 134).[10]

The readers targeted by Neville are old enough to absorb the sorrows experienced by human characters as well. Tom's father has abandoned him for his new family; Kate's only relative, a long-estranged brother, has died. When Dave's mother invites both of Dave's friends to Thanksgiving dinner, Dave compares them to strays: "My family is starting to collect people the way Kate collects homeless cats. Of course, Kate and Tom aren't homeless. They're people-less—not part of any family" (146). Cat, who brought both stray humans into the Mitchells' orbit, proves a conduit for more harmonious relations within the family. When the Mitchells take in two of Kate's stray kittens to prevent trouble with her landlord, it becomes clear that the father-son fights, not pet dander, are "the main cause of Mom's asthma. So we both try to do a little better" (159, 171). Importantly, this is not a story in which the teenager alone is to blame for family strife, but one in which both father and son acknowledge their role in the conflict.

Neville shows us incremental change and believable growth, rather than tying the father-son conflict up with a bow and claiming that all is well now. This comports with her stated aim of providing "insight ... not conclusions" in her books (Ullmann). With no facile closure to the central conflict, though, how is a writer to end her novel? Neville opts for one of the oldest endings in the world: an engagement. In the novel's final chapter, Tom suddenly announces that he and his girlfriend Hilda have become engaged, and that he has enlisted in the Army in order to support his new family (178).[11] Everyone toasts the happy couple, the adults with champagne and Dave with soda, then Dave raises his glass "to Cat! Tom wouldn't even be standing here if it wasn't for Cat" (180). The story has come full circle: a novel that began when a scrappy stray tomcat found a family ends with an abandoned young man, Tom, building a new family for himself. The symmetry works, yet the sudden change of focus, from Dave to Tom, is surprising. Like Frances Hodgson Burnett's *The Secret Garden*, where protagonist Mary is sidelined at the end, reduced to witnessing a father-son reconciliation, *It's Like This, Cat* ends with its protagonist observing from the margins. This is an extremely clever move on Neville's part. Dave's own story retains the open-endedness that would become typical of YA fiction, but he is left to witness his friend's assimilation into two of society's most powerful institutions: marriage and the military. What Dave witnesses is a reminder of how close he is to adulthood—after all, he's only five years younger than Tom. Thanks to his family's support, Dave will surely attend college (61–62); his own adolescent freedom will last a little longer than Tom's. But from the beginning, the novel's conservative tendencies have drawn Dave closer to his parents' ideals, as when he cuts his hair and puts on a suit jacket and necktie (19). Ultimately, Neville implies, Dave himself will get married, and look more and more like Pop. This is the opposite of the exhortation to "stay gold"—to retain the idealism of youth—in S. E. Hinton's *The Outsiders* (113). Returning to Trites's argument that YA fiction is all about negotiating institutions and coming to understand how power works, it is clear that Neville's stance is different from that of other YA origin texts. Hinton, a teenager herself when she wrote *The Outsiders*, demonstrates a keen awareness of the power of social institutions, especially class, but retains a youthful rebelliousness against the tarnish of aging. Salinger, though closer to thirty at the time of authorship, takes a similar stance in *The Catcher in the Rye*. But Neville, writing in her forties, has a different viewpoint entirely: her novel concludes with the sense that it will be perfectly fine for both Tom and Dave to settle into mainstream, middle-class American adulthood.

## From the Newbery to Neglect

*It's Like This, Cat* was lauded in its own time by critics and librarians as a new type of book for teens, a type that would soon take hold as the mainstay of YA literature and last until the recent invasion of vampires and angels and other unreal situations. Why, then, is it not remembered today? Why is it not considered at least a touchstone of YA literature, if not a classic work? Why does *The Outsiders*, published four years later, get credited as the book that ushered in a new era of contemporary realism in YA literature? The answer is multifaceted: we argue that the lack of uptake from teen readers, the author's position as a middle-aged mother, and perhaps even Newbery gold itself were contributing factors.

Few teens embraced Neville's novel at the time of its publication, not to mention in the intervening years. The reasons for early neglect aren't readily apparent. Dave was a likable, sophisticated character who represented a counterculture mindset and spoke directly to teens. As such, he might have developed a cult following. Elizabeth H. Moger, a librarian from Long Island, proffered a hypothesis about the cool reception in an April 1964 letter to the editor of *SLJ*:

> Librarians may be crazy about *It's Like This, Cat* (I am myself) but have you tried to get people to touch it with a 10-foot pole? It's a

*Figure 9.1* Glenn and Marcy Neville on their front stoop.

Source: Photograph by Emily Cheney Neville, from the Neville family collection.

> book about, and presumably for, a 14-year-old boy, but will you look at that fourth-reader print? Why do publishers have to give a book that kind of kiss of death? Not to mention the illustrations which are a great big horrible folksy mess. (Moger 4)

Moger is absolutely right. A librarian trying to sell a fourteen-year-old on the book, with its large type and copious white space, wouldn't stand a chance.

The line drawings that open each chapter aren't as bad as Moger claims; illustrator Emil Weiss actually used Neville's own teenage son, Glenn Jr., as his model. But the illustrated novel, at least for older kids, was on its way out. *Rifles for Watie*, the first Newbery winner that didn't have illustrations, had been published six years earlier. Only four Newbery winners from the sixties were illustrated, and most of those aimed at a much

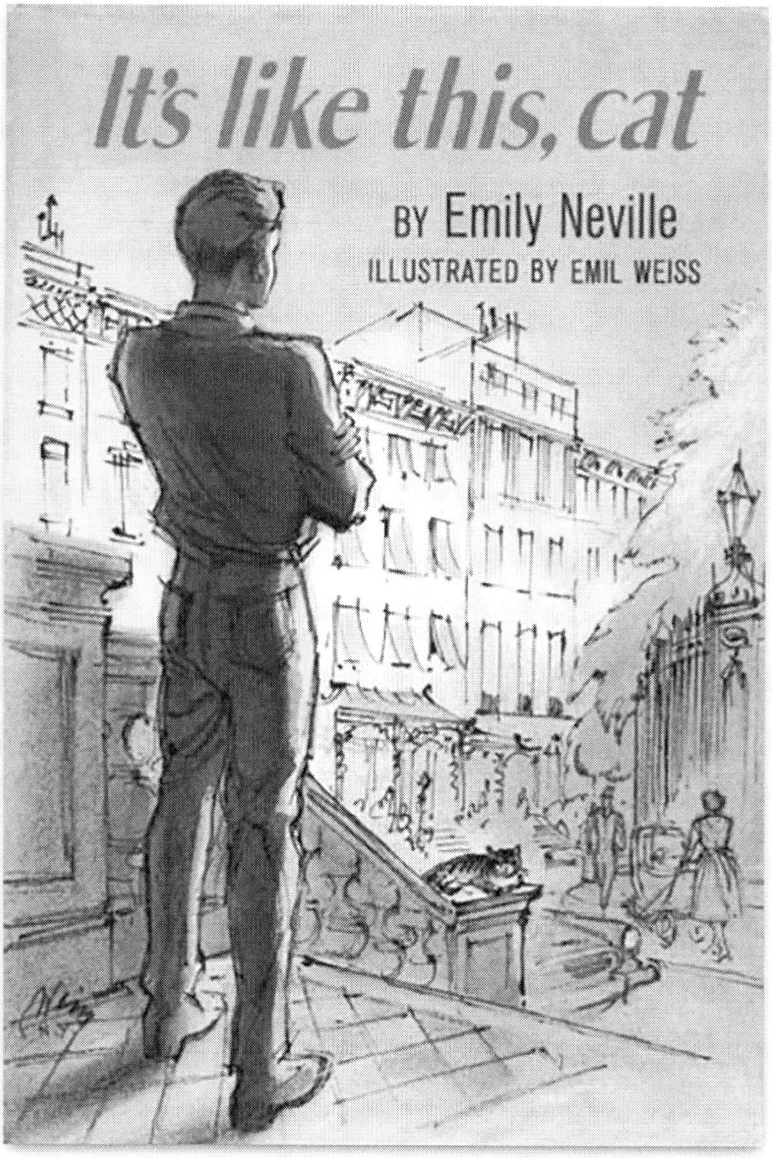


*Figure 9.2* Jacket art by Emil Weiss, based on a photograph of the author's son Glenn (Figure 9.1).

Source: *It's Like This, Cat*, by Emily Neville, with illustrations by Emil Weiss (Harper & Row Publishers, 1963).

younger readership than *Cat*.[12] The contrast between *Cat*'s story, voice, and intended readership on the one hand and the line drawings reminiscent of *Highlights for Children* magazine on the other makes for a jarring disconnect.

With Moger's perceptive remarks on the book's design in mind, we saw *Cat* as we had almost fifty years ago, when we were young readers ourselves. Neither of us read *It's Like This, Cat* as a child or young teen, though Kathleen did read and love two other books by Emily Cheney Neville, *Berries Goodman* and *The Seventeenth Street Gang*.[13] They have the same hallmarks as *It's Like This, Cat*—real kids, flawed adults, humor, a great voice—and Kathleen is sure she would have loved *Cat* back then. We both remember pulling *It's Like This, Cat* off the library shelf, looking at it, and rejecting it. It must have been the look of it. (Jocelyn clearly recalls being turned off by the book's resemblance to the Harper & Row readers used in her school.) Librarians know that kids are very sensitive to typography, perhaps even more so than jacket art, and that teens will quickly reject a book where the type is either too big or too small. The usually savvy Ursula Nordstrom had gotten the text right, but had made a fatal error when it came to book design.

We frequently compare the winners of the Newbery and Caldecott Medals to their corresponding Honor Books, or to the medal winners in previous or subsequent years. But rarely do we compare the Newbery book of any given year to its corresponding Caldecott winner, even though, until 1979, both awards were determined by the same committee. With that in mind, it's especially interesting to look at the winning books of 1964—*Where the Wild Things Are* and *It's Like This, Cat*—in tandem.

Both are about boys rebelling against their parents. Both speak respectfully and directly to young readers, eschewing the "rigid world of good and bad" (Neville, "Newbery" 135). Both embody the truthfulness their authors valued—Neville's embrace of the "real world" and Sendak's rejection of "half-truth [children's] books" in his Caldecott acceptance speech (Neville, "Newbery" 135; Sendak 252). Both were harbingers of change. And both were published by the same formidable editor, Harper & Row's Ursula Nordstrom, who was no stranger to breaking with tradition.[14] Although ultimately the two books were very different from each other in their artistic approaches and, today, one is beloved and the other virtually unread, it is easy to see how the same group of people would choose these two books, even if it took much discussion and many ballots to reach a decision. Clearly, the 1964 Newbery-Caldecott Medal Selection Committee was made up of risk-takers who were able to embrace a changing world, even if they were unsure of what that terrain would be like, out beyond the library shelves of sunny, happy stories published in the golden age of children's books, out here in the future, where the wild things and the real people are.[15]

And yet, the Newbery Award itself may have been, in some sense, the kiss of death, preventing *It's Like This, Cat* from gaining traction and longevity. One of *Cat*'s liabilities is evident from the reviews and author profiles published in the wake of Neville's 1964 Newbery win. These depictions of the middle-aged first-time author emphasized her subject position as "mother," explaining, for example, that she wrote the manuscript during the morning hours when the youngest of her five children was in kindergarten (Start 31). Such descriptions were common for female authors at the time; journalists penned similar copy when Elizabeth George Speare won the Newbery for *The Witch of Blackbird Pond* (1958; 1959 Newbery Medal), and again when Madeline L'Engle won the prize for *A Wrinkle in Time* (1962; 1963 Newbery Medal). During the postwar years, middle-class White motherhood was an asset for children's authors, lending an air of "wholesomeness" to their craft while enabling them to outwardly conform to expectations of women's primary role being within the home, as wife and mother.[16] The benefits motherhood brought to *children's* literature, however, were disadvantages for an author of *young adult* literature: being positioned as a middle-aged mother put Neville on the wrong side of the generation gap.

Then, too, the Newbery Award itself may have underscored the disconnect between the book and its intended readership—a great irony, since the Award was, from its inception, about creating a market for youth literature. In the case of the 1964 Newbery winner, the question of target age range is central. The Newbery recognizes a work for readers "of ages up to and including fourteen," according to the ALA (Association). Perceptions have changed, even if the ALA's criteria haven't, and today's teens may think *Cat* is a book for younger kids simply because it won the Newbery. But the landscape may already have been shifting at the time of *Cat*'s publication in 1963. Even then, that shiny gold sticker on the cover—the symbol of approval from the literary establishment—may have been a turn-off for teens.

## *Notes*

Portions of this chapter are revised and reprinted from "A Second Look at *It's Like This, Cat*" by Kathleen T. Horning, *The Horn Book Magazine* 91.4 (July/Aug. 2015): 80–86.

1 Gerhardt's review did not refer to the Newbery Award by name, but with relatively few awards for children's literature available at the time, the Newbery reference was implicit.

2 The urban setting was an innovation: Neville was one of the first youth novelists to set her contemporary story outside the typical "affluent suburbs or bucolic countryside" (Goodwin 449).

3 When vouching for the novel's accuracy, Neville described the New York locales as places she had visited with her children ("Emily" 169). The author's kids didn't roam as freely as her protagonist, it seems, so there may be a touch of fantasy in Dave's solo wanderings.

4 In children's literature published before the 1960s, first-person narration was typical only in historical fiction, Gerhardt notes ("Argument" 7).

5 Dave, a White teenager, considers it appropriate for him to "correct" the older man's errors and police his language (71).

6 This certainly seems plausible for Fitzhugh's 1964 novel *Harriet the Spy*, which mirrors *It's Like This, Cat* in many ways, from the urban setting down to a man who has dozens of cats—the counterpart of Neville's cat lady Kate.

7 Eric L. Tribunella interprets Dave's longish hair, work as a babysitter, and decision to adopt a cat rather than a dog as evidence that Dave's "boyhood deviance" from his father's norms is "coded in gendered terms" ("Boy" 167n3). The gendered associations with cat ownership are reflected in a scene where Dave is carrying Cat along the roadside and nearby kids yell "Lookit the sissy with the pussy!" (96).

8 Friends also served as intermediaries in Neville's depiction of teen characters, since the author gleaned details of adolescents' "language, clothes, food, and friends" from her own teenagers and their friends (Neville, "Emily" 169). "Sometimes you get more details from your children's friends than from the children themselves," she reported (Start 31)—not just material details of teens' lives, perhaps, but also the empathy that comes from seeing her own adolescent children through the eyes of their peers.

9 Megan L. Musgrave's essay in this volume explores the similarly parental relationship between a stable boy and his horse in Marguerite Henry's *King of the Wind* (1948; 1949 Newbery Medal).

10 Neville's acceptance speech is notable for its early use of the term "young adult."

11 Although *Cat*'s action takes place some years before the Vietnam War-era draft became a major concern in the United States, Tom believes that he will "get drafted in a year or two, anyway" (178).

12 Among Newbery winners of the 1960s, Joseph Krumgold's *Onion John* (1959; 1960 Newbery Medal) has the same kind of line drawings seen in *Cat*; in the manner of a scientific textbook, Madeleine L'Engle's *A Wrinkle in Time* (1962; 1963 Newbery Medal) has line drawings only to illustrate the concept of the tesseract; and E. L. Konigsburg's *From the Mixed-Up Files of Mrs. Basil E. Frankweiler* (1967; 1968 Newbery Medal) includes the author's own illustrations, which are quirkier and more personal than the generic line drawings in the Krumgold and Neville books.

13 *Berries Goodman* deals with what Eric A. Kimmel calls "polite suburban anti-Semitism" (qtd. in Goodwin 452).

14 In the turbulent 1960s "it was far from clear where children's literature was headed," says children's literature scholar Leonard S. Marcus, but "Nordstrom, more than any of her colleagues, seemed to know the answer"—witness the "double success" of *Cat* and *Wild Things* in 1964. Nordstrom was only the second editor to capture both the Newbery and Caldecott the same year (231).

15 The committee was clearly aware at the time of the distinctiveness of their choices. Dickinson quotes a fellow committee member as saying, "We'll go down in history as the cuckoo Newbery-Caldecott Committee!" (7).

16 In reality, this respectability provided cover for mother-authors to break norms and challenge conventions; Speare's *The Witch of Blackbird Pond*, for example, is an anti-McCarthy text that critiques witch-hunting (Schwebel 209).

## Works Cited

Arbuthnot, May Hill, and Zena Sutherland. *Children and Books*. 4th ed. Glenview, IL: Scott, Foresman and Company, 1972. Print.

Association for Library Service to Children. "Terms & Criteria: John Newbery Medal." *American Library Association*. 1987. ALA, n.d. Web. 14 July 2020.

Bird, Betsy, Julie Danielson, and Peter D. Sieruta. *Wild Things! Acts of Mischief in Children's Literature*. Somerville, MA: Candlewick Press, 2014. Print.

Cadden, Mike. "The Irony of Narration in the Young Adult Novel." *Children's Literature Association Quarterly* 25.3 (Fall 2000): 146–154. *Project Muse*. Web. 14 Dec. 2020.

Dalgliesh, Alice. "Books for Young People: 'In All of Our Daily Lives.'" *The Saturday Review* 20 (July 1963): 33–34. Print.

Davis, David C. "It's This Way, Kid!" *Horn Book Magazine* 40 (Sept./Oct. 1964): 523–527. Print.

Dickinson, Sarah G. "I Was There on the 1964 Newbery-Caldecott Awards Committee." *Library Leads* 14 (Nov. 1964): 4–7.

Gerhardt, Lillian N. "An Argument Worth Opening." *School Library Journal* 99 (May 1974): 7. Print.

[Gerhardt, Lillian N.] Rev. of *It's Like This, Cat,* by Emily Neville. *Kirkus Reviews*. 22 May 1963: n. pag. Web. 10 Aug. 2020.

Goodwin, Polly. "Emily Cheney Neville. 1919–." *Contemporary Literary Criticism*. Ed. Dedria Bryfonski. Vol. 12. Farmington Hills, MI: Gale, 1980. 449–454. *Gale Literature Criticism*. Web. 6 Aug. 2020.

Hinton, S[usan]. E[loise]. *The Outsiders*. 1967. New York: Penguin Books, 2006. Print.

Hinton, Susan. "Teen-Agers are for Real." *New York Times* 27 Aug. 1967: BR 14, 28–29. Web. 6 Aug. 2020.

Hood, Robert. "... and for Boys Some Stories That Come Close to Themselves." *New York Times* 12 May 1963: 2, 26. Web. 8 Aug. 2020.

Kingston, Carolyn T. *The Tragic Mode in Children's Literature*. New York: Teachers College Press, 1974. Print.

Marcus, Leonard S. *Minders of Make-Believe: Idealists, Entrepreneurs, and the Shaping of American Children's Literature*. Boston: Houghton Mifflin, 2008. Print.

Moger, Elizabeth H. "A Dead Cat?" *School Library Journal* 10 (Apr. 1964): 4. Print.

Neville, Emily. *It's Like This, Cat*. New York: Harper & Row, 1963. Print.

Neville, Emily. "Newbery Award Acceptance: Out Where the Real People Are." *Newbery and Caldecott Medal Books: 1956–1965, with Acceptance Papers, Biographies & Related Material chiefly from the* Horn Book Magazine. Ed. Lee Kingman. Boston: The Horn Book, 1965. 131–136. Print.

Neville, Emily Cheney. "Emily Cheney Neville (1919–)." *Something about the Author Autobiography Series*. Ed. Adele Sarkissian. Vol. 2. [Farmington Hills, MI]: Gale, 1986. 157–173. *Gale Literature*. Web. 31 July 2020.

Nordstrom, Ursula. "Honesty in Teenage Novels." *Top of the News* 21 (Nov. 1964): 35–38. Print.

Schwebel, Sara L. "Historical Fiction and the Classroom: History and Myth in Elizabeth George Speare's *The Witch of Blackbird Pond*." *Children's Literature in Education* 34.3 (Sept. 2003): 195–218. Print.

Sendak, Maurice. "Caldecott Award Acceptance." *Newbery and Caldecott Medal Books: 1956–1965, with Acceptance Papers, Biographies & Related Material chiefly from the* Horn Book Magazine. Ed. Lee Kingman. Boston: The Horn Book, 1965. 247–253. Print.

Start, Clarissa. "Prize-Winning Book by a Mother of Five." *St. Louis Post Dispatch* 2 July 1964: 31. *ProQuest Historical Newspapers*. Web. 8 Aug. 2020.

Sutton, Roger. "Principles in Print: A Conversation with 1995 Grolier Award Winner Lillian N. Gerhardt." *School Library Journal* 83.9 (Sept. 1995): 118–122. Print.

Taylor, Mark. "Children's Literature—The Cream of the Crop." *Los Angeles Times* 15 Mar. 1964: D20. *ProQuest Historical Newspapers*. Web. 8 Aug. 2020.

Thomas, Jane. "Straight Talk: Juvenile Books Tackle, Tussle, Emerge Mature." *Minneapolis Tribune* 31 Oct. 1965: E7. *ProQuest Historical Newspapers*. Web. 8 Aug. 2020.

Tribunella, Eric L. "A Boy and His Dog: Canine Companions and the Proto-Erotics of Youth." *Children's Literature Association Quarterly* 29.3 (Fall 2004): 152–171. *Project Muse*. Web. 31 July 2020.

Tribunella, Eric L. "Children's Literature and the Child Flâneur." *Children's Literature* 38 (2010): 64–91. *Project Muse*. Web. 31 July 2020.

Trites, Roberta Seelinger. *Disturbing the Universe: Power and Repression in Adolescent Literature*. Iowa City: U of Iowa P, 2000. Print.

Ullmann, Nadine. "Book for Teens Wins Mother Prize." *Newsday* 19 Mar. 1964: 59. *ProQuest Historical Newspapers*. Web. 7 Aug. 2020.

Wilkin, Binnie Tate. *African and African American Images in Newbery Award Winning Titles: Progress in Portrayals*. Lanham, MD: The Scarecrow Press, 2009. Print.

# 10 Vision, Visibility, and Disability

## Re-Seeing *The Summer of the Swans* (1971) and *The Westing Game* (1979)

*Sara K. Day and Paige Gray*

As "bookends" for the Newbery Medal in the 1970s, Betsy Byars's *The Summer of the Swans* (1970; 1971 Newbery Medal) and Ellen Raskin's *The Westing Game* (1978; 1979 Newbery Medal) would seem at first glance to have very little in common. The former is a domestic drama focused on adolescent Sara's search for her missing younger brother Charlie, while the latter is a puzzle mystery that follows sixteen people competing to win a massive inheritance. However, the texts share a common interest in the metaphorical invisibility of young people with disabilities; they both emphasize questions of seeing, watching, and looking that ultimately shape their characterizations and plot.[1] *The Summer of the Swans* and *The Westing Game* engage with larger discourses of vision and visibility that have particular relevance to the disability community because—as scholars, advocates, and activists have long asserted—their continued marginalization depends on and reinforces the perceived *invisibility* of disability and illness.

Byars and Raskin seemingly use this discourse as a means of destabilizing the concept of disability, redefining what constitutes active and passive participation in the social world, and subverting notions of self-awareness, agency, and fulfillment. At the same time, however, both novels also reify ableist ideologies about the nature of disability. To some extent, the simultaneously progressive and problematic nature of these representations reflects the era in which the novels were published: the 1970s, a decade that fundamentally altered discourse about disability in the United States and elsewhere. In the years between the publications of *The Summer of the Swans* and *The Westing Game*, the United States witnessed the rise of the disability rights movement and the passage of the Rehabilitation Act of 1973 and the Education of All Handicapped Children Act of 1975. Byars's and Raskin's novels thus reflected a growing awareness of the issue of disability and a growing recognition of the importance of the representation of disability in books and media for youth.

While by no means the first or only Newbery winners to feature characters with disabilities, *The Summer of the Swans* and *The Westing*

DOI: 10.4324/9780367337223-10-11

*Game* serve as particularly effective examples of not only evolving representations of disability in literature for young audiences but also the ways in which children's literature scholarship has, to some extent, failed to reckon with disability as a vital category of analysis.[2] Notably, neither of these Newbery winners has been the subject of much critical discussion in the decades since their publication (particularly surprising in the case of the perennially popular *The Westing Game*), and what scholarship does exist generally does not engage extensively, if at all, with the portrayals of young people with disabilities. Considering their chronological relationship to crucial legislation about access, as well as the fact that the 1970s roughly mark the "halfway point" of the award's now-one-hundred-year history, these Newbery Medalists offer insights into how the disability rights movement has influenced and continues to shape both the creation and reception of literature for young people. At the same time, the relative critical silence surrounding each book's representation of disability highlights larger questions about how ableism may affect which texts and characters receive critical attention.

## Re-Imagining Disability Rights and Representation

For much of the twentieth century, those living with disabilities were largely not seen, made invisible figuratively through lack of representation and literally through institutionalization. This came about, in part, through Progressive Era efforts that sought to address the frequently terrible conditions into which many people with disabilities had been forced (e.g., homelessness, incarceration, exhibition in freak shows) by establishing institutions that ostensibly provided better care and, for children, education. Despite their charitable goals, however, Progressive Era reformers reinforced existing attitudes that marginalized people with disabilities. This led to a problematic "mixture of the protection *of* children and the protection *from* those with disabilities," notes special education scholar Margaret Winzer (7). Then, too, the rise of the eugenics movement provided an important backdrop to Progressive Era reform, as adherents within and outside the academy ultimately worked not to improve the lives of people with disabilities but to eradicate them. While the mass killings undertaken by the Nazis remain the best-known of these attempts, American scientists and lawmakers during the 1920s and 1930s also argued for the elimination of "negative" traits through processes such as forced sterilization. Unsurprisingly, in the United States as in Nazi Germany, understandings about acceptable bodies (and hence ability/disability) intersected with other identity markers, including race, class, sexual orientation, and national origin (Stern 12–13). Thus, the long shadow of eugenics lingers behind many twentieth-century policies, including the National Origins Act, the Tuskegee experiment, and nonconsensual sterilization of people with disabilities, immigrants, unmarried mothers, people of color, and people living in poverty.

The pseudoscience of eugenics viewed disabilities as a contaminant in the body politic. In the early twentieth century, this view existed alongside other frameworks. For example, older understandings of disability included the idea that variants ("flaws") in physical bodies were a condemnation from God or test of faith (now frequently termed "the moral or religious model" of disability), while more modern ideas (now frequently termed "the medical model") viewed such variants as aberrations that could and should be "fixed" via scientific intervention (see Smart for one overview of these models). During the 1970s, however, a new framework for understanding disability emerged: the "social model," a term coined by sociologist and disability rights activist Mike Oliver. It recognized disability as a cultural construct—not a fixed biological category but a consequence of social systems that deny people access based on physical, intellectual, and emotional difference. The social model has gained acceptance in the decades since its inception, but it continues to exist alongside the medical model; as a result, people with disabilities continued to be isolated and institutionalized well into the twenty-first century. The social model was promulgated by the disability rights movement that emerged in the 1970s, in the wake of other Civil Rights movements. Yet in comparison to the (admittedly incomplete) progress achieved by other movements, the pace of social change with regard to disability has been disappointing, many activists argue. Moreover, change has at times been superficial, extending to media representations without penetrating the structures of society. As disability scholars David T. Mitchell and Sharon L. Snyder argue, "disabled people's marginalization has occurred in the midst of a perpetual circulation of their images. Curiously, a social erasure has been performed even as a representational repertoire has evolved" (6). This erasure has become a central focus in the work of literary scholars examining representations of disability.

As a medium that reflects and reinforces society's dominant cultural beliefs, children's literature both reveals evolving approaches to disability and plays a significant role in shaping how we understand disability and ableness. Historically, children's literature has deployed depictions of disability for largely didactic purposes: characters with disabilities most often function as villains, like Captain Hook in *Peter and Wendy* (1911), or objects of pity, like Tiny Tim in *A Christmas Carol* (1843). In cases such as Susan Coolidge's *What Katy Did* (1872) or Eleanor Porter's *Pollyanna* (1913), disability serves as punishment for free-thinking young girls, with suffering figured as a means of self-improvement. Classic children's literature, then, may be seen as perpetuating ideas about "saintly invalids." In such cases, disability functions as a means to build character and aid in spiritual development, though developmental psychologist Ann Dowker notes that the nineteenth- and early-twentieth-century texts that have *not* become classics often offered more nuance than such an overview might suggest. In other words, the prevalence of the religious model of disability in nineteenth-century children's literature may obscure more progressive representations, indicating that representations of disability have not followed a straightforward path toward the respectful and authentic. More recently, portrayals of characters with disabilities have participated in a trend colloquially called "inspiration porn," a term credited to comedian Stella Young that critiques the tendency to treat the experience of living with a disability as inherently inspiring to able-bodied people (Grue, "Problem"). Whether classic or contemporary, children's fiction that portrays disability frequently centers on able-bodied characters and uses characters with disabilities primarily for didactic or motivational purposes.

The history and uses of disability in children's literature are, broadly speaking, replicated in that subset of works granted Newbery Awards. The Newbery has, as yet, infrequently recognized books featuring characters with disabilities:[3] in their analysis of Newbery winners since 1975, Melissa Leininger et al. find that only a quarter of winners or Honor Books feature main or supporting characters with disabilities, and the vast majority of those texts were published after 1990 (586).[4] Sociologists Adie Nelson and Veronica Nelson, meanwhile, consider how representations of disability in Newbery winners are often gendered, racialized, or both; the authors also note that nearly half of these characters with disabilities are "Othered and presented as 'roleless'" within their texts (94). Moreover, trends among the Newbery honorees reflect two key considerations about representations of disability at large, both of which relate to questions of vision and visibility. First, especially prior to 1975, books featuring characters with disabilities overwhelmingly portrayed physical (generally visible) disabilities. Among Newbery winners, these are most often what education scholar Casey Lin Pehrson describes as "orthopedic impairment" (10)—as in Marguerite de Angeli's *The Door in the Wall* (1949; 1950 Newbery Medal)—rather than "invisible" emotional or intellectual ones. In the case of *The Summer of the Swans*, Charlie's cognitive impairment might be understood as an "invisible" disability, while *The Westing Game*'s Chris uses a wheelchair, thus making some aspects of his neurological disorder visible to those around him.[5] Second, unlike the characters discussed by Dowker, the characters with disabilities featured in much twentieth-century children's literature, award-winning or otherwise, are most often supporting or peripheral rather than protagonists or narrators. This has only recently begun to shift in a notable way with the publication of works like Sharon Draper's *Out of My Mind* (2010),

Kathryn Erskine's *Mockingbird* (2010), and CeCe Bell's *El Deafo* (2014; Newbery Honor 2015), in which children with disabilities are both protagonist and narrator. We argue that *The Summer of the Swans* and *The Westing Game* anticipate the move toward centering disabled characters and their points of view through third-person narration that shifts between multiple perspective-holders, including Charlie and Chris, respectively.

The growing but still limited body of scholarship at the intersection of children's literature and disability studies tends to examine a relatively small number of texts, usually titles that have come to be understood as exemplary, many of which are also seen as canonical children's literature. Such scholarship, at times, uncritically celebrates depictions of characters with disability as inspirational, centering on the "surprising" successes or positivity of such characters and thereby participating in "inspiration porn." Rather than questioning the authenticity and intent of works like R. J. Palacio's popular, frequently taught *Wonder* (2012), such readings confirm the value of these texts to able-bodied readers. To consider just one example, literature and disability studies scholar Elizabeth Wheeler argues that with its portrayal of Auggie, a boy with severe craniofacial disfigurations due to Treacher Collins Syndrome, "*Wonder* shows how the public presence of people with disabilities benefits a whole society" (335). However, more recent commentary on the book and its film adaptation pushes against this; for example, activist Ariel Henley notes, in her discussion of *Wonder* in both media, that academic and cultural efforts to affirm the value of people with disabilities often treat them as distinct from society rather than recognizing that disability is a social construction.

In their discussion of *Wonder* and Francisco X. Stork's *Marcelo in the Real World* (2009), which follows a young man with an autism spectrum disorder, literary scholars Abbye Meyer and Emily Wender contend that recent novels featuring young people with disabilities should not be read uncritically simply because they attempt to destabilize stereotypes about disability. Rather, readers must read *against* the efforts of such novels when they are problematic. Meyer and Wender write that while Palacio and Stork work to challenge stereotypes about people with disabilities being "freaks," their novels also assume an able-bodied readership and, in each case, inadvertently reinforce ideas about difference and deficiency.[6]

Likewise, *The Summer of the Swans* and *The Westing Game* both offer useful opportunities to read with and against their efforts to portray people with disabilities. One such opportunity comes through thinking about how the two novels explicitly link their characters with disabilities to birds and birdwatching, a move that helps to establish their more general use of sight semantics. *The Summer of the Swans* hinges on the fascination that ten-year-old Charlie, who has a nonspecific cognitive disability and is nonverbal, holds for the graceful birds of the title. After arriving at the lake where the swans have recently taken up residency, Charlie quickly becomes enamored with watching the birds, and after returning home, he believes he "se[es] one of the swans outside his window" (56) and goes "looking for the swans" (57), getting lost in the process. Meanwhile, in *The Westing Game*, Chris, who has a condition that affects his speech and mobility, identifies himself as a "bird-watcher" (21). Throughout the novel, Chris uses his binoculars to trace the flight of geese and purple martins from his window—an activity for which he has plenty of time, as he is frequently left alone in his family's apartment.

Reading *with* the novels allows a consideration of the boys' active engagement with the world around them, potentially undercutting assumptions about intellectual disabilities in particular. The use of birds and birdwatching also highlights the importance of visibility: the texts do not just position their young birdwatchers as *seeing* but also consider the ways in which Charlie and Chris may or may not be *seen*. Early in *The Summer of the Swans*, it is only the titular birds that see Charlie: "The swans are coming over here, Charlie. They see you, I believe" (Byars 41). In *The Westing Game*, on the other hand, Chris is positioned as an observer who goes unseen. The "special glass windows" through which he tracks the behavior of both birds and humans are reflective, and hence, one-way: "He could see out, but nobody could see in" (9). Chris's metaphorical invisibility to the other residents of Sunset Towers plays a key role in Raskin's construction of his character and the plot of the novel as a whole. However, reading *against* the novels' efforts requires an awareness of problematic assumptions about vision and visibility. Even as the novels use ideas about sight to emphasize their characters' subjectivity, they rely on a framework that connects vision to knowledge in ways that have been challenged by Blind activists and disability studies scholars.[7] Moreover, the birdwatching metaphor links disability to ideas of limitation and dependence by holding the two boys in contrast to the freedom and mobility suggested by the birds' flight.

This type of Othering—highlighting the ways in which some minds and bodies are deemed to be outside the arbitrary markers of normalcy—is, of course, unremarkable for children's literature of the 1970s (or, indeed, more recent years). Yet the treatment of disability in *The Summer of the Swans* and *The Westing Game* is amplified by the Newbery Award: when the Newbery committee chooses to honor texts that depict disability, the honor makes those texts' representations of disability more visible—whether or not those representations are respectful, accurate, or authentic. The notions of normalcy and disability conveyed by Byars and Raskin have, moreover, been codified by decades of critical silence. In further unpacking these texts, our aim is twofold: we want to bring forward the authors' innovative treatment of disability while using the social model of disability to unsettle their heretofore unquestioned attitudes toward ability.

## Revisiting Visibility in The Summer of the Swans

In their remarks about the selection of *The Summer of the Swans* for the Newbery Medal, the 1970–1971 Newbery-Caldecott Awards Committee underscores that, among their other reasons for selecting this novel, Charlie "is shown as a real family member" to his older sisters Sara and Wanda and to their guardian, Aunt Willie, in their West Virginia home ("Supporting Statements" 2). Although the committee praises the book for depicting youth disability, these remarks focus more on protagonist Sara and on how Byars effectively blends "humor and 'tension'" in a way that feels "appropriate to the emotional stress experienced" during adolescence ("Supporting Statements" 2). The novel "lets us look into the mind and heart of a normal, predictably ambivalent adolescent girl," the committee writes, and in doing so, it manages to highlight the ostensible callousness of her feelings by thoughtfully rendering the plight of her nonverbal younger brother ("Supporting Statements" 2). Notably, the committee's comments privilege Sara's experiences, presenting a reading of the novel as one that primarily advances ideas about "normal" adolescence. In one of the very few scholarly discussions of Byars's novel, Karen Coats addresses this slippery aspect of the text, arguing that "Charlie's presence in the novel as a mentally handicapped child is simply to facilitate his sister Sara's growth from an egocentric preadolescent into a sensitive, benevolent girl" (13). Coats goes on to posit that the "disabled character acts as catalyst for normativizing her identity as girl-benevolent, sensitive, other-centered, and actively heterosexual," in that Sara's search for Charlie brings her closer to male classmate (and initial antagonist) Joe Melby (13). Coats's reading is productive and compelling, but might the text also work to challenge ideas about disability? Specifically, might *The Summer of the Swans* suggest a social model of disability through its attention to questions of perception?

Certainly, *The Summer of the Swans* does, at times, indiscriminately connect sight to concepts of metaphorical vision and knowledge. But it also problematizes the notion that the ability to "see" constitutes individual agency or a recognition of one's individual identity. Byars achieves this, at least in part, by setting up a narrative architecture that permits interrogation of sight semantics. Throughout the novel, the third-person limited narration switches between Sara and Charlie, giving the reader access into Charlie's thoughts. Doing so not only provides characterization and detail that would not be possible from Sara's perspective but also invalidates (or attempts to invalidate) presumptions about Charlie's intellect or emotional depth as a result of his "mentally handicapped" label (Byars 97). While the text relies on a series of its characters mis-seeing or misunderstanding one another—Sara and her older sister Wanda, Aunt Willie and Wanda, Sara and Joe Melby—it puts a special focus on how Charlie and Sara "see": that is, the manner in which they encounter and interpret the world. The novel underscores Sara's misreading of people and situations despite her intense concentration on appearances.[8] Over the course of the novel, Sara learns to "see" more clearly. The Newbery judges applauded the book for showing the brother who lives with disability "as a real family member" and for detailing "the heart and mind of a *normal* ... adolescent girl" as she accepts Charlie after the threat of losing him ("Supporting Statements" 2; italics for emphasis). This assessment suggests a somewhat simplistic ableist narrative. Yet the text allows room for a more nuanced reading than that of Sara just overcoming her "normal" teenage ideas. More specifically, it opens space for a social model of disability, or at least its suggestion, by showing the fluidity of people's characteristics and identities. Early in the story, Sara lays out her philosophy to Charlie, telling him, "'I think how you look is the most important thing in the world'" (31). She goes on to explain, "'If you *look* cute, you *are* cute; if you *look* smart, you *are* smart, and if you don't look like anything, then you aren't anything'" (31). On the one hand, this can be read as young vanity or callousness. On the other hand, the idea that identity depends on others' perceptions points toward a constructivist vision: if people perceive you as capable, you *are* capable, but if other people can make you "cute" or "smart" or capable, might they also make you "disabled?"

The text additionally depicts Charlie's disability as a problem for *others*—a problem that is, we argue, of their own making. While the novel acknowledges that Charlie has limitations, these frequently seem to reflect his family's perception that he needs to be fixed. Moreover, the family's habit of doing things for him rather than letting him do them himself has rendered him less capable than he might otherwise be. Since the novel gives us Charlie's perspective, we understand him to be reasonably adept at navigating the world around him, or at least in environments with which he is familiar. It is only through Sara's perspective and behavior that Charlie's disability is made explicit. For example, an early chapter from Charlie's perspective notes that he "had been eating a lollipop and the stick had come off and now he was trying to put it back into the red candy" (13). The text does not indicate that Charlie acted in distress or dismay. However, Sara takes control and says, "I'll do it for you," in a move that assumes his inability to complete the task himself (13). Later, in a conversation with Wanda, Sara lashes out at her sister for discussing Charlie with a college classmate. She asks Wanda, "What do you say? 'Let me tell you all about my retarded brother—it's so interesting'?" (22). The narrative immediately notes that "it was the first time in her life that she had used the term 'retarded' in connection with her brother," and that Sara "looked quickly away" from her brother (22). It is unclear whether Sara's discomfort stems from her open acknowledgment that her brother has an intellectual disability, from her use of a term that was already coming to be seen as derogatory, or from her sister's public discussion of their brother. Whatever the case, she continues to Other Charlie through her language, describing him moments later as the family's "problem" (23).

Charlie's disability is, paradoxically, both central and largely unacknowledged. The chapters narrated from his point of view are based partly around the conceit of his disability, something he has lived with since he was three years old, the result of "two illnesses, one following the other, terrible high-fevered illnesses, which had almost taken his life and had damaged his brain" (52). The narration and plot depend on Charlie's inability to speak. But the narration also treats Charlie as a whole person, not one who lacks or who needs to be "fixed" because of his disability. Understandably, some readers may be uncomfortable with the text "speaking" for a speechless boy, presuming to know how nonverbal individuals think or feel. Be that as it may, the novel relates Charlie's point of view in a manner that reveals his acuity, countering ideas about his supposed mental deficiency. Through the text's narration, Charlie displays his ability to both communicate and find existential significance by means other than his literal voice. For instance, he uses the tent that he and Sara set up in their backyard as a means of agency, as he can choose whether or not to be visible to others. Charlie can readily identify what makes him feel safe: "The warmth of the sun coming through the thin cotton blanket, the shadows of the trees moving overhead had made him drowsy and comfortable and now he wanted to be back in the tent" (19). This self-awareness, even if it primarily describes his responses to physical comfort, serves to emphasize the contrast between Charlie's composure and Sara's perpetual bewilderment.

By juxtaposing Sara's supposed ableness and inner turmoil against her brother's disability and seemingly clear sense of self, the text troubles conventional designations of disability, primarily by using language connected to sight and seeing. Sara, who prioritizes exterior appearances (a trait not atypical during adolescence), not only feels unseen but also lacks an ability to "see" others. Charlie's disappearance, meanwhile, propels the story, and enables him to be seen within the world of the story—his disappearance makes him the concentrated focus of his community. Indeed, the central action of *The Summer of the Swans* pivots on the very idea of Charlie's visibility by way of his disappearance. One evening after Sara takes Charlie to see the swans at a local lake, he has trouble sleeping because of a missing button on his pajamas. Neither his aunt nor his sister is willing to address the missing button that night. The missing button, in some ways, reflects the larger invisibility Charlie feels. While this could be read as Charlie simply wanting attention from his family, it could also be taken as Sara's and Aunt Willie's inability to understand the anxiety that the situation creates for Charlie.

Comforted by the "memory of [the swans'] soft smoothness in the water," the still unsettled, restless Charlie decides to go in search of the swans (56). His pursuit, however, results in his becoming lost in the nearby woods. The story then switches between Sara's dogged search for her missing brother and Charlie's attempts to return home. In the pivotal moment when Sara finds her draggled younger brother in the forest, the novel once again emphasizes the role of sight. Yet it notably subverts expectations by focusing not on Sara alone but on the siblings' mutual gaze of recognition and pleasure. On seeing his sister, Byars writes, "a strange expression came over [Charlie's] face, an expression of wonder and joy and disbelief, and Sara knew that if she lived to be a hundred no one would ever look at her quite that way again" (126). When Aunt Willie arrives, she reinforces this emphasis on visibility, saying, "Charlie, my Charlie, let me look at you.... Oh, you are a sight" (130). As Claudia Mills points out, Aunt Willie's reaction—both her distress at his going missing and her relief at his return—signals that the loss of a child with disabilities is just as devastating as the loss of a "normal" child, a shift from earlier representations and a potential disruption of social norms (537).

To revisit the Newbery committee's comments, *The Summer of the Swans* indeed offers a story in which an adolescent girl remedies her "predictably ambivalent" behavior thanks to her brother's impending peril. But Sara's physical recovery of her brother represents a figurative discovery as well: she recognizes him as a person, not a "problem" (23). After finding Charlie, "Sara could not understand why she suddenly felt so good. It was a puzzle. The day before she had been miserable. She had wanted to fly away from everything, like the swans to a new lake, and now she didn't want that any more" (130). Despite her confusion, Sara does not attempt to *solve* that puzzle, a point that reinforces that novel's larger recognition that Charlie himself is not a problem to be solved. This reunion thus suggests the radical idea that disability and ableness do not have fixed meanings, nor meanings that easily correspond to the constraints of verbal language or rational knowledge. The novel instead suggests that neither she nor Charlie needs to "fly away" or solve the "puzzle." Indeed, the conclusion of the novel insists that Charlie is "all right"—full, complete, and able—just as he is (130).

## Replaying The Westing Game

Unlike *The Summer of the Swans*, which offers a fairly conventional domestic drama, *The Westing Game* sets itself apart from other Newbery winners as the first mystery to have claimed the award. Unfolding on the shore of Lake Michigan in a fictionalized Sheboygan, Wisconsin, this novel follows the sixteen heirs of Sam Westing's fortune as they attempt to solve the late millionaire's murder case. In addition to deciphering Westing's puzzling last will and testament—a riddle-filled document that is read to the heirs only once and on which only the eccentric secretary Sydelle Pulaski has thought to take notes—they find themselves investigating clues, a series of small thefts, and a few minor bombings. Just as notably, though, the heirs come to learn about and develop sometimes surprising relationships with one another. The contrast between Byars's seemingly straightforward portrayal of Charlie and Sara and the more complicated network of characters and representations in Raskin's novel suggests that the latter might provide a more nuanced take on disability. However, while Byars's text argues for recognizing Charlie's personhood without attempting to cure or "fix" him, *The Westing Game*'s genre places emphasis on solving not only the central mystery but also Chris's disability, reflecting the medical model's ongoing influence on representation in the late 1970s.

The novel's complex plot, characterization, and humor likely account for its continued popularity (and have inspired more recent works for children, such as Varian Johnson's 2018 puzzle mystery *The Parker Inheritance*), but critical discussion of *The Westing Game* has been surprisingly limited.[9] Moreover, despite the fact that several characters live with (or feign) disability, this aspect of the novel and the specific representation of Chris as a young person with a neurological disorder have received little attention. Even literature scholar Adrienne E. Gavin, who notes that "Raskin's novel is innovative ... in its acute and witty observations of characters' public facades and the private truths that lie beneath," focuses her argument more on issues of class and age than on disability. She concludes that the novel allows each character to "live out successfully the American dream" without interrogating the ways in which access to that dream is affected by various systems of oppression, including ableism (214).

The fact that Chris has an acquired disability (as does Charlie in *The Summer of the Swans*) reinforces the novel's ableist perspective and adherence to the medical model. Older brother Theo explains that fifteen-year-old Chris had been "a perfectly normal kid, a great kid. And he's smart, too. About four years ago he started to get clumsy, just little things at first" (87). As Theo's wording suggests, Chris is no longer perceived as "normal" because of his neurological disorder. The text notes on multiple occasions that Chris's parents have made great financial sacrifices for his treatment, and when Dr. Denton Deere learns that he has been paired with Chris in the titular game, he assumes that their partnership is meant to manipulate him into offering medical help (which he ultimately does). Such plot devices foreground the question of whether Chris's condition can be fixed, rather than considering how he could be recognized and treated as a complete person with his disability.

Just as Byars problematizes visibility in *The Summer of the Swans*, Raskin emphasizes metaphorical, sometimes willful, blindness throughout her novel. In the opening pages, real estate agent Barney Northrup announces to prospective buyers that the windows of Sunset Towers are made of one-way glass. This comment is immediately followed by a description of potential tenants being "blinded by the blast of morning sun that flashed off the face of the building" (3). *The Westing Game* thus establishes the importance of sight—a common feature of mysteries, which depend on those powers of observation belonging to both their characters and their readers. In many cases, the novel seems to directly critique characters' seeming unwillingness to see Chris. When Chris experiences convulsions during the heirs' first meeting, for example, the narration notes that "[s]ome stared at the afflicted child with morbid fascination, but most turned away. They didn't want to see" (29). And when some other heirs *do* see Chris, they often fail to do so accurately or effectively, generally assuming that his physical disability also signals an intellectual disability. Raskin's text interrogates the relationship between disability and vision by drawing attention to Chris's powers of observation: Chris's birdwatching enables him to see the goings-on in and around Sunset Towers, making him a potentially valuable ally in solving the mystery, though no one seems to realize this. In fact, Chris's observations lead him to a conclusion that the novel will ultimately bear out: "Nobody here looks like a murderer, they're all nice people" (71). While the other heirs become increasingly suspicious and accusatory of one another, Chris alone recognizes the true character of the players in the game, and his certainty about the heirs' collective innocence provides a key insight to its solution.

An effort to normalize and make visible multiple experiences of disability runs throughout *The Westing Game*, as the novel conspicuously incorporates characters with disabilities both real and feigned. Seamstress Flora Baumbach frequently speaks about her late daughter Rosalie, who had Down syndrome. Otis Amber, who acts as the delivery boy to Sunset Towers but is, in fact, a private detective, allows those around him to believe that he has intellectual disabilities. His partner and eventual wife, Berthe Erica Crowe, is a recovering alcoholic, and the text implies that Crowe's daughter experienced depression before dying by suicide. Multiple characters experience or are associated with disability, then, and those disabilities may be intellectual or emotional as well as physical. The text thus situates Chris within a larger awareness of the variability of bodies and ability. However, the fact that at least two of these characters (Otis and Sydelle) actively deceive others complicates this reading. For instance, Otis treats his assumed lack of intelligence as a disguise that permits him to capitalize on other characters' tendency to dismiss or ignore him. While Raskin may position this character as a counterpoint to Chris, who experiences similar erasure, the association between disability and deception nonetheless depends on and perpetuates myths about disability—and, in particular, perpetuates the harmful misconception that many people with disabilities are "faking it," perhaps in order to avoid work.

Such considerations particularly inform the character of middle-aged secretary Sydelle Pulaski, whose frustration with her continual dismissal by the other heirs leads her to buy crutches and falsely claim to have a "wasting disease." This strategy reveals a set of existing, and deeply flawed, assumptions about living with disability, as she presumes that she will now be recognized by the heirs who have previously overlooked her. The strategy *does* draw their attention, but it does not increase their respect for her (or for her notetaking abilities—another mistake on the part of the able-bodied heirs). At the same time, Sydelle's misguided efforts create space for a friendship with Chris, such as when the two end up sitting next to each other at dinner one night. Rather than politely ignoring Chris's wheelchair, Sydelle asks, "Can you stand on your legs? ... Can you walk at all?" (90). Pleased with the fact that she is asking him these questions directly, not "whisper[ing] them to his parents behind his back" as people often do, Chris decides that "they really were friends" (91). The older woman's loneliness, desire for connection, and potential as an amateur detective reflect Chris's own situation. In this way, Raskin's text echoes Byars's emphasis on seeking sameness between characters regardless of their (dis)ability.

The relationship between Sydelle and Chris ultimately captures the tension between progressive and problematic ideas in the novel.[10] Some of these problems come with the rhetoric and the language colloquially used to describe disability at the time of the book's publication—in his notes on Flora Baumbach, for example, doorman Sandy refers to her daughter Rosalie as a "Mongoloid child," though the term Down syndrome came into common usage earlier in the 1970s. The language applied to Otis likewise disrespects those with intellectual disabilities, and his performance relies on insulting exaggeration that nonetheless goes unquestioned by the other characters, indicating that he is playing into their own preconceived notions about disability. And the general sunniness and sweetness of Chris's personality certainly call to mind nineteenth-century "saintly invalids" enduring their pain with a smile. However, the most troubling moment in the novel appears in its final pages. The epilogue presents an adult Chris who has turned his birdwatching into a successful academic career. The novel undercuts this supposed happy ending with a throwaway line about Chris's older brother and his wife: "Turtle and Theo had decided against having children because of the possibility of inheriting Chris's disease" (215). This decision ignores Chris's own fulfilling life and the apparent success of the treatments he continues to take (and it ignores Turtle and Theo's wealth, which would make possible any required medical care for children, should they need it). It assumes that life with a disability isn't worth living, a concept that suggests the ongoing influence of eugenicist beliefs. And though Chris is now happily married himself, the text does not include any reference to *his* decisions about having children, potentially reinforcing the widespread tendency to desexualize and infantilize people with disabilities by assuming that parenthood is out of the question.

Although Raskin herself does not emphasize disability in her descriptions of the novel, it's important to recognize that the author's own struggle with "a disease of the connective tissues"—which, as her editor and friend Ann Durell notes, led to Raskin's death only six years after she finished *The Westing Game*—may have informed the ways in which the book represents experiences of visible and invisible disabilities. In her Newbery acceptance speech, Raskin notes that during the process of developing the large cast of *The Westing Game*, she decided that "[m]y characters will be imperfect, each handicapped by some physical, emotional, or moral defect. Defects which will make them easier to remember, imperfect because aren't we all?" (Raskin, "Newbery" 55). This underlying goal signals both a desire for inclusivity and a problematic conflation of "imperfections." It suggests that Chris should not be seen as different, but it also treats his "handicap" as a "defect." This ambivalent depiction of disability fluctuates between a resistance to ableist assumptions and an implicit reinforcement of them. *The Westing Game* thus serves as a crucial reminder that it can be productive to read *against* popular culture's representations of disability in order to interrogate entrenched ideologies.

## Re-Seeing the Future

Given the cultural visibility conferred by their Newbery wins, *The Summer of the Swans* and *The Westing Game* present us with the opportunity to reassess approaches to disability in children's literature and in children's literature scholarship. By looking back at prize-winning literature of an earlier era—in this case, novels that provide a snapshot of fictional representations of disabilities during the 1970s—we can formulate a forward-looking agenda, one that challenges today's readers and scholars to cultivate new critical practices. Such practices can address the "peril" that education scholar Santiago Solis has identified in "children's books that have disability as a theme": namely, "the degree to which it can authenticate its presumed opposite: normality" (Solis). This is borne out by the most common readings of *The Summer of the Swans* and *The Westing Game*—readings that emphasize the texts' inclusiveness in terms of disability—especially when the reader's identity matches that of the implied, able-bodied audience. Yet we suggest that other, more nuanced readings are possible. By reading both *with* and *against* the grain, one can articulate these novels' successes as well as their shortcomings, the ways in which they simultaneously disrupt and entrench ableist norms.

The reading strategies we advocate may allow readers and scholars alike to understand disability not as a form of Otherness, but as a central part of the human experience. As we re-evaluate these Newbery novels and other works that deal with disability, we can better assess the culturally constructed idea of "normality"; we can also discern the ways in which children's literature and media can both perpetuate this concept and destabilize it through diverse, multi-dimensional characters and stories. Crucial to this project is the imperative "Nothing about us without us," which continues to inform demands for better representation in literature and other media and is exemplified by the Own Voices movement originated by autistic author Corrinne Duyvuis.[11] Duyvuis co-manages the website Disability in Kidlit, which features works by authors with disabilities, such as Harriet McBryde Johnson's *Accidents of Nature* (2006), Bell's *El Deafo*, and Duyvuis's *On the Edge of Gone* (2016)—works that put forward representations informed by personal experience and help to make the social model of disability more visible to young readers.

Thus far, scholarship and activism have focused, of necessity, on increasing representation, correcting stereotypes and ableist attitudes, and putting Own Voices works first. Yet we dare to imagine further progress. There is a need for nuanced engagement with disability that shows it as a social construct rather than a moral failing or a problem to be fixed. And understanding disability as a construct is one step toward using it as a transformative lens, as historian Catherine J. Kudlick would have us do. Forty years after the rise of the disability movement, Kudlick asserted that the paucity of disability scholarship inhibits any full understanding of the human condition. "[D]isability is not just another 'Other,'" Kudlick says; rather, disability "reveals and constructs notions of citizenship, human difference, social values, sexuality, and the complex relationship between the biological and social worlds" (793). In other words, because disability plays a significant role in the drama of human experience, using disability as a critical lens lets us understand humanity in a more complete, accurate way. Kudlick provides an admirable goal—one that scholarship in children's literature has yet to attain. Reckoning with disability as a category of analysis for children's literature has the potential to transform our entire worldview. As such, it is essential not only in reconsidering existing representations of disability but also in establishing expectations for those that have yet to be written. These expectations apply to literary scholarship as well as to literature itself, we contend: children's literature as an academic field should aim to advance the larger project of creating structural change through its scholarship.

## Notes

1 Here and elsewhere, we employ the term "people with disabilities," but it is important to acknowledge that some individuals and communities—such as the Deaf and autistic communities—have worked to resituate identity-first language (e.g., "autistic person" rather than "person with autism"). More generally, we acknowledge that the language we use throughout this essay is part of a changing vocabulary for discussing disability; while we have worked to employ accurate and respectful terminology, we join scholars across fields in recognizing the ongoing need to concentrate on and address the role of language in shaping experiences, especially those of people with disabilities and other marginalized groups.

2 Our theoretical framework draws inspiration from the valuable models of Joan Scott's "Gender: A Useful Category of Historical Analysis," which called for a fundamental shift in how historians approached the question of gender in their scholarship, and Catherine J. Kudlick's "Disability History: Why We Need Another 'Other,'" which similarly intervenes in critical conversations to highlight the role disability plays in constructions of culture and history.

3 In contrast to the occasional awarding of the Newbery to books featuring characters with disabilities, the American Library Association's Schneider Family Book Awards (established in 2004) and the Dolly Gray Awards (awarded since 2000 by the Division on Autism and Developmental Disabilities of the Council for Exceptional Children) both exclusively honor works that represent disabilities, highlighting the growing demand to recognize the value of such portrayals and identify particularly effective works for young audiences.

4 For context, the American Community Survey reported in 2017 that 12.8 percent of Americans have disabilities (Kraus, et al.), while the Center for Disease Control reported in 2018 that one in four adults lives with a disability. These numbers suggest that one consideration worth investigating is the underrepresentation of *adult* characters with disabilities in literature for young readers.

5 In the field of disability studies, writes literature and disability scholar Susannah B. Mintz, "Invisibility ... can refer to a range of exclusions that reinforce the marginalizing of disability" (113). At the same time, the discourse of visibility can also highlight ableist assumptions about what constitutes disability, as invisibility "also refers to diseases, conditions, and sensations that cannot be observed externally, such as chronic pain, cognitive or psychiatric impairment, or Deafness" (113).

6 In her groundbreaking *Extraordinary Bodies: Figuring Physical Disability in American Culture and Literature* (1997), literature and disability studies scholar Rosemarie Garland Thomson "investigates how representation attaches meaning to bodies" and validates the identity of "corporeal otherness" (5), which in turn challenges our reliance on damaging stereotypes that actively construct disability as a means of reaffirming "normalcy" and perpetuating ableist ideology. Indeed, disability studies scholar Jan Grue posits that ableist culture attempts to account for people with disabilities by way of a framework structured on the idea that "bodies with impairments require explanation and action: an explanation of what went wrong, how deviance came about, and actions aimed at restoring normalcy in one way or another" (*Disability* 113).

7 As Mintz and others have noted, language about sight and vision frequently "reinforces the symbolism of vision, long entrenched in Western thought, in

which knowledge, intelligence, and control are linked to sight," a metaphor so common that its bias often goes unnoticed (113–114).

8 Charlie, in contrast, does not misread. Though he is nonverbal, the chapters narrated from his point of view bring forward his ability to see and understand.

9 Literary scholars such as Carol Billman and Ann Grieve have investigated the text primarily in terms of genre and the specific challenges and pleasures that the mystery offers young readers—an approach that centers Turtle, the intellectually gifted girl who eventually wins the game, and that positions her as the proxy for a presumably able-bodied child reader.

10 *The Westing Game* also features diverse representations of gender, race, and class, though these representations—like the novel's portrayal of disability—are fraught. To offer one brief example, Raskin's treatment of the Chinese American Hoo family, especially recent immigrant Sun Lin, relies on but does not always clearly challenge or subvert stereotypes about strict Asian parents and the speech patterns of non-native English speakers.

11 "For the first time in recorded human history," activist James I. Charlton argued in 1998, "politically active people with disabilities are beginning to proclaim that they know what is best for themselves and their community. This is a militant, revelational claim aptly capsulized in the slogan 'Nothing About Us Without Us'" (4). It is worth noting that Charlton's assessment does not account for earlier activism, such as that undertaken by Helen Keller.

## Works Cited


Billman, Carol. "The Child Reader as Sleuth." *Children's Literature in Education* 15.1 (1984): 30–41. Print.

Byars, Betsy. *The Summer of the Swans*. New York: Viking-Penguin, 1970. Print.

Centers for Disease Control and Prevention. "CDC: 1 in 4 US Adults Live with Disability." *CDC Newsroom*, 16 Aug. 2008. Web. 8 Aug. 2018.

Charlton, James I. *Nothing About Us Without Us: Disability Oppression and Empowerment*. Berkeley: U California P, 1998. Print.

Coats, Karen. "The Reason for Disability: Causes and Effects in the Construction of Identity in Contemporary American Children's Books." *Bookbird* 39.1 (2001): 11–16. Print.

Dowker, Ann. "The Treatment of Disability in 19th and Early 20th Century Children's Literature." *Disability Studies Quarterly* 24.1 (2004). Web. 25 Feb. 2019.

Durrell, Ann. Introduction. 2003. *The Westing Game*. By Ellen Raskin. 1978. New York: Penguin, 2008. Kindle file.

Gavin, Adrienne E. "Enigma's Variation: The Puzzling Mysteries of Avi, Ellen Raskin, Diana Wynne Jones, and Chris Van Allsburg." *Mystery in Children's Literature: From the Rational to the Supernatural*. Ed. Adrienne E. Gavin and Christopher Routledge. New York: Palgrave, 2001. 210–218. Print.

Grieve, Ann. "Metafictional Play in Children's Literature." *Papers* 8.3 (1998): 5–15. Print.

Grue, Jan. *Disability and Discourse Analysis*. London: Ashgate, 2015. Print.

Grue, Jan. "The Problem with Inspiration Porn: A Tentative Definition and Provisional Critique." *Disability and Society* 31.6 (2016): 838–849. Print.

Henley, Ariel. "What 'Wonder' Gets Wrong About Disfigurement and Craniofacial Disorders." *Teen Vogue*, 9 Aug. 2017. Web. 17 June 2019.

Henley, Ariel. "'Wonder' Is a Feel-Good Movie That Needed More Realism." *The Atlantic*, 21 Dec. 2017. Web. 30 Mar. 2020.

Kraus, L., et al. "2017 Disability Statistics Annual Report." *Institute on Disability/UCED*, 2018. Web. 10 Jan. 2020.

Kudlick, Catherine J. "Disability History: Why We Need Another 'Other.'" *American Historical Review* 108.3 (2003): 763–793. Print.

Leininger, Melissa, et al. "Newbery Award Winning Books 1975–2009: How Do They Portray Disabilities?" *Education and Training in Autism and Developmental Disabilities* 45.4 (2010): 583–596. Print.

Meyer, Abbye, and Emily Wender. "Teaching and Reading *Wonder* and *Marcelo in the Real World* with Critical Eyes." *Lessons in Disability: Essays on Teaching with Young Adult Literature*. Ed. Jacob Stratman. New York: MacFarland, 2019. 72–99. Print.

Mills, Claudia. "The Portrayal of Mental Disability in Children's Literature: An Ethical Appraisal." *Horn Book Magazine* 78.5 (Sept./Oct. 2002): 531–542. Print.

Mintz, Susannah B. "Invisibility." *Keywords for Disability Studies*. Ed. Rachel Adams, Benjamin Reiss, and David Serlin. New York: New York UP, 2015. 113–114. Print.

Mitchell, David T., and Sharon L. Snyder. *Narrative Prosthesis: Disability and the Dependencies of Discourse*. Ann Arbor: U of Michigan P, 2000. Print.

Nelson, Adie, and Veronica (Ronnie) Nelson. "'Other' Characters: The Gendering and Racialization of 'Disability' Within Newbery Award-Winning Books, 1922–2012." *Canadian Journal of Family and Youth* 8.1 (2016): 73–101. Print.

Oliver, Mike. *The Politics of Disablement*. London: Palgrave MacMillan, 1990. Print.

Pehrson, Casey Lin. "Portrayal of Characters with Disabilities in Newbery Books." Thesis, Brigham Young University, 2011. BYU ScholarsArchive. Web. 8 Aug. 2018.

Raskin, Ellen. "Newbery Medal Acceptance." *Newbery and Caldecott Medal Books 1976–1985, with Acceptance Papers, Biographies & Related Material chiefly from the* Horn Book Magazine. Ed. Lee Kingman. Boston: The Horn Book, 1986: 51–57. Print.

Raskin, Ellen. *The Westing Game*. New York: E. P. Dutton, 1978. Print.

Saunders, Kathy. "What Disability Studies Can Do for Children's Literature." *Disability Studies Quarterly* 24.1 (2004). Web. 8 Aug. 2018.

Smart, Julie F. "The Power of Models of Disability." *Journal of Rehabilitation* 75.2 (2009): 3–11. Print.

Solis, Santiago. "The Disabilitymaking Factory: Manufacturing 'Difference' through Children's Books." *Disability Studies Quarterly* 24.1 (2004). Web. 8 Aug. 2018.

Stern, Alexandra Minna. *Eugenic Nation: Faults and Frontiers of Better Breeding in Modern America*. Berkeley: U of California P, 2005. Print.

"Supporting Statements." 1–8. Record Series 24/2/6, Box 35, Folder 39. American Library Association Archives. University of Illinois Archives, Urbana-Champaign, IL.

Thomson, Rosemary Garland. *Extraordinary Bodies: Figuring Physical Disability in American Culture and Literature*. New York: Columbia UP, 2017. Print.

Wheeler, Elizabeth A. "No Monsters in This Fairy Tale: *Wonder* and the New Children's Literature." *Children's Literature Association Quarterly* 38.8 (2013): 335–350. Print.

Winzer, Margret. *From Integration to Inclusion: A History of Special Education in the 20th Century*. Washington, DC: Gallaudet UP, 2009. Print.

# 11 The Women's Poetry Movement and the Affordance of the Lyric

## *A Visit to William Blake's Inn* (1982)

*Donelle Ruwe*

In a 2008 interview, Nancy Willard recalled the exact moment when *A Visit to William Blake's Inn: Poems for Innocent and Experienced Travelers* (1981; 1982 Newbery Medal) became a possibility. During a conversation with her Harcourt editor Barbara Lucas, Lucas asked: "How about writing a collection of poems for children?" Willard found herself in a quandary:

> I had never written a collection of poems for children and hardly knew how to go about it. My books of poetry for adults were written in the way such books are usually written. For several years you publish poems in this quarterly, in that review, in this little magazine, with a lot of rejections along the way, and at some point you make a selection and arrange them, and send the manuscript out into the world.... But for children's books, it's a different story. The poems in a collection for children are often related, either by subject or theme, and for this reason the poems might be written all at one go, not over the long period that the adult collection requires. (*Left-Handed Story* 26)

There is something strange happening here. Why would Willard, a scholar, novelist, award-winning poet, and children's book author, assume that children's poetry books should have a single topic? Famous children's collections, such as Christina Rossetti's *Sing-Song: A Nursery Rhyme Book* (1872), Robert Louis Stevenson's *A Child's Garden of Verses* (1885), and Shel Silverstein's *Where the Sidewalk Ends* (1974), consist of miscellaneous poems. Prior to this conversation with her editor, Willard had already published twelve children's books, including the charming book of rhymes, *The Merry History of a Christmas Pie: With a Delicious Description of a Christmas Soup* (1974), in which the puppet-master Punch introduces pie ingredients. Each ingredient parades across a stage, reciting a brief nonsense poem about itself: "Here I come, Old Man Dill / I eat my lunch on the windowsill (n. pag.)." Further, Willard had already won the 1977 Lewis Carroll Shelf Award for *Sailing*

DOI: 10.4324/9780367337223-11-12

*to Cythera: and Other Anatole Stories* (1974), the first of her series of children's books inspired by her son, James Anatole Willard. Willard was clearly not suffering from what Beverly Lyon Clark terms "anxiety of immaturity," that fear experienced by women writers who are so afraid of being associated with literary creation as a form of baby-making that they resist writing children's books (6).[1]

Willard's resistance to the very idea of writing a poetry collection for children may have had something to do with the intimate connection that a writer feels to her genre and her established habits of writing. In her mind, playful nursery works such as *The Merry History of a Christmas Pie* are a different species from the adult collection. *The Merry History* adopts a single topic (pie ingredients) and a nursery rhyme style—silly images, strong rhyme, strong beats, and an oral orientation.[2] By contrast, according to Willard, poetry collections are compilations of individual lyrics written over time and tested in the competitive literary journal market. Willard doubts that this sort of collection even exists in the children's book market.[3] It is true that children's verse in the 1960s and 1970s was increasingly oriented towards playground poetry and "urchin verse," a genre that resists subtle lyricism and flouts conventional hierarchies and conventions (Thomas 62). Such verse seems diametrically opposed to adult poetry. As Peter Hunt has written with a fine sense of irony, "many people fundamentally do not believe that children's poetry exists.... There is a common, basic assumption that poetry—at least, post-romantic poetry—although essentially indefinable, is static, thoughtful, sophisticated, skilled, philosophical—and concerned with sex and death and interiority. The general concept of children is that they are NOT any of those things" (17). Hunt's description of poetry—static, philosophical, indefinable, and interior—best fits the lyric. Such verse emphasizes the imitation of feelings (rather than imitations of actions) and is neither narrative (epic) nor dramatic. It encompasses shapes as varied as sonnets, elegies, haiku, villanelles, effusions, ghazels, and lines. The lyric is, in the words of Gérard Genette, "a negative catchall (for everything that is neither narrative nor dramatic)" (24). The lyric in this sense is not a successful children's genre, for children much prefer narrative and dramatic modes. Prior to publishing *A Visit to William Blake's Inn*, Willard had written children's narratives (*Sailing to Cythera*) and nonsense verse (*A Merry History*); she had yet to write lyric poetry for any audience but adults.

*A Visit to William Blake's Inn* falls decidedly in the zone of the lyric with only brief segues into other poetic genres. Hence this essay's central query: What is gained by writing children's verse in a lyric form? Or, to put it another way, what are the affordances of the lyric that Willard brings to bear in *A Visit to William Blake's Inn*? Caroline Levine, in her discussion of the usefulness of form in literary analysis, borrows the idea of "affordances" from design theory. Affordance refers to the potential uses or actions latent in materials and designs. The fork, for example, "affords stabbing and scooping" (6). Rhyme affords "repetition, anticipation, and memorization" (6). The sonnet, with its brief and condensed form, "best affords a single idea or experience, 'a moment's monument'" (6). The lyric best affords intensity within brevity. It also traditionally affords the use of a lyric "I" mode of address and is often a site for working through a poet's own memories and emotions. According to Northrop Frye, the lyric poet "pretends to be talking to himself or to someone else," and in so doing the poet turns his back on his listeners; in other words, lyric poetry expresses the poet's own persona (32).

*A Visit to William Blake's Inn* partakes in the special status of the lyric as an expressive and personal mode, while simultaneously clawing back the lyric from a masculine tradition by aligning it with feminine aesthetic and poetic approaches. The feminine lyric tradition celebrates the productive fragmenting of the lyric "I" rather than a universalizing and totalizing "I." In place of the lyric's usual talking-to-oneself mode, the feminine lyric offers the intimacy of close contact and dialogue with others even as it explores the interiority of home spaces and re-envisions canonical works. This essay begins by placing Willard's creation of a handmade dollhouse (it was the inspiration for the inn depicted in *A Visit*) within the 1970s women's art movement as articulated by the feminist art collective and its journal *Heresies*. It then argues that Willard's verse reflects the feminine aesthetics of the 1970s women's poetry movement as identified by her contemporaries Adrienne Rich and Alicia Ostriker, two leading voices of the movement. The chapter concludes by placing Willard's *A Visit to William Blake's Inn* within Blake studies of the 1970s, demonstrating how Willard adopts a feminist empowering act of "talking back" to canonical male writers while simultaneously finding strength in a sisterhood of female predecessor poets.

## The Women's Art Movement and the Physical Inn as Femmage

*A Visit* consists of sixteen fantastical poems (seventeen if one counts the epigraph) that take place in an imaginary inn, gloriously illustrated by Alice and Martin Provensen. The collection of lyric verse is loosely organized to form a narrative of sorts: a young boy arrives at Blake's inn in a marvelous limousine and meets bears, rats, rabbits, angels, tigers, and sunflowers. He meets Blake, and Blake takes him on a trip to the Milky Way. *A Visit* was the first poetry collection to win the Newbery. Further, it was the first Newbery to also receive a Caldecott Honor, a feat only recently matched by Matt de la Peña's *The Last Stop on Market Street*, illustrated by Christian Robinson (2015).

Willard discussed her inspiration for *A Visit to William Blake's Inn* in her Newbery acceptance speech. Although Willard initially rejected her editor's suggestion of writing a children's collection of poems, the idea had been planted. Willard during that time had been building a house of cardboard boxes or crates (she has variously described her building materials): about six feet tall, tidy, and appealing to her cat, who kept knocking it down by trying to play in it. Willard, like many writers, found that activities such as baking, knitting, and wood-crafting allowed her mind to recharge and open up space for inspiration and creativity. Willard rearranged her house of crates while listening to a recording of Blake's poetry by the British actor Ralph Richardson.[4] Through a strange alchemy of the two activities—handwork and listening—she found inspiration for *A Visit*.

In order to write *A Visit to William Blake's Inn*, Willard as a female writer needed to feel some control over the towering voice of Blake. Her personal mode of empowerment was to experience Blake not as a distant figure, but as a voice coming from a record player in her living room, as well as the imagined proprietor of a dollhouse that she, herself, had created. Willard's editor, Barbara Lucas, recalled seeing the inn of crates in Willard's living room:

> I remember very well a lopsided four-room dollhouse which Nancy had made from bits and ends and furnished in a most intriguing way.... Months later many of the furnishings were moved into a startling seven room house, sturdily built of wood by a friend, Ralph Gabriner. The grand edifice became the inn of William Blake. Its rooms were papered with Blake's engravings, Kate Greenaway's illustrations, and Lewis Carroll's photographs of Alice. New inhabitants included two green rabbits; a staff of Dutch girls with silver shoes and cooks with silver spoons monogrammed with moons; a Wise Cow; a dragon; and other assorted animals. I cannot list the hundreds of objects which reside in this inn, but I do have some favorites. For example, there is a prophet with gold hands and a silver star-moon pendant around his neck. (378)[5]

The physical inn was a shared act of intimacy—a physical object created both by herself and by a friend and enjoyed with visitors to her home. This hand-crafted inn was of such significance to Willard that she brought it with her, despite its encumbering size, to display when she accepted the Newbery Medal. In her acceptance speech, she recounted an anxious dream about her fears of losing the inn. In the dream, Blake reassures her that she hasn't lost the inn, she's "just lost sight of it," and that she should attend to the important things: the inn's irreplaceable guests of "birds, beasts, air, water, flowers, grass. Me. You" (*Telling* 175). In other words, the inn's importance is not about the physical structure per se, but rather about how the physical structure incorporates predecessor texts, gestures of friendship, and objects of personal significance. Willard's dollhouse inn was an empowering creation.

The inn of crates or boxes that fired Willard's imagination is a physical/metaphysical site of women's creative work and reflects the women's art movement's valorization of crafting, domestic work, and the decorative arts. As the pioneering feminist art scholar Lucy Lippard explained in her 1973 essay "Household Images in Art," until the women's movement, women artists had avoided "'Female techniques' like sewing, weaving, knitting, ceramics, even the use of pastel colors (pink!) and delicate lines," for fear of being labeled "feminine artists" (57). Male artists such as Andy Warhol could stack Brillo boxes and launch the Pop Art movement, but, as Lippard argued, if "the first major Pop artists had been women, the movement might never have gotten out of the kitchen" (56). Willard's original creation of a dollhouse made of stacked boxes, like Warhol's stack of Brillo boxes, stakes a claim for the imaginative potential of ordinary household objects. Unlike Warhol's work, however, Willard's boxes are not storage objects repurposed as conceptual art but storage objects re-purposed as new kinds of storage and display. Her boxes are still boxes, but instead of holding objects for storage, they hold objects for play and decorative display.

For Willard, inns are magical places of imagination and supernatural possibilities. When Willard was a child, her mother described an inn in Germany in which the ancient cracks in the plaster seem to have stories to tell. Her mother's stories inspired the young Willard to paint "patient angels [going] about their bright business" around the plaster cracks in her own home (*Telling* 171). Willard had a life-long fascination with angels and published two children's picture books featuring them, *An Alphabet of Angels* (1994) and *Among Angels* (1995, co-authored with Jane Yolen). Lest we overlook the subtle feminisms of Willard's verse, it is important to note that angels historically are androgynous, and that explorations of androgyny are part of the women's poetry movement.[6] As suggested by Luce Irigaray in *An Ethics of Sexual Difference*, angels are aligned with mucus, that which is neither fully flesh nor spirit, neither liquid nor solid, and thus always at the exchange of bodies and sexual identity. The angel, like mucus, challenges patriarchal philosophies and metaphors of identity by refusing to affirm old binarisms such as spirit/flesh, male/female, and solid/liquid.

The inn that Willard built out of boxes exemplifies the feminine art mode "femmage." As feminist art critics Melissa Meyer and Miriam Schapiro explain in their seminal essay published in *Heresies* (1977–1978), "femmage" is identified by such characteristics as "saving and collecting," "scraps ... recycled in the work," the incorporation of photographs and printed materials, a functional as well as aesthetic life, an intended audience of intimates, themes taken from women's lives, and the inclusion of objects of personal significance (69). Faith Ringgold's story quilts exemplify femmage: they offer vibrant displays of personal events within a patchwork that celebrates African American quilting, her mother's work as a clothing designer, and Ringgold's own rejection of masculine modes of art-making in preference to feminine modes of story and craft.

Willard's inn of crates is classic femmage in that scraps, texts, and personal objects are joined into a single artistic creation of female crafting-as-art that is then shared with an audience of intimates. For the inn's wallpaper, Willard used engravings, illustrations, and photographs of Blake, Lewis Carroll, and the children's book illustrator Kate Greenaway. She repurposed boxes and oddities as the building blocks and furnishings of a fantastical, miniature domestic space. These recycled scraps are recycled in turn as images and characters in her poems of Blake's inn: in particular, the rabbits, the silver shoes, the cow, the dragon, angels, and the prophet (which can be linked to a character from *A Visit* called the marmalade man).

## Talking Back and the Affordances of Blake

A close association with Blake affords Willard's text sophistication, literariness, and a timely association with a Romantic poet (Blake) whose star was rising. For much of the twentieth century, Blake was considered a "lesser" poet. Prior to Frye's *Fearful Symmetry* (1947), canonical British Romanticism consisted of five poets: Byron, Coleridge, Keats, Shelley, and Wordsworth.[7] After Frye's publication, Blake scholarship grew slowly but steadily until, in 1982, there was enough scholarship on Blake for a major scholarly bibliography (Natoli). Blake finally joined the Romantic pantheon, what scholars today refer to as "the Big Six." Blake Studies was an unstoppable machine. It is hard to recapture the Blakean fervor of the 1970s and 1980s, a time when it seemed that everyone was teaching Blake and writing books about Blake. Into this ferment comes the 1981 release of *A Visit to William Blake's Inn: Poems for Innocent and Experienced Travelers.*

Yet *A Visit* almost failed to be published. It would seem that fantastical lyrics about Blake were not something that Harcourt anticipated. After reviewing the completed manuscript, the new head of the trade division marched into Barbara Lucas's office and "demanded to know why this book was being published. Who would buy it? Who among potential buyers would have even heard of William Blake? Better to cancel the contract and kill the book than to bring out something with no commercial future at all" (*Left-Handed* 28). Lucas reminded the new trade-division head that "a contract is a contract," and, since the illustrators had already submitted their artwork, the book was ready to go to press. The journey from almost-canceled publication to Newbery Award was unexpected. But Willard, by associating her book with Blake, a rising star and prestigious author who was very much not a children's author, accumulated cultural capital and caught the attention of the Newbery Award Selection Committee.

Not only did Willard's book gain significance through its association with Blake, it also presumably appealed to the committee at this historical moment through its implicit feminism. In "domesticating" Blake as the proprietor of an inn (and an inn inspired, no less, by a dollhouse version of an inn), Willard participates in the feminization of the literary canon and engages in the woman poet's act of "talking back" to the male tradition of the canon. As the poet and critic Alicia Ostriker argues in *Stealing the Language* (1986), writers in the women's poetry movement made verse that "talked back" to male poets and reclaimed the canon. For example, Sharon Olds's childbirth lyric, "The Language of the Brag" (1980), opens by directly confronting two male poets who dominate America's poetic landscape: "I have done what you wanted to do, Walt Whitman, / Allen Ginsberg, I have done this thing, / I and the other women this exceptional / act" (45). Willard, by contrast—and perhaps because she is writing for children—is cautious in talking back in *A Visit to William Blake's Inn*; she does not speak directly to the male poet Blake but rather through an intermediary, an innocent boy traveler. To enable her lyric verses, Willard envisions a child narrator with "the broad curiosity of a traveler" who, as an observer, has a safe distance from events: "he recounts what he's seen and heard of the Tiger or the sunflowers, he has enough sense to leave himself out of it and let these creatures speak for themselves, using phrases and stanza forms Blake himself gave them in 'The Tyger' and 'The Sunflower'" ("Tellers" 229).

Willard, in fact, uses these two poems by Blake as an opportunity to talk back: she precisely mimics the form and phrases of Blake's poems but flips the speaker and the addressee. In Blake's "The Tyger" and "Ah! Sun-Flower," Blake apostrophizes silent objects. By contrast, Willard's tiger and sunflower speak to a voiceless Blake. In Willard's "The Tiger Asks Blake for a Bedtime Story," the tiger begins, "William, William, writing late" (a direct rephrasing of Blake's "Tyger, Tyger, burning bright"), and Blake is never given a chance to respond (40). In Willard's two-stanza "Two Sunflowers Move into the Yellow Room," Blake is similarly silent while the sunflowers speak. They address Blake: "Ah, William, we're weary of weather," a phrasing that echoes Blake's opening line, "Ah Sun-flower! Weary of Time" (Willard 28; Blake 25). As in Blake's poem, Willard's sunflowers count the steps of the sun. However, Blake's isolated sunflower lacks agency: it "wishes to go" and join the sun but has no ability to do so (25). By contrast, Willard's sunflowers are a community, and command their own fates. They arrange themselves at the window in a "room with a view," they take root in the carpet, and there they rest. Ironically, given its rejection of Blake's poetics of isolated speakers and silenced objects of address, Willard's poem is so Blakean in its style that it circulates online in elementary school lesson plans as a poem by Blake (Coughlan).

If one reads "The Sunflowers Move into the Yellow Room" in isolation from the illustration of the poem by the Provensens, the poem talks back to Blake. However, the illustrators rejected Willard's feminist slant, for their sunflowers are once again passive objects under Blake's gaze.

The Provensens depict the sunflowers as literally castrated objects, cut flowers artistically arranged in a pedestalled vase for the gratification of a male viewer. A few vines fall from the vase and touch the carpet, but otherwise there is little sense that these sunflowers might be rooted rather than cut flowers. The largest figure on the two-page spread is Blake himself (based on a real-life portrait of Blake) sitting in a chair and holding a quill pen.[8] Blake is clearly in the power position in this illustration: he holds the pen, he sits before a desk about to draw or write on a piece of paper, and he gazes at the blooms. The flowers themselves are trapped in an alcove (not a window with a view). In short, the Provensens' Blake is once more the active subject, and the sunflowers are silent enclosed objects to be painted or written about.[9]

*Figure 11.1* Illustration of "Two Sunflowers Move into the Yellow Room."

Source: *A Visit to William Blake's Inn: Poems for Innocent and Experienced Travelers*, by Nancy Willard, with illustrations by Alice and Martin Provensen (Harcourt Brace Jovanovich, 1981), pages 28–29.

When Willard began *A Visit to William Blake's Inn*, she was fortunate in that she had already developed an intimate relationship with Blake through her dollhouse-sized inn as well as through her childhood reading of Blake's poetry. As a youth, she had pored over a children's edition of twenty Blake poems re-illustrated by Pamela Bianco: *The Land of Dreams: Poems by William Blake* (1928). Bianco was a child prodigy and the daughter of Margery Williams Bianco, author of the *Velveteen Rabbit* and a Newbery runner-up for *Winterbound* (1937).[10] Bianco wrote a preface to *The Land of Dreams* in the form of a four-page letter to Blake, in which she speaks to Blake as if he were a friendly acquaintance, and in which she acknowledges having a "guilty conscience" about re-illustrating works that he had illustrated so masterfully (n. pag.). Willard identified Bianco's preface as a transformative moment for her childhood self: it offered her a way into conversation with Blake and thereby freed her from intimidation and silence. Willard was thus able to talk *with* Blake (rather than "talking back") and create a miniature world of poems in which readers are invited to visit Blake's magical inn. Her sense of intimacy with a living Blake, the sort of person to whom one might write letters, felt like a benediction on her project.

## Feminist Affordances of the Lyric

In the little that has been written about Willard, it is common to distance her from her feminist contemporaries.[11] In 1975, poetry reviewer Stanley Poss wrote that Willard "lacks altogether [Adrienne] Rich's ideology, [and] reveals no overtly feminist positions" (392); in 1978, Francine Danis argued that Willard's poetry does not fit the women's poetry movement because her verse is "not violent or militant, not startling at all—unless one is startled at encountering joy in the work of a female poet of the 1970s" (126). I find that Willard's lyrics (her poetry for adults as well as the poems in *A Visit*) do reflect the women's poetry movement. Women's poetry, particularly feminist poetry as identified by Ostriker, shares "multiple and complex patterns of thought," such as a doubled identity, a re-envisioning of enclosure (confining spaces, domesticity as a prison), and revisionist mythmaking (9).[12]

In Willard's essays on her own writing process, she depicts herself as a doubled persona, as passive and active entities who together enable the act of writing. Feminist scholars have argued that such doubled identities typify the ways that women writers see themselves. For example, in her influential 1976 essay "Vesuvius at Home: The Power of Emily Dickinson," Adrienne Rich suggests that women poets take on double identities (as an object of a poem as well as the creating subject) in order to depict themselves as poets, and that their poetry explores a woman writer's "relationship to her daemon—her own active, creative, power" (x). According to Rich, Emily Dickinson's "My Life had Stood a Loaded

Gun" exemplifies this dual positioning: the female artist is a loaded gun (object) waiting for the owner (subject) to take charge. Such poems allow the female author to explore her creative process while offering her protection from public exposure of her private self by projecting her identity into an "other." In the essay "Camping on the Border," Willard identifies her doubled writing self as "World" and "Dream": the World-self deals with distractions and deadlines while Dream exists in timeless space and waits like a hunter for inspiration (*Left-Handed* 23). In another essay, Willard depicts the divided writerly self "as outside observer" and "inside participant" who are like "two sisters destined to fight with each other": Miss Gatherer memorizes details while Miss Experience understands and contextualizes information (*Telling* 255).

In *A Visit to William Blake's Inn*, Willard offers multiple projections of her divided self, in particular that of a little boy (the point of view character), a bardic marmalade man, and Blake himself as the inn's proprietor. All of these projections are male figures, a classic choice for women writers in their doubled identities. By using male figures as their lyric Others, women poets are afforded great cultural and aesthetic authority. By tapping into the tradition of the male voice and the lyric "I," they can give their creative selves freedom for spatial movement and uncurtailed curiosity, two privileges not typically accorded to women. All three projections of Willard's writing self—the child, the marmalade man, and Blake-the-innkeeper—are Blakean. The innocent child is associated with *Songs of Innocence*, and the bard is associated with the "Experience" poems, most notably the opening poem "Introduction": "Hear the voice of the Bard! / Who Present, Past & Future sees!" (18).

We first meet the boy in "Blake's Wonderful Car Delivers Us Wonderfully Well," a poem modeled after Dickinson's "Because I Could Not Stop for Death," which Willard had memorized in high school (*Left-Handed* 87). Willard's inn is a sort of stopping place between life and death, not unlike the carriage in Dickinson's poem, in which Death, the carriage driver, "kindly stopped for me— / The Carriage held but just Ourselves— / And immortality" (350). Dickinson, dressed in gossamer and tulle, has put away her labor and leisure to take a journey to eternity, and she passes by fields of grain, schoolchildren, the setting sun, and a house that is a bare swelling in the ground. Similarly, Willard's young boy is taken up by a kindly, otherworldly driver: "The driver bowed and took my things. / He wore a mackintosh and wings," and his cap is labeled "Blake's Celestial Limousine" (17). As in Dickinson's poem, the passenger must let go of worldly things before ascending into the carriage. The boy discovers that his luggage is "excessive" and cannot be brought aboard. The suitcases, described as the boy's "fondest hopes," shrink and grow "pale as envelopes" (17). When the boy finally steps into the limousine, what should have been a tight, confining space is instead a spacious place of wonder and imagination. The seats are "green and wide," the grass is soft, the view is vast, and the child compares the car to a wish that can fly (17).

As exemplified in this poem, Willard's *A Visit* presents the escape from enclosure and entrapment through the imagery of journeys, new vistas, and open spaces of imagination. Ostriker suggests that key imagery of the women's poetry movement involved enclosure—confined spaces (coffins), confined roles (housewife, domesticity), and self-enclosures (silence, passivity)—and escape from these enclosures. In Willard's poem, the cramped interior of a limousine becomes a vast interior that takes the boy from anxious reality to a fantastical inn.

Journeys are archetypal symbols of transformation and stages of life, and they are allegories of the passage from life, to death, to the afterlife. Journeys are rife throughout *A Visit*, from the boy's traveling to the inn to journeys taken by the guests at the inn, such as a mysterious visit to the Milky Way. The concept of the journey can be a metaphysical act in which a woman writer seeks out the source of her inspiration. For example, Rich's "Vesuvius at Home" is a pilgrimage—"I am travelling at the speed of time, along the Massachusetts Turnpike"—in which her physical journey to visit Dickinson's home becomes a metaphysical journey as the traveler seeks Dickinson's essence through simultaneous immersions into her verse and life (99). Willard fully exploits the highly allusive nature of the lyric in "Blake's Wonderful Car" and evokes multiple canonical texts about journeys, beginning with Dickinson's "Because I could not Stop for Death." Her phrase "celestial limousine" evokes Hawthorne's "The Celestial Railroad," which itself evokes the most famous of all spiritual journeys, Bunyan's *The Pilgrim's Progress*.

It is worth pausing here to reflect on the feminist act of revisionist mythmaking. According to Rich, women poets take old texts in new directions in order to survive: "Re-vision—the act of looking back, of seeing with fresh eyes, of entering an old text from a new critical direction—is for women ... an act of survival" (*On Lies* 35). What is *A Visit to William Blake's Inn* but a re-envisioning of Blake's corpus? In the eleven couplets of "Blake's Wonderful Car Delivers Us Wonderfully Well," Willard aligns herself with a female predecessor and visionary (Dickinson) and reshapes the work of male writers (Hawthorne and Bunyan). From the very beginning of her writing career, Willard demonstrated a commitment to re-envisioning the canon. For example, her 1963 PhD dissertation from the University of Michigan, "An Experiment in Objectivity: the Poetic Theory and Practice of William Carlos Williams and Rainer Maria Rilke" (published in 1970 as *Testimony of the Invisible Man: William Carlos Williams, Francis Ponge, Rainer Maria Rilke, and Pablo Neruda*) interprets male poets through a feminist lens. Willard presents these writers as understanding that "all a priori systems of thought make a false unity because they leave out the total richness of the concrete" (*Testimony* 3). Willard is, in effect, anticipating the feminist scholars of the 1980s who argued for a female poetic tradition founded on a respect for the irreducible alterity of the Other. This alterity cannot be absorbed into totalizing systems and is expressed by attending to concrete particulars and expresses an "ethic of care," in which the physical and emotional needs of others must be respected and not absorbed into abstract and uncaring systems.[13] In other works, such as her verse picture book *The Sorcerer's Apprentice*, Willard incorporates personal narratives into her revisionist mythmaking. A female-centric retelling of Goethe's "Der Zauberlehrling," *The Sorcerer's Apprentice* features a heroine who works an uncontrollable sewing machine in an old magician's laboratory. This book re-envisions not only Goethe's poem but also Willard's father's chemistry lab at the University of Michigan and her parents' grief at the loss of an infant son. Willard had wanted to write about a girl with her own magical laboratory, a girl who could follow in her father's footsteps and compensate for the son who never had a chance to live.[14]

The innocent boy is only one projection of Willard's doubled identity; another projection is the bardic man in the marmalade hat. This figure of experience is closely associated with Blake himself and is linked to the afterlife and the unknown. Willard first mentions the man during a dialogue between a sleepy bear and the boy, a conversation in which the bear predicts that the sun will rise and the man in the marmalade hat will appear. Indeed, the man arrives just one poem later, in the middle of March. Like a harbinger of spring, his bustling wakes up the hibernating guests—badgers, hedgehogs, and moles. He comes "equipped with a bottle of starch," to straighten out the bends in the road, a bucket, and a mop. In a bardic refrain that is twice repeated in the poem and that seems to be spoken by a disembodied chorus, the people make way for the man:

> Now beat the gong and the drum!
> Call out the keeper
> and waken the sleepers.
> The man in the marmalade hat has come! (22)

Through the use of second-person commands, Willard creates a sense of energy and urgency in this call to the people, a tone that is only enhanced by active verbs and exclamation points. This poem echoes biblical language and motifs, and, indeed, Willard's verse often borrows heavily from the cadences and imagery of the Bible.[15]

This beating of gongs and drums and the waking of sleepers evoke biblical verses that are then feminized within Willard's poetry. The man in the marmalade hat who will straighten the bends in the road with the domestic implements of starch, mop, and water bucket is answering the famous call, "Prepare ye the way of the Lord, make his paths straight" (Mark 1:3). The connection to this biblical verse is made even more explicit in a later poem, "The Wise Cow Makes *Way*, *Room*, and *Believe*," when the Rabbit cries, "Make *Way!* / Make *Way* for William Blake!" (30). Blake, in works such as *Milton*, saw himself as a latter-day John the Baptist, exhorting the people of England to reform and prophesying destruction. In Willard's final poem about the man in the marmalade hat, "The Marmalade Man Makes a Dance to Mend Us," she brings together multiple guests of the inn—tiger, sunflowers, king of cats, cow, rabbit, fox, hound, rat, lamb, and tiger. In a direct apostrophe to the inn's inhabitants, the marmalade man, like John the Baptist and the prophets before him, cries out, "mend your ways, / I the needle, you the thread— / follow me," and the animals follow him, the lamb and tiger walking together as friends. In the illustration accompanying this poem, the Provensens depict the marmalade man as the pied piper—piping across the page, leading the procession of animals across the gutter from verso to recto. The piper is so far to the right side of the recto page that his pipe is cut off as it extends past the edge of the page. The marmalade man observes no boundaries and leads his parade of animals off the page into the possibilities of the unknown. That the marmalade man plays a flute-like instrument as he leads the animals is a clear allusion to Blake's "Introduction" from *Songs of Innocence*: "Piping down the valleys wild / Piping songs of pleasant glee / On a cloud I saw a child. / And he laughing said to me / Pipe a song about a Lamb" (7). Willard's and Blake's poems both allude to Isaiah 11.6, the source text of the Peaceable Kingdom legend, in which the wolf, lamb, leopard, and other creatures lie down together. In the biblical passage, however, it is not a pied piper but a little child who leads the animals: "The wolf also shall dwell with the lamb, and the leopard shall lie down with the kid ... and a little child shall lead them" (Isaiah 11:6). As a further connection between *A Visit* and the Peaceable Kingdom legend, the Provensens published *A Peaceable Kingdom: The Shaker Abecedarius* (1978), an American Library Association (ALA) Notable Book, just before working with Willard's text. Moreover, the Provensens used the same illustration style in this book as they did in Willard's collection.

With her 1982 Newbery book, Willard takes her place in a long line of prominent women writers who re-imagined Blake—an obscure and difficult author—as a children's poet. *Songs of Innocence and Experience* was not a children's book at first, but it became so through the efforts of women who saw its potential. The first instance of Blake's verse appearing in a children's text came in 1814 when the children's author Priscilla Wakefield included "Holy Thursday" in her revised edition of *Perambulations in London*.[16] Four years later, poets Ann and Jane Taylor included "Holy Thursday" in *City Scenes, or a Peep into London*. (Jane Taylor is most famous for writing "Twinkle, Twinkle,

Little Star.") At the end of the nineteenth century, Kate Greenaway prepared rough preliminary sketches for a proposed edition of a re-illustrated *Songs of Innocence*.[17] Pamela Bianco's 1928 *Land of Dreams* achieved Greenaway's dream of a newly illustrated edition of Blake's *Songs*. And Bianco's work, in turn, inspired Nancy Willard's *A Visit to William Blake's Inn*, for it allowed Willard to overcome her anxiety about writing new poems in the style of Blake. As Willard realized, "dreaming your way into history has its problems. To narrate a story from the point of view of Blake—who but the spirit of William Blake could do it?" ("Tellers" 229). Through the suggestions of friends (Barbara Lucas), through femmage (the inn of crates), through her childhood experiences with Blake, and through her own confidence as a lyric poet and successful children's author, Willard was empowered to write children's lyric poetry in a prophetic mode that was inspired—not silenced—by Blake.

## Notes

1 Willard published at least forty-one children's books, sixteen collections of poetry for adults, and eight fiction and nonfiction works. A prolific author, Willard moved between multiple genres and audiences throughout her fifty-two-year writing career.

2 Glenna Sloan notes that children respond to rhythm and rhyme (not free verse), humor, and narrative (54–55).

3 Despite Willard's reservations that children's verse is not tested in the little journal market, "Blake's Wonderful Car Delivers Us Wonderfully Well" from *A Visit* was first published in *The Massachusetts Review* in 1980.

4 The Ralph Richardson recording was probably the 1958 Caedmon LP, *The Poetry of William Blake*.

5 Willard describes the connections between the handmade inn and the imaginary inn of the book as follows: "the book is about a child taking a vacation at this fantastic inn. And the real inn is filled with mirrors, suns, stars, angels" (Rubin 113).

6 See Daniels for discussion of androgyny and the women's poetry movement.

7 Only Wordsworth, Coleridge, Shelley, Byron, and Keats were represented as major authors in the MLA's *The English Romantic Poets: A Review of Research and Criticism* (1972). The 1985 edition included Blake as one of six major Romantic poets.

8 Willard sent a card to editor Barbara Lucas with a request for the Provensens: "Can you ask them, please, to make Blake look like the real Blake? That's my only request regarding the pictures" (qtd. in Lucas, n. pag.). The Provensens based their Blake on Thomas Phillips's 1807 oil portrait in the National Portrait Gallery in London.

9 The Provensens did not consult Willard or Lucas in illustrating *A Visit*. They read Blake's verse, biographies of Blake, and Willard's text. The Provensens began working as children's book illustrators after World War II. Alice's training included engineering studies at UCLA, and Martin worked at Disney Studios creating storyboards and character designs (Willard, "Well-Tempered"). Their first major commission was from Simon and Schuster to illustrate *The Fireside Book of Folk Songs*. They illustrated multiple titles in

the Golden Book series as well as texts by Margaret Wise Brown, Louis Untermeyer, and Walter Dean Myers. Their original *The Glorious Flight*, a recounting of Louis Bleriot's 1909 flight across the English Channel, received the Caldecott Medal. On Martin Provensen's artistic process, see Willard's *Telling Time* (182–184).

10 Walter de la Mare, a family friend, was so inspired by Bianco's artwork that he authored verses to be published alongside selections of her drawings in a collection called *Flora* (1919). Bianco (1906–1994) authored and illustrated multiple children's books, and her mature work is held in major museums.

11 After a flurry of published interviews and book reviews following the Newbery Award, most writings about Willard consist of profiles, interviews, and retrospective biographical essays.

12 In *The Norton Anthology of Literature by Women* (1985), Sandra M. Gilbert and Susan Gubar call this divided identity of the woman writer a double consciousness. Women write with an awareness of their role as female artists while simultaneously writing with an awareness of their vulnerability within a culture hostile to women's voices.

13 See Gilligan's critique of masculine systems of ethics in *In a Different Voice*; she contrasts an "ethic of care" to an "ethic of justice" (30, 174).

14 For discussion of *The Sorcerer's Apprentice* and Willard's subconscious motivations, see Willard's *The Left-Handed Story* (67–73). Willard also authored a children's (and female-centric) version of *Paradise Lost*.

15 For discussion of Willard's use of supernatural imagery, see Larsen.

16 The first republication of Blake's "Holy Thursday" was in Benjamin Heath Malkin's 1806 *A Father's Memoir of his Child*, a book for adults about a child, but not a children's book. On Blake's republication in early children's books, see Levy (95–100). For discussion of Blake as adult (not children's) literature, see Ruwe, Introduction to *British Children's Poetry in the Romantic Era: Verse, Riddle, and Rhyme*.

17 See Essick.

## Works Cited


Bianco, Pamela, illus. and ed. *The Land of Dreams: Twenty Poems by William Blake*. New York: Macmillan, 1928. Print.

Blake, William. *The Complete Poetry and Prose of William Blake*. Revised ed. Ed. David V. Erdman. New York: Anchor, 1988. Print.

Clark, Beverly Lyon. *Kiddie Lit: The Cultural Construction of Children's Literature in America*. Baltimore: Johns Hopkins UP, 2003. Print.

Coughlan, Sean. "School Librarian Finds Fake Blake Poem." *BBC News*. BBC, 20 June 2013. Web. 18 June 2018.

Daniels, Kate. "The Demise of the 'Delicate Prisons': the Women's Movement in Twentieth-Century American Poetry." *A Profile of Twentieth-Century American Poetry*. Ed. Jack Myers and David Wojahn. Carbondale: Southern Illinois UP, 1991. 224–253. Print.

Danis, Francine. "Nancy Willard's Domestic Psalms." *Modern Poetry Studies* 9.9 (1978): 126–134. Print.

Dickinson, Emily. *The Complete Poems of Emily Dickinson*. Ed. Thomas H. Johnson. Boston: Little, Brown, 1960. Print.

Essick, Robert N. "Blake and Kate Greenaway." *Blake: An Illustrated Quarterly* 40.1 (Summer 2006): 44. Print.

Frye, Northrup. "Theory of Genres." *The Lyric Theory Reader: A Critical Anthology*. Ed. Virginia Jackson and Yopie Prins. Baltimore: Johns Hopkins UP, 2014. 30–39. Print.

Genette, Gérard. "The Architext." Trans. Jane E. Lewin. *The Lyric Theory Reader: A Critical Anthology*. Ed. Virginia Jackson and Yopie Prins. Baltimore: Johns Hopkins UP, 2014. 17–30. Print.

Gilbert, Sandra, and Susan M. Gubar. *The Norton Anthology of Literature by Women*. New York: Norton, 1985. Print.

Gilligan, Carol. *In a Different Voice: Psychological Theory and Women's Development*. Cambridge: Harvard UP, 1982. Print.

Hunt, Peter. "Confronting the Snark: The Non-Theory of Children's Poetry." *Poetry and Childhood*. Ed. Morag Styles, Louise Joy, and David Whitley. Trentham: Stoke-on-Kent, 2010. 17–23. Print.

Irigaray, Luce. *An Ethics of Sexual Difference*. Trans. C. Burke and G. C. Gill. Ithaca: Cornell UP, 1993. Print.

Larsen, Jeanne. "'By the Light of the Baseball Moon': The Sublunary Magic of Nancy Willard." *Hollins Critic* 35.4 (Oct. 1998): n. pag. *Gale Literature Resource Center*. Web. 12 July 2017.

Levine, Caroline. *Forms: Whole, Rhythm, Hierarchy, Network*. Princeton: Princeton UP, 2015. Print.

Levy, Michelle. *Family Authorship and Romantic Print Culture*. Houndsmills: Palgrave Macmillan, 2008. Print.

Lippard, Lucy R. *From the Center: Feminist Essays on Women's Art*. New York: Dutton, 1976. Print.

Lucas, Barbara. "Profile of Newbery Medalist Nancy Willard." *Horn Book* 58 (July/Aug. 1982): 374–379. Print.

Mare, Walter de la. *Flora: A Book of Drawings by Pamela Bianco with Illustrative Poems by Walter de la Mare*. New York: Lippincott, 1919. Print.

Meyer, Melissa, and Miriam Schapiro. "Waste Not Want Not: An Inquiry into What Women Saved and Assembled—FEMMAGE." *Heresies* 1.4 (1977–1978): 66–69. Rpt. in *ArtCritical: The Online Magazine of Art and Ideas* (24 June 2015): n. pag. Web. 12 June 2017.

Natoli, Joseph P. *Twentieth-Century Blake Criticism: Northrop Frye to the Present*. New York: Garland, 1982. Print.

Olds, Sharon. *Satan Says*. Pittsburgh: U of Pittsburgh P, 1980. Print.

Ostriker, Alicia Suskin. *Stealing the Language: The Emergence of Women's Poetry in America*. Boston: Beacon, 1986. Print.

Provensen, Alice and Martin, illus. *A Peaceable Kingdom: The Shaker Abecedarius*. New York: Viking, 1978. Print.

Rich, Adrienne. *On Lies, Secrets and Silence*. New York: Norton, 1979. Print.

Rubin, Stan Sanvel. "'From the Odd Corner of the Imagination': A Conversation with Nancy Willard." *The Post-Confessionals: Conversations with American Poets of the Eighties*. Ed. Earl G. Ingersoll, et al. Madison, NJ: Fairleigh Dickinson UP, 1989. 109–120. Print.

Ruwe, Donelle. *British Children's Poetry in the Romantic Era: Verse, Riddle, and Rhyme*. Houndsmills: Palgrave Macmillan, 2015. Print.

Sloan, Glenna. "But is It Poetry?" *Children's Literature in Education* 32.1 (2001): 45–56. Print.

Thomas, Joseph T., Jr. *Poetry's Playground: The Culture of Contemporary American Children's Poetry*. Detroit: Wayne State UP, 2007. Print.

Willard, Nancy. "Blake's Wonderful Car Delivers Us Wonderfully Well." *The Massachusetts Review* 21.4 (Winter/Fall 1980): 780.

Willard, Nancy. *The Merry History of a Christmas Pie: With a Delicious Description of a Christmas Soup*. Illus. Haig Shekerjian and Regina Shekerjian. New York: Putnam, 1974. Print.

Willard, Nancy. *Testimony of the Invisible Man: William Carlos Williams, Francis Ponge, Rainer Maria Rilke, and Pablo Neruda*. Columbia: U of Missouri P, 1970. Print.

Willard, Nancy. *The Left-Handed Story: Writing and the Writer's Life*. Ann Arbor: U of Michigan P, 2008. Print.

Willard, Nancy. *The Sorcerer's Apprentice*. Illus. Leo and Diane Dillon. New York: Blue Sky, 1993. Print.

Willard, Nancy. *The Tale of Paradise Lost: Based on a Poem by John Milton*. Illus. Jude Daly. New York: Atheneum, 2004. Print.

Willard, Nancy. "Tellers and Travelers: The Voices of *A Visit to William Blake's Inn* and *The Voyage of the Ludgate Hill*." *The Voice of the Narrator in Children's Literature: Insights from Writers and Critics*. Ed. Charlotte F. Otten and Gary D. Schmidt. Santa Barbara: Greenwood, 1989. 228–230. Print.

Willard, Nancy. *Telling Time: Angels, Ancestors, and Stories: Essays on Writing by Nancy Willard*. San Diego: Harcourt Brace Jovanovich, 1993. Print.

Willard, Nancy. *A Visit to William Blake's Inn: Poems for Innocent and Experienced Travelers*. Illus. Alice and Martin Provensen. San Diego: Harcourt Brace Jovanovich, 1981. Print.

Willard, Nancy. "The Well-Tempered Book." *Picturing the World: The Art of Alice and Martin Provensen*. Amherst: The Eric Carle Museum of Picture Book Art, 2005. 6–15. Print.

# 12 "One Jew, One Half-Jew, a WASP, and an Indian"

## Diversity in *The View from Saturday* (1997)

*Adrienne Kertzer*

The complex representation of diversity in E. L. Konigsburg's *The View from Saturday* (1996; 1997 Newbery Medal) has received little scholarly attention. According to Konigsburg, the novel's sixth-grade teacher Mrs. Eva Marie Olinski offers a "response to political correctness" ("Newbery Medal") in her reply to District Superintendent Dr. Clayton Rohmer's inquiry about how she chose the four members of her successful Academic Bowl team. "In the interest of diversity," she informs him, she chose "one Jew, one half-Jew, a WASP, and an Indian" (22). Marah Gubar contextualizes this satirical response by situating the novel as the first in a series of four loosely linked books that demonstrate how "Konigsburg's commitment to representing young people as enmeshed in diverse communities only intensified over the course of her career" (411).[1] She also asserts that *The View from Saturday*, like Konigsburg's novel *About the B'nai Bagels* (1969), "prompts readers to notice that ethnicity is not something that only dark-skinned people have" (413). However, when educational researcher Leif Gustavson asked four White upper-middle-class students to discuss *The View from Saturday* in the absence of a teacher, the students did not address the novel's attention to "issues of race, culture, and disability" (23). He speculates that their silence might be attributed to reasons that include the fact that teacher-led discussions examine race only when "the text is written by an author of color" (28).

Gustavson's belief that the novel won the Newbery in part because of its attention to diversity (30) is not supported by the American Library Association (ALA) announcement "1997 Newbery Medal Winner." Instead, the announcement identifies Konigsburg as the only writer to date who has received a Newbery Medal (for *From the Mixed-Up Files of Mrs. Basil E. Frankweiler*) the same year (1968) that she also won a Newbery Honor (for *Jennifer, Hecate, Macbeth, William McKinley, and Me, Elizabeth*), and praises her superior "command of every tool in the writer's cabinet." More recently, *New Yorker* columnist Jia Tolentino

DOI: 10.4324/9780367337223-12-13

has celebrated *The View from Saturday* as "less an exemplary children's novel than a perfect novel, full stop" (Tolentino). Her appreciation of the novel's "stylistic grace notes" and the "charming formality [that] unites the five different narrative voices" lends support to scholars who view the Newbery as "the last bastion of aesthetics" (Bittner and Superle 73).

Rather than accept this conclusion, my essay analyzes how Konigsburg's use of "every tool in the writer's cabinet" presents a corrective to the multiculturalism that the novel satirizes. Locating its understanding of "true diversity" (Konigsburg, "Newbery Medal") through its criticism of the institutional language of diversity, its reliance on narrative techniques that problematize visibility, and its complex treatment of courtesy, I focus on the novel's inclusion and representation of Jewish characters for multiple reasons. The first is that such inclusion highlights how multiculturalism "often privileges certain kinds of diversity over others" (Goldstein 221); the second is that Newbery Medal books have very rarely featured Jewish American protagonists. More importantly, Konigsburg's lengthy career coincided with a period of intense debates regarding Jewish American identity, including but not limited to those prompted by the dramatic increase in intermarriage rates. Prior to 1970, only seventeen percent of Jewish Americans married non-Jews. Between 1995 and 1999, fifty-five percent did so, and by the time Konigsburg published her final three novels, the rate had risen to fifty-eight percent (*A Portrait* 9).

Although it is unclear whether intermarriage "tends to make U.S. Jews less religious" (*A Portrait* 9) or vice versa, Konigsburg's fiction also reflects a concurrent shift away from a faith-based definition of Jewish American identity. In *About the B'nai Bagels*, the Jewish child protagonist faces a dilemma every Saturday. Preparing for his forthcoming bar mitzvah, he is expected by his parents to attend Shabbat services when he would rather play baseball. In contrast, in *The View from Saturday*, the only Jewish religious ceremony occurs during Noah Gershom's visit to Century Village. Although Noah never quite abandons his belief that the inhabitants of this gated retirement community are not part of "the real world" (19), he learns to value the elderly who live there, as is evident when he participates in a rabbi-conducted wedding between the Jewish Izzy Diamondstein and the non-Jewish Margaret Draper. The next time that Noah sees the newlyweds, they are visiting Epiphany "to celebrate Christmas" (106). Is Christmas a religious holiday or has it become like Epiphany, a fictional town whose name no longer evokes the celebration of a specific Christian festival?[2]

Finally, *The View from Saturday* is significant for what it excludes. Published during a decade that saw the awarding of the Newbery Medal to Lois Lowry's Holocaust novel *Number the Stars*, and a tremendous growth in Holocaust literature for American youth, *The View from Saturday* never mentions the Holocaust. This exclusion does more than raise questions about the role Holocaust memory plays in Jewish

American identity; it also directs attention to the complex relationship between the premises underlying *The View from Saturday* and the depiction of the Holocaust in Konigsburg's final fiction.

## "Monolithic Whiteness" and Jewish American Identity

In the speeches collected in *TalkTalk: A Children's Book Author Speaks to Grown-Ups*, Konigsburg often reflected upon changing perceptions of Jewish American identity. These changing perceptions are also evident in Bonnie J. F. Miller's criticism of the Newbery Medals and Karen Brodkin's work on Jewish American identity. In her 1998 essay "What Color Is Gold? Twenty-One Years of Same-Race Authors and Protagonists in the Newbery Medal," Miller condemns the "conspicuous absence of non-white protagonists and authors" (34) among the medal winners since Mildred Taylor received the medal in 1977 for *Roll of Thunder, Hear My Cry*. Advising the winners that unless they "model multi-cultural diversity ... they will be linked, however unwillingly, in monolithic whiteness" (37), she does not hesitate to include Jewish American authors in this group. Brodkin provides a context for Miller's perspective. In her 1998 study *How Jews Became White Folks and What That Says about Race in America*, Brodkin traces the shift of Jewish American identity from the late nineteenth and early twentieth centuries when Jewish Americans were not regarded as White, to the period following World War II, when they "had been socially assigned to whiteness and accorded its privileges" (173).

Brodkin acknowledges that not all Jewish Americans will agree with her. One factor contributing to their ambivalence may derive from her distinction between ethnoracial assignment and ethnoracial identity: "Groups fashion their identities for themselves, even though they do so in response to ethnoracial assignments" (103). Despite how "In the last hundred years, Jews in the United States have been shuttled from one side of the American racial binary to the other" (175), Jewish Americans may continue to feel that their current ethnoracial assignment is precarious precisely because ethnic groups cannot control what side of the binary they are shuttled to. As many have observed, anti-Semitism demonstrates that the "categories of white and color don't correspond neatly to Jewish reality" (Kaye/Kantrowitz 123). The role of anti-Semitism in problematizing ethnoracial assignment is confronted by Brodkin who immediately following the American presidential election in 2016 published an opinion piece provocatively titled "How Jews Became White Folks—and May Become Nonwhite under Trump."

Konigsburg portrays anti-Semitism as a significant aspect of American life in only one novel, *About the B'nai Bagels*, but Jewish identity continues to interest the author in evolving, if less overt, ways. By the time she published *The Outcasts of 19 Schuyler Place* (2004) a question about whether the neighbors are anti-Semitic is regarded as a joke. Nor does she always identify her characters as Jewish Americans. It is widely recognized that *From the Mixed-Up Files* was inspired by her children, and she even used them as models for her illustrations (Sauer), but when the novel's protagonists wake up on Sunday, they discuss whether they ought to go to church. *The View from Saturday* is very different. In labeling two of the child protagonists, Noah Gershom and Nadia Diamondstein, as respectively Jewish and half-Jewish, the novel contests Miller's confidence that the Newbery Medals are interested in "only one ethnicity and one culture" (37).

What are the correct terms to describe the ethnicity of Noah and Nadia and of a cultural heritage that makes Noah familiar with Yiddish phrases and Nadia long for the Jewish dessert that her new Protestant grandmother has never heard of? According to Brodkin, ethnicity came into use after World War II "to describe those who had been formerly discussed as members of a less-than-white race, nation, or people" (144). Konigsburg supports this account when she writes that growing up during the 1930s and early 1940s, she and the other children "didn't know we were ethnic" (*TalkTalk* 141). What complicates the concept of ethnic identity is that the relationship between ethnicity and race is hard to pin down. Like Brodkin (189n1), Miller sometimes treats ethnicity as synonymous with race and sometimes as different. The slipperiness of her usage is particularly noticeable in the two sentences that conclude her article: "The Newbery should be awarded to non-white authors. Even more important, the Newbery books should have positive, ethnically diverse protagonists" (37). In the latter sentence, what does Miller mean by ethnically diverse?

Konigsburg is the only Newbery winner featured in Miller's footnotes. In one of those notes, Miller ambiguously acknowledges that *The View from Saturday* may challenge her statement that "all award books ... essentially feature white protagonists" (36). Admitting that she uses "'essentially' ... to describe a situation that is somewhat difficult to classify" (38n11), she states that how one reads *The View from Saturday* determines whether it has "four white and one Indian American central characters" or "one white central character" (38n11). Calling the White character, Mrs. Olinski, "a genuine contribution to the literature of another vastly under-represented minority group: the physically challenged," Miller does not explain why she believes that "the majority of readers are perhaps likely to view this story as having only a single (White) protagonist" (38n11). One obvious advantage is that this judgment allows her to discredit the possibility that the child Julian Singh, who has skin "the color of strong coffee with skim milk" (*The View* 66), is one of the novel's protagonists. The disadvantage is that it sets aside the narrative structure that is so significant to Konigsburg's treatment of diversity.

## Narrative Structure, Visibility, and Courtesy

Konigsburg has described the structure of *The View from Saturday* as "a risk" ("Newbery Medal"). Miller's reading demonstrates what is at risk. Possibly because each of the interior monologues has a title, Miller concludes that readers may view the book "as a compilation of short stories" (38n11). Should they do so, they will ignore how the monologues articulate the novel's treatment of diversity. The intricate relationship between the third-person narration and the monologues of the child protagonists produces a structure that resembles the puzzles that Julian enjoys. Although Konigsburg trusts that her readers are capable of working out many aspects of the puzzle, she provides an important clue when Noah protests the number of steps he must take before Tillie Nachman begins teaching him how to use a calligraphy pen. Tillie corrects him: "You must think of those six steps not as preparation for the beginning but as the beginning itself" (10). Her advice is equally applicable to the novel's structure, for the story of how the children become members of a winning team commences long before they encounter Mrs. Olinski on their first day in sixth grade.

The monologues serve multiple purposes. First, they reveal the experiences that enable the children to succeed at the Academic Bowl. According to Konigsburg, there is a "critical age" when children's brains must be "jump-started with experience" ("Newbery Medal"). Believing that the critical age for learning kindness occurs during "the cruelest year—grade six," she uses the monologues to reveal how the children's experiences jump-start their brains. In addition, the monologues by Ethan Potter and Julian demonstrate how the kindness that they experience during the children's weekly tea parties—first convened by Julian before the four children became a team—alters their relationship with each other and informs their view of Mrs. Olinski. Throughout the novel, Mrs. Olinski is frequently asked how she chose the members of her winning team. At the novel's conclusion, she asks the children "Did I choose you, or did you choose me?" (160). Their ambiguous answer "Yes!" indicates that while they chose her, they are also aware that she chose them, a choice that Julian's father attributes to her intuitive recognition that the children had all been on transformative journeys (156–157).

Just as Mrs. Olinski cannot explain how Mr. Singh knows that she nearly did not choose Julian, her insight into what the children bring to the competition is puzzling. She has no conscious knowledge of their journeys nor the transformative impact of their weekly visits to Sillington House, a property that Julian's father has purchased in order to open a bed and breakfast inn. For example, she does not know why one Monday the previously quiet Nadia enters her classroom smiling and happy to engage in conversation. Ethan's monologue provides a likely answer in that it reveals that Nadia's first visit to Sillington House took place the previous Saturday. Although Mrs. Olinski first visits Sillington House in late December, she does not learn about the weekly tea parties until months later when she attempts to schedule a practice on a Saturday afternoon. And just as she knows very little about what the children reveal about themselves in the monologues, the children do not have access to the thoughts the third-person narrator attributes to Mrs. Olinski.

One major difference between the two narrative techniques—the third-person narration about Mrs. Olinski and her team and the children's first-person monologues—is that the narrator is much more assured about what Mrs. Olinski is feeling than the children are in their monologues. The monologues frequently imply that the children are not always capable of probing the motives prompting their own behavior. According to Gustavson, "There is a reason why Ethan loves musical theater and costumes" (28), but the narrative suggests that if this is the case, then Ethan is not prepared to acknowledge it. For Gustavson to hint that Ethan must be gay because he wants to work in the theater is problematic for several reasons. Not only is Ethan's monologue silent on this point, but Gustavson's statement also relies on a dubious stereotype that all boys who want to work in the theater must be gay. How then should readers understand the fact that Ethan is as attracted to "the halo the sunlight made of [Nadia's] hair" (70) as he is to the halo that appears when Julian tries to cover over the abusive message scrawled on his book bag? Ethan doesn't analyze what draws him to the latter. His admission is simply followed by "I guess I like halos" (73).

What the narrative techniques emphasize is how the characters' self-perception undercuts the labels others apply to them. Those self-perceptions are rarely shared with other characters. Just as the narrator reveals what Mrs. Olinski thinks when people use the word "cripple," the monologues reveal that what the children are unwilling to share with others is precisely what makes them feel most different. Again, Ethan's monologue offers the best example. On the surface, he looks like the WASP that his family heritage confirms. But he never tells anyone how constant comparisons to his multitalented older brother Luke have driven him to years of painful silence. Convinced that he has been "a disappointment to every one of [his] teachers" (63), he also admits that he cannot "tell anyone" (74) about his desire to work in the theater. Since this admission comes immediately after a paragraph in which he refers to himself as the son "scheduled to inherit the farm because Luke was scheduled for greater things" (74), the narrative perspective contests Gustavson's understanding of the nature of the desire that compels Ethan. Perhaps Ethan wants to work in the theater because he is gay, but maybe he wants to do so because it would enable him to defy family and community expectations about Potter children. Referring to himself in the third person, he states "No one in Epiphany would believe that Ethan Potter wanted to go to New York City to work in the theater" (74).

The result is a novel that both acknowledges the significance of visibility as a sign of difference, particularly in the depiction of Julian and Mrs. Olinski, and simultaneously undercuts this significance. This suggests that when Dr. Rohmer asks Mrs. Olinski how she chose the members of her team her answer is wrong because it does not get at the diverse strengths that each protagonist brings to the competition. The four children are indeed members of a "diverse group" (23), but their ethnic and/or racial identity is a very small component of that diversity.

According to the narrator, Mrs. Olinski has a good reason for giving her "bad answer" (1). In fact, her answer has two parts and the narrative provides at least two good reasons. The first is that when Dr. Rohmer asked his question, Mrs. Olinski "did not know how she had chosen her team" (1). The second is that he has just completed "a three-day workshop on multiculturalism for *ed-you-kay-toars*" (22; italics in original). Having "always been amused by educators who called themselves *ed-you-kay-toars*" (22) and convinced that Dr. Rohmer expects an answer that will confirm the lessons he has learned at the workshop, Mrs. Olinski first tells him that she chose her team members on the basis of their diverse hair color. Assuredly false in that this answer has nothing to do with how she chose her team members, the answer certainly pays attention to visible differences.

Dr. Rohmer proceeds to give Mrs. Olinski "a capsule lecture on what multiculturalism really means" (22). The novel does not provide that lecture; instead, it recounts the increasingly fraught conversation that follows. After she tells him the second version of her answer—"the Epiphany Middle School team has one Jew, one half-Jew, a WASP, and an Indian" (22)—he responds "Jews, half-Jews, and WASPs have nothing to do with diversity, Mrs. Olinski. The Indian does. But we don't call them Indians anymore. We call them Native Americans" (22–23). He does not say why Jews and half-Jews have nothing to do with diversity; nor does he consider that his use of the royal we—"we don't call them Indians anymore"—objectifies the very people he believes that his new vocabulary recognizes.

The dialogue between Mrs. Olinski and Dr. Rohmer provides a nuanced example of the novel's interest in misleading assumptions about identity. At one point, Julian realizes he has erred in assuming that a veterinarian with a gender-neutral name is a man. Similarly, since the novel has not yet introduced the character whom Mrs. Olinski insists is Indian, Konigsburg sets up a situation where readers may wonder why she is so insistent. What complicates this situation is that unlike readers, Dr. Rohmer already knows that Mrs. Olinski uses a wheelchair because of a car accident a decade earlier. Not aware of this, readers may take for granted that she is able-bodied. However, the revelation that she is a paraplegic may be less likely to disturb them than the manner in which they learn this fact. For Dr. Rohmer replies to her repeated insistence that one team member is Indian by condescendingly asking her "Mrs. Olinski ... would you like it if people called you a cripple?" (23). Once again, he is sure that he has the answer.

The comment illustrates more than Dr. Rohmer's arrogance. If his three-day course has taught him that it is impolite to call people cripples, then surely his desire to prove his superiority to Mrs. Olinski leads him to forget this lesson. His question immediately silences Mrs. Olinski, not because she is shocked but because she realizes that he is incapable of understanding her complex response to the word he is so sure will offend her. She cannot explain to him that "the word itself does not hurt, but the manner of its delivery can" (23). Her distinction is reinforced by her experience the first day of school when she returns to her classroom and sees on the blackboard that one of her students has written "cripple" where she had written "paraplegic" (71). Nor is he capable of understanding the error of generalizing about group identity on the basis of surface resemblances: "For all of his training, Dr. Rohmer would never believe that cripples themselves are a diverse group, and some make jokes" (23).

The episode also sets up a major contrast between Dr. Rohmer's silencing of Mrs. Olinski and the conversations that Sillington House facilitates. In her Newbery Medal acceptance speech for *The View from Saturday*, Konigsburg praises the "Third Places" in her life, third because they are "neither work nor home" but rather "where we learn to listen to different voices and where we learn how to agree to disagree." Admitting that she is not sure "if suburban America even has a Third Place," she creates one in Sillington House (Konigsburg, "Newbery"). This is where Ethan gains "permission to do things [he] had never done before" (Konigsburg 1996 *The View* 93), where Nadia and Noah learn to enjoy their constant bickering (101), and where Julian shows the three children a sculpture of a "small ivory monkey, only two inches high" (97). Demonstrating that the monkey can do tricks in that it "can balance on any one of its four limbs" (97), he persuades them to join in assisting Mrs. Olinski to deal with the people in the school "who try to get her off balance" (97). Their decision to help her exemplifies how a Third Place enables them to "learn to identify—or not identify—with people whose lives are not [their] own" ("Newbery Medal").

Although the novel portrays Sillington House as a place of true courtesy, Dr. Rohmer's assertion—"we don't call them Indians anymore" (23)—indicates that multicultural discourse has its own code of polite speech. It also has a code of manners. After Julian identifies himself to Dr. Rohmer's deputy superintendent, Homer Fairbairn, as being "in part what is called East Indian" (137), Fairbairn asks him what his tribe is. Rather than comment on his failure to distinguish between East Indians and Native Americans, the narrator interjects: "Everyone ...

knew that even though it was correct to recognize a person's ethnicity, it was not correct to comment upon it in public" (137). Why is it correct to do one, but not the other?

Initially, the novel satirizes traditional good manners as something adults use to berate children whose ignorance of these manners proves "how Western Civilization was in a decline" (5). In his monologue, Noah mocks his mother who uses this phrase after he admits that he does not know that a B and B letter is "a *bread and butter letter* you write to people to thank them for having you as their houseguest" (5). Recalling that Tillie Nachman makes the same comment in reference to the invention of the ballpoint pen, he thinks that the two women should get together: "Between them, they have come up with the two major reasons why Western Civilization is about to collapse" (6–7). Mrs. Olinski also uses this phrase during her first visit to Sillington House. Observing the children listen to each other, she thinks that "maybe—just maybe—Western Civilization was in a decline because people did not take time to take tea at four o'clock" (125). While the "maybe" hints that she is being ironic, a more significant irony is that the manners symbolized by the tea parties are proposed by Julian, the character whose "ever polite" (92) behavior has contributed to the harassment he has endured.

Unlike the other monologues, Julian's does not dwell on events that take place prior to meeting Mrs. Olinski. Instead, it is set two months after the weekly tea parties commence, and focuses on the temptation he experiences when he uncovers a malicious plot to disrupt a school production. Realizing that he has the opportunity to take revenge on the two boys who harassed him when he first moved to Epiphany but choosing not to take revenge, he is unable to resist breaking the rule taught him by his mentor, the cruise-ship magician Gopal, that "magicians never reveal the secrets of their trade to laymen" (117). Using his magical tricks to reveal to the instigator that he is aware of the plot, he recalls how Gopal once told him that he had "chops" (93).

Because Julian's monologue focuses primarily on what he observes, readers must decide for themselves why the day Julian heard this praise from Gopal remains so important to him. One possible clue is that Gopal told him that he had chops the day before Julian was to start his education at a British boarding school. But readers cannot know if Gopal's words helped Julian adapt to the boarding school, since Julian says nothing. Rather than view his silence as evidence of the novel's "strain of Orientalism" (Erickson 276), I regard it, along with his politeness and his magical expertise, as part of the mask he wears to protect himself. But if "there are times when the only way you can be yourself is to hide behind a mask" (Konigsburg, *TalkTalk* 148), the manners he has learned offer little protection upon his arrival in Epiphany.

As Ethan watches Julian and his father waiting for the school bus on the first morning of school, Ethan does not know how to categorize the people he sees. The adult is wearing a white turban; the boy with him is wearing shorts and knee socks. When the boy boards the bus, Ethan cannot reconcile his accent with the color of his skin: "He didn't look British" (66). Despite this statement, Ethan's perspective implies that Julian's harassment is driven not primarily because of the color of his skin, but because of the clothes he wears, the manners he has learned, and the accent and vocabulary that mark him as different from the others. Although Ethan envies Julian's accent—"What is there about an English accent that makes people seem more intelligent than they maybe are?" (67)—he wants nothing to do with a boy whose attire, ways of speaking, and behavior defy the norms of what is done in Epiphany. Unwilling to share his bus seat or walk into the school with him, for the most part, Ethan remains a silent observer of the abuse Julian experiences.

All of this changes after Julian sends Noah, Nadia, and Ethan invitations using clues taken from *Alice's Adventures in Wonderland*. In effect, Julian reinvents the mad tea party as the occasion for weekly tea parties that are performed far more respectfully than in *Alice's Adventures*. During the first party, Ethan notices that the tea is so hot that the four children cannot gulp but must slow down and sip. That the ceremony produces more than a calming effect upon its participants is apparent the second time Mrs. Olinski visits Sillington House. As she drinks tea, the narrator highlights how strange she feels: "She could not remember a time since her accident—maybe even before it—when she had not forced herself not to notice people noticing her" (141). Aware that the children are watching her, "she [does] not feel at all self-conscious" (141). In contrast to Dr. Rohmer, the children see her disability but that is not all they see.

The tea parties initiate the transformation of children, who were once silent observers of the malice directed towards Julian and Mrs. Olinski, into children who celebrate how Mrs. Olinski regains control of the classroom. After two classmates rudely challenge Mrs. Olinski's authority (129), the children mimic the posture of the ivory monkey—Nadia thrusting her left leg into the aisle; Noah sticking out his right (131)—an obvious contrast to the way the students on the bus had stuck their feet into the aisle in order to trip Julian. Leading their classmates in lifting her wheelchair triumphantly following their victory in the district finals (138), and ensuring that everyone applauds her when they win the Academic Bowl, they come off the stage so that they can stand beside her in her wheelchair, and thereby compel the commissioner to "come down off the stage to give them their trophy" (154). Drawing on the lessons in courtesy and community that they have learned at Sillington House, the children enable Mrs. Olinski to feel at home in the world.

## Nadia's Rugelach and Jewish American Identity

That the color of Julian's skin matters more than Ethan perceives is supported by the novel's ambiguous treatment of Julian's hybridity. When Konigsburg says that she "[has] been allowed to wear many masks because Western civilization—flawed though it may be—has given [her] the privacy and privilege to do so" (*TalkTalk* 143), she, intentionally or not, acknowledges the White privilege that allows her to benefit from wearing masks. However, the mask that Julian wears does not prevent Mrs. Olinski from referring to him as an Indian. Her reference to Julian as an Indian and Nadia as a half-Jew is undoubtedly intended to mock the language of multicultural discourse, but it is also contested by Julian's self-description when he informs Mr. Fairbairn that he is "a hybrid" (137). Until then, because of how Ethan had described the color of Julian's skin, readers might set aside the possible implications of the "skim milk" (66) that lightens his coffee-colored skin, and assume that both of Julian's parents must also be dark-skinned. The possibility that these assumptions are mistaken emerges during Ethan's first visit to Sillington House. After Ethan notices a poster of a "dark-haired" (84) woman named Simonetta (which may be a stage name), Julian informs him that the woman is his dead mother and that she was "an American by birth" (85). He says nothing more about her. Instead, he jokes that because his father was also American "by naturalization" (85), his own birth "on the high seas" (85) makes him "as American as pizza pie" (85). Since an "American by birth" could also have dark skin, Julian's refusal to comment on his mother's racial identity, along with his conversation with Fairbairn, raises two issues. The first is that when he says that he is "in part what is called East Indian" (137), he does not explain whether this refers to his being an American of East Indian descent or to the fact that one of his parents was not East Indian. The second issue is that the novel's vagueness about what constitutes Julian's hybridity is radically unlike its precision in identifying how many Jewish parents Noah and Nadia have.

In calling himself a "hybrid" (137), Julian uses a word that clearly links him to Nadia. When Nadia meets Ethan, readers already know that she is "the product of a mixed marriage" (26). After she reveals her "Half-Jewish, half-Protestant" parentage (35), he observes that his "thoroughbred Protestant" (36) grandmother's marriage to Nadia's Jewish grandfather is the only claim to hybridity that his family can make. He also embarrasses Nadia by saying that since this is a late second marriage, the newlywed couple "don't plan on breeding" (36). His observation resembles Noah's earlier comment that because of the age of the bride and groom, "there wouldn't be any concern about what religion they should choose for their children since all their children were already … chosen" (8).

It is remarkable that in a novel which suggests that the primary challenge with mixed marriages is deciding what religion the children should be, Konigsburg never actually reveals what Julian or Nadia's religion, if any, is. While the turban Julian's father always wears and his name might signify that he is Sikh, the novel never uses that word. Nor does it clarify whether Julian shares his father's faith. As for Nadia, her monologue demonstrates no concern about her religious status. Resentful at having a new grandmother at a time when she is overwhelmed by the consequences of her parents' divorce, she misses her dead Jewish grandmother's homemade rugelach and consoles herself that knowledge of rugelach "is a hybrid advantage" (39). Because her parents have just divorced, she is split in half, constantly traveling between her new home in upstate New York where her mother has moved and her father's new home in Florida. The anxieties that concern her relate less to ethnic identity and more to her displacement and loneliness. Her uncertainty about where she fits may explain why, in moving to Epiphany, she initially finds Noah's self-confidence overbearing. One advantage to discussing Jewish identity in relation to more than one protagonist is that it challenges the assumption that all Jews are alike.

Hybrid characters like Nadia appear in each of the three novels that Konigsburg published following *The View from Saturday*. *Silent to the Bone* (2000) is set in 1998; *The Outcasts of 19 Schuyler Place* (2004) focuses on Margaret Kane's memories of events that occurred in 1983; *The Mysterious Edge of the Heroic World* (2007) takes place in the late 1990s.[3] However, although each novel defines Jewish American identity as a matter of hybridity, heritage, and culture, Jewish heritage receives less narrative attention than other kinds of heritage.

Margaret Kane, the narrator of *The Outcasts of 19 Schuyler Place* (and an important adult character in *Silent to the Bone*), is a good example. Whereas *The View from Saturday*'s Noah translates Yiddish phrases and Nadia laments the loss of homemade rugelach, Margaret translates Hungarian and explains that *palacsinta* are Hungarian crepes (123). Revealing her Hungarian heritage long before she mentions that her Hungarian uncles and her American-born mother are Jewish, Margaret is delighted to discover that the man to whom she discloses this fact is also half-Jewish, but in contrast to the narrative attention given to the revelation in *The View from Saturday* that Mrs. Olinski is a paraplegic, Margaret never dwells on the significance of her Jewish heritage. Instead, Konigsburg uses Margaret's misery at summer camp as further evidence of the limitations of identity labels. As Margaret says, "everyone ... had a name for me but none of them knew me" (50).

## Identity Labels, Visibility, and the Holocaust

Holocaust references in *The Outcasts of 19 Schuyler Place* often juxtapose the benefits of Jewish ethnoracial assignment in America beside the disastrous consequences of being identified as Jewish during the Holocaust. Thus, the uncles are perplexed that Americans would choose to have tattoos, and when Margaret plans an act of civil disobedience, she inspires herself by thinking of "Anne Frank (but not her fate)" (164). At the same time, the relationship between the Holocaust and the circumstances leading to the uncles' immigration remains uncertain. Uncle Morris says that they began building the towers that make them outcasts in their Epiphany neighborhood shortly after they bought the house. Margaret states that they have been constructing them for forty-five years. This duration suggests that they began in 1938, a year in which it was increasingly difficult for European Jews to ignore the threat posed by Nazis, or to find refuge elsewhere. But it is impossible to establish when exactly the uncles immigrated. According to Uncle Alex, building the towers "kept Morris and [him] going through some bad times" (204–205), but readers never learn how many, if any, of the friends Morris and Alex lost during those "bad times" were lost because of the Holocaust.

*The Mysterious Edge of the Heroic World* is far more explicit regarding the relationship between characters and the Holocaust. Published only six years before a Pew Research Center study reported that seventy-three percent of Jewish Americans regarded "remembering the Holocaust [as] … an essential part of what being Jewish means to them" (*A Portrait* 55), *The Mysterious Edge* resists this way of understanding Jewish American identity. Although its child protagonist Amedeo Kaplan has one Jewish grandfather (and is thus a "hybrid" like Nadia), this matters less than a sexual orientation which critic Michelle Robinson describes as "simultaneously obscure and plain" (390).[4] Nor does Amedeo's quest to discover something lead to a revelation about the Holocaust's impact upon his family. Instead, he fulfills his quest by uncovering the provenance of Nazi-stolen art through a plot that links his Florida neighbor Mrs. Zender to documents once in possession of a former resident of Epiphany and emphasizes the horrific consequences when the Nazis applied identity labels to those they regarded as degenerate, including but not limited to homosexuals, modern artists, and Jews.

Mrs. Zender plays a key role in this plot. While her belief that "Ninety percent of who you are is invisible" (102) supports the treatment of visibility in *The View from Saturday*, it also ironically applies to her decades-long silence about how a Modigliani drawing that "a senior officer of an *Einsatzgruppen*" (225) stole ended up in her possession.[5] She has been similarly quiet about how she used the threat of exposing this man's Nazi past in order to compel him to install a superb sound system in her home. Her behavior has striking parallels to the Austrian official who was equally willing to overlook this past once the man bribed him with a Klimt drawing he had stolen. It also demonstrates the novel's resistance to conventional narratives about how and why Americans remember the Holocaust. Mrs. Zender remembers in order to profit by it.

Like *The View from Saturday*, *The Mysterious Edge* strongly objects to identity labels and problematizes visibility. Certainly, Konigsburg never claims that the multicultural discourse she satirizes is equivalent to the Nazi discourse she condemns. However, the omission in *The View from Saturday* of Dr. Rohmer's lecture on "what multiculturalism really means" (*The View* 22) obscures this distinction. While the novel's satiric intent likely encouraged Konigsburg to set aside how multicultural discourse is intended to create a more inclusive society and to respect cultural difference, the difference between this discourse and a Nazi discourse designed to humiliate, exclude, and destroy is crucial. When Dr. Rohmer restricts the meaning of diversity to certain groups, he does not harm those he excludes. In contrast, in *The Mysterious Edge*, courtesy offers no protection to those the Nazis label as "degenerate"; nor does hybridity have any place under the Nuremberg Laws that forbade marriage between Jews and non-Jews. The same is true of intersectional identities, as the young protagonists learn through reading John Vanderwaal's memoir: the Nazis decided that one man must wear a yellow star rather than a pink triangle because they hated his Jewish identity more than his homosexuality (194–195).

The reading of the memoir prompts everyone, including Mrs. Zender, to weep. Undoubtedly, Vanderwaal's lament about his beloved brother—"*The Nazis knew as much about Pieter ... as the amount of him that the Rosa Winkel covered: a small, flat Pink Triangle*" (219)—strongly evokes the objections to identity labels in *The View from Saturday* and demonstrates how Konigsburg's late oeuvre engages with issues of labeling and identity, hybridity, and visibility. At the same time, the weeping that follows the reading of the memoir marks Konigsburg's recognition of the difference between satirizing the limitations of multicultural identity labels and tracing the murderous consequences of the labeling and categorizing of Pieter. *The Mysterious Edge of the Heroic World* has numerous satiric moments, but the comic mode Konigsburg utilizes to satirize multicultural discourse in *The View from Saturday* has no place in her representation of the Holocaust.

## Notes

1 What loosely links the four novels is that three of them—*The View from Saturday*, *Silent to the Bone* (2000), and *The Outcasts of 19 Schuyler Place* (2004)—are set in the fictional town of Epiphany. Although *The Mysterious Edge of the Heroic World* (2007) is set in Florida, several characters have a family connection to characters in *Silent to the Bone* and *The Outcasts of 19 Schuyler Place.*

2 Unlike Epiphany, Century Village is a real community whose current website supports Noah's view that it resembles "a theme park for old people" (7). Although the website boasts that "South Florida is known worldwide as a cultural mixing-pot" ("Welcome"), nearly all of the residents Noah encounters there are Jewish.

3 Specific historical events establish that the memories Margaret recalls in *The Outcasts* occurred in 1983. My estimates for the dates of the two other novels are based on familial relationships between the characters. For example, the sixth-grade protagonist in *The Mysterious Edge* is the child of characters who "met and fell in love" (127) during the events narrated in *The Outcasts.*

4 Robinson's reading of Amedeo's desire and the novel's "queer possibilities" (391) is much more persuasive than Gustavson's reading of Ethan's sexual identity.

5 *The Mysterious Edge* depicts the *Einsatzgruppen* as thieves who competed "to steal things that would please Hitler or Reichsmarschall Hermann Goering" (225). They are better known for being "key perpetrators of mass shooting operations in which more than a third of Jewish Holocaust victims died" ("Einsatzgruppen").

## Works Cited

Bittner, Robert, and Michelle Superle. "The Last Bastion of Aesthetics? Formalism and the Rhetoric of Excellence in Children's Literary Awards." *Prizing Children's Literature: The Cultural Politics of Children's Book Awards*. Ed. Kenneth B. Kidd and Joseph T. Thomas, Jr. New York: Routledge, 2017. 73–86. Print.

Brodkin, Karen. "How Jews Became White Folks—and May Become Nonwhite under Trump." *Forward* 6 Dec. 2016. N. pag. Web. 11 Aug. 2020.

Brodkin, Karen. *How Jews Became White Folks and What That Says about Race in America*. 1998. New Brunswick: Rutgers UP, 2000. Print.

"Einsatzgruppen: An Overview." *Holocaust Encyclopedia*. United States Holocaust Memorial Museum. Web. 12 Aug. 2020.

Erickson, Anne K. "The View from Saturday by E. L. Konigsburg." *American Post-Modernist Novels*. New York: Grey House Publishing/Salem Press, 2013. 273–279. Print.

Goldstein, Eric L. *The Price of Whiteness: Jews, Race, and American Identity*. Princeton: Princeton UP, 2006. Print.

Gubar, Marah. "The Mixed-Up Kids of Mrs. E. L. Konigsburg." *Think in Public: A Public Books Reader*. Ed. Sharon Marcus and Caitlin Zaloom. New York: Columbia UP, 2019. 409–420. Print.

Gustavson, Leif. "Normalizing the Text: What Is Being Said, What Is Not and Why in Students' Conversations of E. L. Konigsburg's *The View from Saturday*." *Journal of Children's Literature* 26.1 (2000): 18–31. Print.

Kaye/Kantrowitz, Melanie. "Jews in the U.S.: The Rising Costs of Whiteness." *Names We Call Home: Autobiography on Racial Identity*. Ed. Becky Thompson and Sangeeta Tyagi. New York: Routledge, 1996. 121–137. Print.

Konigsburg, E. L. *About the B'nai Bagels*. Illus. E. L. Konigsburg. New York: Atheneum, 1969. Print.

Konigsburg, E. L. *From the Mixed-Up Files of Mrs. Basil E. Frankweiler*. Illus. E. L. Konigsburg. New York: Atheneum, 1967. Print.

Konigsburg, E. L. *Jennifer, Hecate, Macbeth, William McKinley, and Me, Elizabeth*. Illus. E. L. Konigsburg. New York: Atheneum, 1967. Print.

Konigsburg, E. L. *The Mysterious Edge of the Heroic World*. 2007. New York: Atheneum Books for Young Readers-Simon and Schuster Children's Publishing Division, 2009. Print.

Konigsburg, E. L. "Newbery Medal Acceptance." *Horn Book Magazine* 73.4 (July/Aug. 1997): 404–415. *Academic Search Ultimate*. Web. 14 May 2021.

Konigsburg, E. L. *The Outcasts of 19 Schuyler Place*. New York: Aladdin-Simon and Schuster Children's Publishing Division, 2004. Print.

Konigsburg, E. L. *Silent to the Bone*. 2000. New York: Simon Pulse-Simon and Schuster Children's Publishing Division, 2004. Print.

Konigsburg, E. L. *TalkTalk: A Children's Book Author Speaks to Grown-Ups*. New York: Atheneum-Simon and Schuster Children's Publishing Division, 1995. Print.

Konigsburg, E. L. *The View from Saturday*. New York: Atheneum Books for Young Readers-Simon and Schuster Children's Publishing Division, 1996. Print.

Miller, Bonnie J. F. "What Color Is Gold? Twenty-One Years of Same-Race Authors and Protagonists in the Newbery Medal." *Journal of Youth Services in Libraries* 12.1 (1998): 34–39. Print.

"1997 Newbery Medal Winner." *American Library Association*. N. pag. Web. 8 Apr. 2018.

*A Portrait of Jewish Americans: Findings from a Pew Research Center Survey of U. S. Jews*. Pew Research Center. 1 Oct. 2013. Web. 24 Oct. 2018.

Robinson, Michelle. "Lovebugs and Queer Boys in E. L. Konigsburg's *The Mysterious Edge of the Heroic World*." *Children's Literature Association Quarterly* 37.4 (2012): 389–399. Print.

Sauer, Patrick. "The True Story behind Mrs. Basil E. Frankweiler and Her Mixed-Up Files." *Smithsonian Magazine* 16 May 2017. N. pag. Smithsonian.com. 28 Sept. 2018.

Tolentino, Jia. "'The View from Saturday,' by E. L. Konigsburg." "The New Yorker Recommends." *The New Yorker* 17 July 2018. N. pag. newyorker.com. 29 July 2018.

"Welcome to Your Dream Gateaway [sic]." Centuryvillage.com. Century Village Real Estate, Inc. 2021. Web. 12 Apr. 2021.

# 13 Ghosts of Japanese/American History in *Kira-Kira* (2005)

*Giselle Liza Anatol*

Cynthia Kadohata's Newbery Award-winning *Kira-Kira* (2004; 2005 Newbery Medal) describes the experiences of the Japanese American Takeshima family in the 1950s and 1960s US South. Given its postwar setting, it is striking that the author chooses not to mention the forced relocation and internment of more than 100,000 Japanese immigrants and Japanese Americans during World War II, following President Franklin D. Roosevelt's issuance of Executive Order 9066, or to acknowledge the US nuclear attacks on Hiroshima and Nagasaki.[1] One might initially interpret the absence of these references as promoting Japanese American—and, more broadly, pan-Asian—assimilation into Eurocentric US culture. In other words, Kadohata might seem to participate in "the persistent ghosting from official United States history" of events that, instead of being remembered, atoned for, and learned from, "haunt the United States ... as collective hallucinations" (McClintock 819).[2] This chapter reveals, however, that while the novel only faintly alludes to Japanese American history of the mid-twentieth century, these incidents possess the text of *Kira-Kira* as a powerful spectral presence. Importantly, the ghosts of Japanese/American[3] evacuation and detention that lurk beneath the surface of the story primarily come to light in a Southern setting.[4] The US South, haunted by the atrocities of slavery, Jim Crow, and ongoing racial violence, is commonly assumed to be a site of trauma only for African Americans, erasing all other racialized subjects.[5] *Kira-Kira*, however, explores the trauma experienced by Japanese/Americans in the South; in doing so, Kadohata's debut novel counters previous erasures in the Southern landscape as she develops characters who refuse to fully assimilate into Eurocentric norms. She simultaneously rejects a model that lumps all people of color together, calling for a recognition of distinct experiences in the collective fight against racism.

*Kira-Kira* introduces the Takeshima family through the eyes of Katie, who was born in Iowa in the early 1950s as the younger sister of Lynn, whom she adores. When their parents' small grocery store fails, the family moves to Chesterfield, Georgia, where the girls' paternal uncle

DOI: 10.4324/9780367337223-13-14

works in the thriving poultry industry and can secure jobs for Mr. and Mrs. Takeshima. Over the course of the novel, the sisters experience the birth of a baby brother, friendships outside the Japanese/American community, racial and class discrimination, and Lynn's tragic illness and death. *Kira-Kira* has been heralded as a "beautifully handled and emotionally satisfying" story (Tillotson) that "speak[s] to readers who have lost someone they love—or fear that they could" (Rochman). Identifying Kadohata's novel as primarily about Katie's relationships with family, friendships, and loss, instead of about her navigation of complex racial and cultural challenges, might appeal to readers seeking a "universal" or "apolitical" story. And this interpretation is understandable: the novel opens in a pastoral version of the Midwest, and the most harrowing incident the Takeshima sisters face involves an encounter with a snarling dog. Once the family leaves their bucolic Iowa home, upsets and distress wrapped up in racist experiences do emerge, yet the greatest tragedy, Lynn's illness and death, stands apart from any racialized episodes. Moreover, Kadohata carefully avoids a narrative that pivots around the physicality of racist violence (e.g., the whippings of enslaved people or lynchings in the deep South), or around the brutality, death, and destruction of World War II. Her exploration of racism, in other words, unfolds in an unobtrusive manner, different from the ways readers typically learn about the topic.[6]

Yet the description of *Kira-Kira* as a "universal" or "apolitical" story is problematic and deceptive. As literary scholar and teacher-educator, Peter Morgan has argued about other Asian American texts, *Kira-Kira* is not simply youth literature about teenagers fitting in. Presenting it as such, in fact, incorrectly renders generic adolescent conformity as a "stepping stone to a much more profound assimilationist ideology" (Morgan 20). The novel is decidedly about the personal—both in the pathos of the "dying girl" story, and in the protagonist's physical, intellectual, and emotional development—but it is also about the collective trauma of the Japanese/American community.

Valuing the collective as much as, if not more than, the individual is key to the work of many ethnic authors and writers of color; ignoring its significance in *Kira-Kira* "ghosts," or obscures, an important element of the book and causes culture, race, and heritage to fade away, becoming merely setting or backdrop. Moreover, the novel is about a communal history that has been "ghosted": the traumatic experience of Japanese/Americans during World War II. This history haunts *Kira-Kira* much as Lynn "haunts" Katie after her death. While Katie actively claims both her Japanese cultural heritage and certain aspects of Southern culture, seeing no conflict between them, she also reckons with—albeit unknowingly—ghosts of the past that clamor for recognition.

In writing *Kira-Kira*, Kadohata confronts the pressures that minority writers of literary fiction face in order to get their stories published or prized: trends that obligate authors to craft predominantly historical narratives and fiction set in the time periods and places associated with their ethnic or racial identity groups (e.g., the prevalence of African American novels and picture books set during slavery or the Civil Rights Movement, either in inner cities or in the rural Deep South). When authors conform to these expectations, editors are more inclined to see their works as publishable, and readers are more likely to recognize historical topics that are already part of school curricula. When authors refuse to participate in this practice, they risk encountering gaps in the knowledge-base of gatekeeping editors as well as audiences. Kadohata's *Kira-Kira* operates in a type of spectral liminal space: it is not set during World War II and the war does not appear to overtly influence or come into the consciousness of the adolescent protagonist. But its effects linger all around her. Just like a ghost, the war is not a tangible, visible presence, but it can still induce trauma in the lives of the living. Thus, while neither of the Takeshima sisters can have any personal memories of the war or the relocation camps, Kadohata sets up the novel to suggest that the parents' experiences can haunt not only them but also their children.

In addition to eschewing the wartime historical setting that many Americans associate most closely with Japanese/Americans, Kadohata rejects the stereotypical turn to a legendary, exoticized past. Lynn and Katie frequently tell each other stories, but these are not traditional Japanese folklore: indeed, Kadohata refuses to participate in "the proliferation of folktales meant to teach [White] Americans about Asian cultures" that simultaneously "reinforces and perpetuates the stereotype of Asians as exotic foreigners" (Manuel and Davis, ix). Instead, *Kira-Kira* is grounded in modern, everyday "Japanese-ness": the children's first names are Lynn, Katie, and Sam, but their middle names, respectively, are Akiko, Natsuko, and Ichiro; Katie's first word is "*kira-kira*," which means glittering, and it is only one of many Japanese words in the narrative. Kadohata describes Japanese foods, like onigiri and pickled plums (38); holiday traditions (193–194); and religious beliefs and practices (222, 225) as part of a mid-century American childhood.

Moreover, *Kira-Kira* accurately portrays attitudes and behaviors in the immediate aftermath of World War II as dictated by Japanese culture: the coping mechanisms of myriad internees after their release from detention centers included refusing to openly discuss evacuation from their homes and subsequent incarceration.[7] In other words, the Takeshima parents' silence on the issue is not specific to Kadohata's fictional characters, or necessarily for the comfort of contemporary, non-Japanese readers. Rather, it is a historically-substantiated generational response to internment. The author has stated that although her own father was detained during the war, she did not capture what he lived through in her writing because "[h]e wouldn't tell me anything about his experiences at Poston [camp]. He didn't like talking about that period"

(Comerford). This reluctance to talk about the war is reflected in *Kira-Kira* through the fact that Katie knows that her Uncle Katsuhisa "saved [a man's life] during World War II" (37) but does not seem privy to any of the details of the incident, or the context. The scarcity of overt wartime references in the novel serves multiple purposes. It encourages readers to think beyond preconceptions that ethnic writers can only address the struggles of negotiating their heritage and must concentrate on the past (books about Japanese Americans must focus on World War II, for example) and it presents silence about painful histories as a powerful cultural expression and potentially subversive act.[8]

The text significantly begins with an act of speech but also exposes important gaps in what is revealed: Katie notes, "My sister, Lynn, taught me my first word: *kira-kira*" (1). This introduction indicates an intense bond between the siblings, as well as an immediate cultural marker of the Takeshimas' heritage, in that this first word is Japanese, not English. The verb tense of this first sentence, coupled with that in the lines that follow, also subtly divulges that Lynn has died: Katie recalls that her sister's "eyes *were* deep and black" (4; italics for emphasis). By establishing Lynn as deceased, Kadohata renders the character as a ghostly presence that haunts the novel, a narrative of Katie's memories.

The story of Lynn's illness and premature death follows in the tradition of the "dying girl" narrative popularized in the nineteenth century. Victorian novels like Dickens's *The Old Curiosity Shop* and Alcott's *Little Women* present fetishized depictions of dead and dying women and girls, imparting lessons about the ideal victim: innocent, beautiful, devout, and serenely accepting of her death. Contemporary titles typically address terminal illness in more nuanced ways—Kadohata's depiction addresses "imperfect" emotions like rage and depression—but still overwhelmingly center on the individual growth and experiences of patients and their loved ones.[9] While *Kira-Kira* has roots in the Anglo-American literary tradition of the "dying girl" trope, it also subverts it by implicitly connecting Lynn's story to historical traumas experienced by an entire community of Japanese/Americans. Descriptions of Lynn's illness can be read on a purely literal level, but they can also be interpreted symbolically. Notably, Katie's sister dies of lymphoma, a cancer experienced in elevated rates in atomic bomb survivors. Additionally, her gradual fading away echoes the effects of nuclear poisoning on survivors of the Hiroshima and Nagasaki attacks.[10] The Takeshima family's mourning reflects the emotional pain of Japanese/Americans before, during, and after the war, which can be directly related to the suffering endured because of racism.[11]

Unlike many "dying girl" novels, *Kira-Kira* places its tale of individual and familial suffering within a specific social context: the family faces racial discrimination and exploitation as Japanese/Americans in the Jim Crow South. This element of the novel's anti-racist perspective is not always obvious to readers. My own graduate students, contemplating why *Kira-Kira* won the Newbery Award in 2005, have recognized that the book definitely features the traits valued by Newbery committees of its era—complex characters who experience moral growth, rich historical settings, beautiful language, and lyrical prose—but this would have been true of many of the nominees. Some have wondered whether committee members were captivated by what could be perceived as "diversity lite"—a story in which the characters "just happen" to be Japanese American, so that readers can lose themselves in the "universal" story of two sisters. Others hypothesize that the committee, whether consciously or not, may have been attracted to the ways that the novel spoke to a particular social and cultural moment for Asian Americans at the turn of the millennium, when Asian American histories, experiences, and personalities were increasingly inching from the margins to the center, inhabiting spaces where diverse people, events, and practices could be rendered more accurately and more fully.[12] Teasing out the richness of the Japanese American experience in *Kira-Kira* requires one to look beyond the coming-of-age narrative and dying-girl story to the larger historical context of the United States, both at mid-century and in the early 2000s.[13]

Katie's and Lynn's birthdates (1951 and 1947, respectively) and the fact that they are *Sansei*, or the second generation born in the States, suggest that their parents were likely to have been incarcerated in one of the camps established after the Japanese attack on Pearl Harbor. Mr. and Mrs. Takeshima are *Nisei*—first-generation US-born—but more specifically, Kadohata identifies them as *Kibei*, born in the States but educated for part of their lives in Japan. This would have rendered them even more suspect in the eyes of US authorities, who already viewed all people of Japanese heritage living in the States as possible traitors and spies. Readers learn near the end of the novel that Mr. Takeshima initially moved to Iowa from the West Coast when he was twelve years old, and it was there that he met his wife. Most people of Japanese heritage living in California, Oregon, and Washington state were sent to internment camps in the nation's interior, providing a clear explanation for Mr. and Mrs. Takeshima's residence in the Midwest just prior to Lynn's and Katie's births.[14] Yet Mr. Takeshima's description of the move is ambiguous: he wonders whether "he would have ended up staying in California instead of going to Iowa with his family" if he had run away as an adolescent and struck out on his own (240). He goes on to surmise that he might have been wealthier, and thus able to keep Lynn healthy, had he made different decisions in life (241). Readers can intuit that his consideration of this alternate reality is a way for him to cope with his daughter's death. His wishful thinking—leaving the actual details of the move unstated—allows the "ghosts" of the novel to rattle their chains without fully articulating their presence: why does his family move all the way to Iowa, over a thousand miles away from their West Coast home and a denser population of Japanese/Americans? And how did Mr. and Mrs. Takeshima meet in Iowa? Answers are not found in the novel; they are buried in the history of compulsory relocation. The novel's silence around Mr. Takeshima's relocation with his parents and brother is noteworthy in contrast to the explicitly economic reasons given in the text for the family's later move to Georgia.

Katie learns that before she was born, her father had acquired the trade of chicken sexing—the process of separating male from female chicks to prioritize space and feed for egg-layers; this training allows him to secure work in a hatchery in Georgia when his grocery business fails in Iowa. Katie notes: "Chicken sexing was invented in Japan. Then a Japanese man came to Chicago and started a school to teach Japanese Americans how to sex chickens. That's where my father had learned, before" opening his store (162). Again, there is silence: why did her father learn chicken sexing? World War II again suggests a possible answer: some Japanese Americans traveled voluntarily to "free zones" in the Midwest for employment opportunities—and the chick sexing industry in particular—just prior to mass internment (Azuma 252), while others were permitted to move for jobs in the Midwest after being held in California, investigated by the government, and proving that they were loyal, patriotic citizens.

As historian Eiichiro Azuma maintains, expertise in chick-sexing is part of a larger Japanese/American response to the long history of US racism: it was an employment path that allowed the community to highlight its racial heritage rather than stifle it, supplanting negative conceptualizations of Japanese identity with "ideas of racial desirability" (242). Job advertisements, newspaper articles, and other documents demonstrate how Japanese Americans strategically inverted the racism of the day in order to corner the market on chick sexing and emphasize connections between science, industrial development, profitability, and Japanese workers, thereby making the Japanese "race" (when coupled with native-born US citizenship) "acceptable to white America and to themselves" (242). Whatever the particulars of Mr. Takeshima's career path, the loose threads of the fictional parents' history and livelihood imply historical links to the virulent racism of the United States. That racism, including its greatest manifestation in World War II incarceration, can be seen to haunt Kadohata's text.

This analysis is not obvious in a surface-level reading of *Kira-Kira*, making it strikingly different from Kadohata's second book, *Weedflower* (2006), which provides an explicit history lesson about internment in a style more typical of Newbery Award-winning historical fiction. Interestingly, *Weedflower*, which relates the story of Sumiko Yamaguchi, a Japanese American sixth grader who is evacuated from her home with her extended family and then detained in Poston, Arizona, is itself "haunted" by an earlier novel about Japanese relocation, which it closely resembles—down to both protagonists being named "Sumiko." In 1945, Florence Crannell Means, one of a minority of White Americans in the 1940s who questioned the government's racist practices of "forced Americanization and ethnic dispersal," in Azuma's words (252), published *The Moved-Outers* (1945; 1946 Newbery runner-up).[15] Literary scholar Suzanne Rahn, writing about Means in the 1980s, discusses the increasing prominence of what we today call Own Voices authors—noting a marked shift away from awarding literary prizes to White authors of books about non-White characters (98–99). Rahn took the position that Means's *The Moved-Outers* is still worth reading, not as a "substitute ... for the author who is actually a member of the minority group," but rather "as the interpret[ation] of one group to another.... [As] a member of the white majority, Means knew what assumptions white readers would make about ... Japanese-Americans; what deep-seated prejudices would have to be overcome; what techniques would help these readers step into the shoes of another race" (114–115). This is a salient explanation for why Means begins her novel by occluding her protagonist's racial and ethnic identity. Readers are likely to assume that "Sue Ohara," a teenager coming home from school to an energetic dog, freshly baked cookies, and a stay-at-home mother in a beautiful, two-story house, is White, that "Sue" is short for "Susan" (instead of "Sumiko"), and that the family's surname is a marker of Irish roots instead of Japanese ancestry. Writing at a tenuous moment in history—*The Moved-Outers* was published before the closing of the last internment camp, at Tule Lake, CA—Means painstakingly attempts to build mainstream readers' identification with the Japanese American protagonist. This reader identification facilitates empathy and anger when the protagonist's family is subject to animalization by the US government: before being relocated to more permanent internment camps, they must report to the temporary assembly center established in the Santa Anita racetrack grounds, where they are lodged in stables that reek of the horses formerly kept there. Kadohata includes a similar scene in *Weedflower*, where her protagonist Sumiko states that "the government moved her people around like they were animals"—putting the verb in the passive voice to emphasize the way the people were treated as objects rather than having the agency of active subjects (234).

Compared to Means's Ohara family, *Kira-Kira*'s Takeshima family is less likely to be misread as White, but the characters similarly undermine stereotypes and invite broad reader identification, thus setting the groundwork for anger and outrage at their treatment. As *Kibei*, Mr. and Mrs. Takeshima are crafted realistically, with ties to both Japan and the United States: they are neither wholly assimilationist, anxious to relinquish their cultural heritage for absorption into Eurocentric mainstream culture, nor absolute about adhering to the "old ways" and refusing to acclimatize. And while the oldest daughter Lynn might be seen as a representative of the racialized "model minority" stereotype that leaves many twenty-first-century Asian American children feeling trapped, she is the sister who perishes.[16] Katie is portrayed in ways that consistently prevent the reader from pigeonholing her as the obedient, humble, and studious Asian/American subject: she steals nail polish (171), struggles to get Cs in school (62), speaks with a Southern drawl (48), and fantasizes about a love life with the made-up Joe-John Abondondalarama (79).[17]

Kadohata's nuanced portraits of the Japanese American Takeshimas include several scenes that articulate racial discrimination against the family. When they seek a motel room during their long drive from Iowa to Georgia, they are confronted by a White woman at the check-in desk who ignores Mr. Takeshima in order to continue a personal phone conversation. Refusing to adopt a professional attitude for the transaction, she eventually moves the receiver away from her mouth to say: "Indians stay in the back rooms" (27). When Katie replies, "We're not Indian," the woman continues to engage in a racist refusal to distinguish non-White groups, commenting, "Mexicans, too." Katie, indignant, states, "We're not Mexican," and is promptly scolded by the older woman, who goes on to assert that back rooms—clearly the least desirable—also cost two dollars more than standard ones. Mr. Takeshima pays without complaint, but the length of the scene reveals the weighty significance of the bigotry and exploitation the family faces.

Later, Lynn tries to explain prejudice to Katie in anticipation of her first day at a primarily White school: "Have you noticed that sometimes people won't say hello to Mom when we're out shopping? ... Well, some of the kids at school may not say hello to you, either.... Haven't you noticed that Mom and Dad's only friends are Japanese? ... That's because the rest of the people are ignoring them" (49–51). In a corresponding scene, Katie notices that when her baby brother is born, hospital nurses take turns coming to gaze at him as if he is a circus sideshow. She is now cognizant enough to remark on the irony of the situation: "It was funny how so many people ignored my mother, but they were all fascinated by this little Japanese baby. Then, when he grew up, they would probably ignore him" (56).

Taken together, *Kira-Kira* and *Weedflower* develop the theme of racism and oppression in the United States and ground discussions of Japanese/American experiences in the context of Native and African American histories. In *Kira-Kira*, the focus is primarily on the Japanese/American experience in relation to that of African Americans (although Native American history also figures); in *Weedflower*, Kadohata more fully develops the parallel World War II experiences of Indigenous and Japanese/American communities. *Weedflower* unequivocally connects the forced relocation of Japanese/Americans to that of other disenfranchised peoples in US history: the narrator explains that internees in the Poston camp have displaced the Mohave Indians, and the federal government has transported Chemehuevi, Navajo, and Hopi peoples onto the land as well. At the book's end, Hopi people are being transferred into the barracks that Japanese/Americans vacate. Kadohata thus inspires readers who are thinking about the internment of Japanese/Americans to contextualize the government's actions within a centuries-long history of the forced movement inflicted on Native peoples.

In *Kira-Kira*, that linkage is implicit when Katie mentions Okefenokee Swamp, which she knows means "'Land of Trembling Earth' in Seminole" (87). The Seminole people are acknowledged, but they no longer live in this region, largely as a consequence of the Seminole Wars and Indian Removal policies. Katie apparently cannot relate to the Seminoles' stories in the same way that she connects with the tale of a young girl named Brenda, who, according to local myth, died in a marsh that became named for her "way back before I was born. Her ghost lived in the swamp" (87). Katie has heard about this girl as an individual: "She was ten when she died" (88). She knows details about her family relationships: the ghost "was looking for her parents" (87). Later in the novel, Kadohata's protagonist believes she actually sees Brenda, wearing a white dress and weaving between the trees as she runs with a dog (105). She is part of Katie's imaginative world in a way that the victims of Indian wars, Indian removal, Japanese internment, and the nuclear attacks are not.

Yet Katie processes family trauma in part by relating it to the history of dispossession and genocide with which she is familiar. When Lynn dies, Katie finds reassurance in the idea that millions of people had been sad before her because of the deaths of people they cherished: "the people of the great Incan city of Cuzco, which was ransacked by foreigners in the sixteenth century," about whom she had written a school essay, as well as "all the millions of people in all the many wars throughout history and throughout the world, and all the millions of people with loved ones killed by millions of other people" (199–200). Again implicit, the US mistreatment of Japanese/Americans during World War II and the bombings of Hiroshima and Nagasaki drift as apparitions through the text.

Even more than the linkage to the Native American experience, it is the ghosts of the African American past that become a central point of reference in *Kira-Kira*, in part because of the novel's setting in the Southern United States. The wealth and social prominence of Mr. Lyndon, Mr. Takeshima's employer in Chesterfield, Georgia, are established by Katie's report that President Eisenhower once dined at the Lyndon estate. As a five-star general and commander of the Allied Forces in Europe during World War II, Eisenhower's presence symbolizes US wartime policy, including Japanese/American internment, and that violence is linked to the systemic racism that has defined and elevated the

Lyndon's family status over centuries. The Lyndon house is not just large; it carries the history of once having been a plantation Big House. As such, it is haunted by the ghosts of the forced and stolen labor of African/Americans that went into building the Lyndon fortune and of the African peoples who were involuntarily transported—like evacuated Japanese/Americans and numerous Indigenous communities—but this time across the Atlantic and from plantation to plantation during the slavery era. Kadohata further hints at these phantoms of the past and the way slavery's legacy endures in the present by noting that the Lyndon family employs a Black maid.[18]

In Katie's day, the Lyndon property no longer has slave quarters: Mr. Lyndon has "torn [them] down" and "in [their] place his wife had hired gardeners to create an azalea garden that was supposed to be gorgeous" (86). In referencing the garden, Katie's phrase "supposed to be" signals either that she has not seen the property herself, or that she contests its beauty. The latter interpretation posits a rebellious, anti-colonial reading; the former sets up her lack of access to the space—one the protagonist's family and the rest of the Japanese/American community are unable to penetrate. They are "ghosted," so to speak—rendered invisible and insignificant in White America, despite their arduous labor and the sacrifices they make as they attempt to achieve financial success by working for Mr. Lyndon.[19] Their hard work contrasts sharply with the fact that "Mr. Lyndon inherited everything he owns!" (139); his property and status are unearned. Moreover, Mr. Lyndon takes proprietorship so much for granted that he extends the concept to those under his employ. At one point, the wealthy factory owner asks Katie's father, "Are you one of my sexers?" to which Takeshima responds, "I'm one of *the* sexers" (234; italics in original). Mr. Takeshima can resist Mr. Lyndon's implied claim of ownership because he has options for mobility: he can obtain work at another hatchery. This opportunity, of course, was denied the enslaved African/American people once owned by Mr. Lyndon's family. In a region that has historically construed race as dichotomous points on a Black/White axis, the two men's exchange exposes a reality that is historically complex and nuanced. While this complexity is frustrating to Mr. Lyndon—Mr. Takeshima operates outside a system of race relations begun during slavery whereby White people could legally own Black labor—it illustrates how the Japanese/American community used the professional subculture of chick sexing as an opportunity to negotiate a space for themselves.

The profession of chick sexing is thus linked to cultural identity and providing Japanese/Americans physical and economic mobility, both in US history and in Kadohata's fictional narrative; however, Katie's strong reaction to the imprisonment and slaughter of the chicks allows for the ghosts of wartime internment to flicker once again, even while Katie herself is unaware of that historical trauma. As a *Sansei*, the protagonist knows little about the Japanese/American experience during World War II both because the elders in her community refrain from discussing it and because it is absent from school instruction. When the Takeshima children eventually make their way onto the Lyndon property for a picnic, Katie notes, "A field is a magical place. I could imagine what the past held: cows grazing, a Civil War battle, maybe even dinosaurs" (140).[20] Her sense of time is restricted to the immediate past (cows), the distant prehistoric world, and the Black/White binary implied by her reference to the Civil War.[21] Yet while Katie, who is not yet capable of independent critical thinking, sees only what she has been formally taught, Kadohata carefully prepares the reader to see the specters of American history on the Southern landscape. When Katie steals a few male chicks from the hatchery where her father works in order to free them in a field, she pointedly understands this as an act of liberation, declaring "Be free!" (167–168). Like her *Nisei* parents, Katie has absorbed the practice of processing wartime trauma silently. Her freeing of the birds expands the significance of chick sexing in the novel from a marker of cultural identity to a symbolic reflection on the Japanese/American incarceration and a defiant gesture against imprisonment. Within the larger context of the novel's commentary on the shared historical experiences of oppressed groups, it also stands as a critique of the violence enacted on Indigenous and African American communities.

US children's literature remains dominated by images of Whiteness, reflecting assumptions that an American, by default, is White. By telling a story about everyday Japanese/Americanness in the Deep South—a setting that highlights the ways in which Whiteness has been constructed within a Black/White dichotomy that erases complexity—*Kira-Kira* addresses a failure in the cultural imagination. In doing so, Kadohata simultaneously challenges assumptions that narratives about non-White groups must be set in expected places, during expected times, and illustrates how shared American landscapes boast a plurality of histories, both seen and unseen. The American South is haunted by the horrors of slavery, yet as Kadohata shows, the ghosts of that painful past mingle with other spectral presences. In her 2005 Newbery Award acceptance speech, Kadohata reflected on an insight born from a cross-country bus trip: "in my heart was a sense of what it meant to me to be an American in general, and in particular, an American writer. It did not mean shared history or even shared values with other Americans, but a shared landscape.... I understood then that I could write about my section of that shared landscape" (87).

*Kira-Kira* may read as universal because it depicts everyday life on familiar Georgia soil; nonetheless, spirits of the past lurk in that shared American landscape. In evoking the *particular* history of Japanese/Americans in the South—a history shaped by an omnipresent racism that manifested in World War II internment—Kadohata also suggests commonalities with other minority groups. The ghosts of internment circulate with those of Indian Removal and slavery. And the haunting generated by each of these traumas points to contemporary racist oppression. Like the nearly contemporaneous Newbery novel *Holes* by Louis Sachar (1998; 1999 Newbery)—in which incarcerated youth perform forced manual labor in a contemporary landscape cursed by the lynching of an African American man—*Kira-Kira* asks readers to pay attention to ghosted history.[22] Just as *Holes* invites readers to attend to history's ghosts by filling in the "missing holes" that constitute the story's mystery, so, too, I argue, does *Kira-Kira* invite readers to fill gaps in the "dying girl" story. Kadohata's narrator Katie, from the novel's opening pages, intimates that her sister has died. In doing so she primes readers to wonder what happened to Lynn and to feel the heightened significance and poignancy of Katie's memories. From the beginning, then, readers are hunting for ghosts—and explanation. The answers that readers find come from both Katie—who feels equal hurt and confusion about her sister's death and the racism she observes—and from Mr. Takeshima, whose wishful thinking implies that Lynn would not have died if war between the United States and Japan had never happened. Thus, while *Kira-Kira* avoids overt treatment of the historical events most closely associated with Japanese/Americans in children's literature, it does address the incarceration—and other racially motivated wrongs—through a skillful merging of private grief with a broader critique of US racism.

## Notes

1 Under the claim of domestic security risks, the US government established camps to incarcerate people of Japanese ancestry who were living on the West Coast of the United States. The first to open, Manzanar, was built in Southern California while others were located at Tule Lake, CA; Honouliuli, HI; Granada, CO; Topaz, UT; Minidoka, ID; Heart Mountain, WY; Jerome and Rohwer, AR; Gila River and Poston, AZ.

2 In her essay exploring 9/11, literary scholar Anne McClintock identifies the "forgettings" of historical events such as slavery, the genocide of Indigenous peoples, and the atomic annihilation of Hiroshima and Nagasaki as acts of "imperial ghosting" that haunt the nation (819).

3 I use the slash to indicate a mixed group of Japanese immigrants and Japanese American citizens of the United States.

4 Kadohata knows this setting intimately. She was born in Chicago in 1956 but her family moved to Georgia, where they lived briefly, then settled in Arkansas. Her father, like the fictional Mr. Takeshima, was employed as a chicken sexer (Cha 108).

5 Scholars of Asian American Studies have highlighted how American narratives—especially those set during the Jim Crow era and in the deep South—typically operate within a distinct "black-white racial binary" which negates how racial and ethnic groups like Asians Americans lived both "within *and* outside the system of segregation" (Cha 105, 106).

6 Literary scholar Amina Chaudhri asserts that Kadohata's novel "breaks from convention by naming whiteness, challenging individualism, and locating capitalism as a site of racism and injustice" (161). While this is true, the "break," "naming," and "challenging" are markedly calm and quiet.
7 See, for instance, Tanaka and Matsumoto.
8 Kadohata's oeuvre as a whole challenges this idea; *The Thing About Luck* (2013), winner of the 2013 National Book Award, for example, situates its Japanese American family as residents of Kansas who work as wheat harvesters throughout the Midwest in the present day.
9 Consider Lois Lowry's *A Summer to Die* (1977), which, like *Kira-Kira*, is narrated by the younger sister of a teenage girl who dies of cancer; *Me and Earl and the Dying Girl* by Jesse Andrews (2012); *The Fault in Our Stars* (2012) by John Green; and the extensive oeuvre of Lurlene McDaniel, who writes YA novels about characters facing serious illness and death.
10 Eleanor Coerr's *Sadako and the Thousand Paper Cranes* (1977) deals directly with a cancer death caused by the US nuclear bombing of Hiroshima: it recounts the story of young Sadako Sasaki, who died of leukemia caused by radiation from the bomb.
11 Valerie Matsumoto makes a similar claim about Janice D. Tanaka's documentary film, *When You're Smiling: The Deadly Legacy of Internment* (1999): "The premature deaths of … men like Tanaka's father, her mother's reliance on prescription medication, and a high number of drug-overdose deaths among [second-generation US-born] Sansei—especially young women—in the early 1970s mirrored the persisting pain of World War II forced removal and the difficulties of gaining acceptance in the mainstream" (223).
12 A handful of striking examples: in politics, President Ford declared the World War II-era incarceration of Japanese/Americans unethical in 1976; President Carter's 1980 Commission on Wartime Relocation and Internment of Civilians affirmed that internment was sparked and sustained by racism; in 1988, President Reagan signed the Civil Liberties Act, not only apologizing for the camps but paying damages to former internees. In sports, Michael Chang, the first Chinese American to win the French Open, rose to #2 in the world; Kristi Yamaguchi won the US Figure Skating title and the Olympic gold medal in 1992; figure skater Michelle Kwan earned World Champion status five times shortly thereafter. In the literary arts, a host of titles for young people on the subject of Japanese/American internment appeared in the 1990s, including Yoshiko Uchida's *The Invisible Thread* (1991); Ken Mochizuke's *Baseball Saved Us* (1993); Marlene Shigekawa's *Blue Jay in the Desert* (1993); and Steven Chin's *When Justice Failed* (1993). Asian American authors of adult fiction also received acclaim in the late twentieth century: Maxine Hong Kingston's *The Woman Warrior* (1976) became one of the most frequently taught books in US college classes, and Amy Tan's *The Joy Luck Club* (1989) was adapted as a major motion picture in 1993. In popular culture, Disney produced *Mulan* (1998), its first animated "princess" feature with an Asian heroine.
13 As Sara Schwebel astutely notes of the "doubly historical" nature of children's historical fiction, it often provides insights into *two* periods in history, although K-12 classrooms rarely—if ever—explore that second, more contemporary historical context (21–22).
14 Cha aligns the Takeshima family's history with the Jerome Relocation Center in Dermott, Arkansas because of that camp's proximity to Tyson Foods

headquarters in the northern part of the state, as well as Kadohata's childhood residence in Arkansas (103). However, an equally compelling case can be made for the family's internment in Iowa, which had a number of incarceration facilities. Kadohata's Chicago birth could explain her semi-autobiographical character's birthplace in the Midwest.

15 *The Moved-Outers* also won the Child Study Association Award for best book tackling contemporary problems. Kenneth Kidd discusses the book as part of a "shadow canon" embedded in Newbery Honor titles (formerly Newbery runners-up) in his important 2007 article on literary prizing (177).

16 The notion of the "model minority" gained traction in the 1980s and 1990s; it is recognizable to contemporary readers but was not present in the mid-century setting of the novel.

17 Summer, the first-person Japanese American narrator of Kadohata's *The Thing About Luck*, also defies the "model minority" label. She hates homework (25), identifies as not good at math (105), and mentions "iffy grades" (4).

18 Katie observes, "She was very beautiful. Her skin was the same color as my brown silk hat" (232). In this reflection, Katie resists the American beauty standards of her time that would have celebrated Whiteness and denigrated features associated with African ancestry, from complexion to the size of nose and lips to body frame and shape.

19 When considering Mrs. Lyndon's luxurious garden plot, the most Katie can hope for is a single flowering bush: "Someday when we owned a house, I would get my mother an azalea plant so she could start her own garden" (86). Katie's modest plan underscores both the financial inequality between the Lyndons and Takeshimas and the fact that the Lyndons—wealthy descendants of White enslavers—provide the model for Katie's "American Dream."

20 Her limited vision of US history does not include any Asian Americans, though their presence in the South dates back to the late eighteenth century with the Filipino Saint Malo settlement in Louisiana, followed by the nineteenth-century arrival of Chinese workers from Cuba and California to the Mississippi Delta. Cha reads this scene more optimistically: he interprets Katie's "innocent ruminations on history" as peering "beyond the mythologized constructions of the Old South and the ghosts of the Confederacy" to a prehistoric moment "devoid of racial prejudice and class disparities" (116).

21 Kadohata raises the issue of a slanted education more explicitly in *Weedflower* and *The Thing About Luck*. In *Weedflower*, when Sumiko learns that Native Americans in Arizona do not have the legal right to vote, she is stunned, having had the ideals of democracy ingrained in her through formal schooling: "[T]he class had learned that all grown-ups born in the United States could vote" (214). And even in the contemporary time period of *The Thing About Luck*—an era with jet planes, DEET, LEGOs, and cell phones—the Japanese American narrator, Summer, perceives the gaps in the history published in texts assigned by her teachers. "I'll bet all sorts of things happened in history that were more interesting than the stuff in this book. In fact, I was sure of it, because Jiichan [my grandfather] was reading my history book once and said, 'This not history. This public relation document'" (147).

22 As Kirsten Møllegaard has shown, haunting is a central structuring device in *Holes*, which is set in the American Southwest.

## Works Cited


Azuma, Eiichiro. "Race, Citizenship, and the 'Science of Chick Sexing': The Politics of Racial Identity among Japanese Americans." *Pacific Historical Reviews* 78.2 (2009): 242–275. *JSTOR*. Web. 17 Jan. 2021.

Cha, Frank. "Migrating to the 'Broiler Belt': Japanese American Labor and the Jim Crow South in Cynthia Kadohata's *Kira-Kira*." *The Mississippi Quarterly* 65.1 (Winter 2012): 103–120. *JSTOR*. Web. 17 Jan. 2021.

Chaudhri, Amina. "'Straighten Up and Fly Right': HeteroMasculinity in *The Watsons Go to Birmingham—1963*." *Children's Literature Association Quarterly* 36.2 (Summer 2011): 147–163. *Project Muse*. Web. 17 Jan. 2021.

Comerford, Lynda. "Children's Bookshelf Talks with Cynthia Kadohata." *Publishers Weekly* 29 Mar. 2006. Web. 13 Apr. 2021.

Kadohata, Cynthia. *Kira-Kira*. New York: Atheneum Books for Young Readers, 2004. Print.

Kadohata, Cynthia. Newbery Acceptance Speech. "2005." *In the Words of the Winners: The Newbery and Caldecott Medals, 2001 – 2010*. Association for Library Service to Children and The Horn Book. Chicago: American Library Association, 2011. 86–105. *Google Books*. Web. 17 Jan. 2021.

Kadohata, Cynthia. *The Thing About Luck*. New York: Atheneum Books for Young Readers, 2013. Print.

Kadohata, Cynthia. *Weedflower*. New York: Atheneum Books for Young Readers, 2006. Print.

Kidd, Kenneth B. "Prizing Children's Literature: The Case of Newbery Gold." *Children's Literature* 35 (2007): 166–190. *Project Muse*. Web. 12 June 2018.

Manuel, Dolores, and Rocío G. Davis. "Editors' Introduction: Critical Perspectives on Asian American Children's Literature." *The Lion and the Unicorn* 30.2 (2006): v–xv. *Humanities Source*. Web. 17 Jan. 2021.

Matsumoto, Valerie J. *City Girls: The Nisei Social World in Los Angeles, 1920–1950*. New York: Oxford UP, 2014. Print.

McClintock, Anne. "Imperial Ghosting and National Tragedy: Revenants from Hiroshima and Indian Country in the War on Terror." *PMLA* 129.4 (2014): 819–829. Print.

Means, Florence Crannell. *The Moved-Outers*. Boston: Houghton Mifflin, 1945. Print.

Møllegaard, Kirsten. "Haunting and History in Louis Sachar's *Holes*." *Western American Literature* 45.2 (Summer 2010): 138–161. *Project Muse*. Web. 6 Jan. 2017.

Morgan, Peter E. "A Bridge to Whose Future? Young Adult Literature and the Asian American Teenager." *ALAN Review* 25.3 (Spring 1998): 18–20. *ERIC*. Web. 17 Jan. 2021.

Rahn, Suzanne. "Early Images of American Minorities: Rediscovering Florence Crannell Means." *The Lion and the Unicorn* 11.1 (1987): 98–115. *Project Muse*. Web. 10 Mar. 2020.

Rochman, Hazel. Rev. of *Kira-Kira*, by Cynthia Kadohata. *The Booklist* 100.9 (2004): 858. *Booklist Online*. Web. 17 Jan. 2021.

Sachar, Louis. *Holes*. New York: Farrar, Straus & Giroux, 1998. Print.
Schwebel, Sara L., ed. *Island of the Blue Dolphins: The Complete Reader's Edition*. Oakland: U of California P, 2016. Print.
Tanaka, Janice D. *When You're Smiling: The Deadly Legacy of Internment*. Visual Communications, 1999. Film.
Tillotson, Laura. Rev. of *Kira-Kira*, by Cynthia Kadohata. *Book Links* 14.3 (Jan. 2005): 12–13. *Gale Academic OneFile*. Web. 17 Jan. 2021.

# 14 Playing to Win the Newbery

## Black Boyhood in *The Crossover* (2015)

*Rachel L. Rickard Rebellino and Rebekah May Degener*

In February 2012, seventeen-year-old Trayvon Martin was fatally shot by neighborhood watch coordinator George Zimmerman. The lynching of a Black boy and subsequent acquittal of his murderer was not a new occurrence in the United States. Yet Martin's death and the consequent founding of Black Lives Matter, a movement intervening in violence committed against Black individuals, served as a catalyst for a larger public conversation around twenty-first-century Black boyhood. One touchstone in this conversation was journalist Ta-Nehisi Coates's award-winning 2015 book *Between the World and Me*. As a correspondent for *The Atlantic*, Coates drew large-scale attention to Martin's death. In this book-length work, framed as a letter to his teenage son, Coates considers the impact of historical and contemporary violence against Black men and boys in America: "you are a black boy and you must be responsible for your body in a way that other boys cannot know" (71).

Writing in *The Horn Book*, award-winning author and illustrator Christopher Myers considers how representations of Black children in youth literature might shift this inequitable responsibility: "The rhetoric of [Zimmerman's] trial hinged on precisely this question: whether or not this young black boy, with his bag of candy and his iced tea and his sweatshirt, was a threat. Here is also where I see my responsibility. Although it is unfair, and although it comes with an intricate history, I have the opportunity with every book I make to write this boy as even less a threat than he already isn't" ("Young"). Myers speaks to two interconnected ideas: the possibility that youth literature can shape readers' perceptions of themselves and others and the problem of severely limited literary portrayals of Black boys. The paucity of children's books featuring Black characters and the limited diversity of experiences reflected in existing stories have created what youth literature scholar Ebony Elizabeth Thomas terms a "separate and unequal literary landscape" (14).

The Newbery Medal has historically reified that landscape. As literary scholars Kenneth Kidd and Joseph Thomas explain in the introduction to

DOI: 10.4324/9780367337223-14-15

their collection on prizing children's literature, "Only grudgingly and with mixed results has the Medal responded to the pressures of pluralism and fair social representation" (5). Prior to 2015, only three novels written by Black authors received the Newbery: Virginia Hamilton's *M.C. Higgins the Great* (1974; 1975 Newbery Medal), Mildred Taylor's *Roll of Thunder, Hear My Cry* (1976; 1977 Newbery Medal), and Christopher Paul Curtis's *Bud, Not Buddy* (1999; 2000 Newbery Medal). Taylor's and Curtis's books are historical fiction, and Hamilton's novel is set in rural Appalachia. Focusing on a contemporary Black family living in a city, Kwame Alexander's *The Crossover* (2014; 2015 Newbery Medal) was a departure. Alexander's verse novel—a story told through a series of poems—is written from the perspective of Josh Bell, a tween basketball star. Through masterful poetry, Josh narrates his team's journey toward the county championship, conveys frustration with his twin JB's budding romance, and expresses worry about his father's growing health concerns.

On its surface, *The Crossover* is a fun, fast-paced sports book with a compelling emotional core and the potential to entertain a wide audience. According to reviewers, the story "vibrates with energy and heat" (Parrott 132) and is "massively appealing … for reluctant readers, athletes especially" (Hedeen). Based on these reviews, Alexander's novel might appear distant from Coates's writing, with its explicitly political discussion of Black boyhood and adolescence. However, *The Crossover* enters the same larger conversation by means of its setting, form, and content, which honor Black boys' lives and literacies. The many forms of communication, ways of knowing, and genres of writing associated with the Black community, and with Black boys in particular, have been and continue to be dismissed in formal educational settings. As education scholars such as David Kirkland and Bettina Love argue, these devaluations have substantial ramifications, including the school-to-prison pipeline and the disproportionate number of Black boys who drop out of or are suspended or expelled from school. Alexander's novel speaks to these issues.

*The Crossover* is set in a twenty-first-century Black community, draws on hip-hop techniques and content in its poetry, and utilizes basketball as its predominant metaphor. By establishing these genres of writing and ways of knowing as valuable and by demonstrating the fluency with which protagonist Josh navigates various forms of expression, Alexander's book makes an argument rooted in the politics of literacy: Black boys—their stories, music, and interests—matter.

## A More Expansive Playing Field: Public Conversations Around Race

In 2014, two years after Trayvon Martin's death—and two days before *The Crossover* was published—Walter Dean Myers and Christopher Myers wrote a pair of *New York Times* op-eds in response to the

Cooperative Children's Book Center (CCBC) at the University of Wisconsin-Madison's release of its annual statistical report on books for children and teens published by and about people of color and Indigenous individuals. In their essays, the father and son discuss the continued lack of racial representation in youth literature. The elder Myers questions how this paucity impacts readers: "Where are the future white loan officers and future white politicians going to get their knowledge of people of color? Where are black children going to get a sense of who they are and what they can be?" (W. D. Myers 1). Christopher Myers evokes the metaphor of a map: "I think it's necessary to provide for boys and girls ... a more expansive landscape upon which to dream" ("Apartheid" 1). A month later, the annual fan-focused book conference BookCon announced its speakers, and all thirty invited children's authors were White; the most prominent panel, "Blockbuster Reads: Meet the Kids' Authors That Dazzle," was comprised entirely of White men. The youth literature community saw this blatant exclusion as exemplifying the broader treatment of authors of color, and authors and advocates Ellen Oh and Malinda Lo, along with other stakeholders, began a Twitter discussion addressing the lack of representation in youth literature. Another author, Aisha Saeed, created the #WeNeedDiverseBooks hashtag, which became a rallying cry across social media. Alongside five other authors, illustrators, and members of the publishing industry, Oh and Saeed founded a nonprofit bearing the same name that advocates for increased quality and quantity of diverse youth literature (We Need Diverse Books).

These intersecting events in 2014 echo an earlier history of activist work around diversity in children's books. In many ways, We Need Diverse Books (WNDB) mirrors the Council on Interracial Books for Children (CIBC), an organization devoted to nearly identical goals that was founded in 1965. Like WNDB, the CIBC used a variety of approaches to address the significant problem of absent or negative representations of children of color in youth literature. Among other initiatives, the CIBC created a contest for Black authors intended to increase visibility of excellent unpublished manuscripts. The first published books from Newbery-recognized Black authors Mildred Taylor and Walter Dean Myers were their CIBC-contest-winning manuscripts (Bishop 86). The CIBC's accomplishments were impressive and groundbreaking. In addition to launching the careers of influential authors, the CIBC drew attention to racist (and sexist) images in classic youth literature, from *Pippi Longstocking* to *Charlie and the Chocolate Factory*. But like racism itself, the Whiteness of American youth literature is deeply embedded in national culture. As the 2014 CCBC statistics, launching of WNDB, and paucity of Newbery winners by Black authors attest, the work of publishing, promoting, and prizing children's books by authors of color is ongoing.

In her important 2016 discussion of children's book prizing, youth literature scholar June Cummins explores the work of the CIBC and identity-based book prizing and predicts that industry-wide transformation will materialize only when long-standing institutions such as the Newbery change. Quoting Kenneth Kidd's remarks about the Newbery's foundation—which linked literature with citizenship, character-building, and the public good—she conjectures that "reading about the history and institutionalization of the award may make the judges more aware of what the award set out to do and what they can now do" (102). Notably, Cummins reveals that she has personal knowledge that a 2015 Newbery committee member shared Kidd's "Prizing Children's Literature: The Case of Newbery Gold," which discusses the history and purpose of the award, with fellow deliberators. Though the specifics of the committee's discussions of *The Crossover* are unknown, it is quite possible that knowledge of Newbery's historical concern with social progress—along with 2014's cultural reckoning around the dehumanization and murder of Black boys—influenced the ways in which the committee read and interpreted Alexander's book.

Insofar as the Newbery committee was composed primarily of White librarians, its response to this work of African American children's literature raises questions of how *The Crossover* engages its audience. Children's literature by definition is written for a dual audience of adults and children, but African American youth literature contains a second "dual audience." Drawing upon Henry Louis Gates's discussion of the "double-voicedness" of literature written by Black authors, youth literature scholar Michelle H. Martin argues that children's books written by Black authors often demonstrate an awareness of both Black and White audiences. Historically, books by Black authors that have been well-received by the Newbery have provided specific entry points for White readers. For instance, youth literature scholar Jani Barker details how attention to both Black and White readers is evident in Taylor's *Roll of Thunder, Hear My Cry*, in which the author provides non-racist White characters with whom White readers might identify. While Christopher Paul Curtis's *The Watsons Go to Birmingham—1963* (1995; 1996 Newbery Honor) does not include White characters with whom White readers might identify, it facilitates White readers' identification with the Black characters, Barker explains. In his story of a family's trip to Civil Rights-era Alabama, Curtis uses what Barker describes as a naive narrator who views his Black family as the norm and racism against them as incomprehensible, positioning readers, regardless of race, as similarly perceiving the violence that occurs as unthinkable: "With no other characters with whom to identify, readers of all races are positioned to identify with the human Watsons against the monstrous racism that seeks to devour them" (139). Significantly, both Taylor's and Curtis's prizewinning novels are set in the past. This setting results in books that not only provide substantial historical context for contemporary readers, regardless of their racial or cultural background, but also grant distance, permitting White readers to empathize with those who experienced racism in the past but without necessarily developing an awareness of anti-Black racism as a contemporary reality. *The Crossover* departs from previous Newbery winners in this regard as it centralizes a Black boy's story without qualification or explicit appeals to White readers. Alexander does not provide non-Black readers with a character or narrator who sees the protagonist's actions from a White vantage point. Instead, the story is grounded in a Black boy's perspective and experiences, and readers of all identities—including the readers on the Newbery committee—are expected to see Josh's humanity through this lens.

Notably, while Josh's experiences are specific to his identity as a Black boy, his race is never explicitly named, though Alexander has stated that "race is obvious and evident in all of [his] books" (Malhotra). In *The Crossover*, myriad cultural references point to the Bells as a Black family living within a Black community. Josh wears his hair in locks (14–15), the boys' school has a step team and rap group (54), the family's Christmas meal includes collards and yams (207), and nearly every hero Josh mentions throughout the book is a Black athlete, musician, or celebrity. Through these narrative details, Alexander resists the way American readers have been socialized to assume that characters in youth literature are White until proven otherwise. This tactic calls back to Newbery winner *Bud, Not Buddy*. When that book's protagonist names the race of a woman he encounters as "white," readers are asked to evaluate "assumptions they may have made about characters they've already met, as well as those they will meet: they are black unless specified otherwise" (Smith). Because Alexander never names a character's race and, instead, establishes race through contextual details, he speaks not only to the problem of Whiteness as a default assumption but also to the impossibility of colorblindness. Readers aren't given any explicit racial descriptors, and though they cannot directly "read" color, they read how Blackness permeates Josh's lived experiences.

Similarly, though *The Crossover* does not explicitly address racial inequity, the effects thereof permeate the story. The novel is layered with issues affecting Black boys such as stereotypes of criminality, fear of police brutality, and the deadly health consequences of racism. During a basketball game, Josh's growing jealousy of his twin results in Josh rashly passing the ball to JB with such force that JB's nose gushes blood. A poem entitled "Suspension" records Josh's post-game conversation with his mother. "Boys with no self-control become men behind bars," she warns, inquiring "When did you become a thug?" (138–139). Though she does not say "*Black* boys," Josh's mother implicitly calls upon the permeating positioning of Black boys as deviant in

American society. Her warning recognizes that because of this stereotype Josh needs to make himself "even less a threat than he already isn't" (C. Myers, "Young"). The violence that can occur when Black boys and men are seen as inherently dangerous is suggested in the later poem "Game Time: 6:00 p.m." when Josh's dad is pulled over by a police officer while driving Josh to his basketball game. Josh narrates:

At 5:28 p.m.
a cop
pulls us over
because Dad has
a broken
taillight. (125)

The emphasis on time and the poem's short staccato lines build tension. During the incident Josh doesn't pray that he and his father, Chuck Bell, will arrive at the game on time. His focus is elsewhere: "I pray Dad / won't get arrested" (126). This encounter with the police ultimately resolves peacefully, but the tension that occurs between the lines evokes the countless real-life stories of Black men being killed, injured, or arrested by the police, suggesting the possibility of an alternate, more violent resolution.

In addition to addressing the perceived criminality of Black men, Alexander's novel incorporates the health disparities faced by Black men as Josh and JB later lose their thirty-nine-year-old father to heart disease. Since heart disease is the leading cause of death for all Americans, this cause of death might not initially seem connected to race. But Black men are disproportionately affected, with heart disease among this group being both more prevalent and more severe (Brewer and Cooper).[1] Alexander weaves concern about cardiovascular health throughout *The Crossover*, with two poems that explain cardiovascular-related medical terminology (76; 201), a stated history of family heart disease (97), explicit discussions of healthful eating habits (78–79; 96), and a final section set largely in the hospital after Chuck Bell has a heart attack. Smaller details, such as the twins' school's name, Reggie Lewis Junior High (27), also hint at this topic; Lewis was a basketball player who died of heart disease at age twenty-seven. In the chapter "Conversation," Josh narrates:

In the car
I ask Dad
if going to the doctor
will kill him.
He tells me

he doesn't trust doctors,
that my grandfather did
and look where it got him:
six feet under
at forty-five. (123)

Mr. Bell repeatedly refuses to visit the doctor, reflecting many Black men's hesitance to rely on medical experts because of past experiences of healthcare discrimination, such as the inadequate care implied to have led to Josh's grandfather's death.

The book's engagement with these systemic issues burdening the Black community creates a nuanced and specific portrayal of a twenty-first-century Black family. Though Alexander offers subtle discussion about criminalization and healthcare, he weaves a more explicit argument around youth literature's potential to validate the lived experiences of children from historically marginalized groups. *The Crossover*'s overarching story humanizes the lives of contemporary Black boys, aligning with Alexander's stated aim to demonstrate "that boys in general, black boys in particular, we smile, we laugh, we love, we cry, we hope, we think like everyone else" (NPR). In writing his story with these aims in mind, Alexander recognizes the capacity of child and adult readers of all racial identities to see Josh as having a story worth being told. But the process of humanization does not stop there. Through the very language used to tell Josh's story, Alexander speaks not only to the question of whose stories are meaningful but also to the issue of what kind of writing is worthy as art.

## "You Better Recognize Greatness": *The Crossover* as a Hip-Hop Text

The poetry in *The Crossover* relies heavily on hip-hop, inviting readers to investigate their assumptions around language and the valuation of certain kinds of communication. Though hip-hop is sometimes understood as a genre of music, linguist Geneva Smitherman clarifies the wider meaning of the term: "*hip-hop* refers to urban youth culture in America ... manifested in such cultural productions as graffiti art, break dancing, styles of dress (e.g., baggy pants, sneakers, Malcolm X caps, appropriately worn backward), love of b-ball (basketball), and so forth" (3). Literacy scholar Elaine Richardson extends this understanding of hip-hop culture, coining the term "hiphop literacies" to describe the communication, knowledge, and resistance practices associated with hip-hop, while linguist H. Samy Alim uses the term "ill-literacies" to emphasize the ways such practices are simultaneously positioned as illegitimate or illiterate within formal educational contexts and "ill," or skilled and creative, in hip-hop culture (122). Regardless of terminology, hip-hop as a literacy practice resists oppression and celebrates Black culture even as it is often dismissed within schools. It is into this context that Alexander writes Josh, who loves hip-hop, excels in the English classroom, and, as narrator, fluidly shifts from hip-hop to haiku and everything in between.

The first two poems of *The Crossover* explicitly draw upon hip-hop music, establishing the form's centrality to the text. "Dribbling" opens the book in the middle of a basketball game. The size and position of the words in the concrete poem mirror Josh's on-court action, as when the letters of the word "slipping" are positioned at a diagonal across the page (3). Language such as "crunking" suggests the movement of the game while evoking the "crunk" subgenre of hip-hop, which emphasizes beat and danceability. The rhythm and style of hip-hop music are repeated in the novel's second poem, which introduces Josh:

> Josh Bell
>
> is my name.
> But *Filthy McNasty* is my claim to fame.
> Folks call me that 'cause my game's acclaimed,
> so downright dirty, it'll put you to shame.
> My hair is long, my height's tall.
> See, I'm the next Kevin Durant,
> LeBron, and Chris Paul. (4)

The short lines and repeated sounds might incorrectly be read as simplistic, a mistake common in the evaluation of hip-hop lyrics (Bradley). This poem, though, demonstrates a sophisticated understanding of rhyme, drawing on both internal ("claim to fame") and slant ("acclaimed" and "shame") rhyme. Reading the poem aloud highlights how the various rhymes "shape the rhythm" by encouraging emphasis on particular words (Bradley 62). In turn, the rhyme guides the poem's vocalization in a way that has become increasingly common in rap, a music genre that falls under the larger banner of hip-hop culture (Richardson). Further, in this introduction, Josh compares himself to some of the best-known basketball players of the mid-2010s: Kevin Durant, LeBron James, Chris Paul. In so doing, he utilizes the tradition of braggadocio, a hip-hop technique of boasting in which the "speaker/rapper asserts his or her superb and many times exaggerated characteristics or abilities" (Richardson 11).

Braggadocio figures prominently in another introductory poem bearing Josh's nickname as its title.

"Filthy McNasty" structurally resembles "Josh Bell," with the title functioning as a subject explained in the first line:

Filthy McNasty

Is a MYTHical MANchild
Of rather *dubious distinction*
Always AGITATING
COMBINATING
AND ELEVATING his game (10)

The poem continues, sprawling across the page as Josh shoots a basket. Writing about *The Crossover*, youth literature scholars Lissa Paul, Kate Pendlebury, and Craig Svonkin discuss their reaction of laughter at the poetry's "cute rhymes and 'SLAMMERIFIC shots' at idiom" (339).[2] While the critics view their reaction as a sign of the poem's deficiencies, laughter might be exactly the poem's intent. As Smitherman explains, braggadocio relies on the speaker describing himself "as a powerful, all-knowing, omnipotent hero, able to overcome all odds" (12–13). With his claims of being a "MYTHical MANchild" constantly "ELEVATING" his skills, Josh does just that. Considering the poem in the context of the larger narrative adds nuance to the nickname. In a previous poem, "At first," Josh reveals his initial dislike of the nickname "Filthy McNasty," which he came to appreciate only when it became associated with praise from his father: "And that made me feel / real good / about my nickname" (9). The sharp contrast between Josh's desire for his father's approval, so earnestly revealed here, and the prideful braggadocio present in "Filthy McNasty" hints at family dynamics and power struggles that are complicated and extended throughout the book.

In building Josh's story, Alexander relies on the techniques of signifying and sampling, which Gates sees as interconnected. In his landmark book *The Signifying Monkey*, first published around the time contemporary hip-hop was developing, Gates argues that signifying "functions as a metaphor for formal revision, or intertextuality, within the Afro-American literary tradition" (16). In the introduction to the book's twenty-fifth-anniversary edition, he explains that hip-hop brought attention to signifying through the technique of sampling (xxx). In the process of creating hip-hop, artists draw upon existing music as a way to not only honor previous songs by incorporating portions into new music but also "*to become part of them as they become signal parts of the new composition*" (xxxi, italics in original). This process of signifying and sampling figures heavily in *The Crossover*. Alexander participates in a tradition common to Black creators: "indirectly commenting on the work of earlier Black writers within the narrative structure of their own literary productions," and, thereby, rooting themselves "squarely and unabashedly in the Black musical-cultural tradition, even as they extend that tradition and put their own imprint on the game" (Smitherman 15–16).

# Filthy McNasty

is a MYTHical MANchild
Of rather *dubious distinction*
Always AGITATING
COMBINATING
and ELEVATING his game
*He* *dribbles*
*fakes*
then *takes*
the ROCK to the
*glass, fast,* and on BLAST
But watch out when he shoots
or you'll get SCHOOLed
FOOLed
UNCOOLed
'Cause when FILTHY gets hot
He has a *SLAMMERIFIC SHOT*
It's
Dunkalicious CLASSY
Supersonic SASSY
and D
O
W
N right
in your face
mcNASTY

*Figure 14.1* "Filthy McNasty."

Source: *The Crossover*, by Kwame Alexander (Houghton Mifflin Harcourt Publishing Company, 2014), page 10.

Even Alexander's use of the verse novel form can be understood as a kind of signifying and sampling. Pioneering youth literature scholar Rudine Sims Bishop asserts that poetry was one of the earliest forms used in African American youth literature, and she explores the consistency of themes across time: pride in one's identity, the value of family, and honoring Black culture and history. In the same way that a hip-hop musician might engage in sampling through sonic references to other artists' beats or music, Alexander's verse novel draws upon the rich history of African American children's poetry even as it points to contemporary works, including verse novels, that honor the experiences of Black children. Indeed, Alexander was trained and mentored by poet Nikki Giovanni and, on his website, he lists Coretta Scott King Award-winning Black verse novelists Jacqueline Woodson and Nikki Grimes among his favorite writers ("Q&A").[3] By connecting to founding works of African American youth literature through form and directly invoking Black musicians—Tupac, Horace Silver, John Coltrane, and Jay-Z to name a few—within *The Crossover*, Alexander participates in one of the goals of sampling: fostering a "conscious preoccupation with artistic continuity and connection to Black cultural roots" (Smitherman 15–16).

Even the book's focus on basketball and mention of particular athletes can be read as sampling. Basketball and hip-hop have long been linked, with the sport often considered an important aspect of hip-hop culture (Smitherman). In using hip-hop to write about basketball, Alexander taps into the legacy of sports as a site of resistance (Rodesiler 17). Kevin Durant, LeBron James, and Chris Paul, the figures mentioned in "Filthy McNasty" as Josh's heroes, are not only accomplished athletes but also activists who have utilized their platforms to advocate for racial justice. Although neither Josh as a character nor *The Crossover* as a book explicitly takes on activism, these references—this sampling—links the novel to an activist legacy. By focusing on the connections between hip-hop and basketball, Alexander centralizes important aspects of many Black boys' lives, ones that allow them, like protagonist Josh, to both "shoot" and "inspire."

## "When I Shoot, I Inspire": *The Crossover* as Sports Novel

Just as Alexander asks readers to assess their prior notions of hip-hop, he challenges understandings of the literary merit of sports literature and the false dichotomy between athletics and academics. Despite the significance of sports in children's lives, sports fiction has often been dismissed by educators and critics as having little literary value (Brown and Rodesiler). Yet Alexander's book is not just *about* sports; its entire structure draws from basketball. Modifying the commonly used organization of the school story, Alexander builds his narrative not around the four quarters of the school year but around those of a basketball game, with a warm-up, four quarters, and an overtime. This organization suggests the importance of athletics: it is the lens through which the story is told, the predominant theme of the book, and a key way in which Josh conceptualizes the world and his own identity.

Drawing from his father's imparted wisdom, narrator Josh provides ten basketball rules that highlight concepts he is processing. In an act of signifying, these "rules" poems echo the life-lessons presented by the protagonist of Curtis's *Bud, Not Buddy*.[4] The repeated emphasis on rules within Black-authored books about Black boys can be read as responding to the reality that society heavily regulates Black boys and requires them to "be responsible for [their bodies] in ways that other boys cannot know" (Coates 71). In *The Crossover*, Alexander specifically reframes rules through the Black spaces of hip-hop and basketball. He uses these rule poems in overtly literary ways, as when Josh states, in "Basketball Rule #1":

> In this game of life
> your family is the court
> and the ball is your heart.
> No matter how good you are,
> no matter how down you get,
> always leave
> your heart
> on the court. (20)

This initial rule uses metaphor to emphasize the book's persistent focus on family. At the same time, the repeated use of the word "heart," which in this context reads as symbolic of love or devotion, foreshadows Chuck Bell's heart disease. The rules become more serious as Josh faces life-altering events, including his father's death:

> A loss is inevitable,
> like snow in winter.
> True champions
> learn
> to dance
> through
> the storm. (230)

*The Crossover* invites readers to encounter the theme of loss, thereby combining the kind of seriousness that the Newbery tends to honor with sports fiction, which is often assumed to be trivial. Using a metaphor of athletic persistence assists Josh in understanding how to move forward after his father's death, emphasizing basketball's value as a way of viewing the world.

The convergence of the literary and the athletic is further exemplified in another repeated poetic structure in *The Crossover*, the definition poem. Alexander includes twelve such poems wherein Josh defines a vocabulary word pertinent to significant narrative events. The majority of these are SAT-worthy words, such as pulchritudinous and churlish, or medical terms (e.g., patella tendinitis and hypertension); however, the first definition poem defines the book's eponymous sports term. It offers a largely literal definition, with the first stanza explaining "cross·o·ver" as follows:

> A simple basketball move
> in which a player dribbles
> the ball quickly
> from one hand
> to the other. (29)

Though this definition is straightforward, readers become increasingly aware of alternate meanings of "crossover." It is a euphemism for dying, and, for Josh, of moving from childhood to adolescence. The obvious complexity of these crossings is contrasted with the supposedly "simple" basketball move. Further, by first using the definition poem to define a sports term, Alexander centers sports as an important kind of knowledge in much the same way that opening the book with hip-hop poetry emphasizes its value.

More importantly, these definition poems refute the belief that Black boys are academically unengaged. Through his poetry, Josh demonstrates fluency in a range of communication practices. In each definition poem, he spells words phonetically and names their part of speech before offering multiple definitions or, in a practice commonly recommended by English teachers, using the word in a sentence of his own construction. The seventh definition poem, "tip·ping point," begins with a technical definition that Josh expands through examples. In the second stanza, he references his father's analysis of the 2008 housing crash, in which "housing gamblers" and "greedy bankers" were the tipping point; then, in the third stanza, he uses the phrase in connection with his mother's commitment to her sons' academic success (118). His final example moves to the present moment, describing his emotional tipping point after witnessing JB kissing a girl in the library. Though Josh identifies this event as putting him over the metaphorical edge of jealousy, left unsaid is the fact that this poem also serves as a tipping point in and of itself. Located exactly in the middle of the book, it marks the moment in which the story's tension has reached a climax. The poems that closely follow "tip·ping point" describe Josh's overwhelming frustration when his father refuses to visit a doctor, foreshadowing the shift from Chuck Bell as alive and present to his worsening illness and eventual death.

To further suggest the value of sports as a lens for interpreting the world, Alexander incorporates a reference to another text frequently used for purposes beyond its purported goal: Sun Tzu's *The Art of War*. Josh records his coach quoting Sun in a poem entitled "Practice":

> Coach reads to us from
> *The Art of War*
> *A winning strategy is*
> *not about planning*, he says.
> *It's about quick responses*
> *to changing conditions*. (56, italics in original)

His coach's reference to military strategy is intended to reinforce the flexibility and quick decision-making vital for athletes before he leads the team in drills and sprints where they practice such skills. While explicitly about athletic prowess, the coach's words foreshadow "changing conditions" in Josh's life, ones that will challenge him not just as an athlete but as a child facing parental loss. Here, the coach uses a treatise on war to teach about sports strategy; similarly, Alexander's own book about sports imparts lessons about life off the court.

Children's author and literary scholar Chris Crowe notes that youth literature has long represented athletics as vital to youths' lives, citing, for example, late nineteenth- and early-twentieth-century dime novels by authors such as Gilbert Patten, Ralph Henry Barbour, and William Heyliger (129). Librarian Michael Cart argues that Robert Lipsyte's *The Contender* (1967), about a teenage boxer and high school dropout in Harlem, is a groundbreaking work of young adult literature that moved YA books as a whole toward realism (31). In the late twentieth and early twenty-first centuries, Walter Dean Myers's sports books, including *Hoops* (1981), *Slam!* (1998), and *All the Right Stuff* (2012), feature Black athletes who come to better understand their identity and find meaning in their lives through sports; his legacy can be seen across contemporary sports literature, including Alexander's novels (Schuck).[5] Yet the value of sports books remains contentious, as in the textbook *Literature for Today's Young Adults*, which dismisses the idea that "sports books teach us the game of life," instead stating that a better argument is that "reading for pleasure is a worthy activity and a goal in and of itself" (Nilsen et al. 227). This assessment marginalizes sports fiction in multiple ways. It assumes that such stories are primarily appropriate for readers who won't engage with texts deemed more complex; it relegates these works to the category of entertainment; and, perhaps because of the negative associations that much genre fiction carries, reinforces the idea that sports novels are of inferior literary quality.

## An Expected and Radical Choice: *The Crossover* as Newbery Winner

In many ways, the decision to grant the Newbery to *The Crossover* was groundbreaking. As the story of a contemporary Black tween written by a Black author, Alexander's novel diverges from past Newbery winners. It does not explicitly tackle racism, as previous Newbery winners by African American authors did. Its poetry is aligned with hip-hop rhythms and lyrics, which have historically been seen as lacking literary value, and it is about sports, a topic the Newbery had previously placed on the sidelines.[6] In other ways, though, *The Crossover* shouts its Newbery potential with a protagonist who loves words and reading and a plot that moves fluidly between lighthearted and weighty topics. Through these similarities to other Newbery-winning books, Alexander gestures toward the adult audience for his novel: educators, librarians, and critics who play a substantive role in determining whether a book ends up in the hands of readers. In fact, in a move that seems to speak specifically to a hypothetical Newbery committee, *The Crossover* honors past winners through intertextual references. Josh is assigned to read Lois Lowry's *The Giver* (1993; 1994 Newbery Award); the book's basketball rules call to mind the rules of life laid out in *Bud, Not Buddy*; and Alexander's focus on sibling relationships within a Black family echoes Mildred Taylor's *Roll of Thunder, Hear My Cry*. Beyond these textual details, the entire slate of 2015 Newbery Medal and Honor Books suggests the expectedness of *The Crossover*'s win. In addition to *The Crossover*, both 2015 Honor Books—Jacqueline Woodson's *Brown Girl Dreaming* (2014; 2015 Newbery Honor) and Cece Bell's *El Deafo* (2014; 2015 Newbery Honor)—tell stories of young people from groups that have been underrepresented in youth literature. This set of books indicates that the 2015 committee was attentive to the aims of WNDB.

In a final footnote to her article on the Newbery and Whiteness in children's literature, Cummins speculates on the potential legacy of *The Crossover*'s win: "The selection of Alexander heartens me, but I do not think we'll see the kind of change in the choice of winners that is necessary" (103). Though it would be short-sighted to claim that *The Crossover*'s 2015 win signaled lasting change for the Newbery or American youth literature more broadly, it would be negligent not to acknowledge the Newbery Medal books that followed. Contemporary Own Voices stories of young people of color were routinely prized in the final years of the Newbery's first century: *Last Stop on Market Street* (2015; 2016 Newbery Medal); *Hello, Universe* (2017; 2018 Newbery Medal); *Merci Suárez Changes Gears* (2018; 2019 Newbery Medal); *New Kid* (2019; 2020 Newbery Medal); and *When You Trap a Tiger* (2020; 2021 Newbery Medal). In the years immediately following

*The Crossover*, then, the librarians of the Newbery Selection Committee widened the circle of authors and stories they recognized.

*The Crossover*'s prizing speaks not just to which authors are recognized by the Newbery and which children appear in Medal-winning books, but also to the language and style deemed worthy of Newbery gold. Just as Alim argues that youth utilize hip-hop as a force for reframing "notions of correctness and creativity" (122), so too the Newbery's prizing of *The Crossover* can be understood as a reframing of what eminence and distinction in youth literature might look like. Expressing youth interest in basketball through hip-hop-inflected verse, *The Crossover* made a play for the Newbery and won. The long-term legacy of that win remains unknown, but just five years after *The Crossover*'s victory, another Newbery honoree—Jerry Craft, author of the first graphic novel to win the Medal—acknowledged its impact. Fittingly, the *New Kid* author used a sports metaphor to depict the contributions of Alexander and other award-winning Black authors and illustrators: "they did all the blocking so that I could make it into the endzone" (Maughan). Perhaps, then, *The Crossover* was not just an expected choice but one with radical implications for the next century of the Newbery.

## Notes

1 In their discussion of their research on stress, race, and cardiovascular disease, medical doctors LaPrincess C. Brewer and Lisa A. Cooper articulate some of the interconnecting reasons for the disproportionate prevalence of heart disease among Black individuals: less access to and lower quality healthcare, increased stress levels as a result of racism, and persistent institutional racism and individual bias in medical treatment.

2 This assessment of the poetry in *The Crossover* finds its echo in the broader claim, by numerous literary critics, that verse novels are inferior poetry—or aren't poetry at all. For a refutation of this position, see Coats.

3 Alexander's knowledge and love of children's poetry extending beyond African American children's literature is even more apparent in his follow-up verse novel, *Booked* (2016), where the protagonist reads verse novels such as Ann Burg's *All the Broken Pieces* (2009) and Karen Hesse's *Out of the Dust* (1997; 1998 Newbery Medal).

4 Alexander's familiarity with Curtis's body of work is established in *Booked*, where the protagonist's class reads *The Watsons Go to Birmingham—1963*. The practice of listing rules is echoed by Jason Reynolds in his verse novel *Long Way Down* (2017; 2018 Newbery Honor).

5 In addition to *The Crossover*, sports undergird Alexander's verse novels *Booked* (2016), *Rebound* (2018), and *Swing* (2018), as well as his nonfiction *The Playbook: 52 Rules to Aim, Shoot, and Score in this Game Called Life* (2017) and his picture book *The Undefeated* (2019).

6 Prior to 2015, only one Newbery book substantively incorporated athletics: Bruce Brooks's *The Moves Make the Man* (1984; 1985 Newbery Honor). This book is part of the Newbery Honor Book "shadow-canon" described by Kenneth Kidd—a body that "offset[s] the relative conservatism of the Medal

books" but remains "safely contained," apart from the pantheon of Medal winners (Kidd 177). A similar phenomenon is at play in the partitioning of Walter Dean Myers's oeuvre: while two of his works won Newbery recognition—
*Scorpions* (1988; 1989 Newbery Honor) and *Somewhere in the Darkness* (1992; 1993 Newbery Honor)—his sports-themed books were never recognized. Meanwhile, the Coretta Scott King Award prized two of Myers's sports books, *Slam!* (1996) and *Darius & Twig* (2013), recognizing merit that the Newbery establishment chose to ignore.

## Works Cited

Alexander, Kwame. *Booked*. New York: Houghton Mifflin Harcourt, 2016. Print.

Alexander, Kwame. *The Crossover*. New York: Houghton Mifflin Harcourt, 2014. Print.

Alexander, Kwame. "Q&A." *Kwame Alexander*, 2020. Web. 15 Sept. 2020.

Alim, H. Samy. "Global Ill-Literacies: Hip Hop Cultures, Youth Identities, and the Politics of Literacy." *Review of Research on Education* 35 (2011): 120–146. Print.

Barker, Jani. "Racial Identification and Audience in *Roll of Thunder, Hear My Cry* and *The Watsons Go to Birmingham—1963*." *Children's Literature in Education* 41.2 (2010): 118–145. Print.

Bishop, Rudine Sims. *Free Within Ourselves: The Development of African American Children's Literature*. Portsmouth, NH: Heinemann, 2007. Print.

Bradley, Adam. *Book of Rhymes: The Poetics of Hip Hop*. New York: Hachette Book Group, 2009. Print.

Brewer, LaPrincess C., and Lisa A. Cooper. "Race, Discrimination, and Cardiovascular Disease." *Virtual Mentor: American Medical Association Journal of Ethics* 16.6 (2014): 455–460. Web. 15 Sept. 2020.

Brown, Alan, and Luke Rodesiler, eds. *Developing Contemporary Literacies through Sports: A Guide for the English Classroom*. Urbana, IL: NCTE, 2016. Print.

Cart, Michael. *Young Adult Literature: From Romance to Realism*. 3rd ed. Chicago: American Library Association, 2016. Print.

Coates, Ta-Nehisi. *Between the World and Me*. New York: Spiegel & Grau, 2015. Print.

Coats, Karen. "Form as Metaphor in Middle Grade and Young Adult Verse Novels." *The Lion and the Unicorn* 42.2 (Apr. 2018): 145–161. *Project Muse*. Web. 13 Feb. 2021.

Cooperative Children's Book Center. "Multicultural Children's Literature 2014." *Cooperative Children's Book Center*, 2019. Web. 15 Sept. 2020.

Crowe, Chris. "Young Adult Literature: Sports Literature for Young Adults." *The English Journal* 90.6 (2001): 129–133. Print.

Cummins, June. "The Still Almost All-White World of Children's Literature: Theory, Practice, and Identity-Based Children's Book Awards." *Prizing Children's Literature: The Cultural Politics of Children's Book Awards*. Ed. Kenneth B. Kidd and Joseph T. Thomas, Jr. New York: Routledge, 2016. 87–103. Print.

Curtis, Christopher Paul. *Bud, Not Buddy*. New York: Penguin Random House, 1999. Print.
Gates, Henry Louis. "Introduction: Hip-Hop and the Fate of Signifying." *The Signifying Monkey: 25th Anniversary Edition*. New York: Oxford UP, 2014. xxix–xxxiii. Print.
Gates, Henry Louis. *The Signifying Monkey*. New York: Oxford Press, 1988. Print.
Hedeen, Katrina. Rev. of *The Crossover*, by Kwame Alexander. *The Horn Book Magazine* 9.3 (May/June 2014): 79. EBSCOhost. Web. 10 May 2021.
Kidd, Kenneth B. "Prizing Children's Literature: The Case of Newbery Gold." *Children's Literature* 35 (2007): 166–190. Print.
Kidd, Kenneth B., and Joseph T. Thomas, Jr. "A Prize-Losing Introduction." *Prizing Children's Literature: The Cultural Politics of Children's Book Awards*. Ed. Kenneth B. Kidd and Joseph T. Thomas, Jr. New York: Routledge, 2016. 1–18. Print.
Kirkland, David. *A Search Past Silence: The Literacy of Young Black Men*. New York: Teachers College Press, 2013. Print.
Love, Bettina. "'I See Trayvon Martin': What Teachers Can Learn from the Tragic Death of a Young Black Male." *The Urban Review* 46.2 (2014): 292–306. Print.
Malhotra, Mary. "Mary Malhotra Interviews Swing Author Kwame Alexander." *Good Reads with Ronna*, 16 Nov. 2018. Web. 15 Sept. 2020.
Martin, Michelle H. *Brown Gold: Milestones of African American Children's Picture Books, 1845–2002*. New York: Routledge, 2004. Print.
Maughan, Shannon. "Jerry Craft's Newbery Win Was an Unforeseeable Dream." *Publishers Weekly*, 28 Jan. 2020. Web. 15 Sept. 2020.
Myers, Christopher. "The Apartheid of Children's Literature." *The New York Times*, 16 Mar. 2014: SR1. Print.
Myers, Christopher. "Young Dreamers." *The Horn Book Magazine*, 6 Aug. 2013. Web. 15 Sept. 2020.
Myers, Walter Dean. "Where Are the People of Color in Children's Books?" *The New York Times*, 16 Mar. 2014: SR1. Print.
Nilsen, Alleen Pace, et al. *Literature for Today's Young Adults*. 9th ed. Boston: Pearson, 2013. Print.
NPR. "How to Get Kids Hooked on Books? 'Use Poetry. It Is a Surefire Way.'" 3 Apr. 2016. Web. 15 Sept. 2020.
Parrott, Kiera. "The Crossover." *School Library Journal* 60.3 (2014): 132. Print.
Paul, Lissa, Kate Pendlebury, and Craig Svonkin. "A New Parliament of Fouls: The 2015 *Lion and the Unicorn* Award for Excellence in North American Poetry." *The Lion and the Unicorn* 39.3 (2015): 331–351. Print.
Richardson, Elaine. *Hiphop Literacies*. New York: Routledge, 2006. Print.
Rodesiler, Luke. "Beyond Appealing to Students' Interests: Studying Sports Culture for Critical Literacy." *Talking Points* 29.1 (2017): 12–19. Print.
Schuck, Raymond I. "From Politics to Personal Expression: Representations of Sport in Walter Dean Myers' Young Adult Works." *Young Adult Literature and Culture*. Ed. Harry Edwin Eiss. Newcastle Upon Tyne: Cambridge Scholars Publishing, 2009. 1–20. Print.

Smith, Vicky. "Unmaking the White Default." *Kirkus*, 4 May 2016. Web. 15 Sept. 2020.

Smitherman, Geneva. "'The Chain Remain the Same': Communicative Practices in the Hip Hop Nation." *Journal of Black Studies* 28.1 (1997): 3–25. Print.

Thomas, Ebony Elizabeth. "Critical Engagement with Middle Grades Reads: Who Lives? Who Thrives? Who Tells Your Story?" *Voices from the Middle* 26.2 (2018): 13–16. Print.

We Need Diverse Books. *WNDB*. We Need Diverse Books, 2019. Web. 15 Sept. 2020.

# Index

Made in the USA
Columbia, SC
22 April 2025

1a89cdd8-7d32-4657-a477-8e8f6d39a856R04